TENTING ON THE PLAINS

SMOKING THE PIPE OF PEACE.

TENTING
ON THE PLAINS

GENERAL CUSTER
in KANSAS and TEXAS

By ELIZABETH BACON CUSTER

With an Introduction by Jane R. Stewart
Foreword by Shirley A. Leckie

University of Oklahoma Press
Norman and London

Dedication to Tenting on the Plains.

To him whose brave and blithe endurance made those who
followed him forget, in his sunshiny presence, half the
hardship and the danger.

Library of Congress Cataloging-in-Publication Data

Custer, Elizabeth Bacon, 1842–1933.
    Tenting on the plains, or, General Custer in Kansas and Texas /by
Elizabeth B. Custer ; with an introduction by Jane R. Stewart ;
foreword by Shirley A. Leckie.
    p. cm.
    ISBN 0–8061–2668–X
    1. Custer, George Armstrong, 1839–1876. 2. Custer, Elizabeth
Bacon, 1842–1933. 3. Generals—United States—Biography. 4.
United States. Army—Biography. 5. United States. Army—Mili-
tary life—History—19th century. 6. Frontier and pioneer life—West
(U.S.) 7. West (U.S.)—History—1860–1890. I. Title. II. Title:
General Custer in Kansas and Texas.
F594.C986 1994
973.8′1′092—dc20
[B]   94-11743
                                                  CIP

The paper in this book meets the guidelines for permanence and durability
of the Committee on Production Guidelines for Book Longevity of the
Council on Library Resources, Inc.∞

Published in 1994 by the University of Oklahoma Press, Norman, Publishing Division of the University. First published in 1895 by Harper &
Brothers, New York. Introduction and notes, by Jane R. Stewart, copyright © 1971 by the University of Oklahoma Press. Foreword by Shirley A.
Leckie copyright © 1994 by the University of Oklahoma Press. All rights
reserved. Manufactured in the U.S.A. First printing of the University of
Oklahoma Press edition, 1994.

1 2 3 4 5 6 7 8 9 10

FOREWORD

By Shirley A. Leckie

IN 1971 the University of Oklahoma Press reprinted in three volumes *Tenting on the Plains; Or, General Custer in Kansas and Texas,* a work first published by C. L. Webster and Company in 1887. Jane R. Stewart's Introduction to this remains an invaluable source of background information on Elizabeth Bacon Custer, the author of the book, and its subject, her husband George Armstrong Custer.

Nonetheless, more than two decades have passed, and scholars have uncovered new information regarding Lieutenant Colonel Custer's life and career. Moreover, given the increased awareness of the role of women in history, scholars have a heightened appreciation for the part Elizabeth Custer played in creating her husband's heroic stature following his death. In order to make this work available in a one-volume paperback edition, the University of Oklahoma Press has reissued not the original 702-page work but the condensed 403-page book issued by the original publisher in 1893. Two years later, when Harper and Brothers acquired the rights to *Tenting on the Plains,* it reprinted the

v

smaller version, and this paperback edition is a facsimile of
that work.

In 1973 the late Minnie Dubbs Millbrook explored Custer's role in the near mutiny of volunteer troops in Louisiana
in 1865. While Stewart tells us that Custer was "something
of a martinet," Millbrook reveals that, less than twenty-four
hours after he arrived at Alexandria, he ignited rebellion by
inviting former Confederates to register their complaints
against Union soldiers. Then, when men of the Second
Wisconsin petitioned for removal of their commander, Lt.
Col. Nicholas Dale, for allegedly rejoicing over Abraham
Lincoln's assassination, Custer interpreted their actions as
mutiny. Sgt. Leonard Lancaster, who spearheaded the
drive, was sentenced to death by firing squad along with a
deserter. Lancaster's life was spared when Custer ordered
him pulled aside in the split second between "aim" and
"fire." The other soldier was executed. He was not, however, as Elizabeth claims, "a vagabond and criminal." Instead, Millbrook found that he was eighteen-year-old William A. Wilson, an Illinois farm boy whose records at the
National Archives contain no previous demerits.[1]

In another essay, "The West Breaks in General Custer,"
Millbrook examined Custer's involvement in the campaign
under Gen. Winfield Scott Hancock. She discovered that
his actions in the summer of 1867, including forced marches
over vast prairies, made no sense except in the context of
an overriding desire. Armstrong wanted his wife with
him, and everything else, including obeying orders, was
secondary.

Millbrook also investigated the explanations Custer gave
for leaving Fort Wallace without authorization and rejoin-
ing Elizabeth at Fort Riley. In his 1875 book, *My Life on the
Plains*, Custer stated that when he arrived at Wallace on July
13, 1867, the post was under siege, poorly supplied, and
suffering from cholera. Elizabeth, in *Tenting on the Plains*,
repeats these claims. By examining the War Department's
Report on Epidemic Cholera and Yellow Fever in the Army of the

United States, during the Year 1867, Millbrook discovered that cholera did not appear among Seventh Cavalry troopers until July 22. Moreover, post returns indicate that Wallace was not under siege and had adequate supplies.[2]

In 1988 Robert Utley published his penetrating biography, *Cavalier in Buckskin: George Armstrong Custer and the Western Military Frontier.* In his view, Armstrong was a person in whom the boy and the man were constantly at war. The Civil War had brought out his maturity, but when he faced the frustrations of postwar adjustment and regular army duty on the frontier in 1867, the immature boy prevailed.[3]

Utley also found information that sheds light on Armstrong and Elizabeth's relationship. According to Capt. Frederick Benteen, an anonymous letter informed Custer that Lt. Thomas Weir was paying too much attention to his wife. While Benteen's hatred for his commander must be weighed in evaluating his testimony, another source has verified this accusation. In 1910, Col. Edward G. Mathey told a similar story to Walter M. Camp, a railroad engineer, who interviewed him for a never-completed history of the Battle of the Little Bighorn.[4]

Very likely the relationship between Elizabeth Custer and the alcoholic Lieutenant Weir never amounted to more than flirtation. Still, Custer's willingness to jeopardize his career by leaving Fort Wallace without authorization and appearing unexpectedly at Fort Riley was immensely flattering to his wife. Thus her closing statement in *Tenting on the Plains*, "There was in that summer of 1867 one long, perfect day," assumes greater meaning than most of her contemporaries or subsequent historians imagined.

After Armstrong's death, Elizabeth collaborated with Frederick Whittaker, a dime novelist, by giving him access to her husband's correspondence. As a result, Whittaker published *A Complete Life of Gen. George A. Custer* five months after the Battle of the Little Bighorn. The work extolled Custer as a blameless hero and, more important, inspired similar biographies.

By publishing three books of her own, however, beginning with *"Boots and Saddles"; Or, Life in Dakota with General Custer* in 1885, *Tenting on the Plains* two years later, and *Following the Guidon* in 1890, Elizabeth established her husband's heroic stature firmly in the public eye. All three present him as a painstaking and solicitous commanding officer and a devoted, wise, and humorous family man. Moreover, by portraying her marriage as ideal and doing so with humor and no tinge of self-pity, Elizabeth won not only critical acclaim but a wide personal following. Faced with this situation, those officers and veterans who were critical of Custer were loath to challenge her statements publicly.

Elizabeth, moreover, endeared herself to many in the military by extolling the army's role in westward expansion and praising individual figures. For example, in the latter part of *Tenting on the Plains*, she emphasizes the partnership between the soldier—in this case her husband—and the pioneer, celebrating the heroism of both. She also lauds William T. Sherman, the retired commanding general of the army. Shortly thereafter she obtained from Sherman a testimonial to her husband, which stated that Custer's assistance to the transcontinental railroads had been worth more "than a hundred Richmonds."[5] It is not surprising that by the early twentieth century Armstrong had become, according to President Theodore Roosevelt, "the typical representative of the American regular officer who fought for the extension of our frontier."[6]

Thus, Elizabeth Custer must be considered one of America's most successful mythmakers. Until her death in 1933, her rendition of General Custer predominated in the public mind. A year later, with the appearance of Frederic Van de Water's *Glory-Hunter*, the reassessment of her husband began, and today scholars and the general public see Custer as a flawed and contradictory individual.

This abridged edition of *Tenting on the Plains* differs from the first edition in several ways. Elizabeth's opening biographical sketch of her husband has been deleted, as has the lengthy correspondence between Armstrong and Elizabeth during the Hancock Campaign (originally chapters 16–19). Some readers may miss the Hancock Campaign correspondence, but it is good news that the more tightly knit version of Elizabeth Custer's second book is again available. Whatever her purposes in writing, this woman was a born storyteller. By using self-deprecating humor, she skillfully transforms the reader into her confidant; by carefully selecting the exact details, she brings a lost world vividly to life. Few authors are her equal when it comes to transporting the reader back to the Old West. For these reasons alone, the decision to bring *Tenting on the Plains* back into print has been long overdue.

NOTES TO FOREWORD

1. Minnie Dubbs Millbrook, "The Boy General and How He Grew: George Custer after Appomattox," *Montana:The Magazine of Western History* 23 (spring 1973): 34–43.
2. Minnie Dubbs Millbrook, "The West Breaks in General Custer," *Kansas Historical Quarterly* 36 (summer 1970): 113–48.
3. Robert M. Utley, *Cavalier in Buckskin: George Armstrong Custer and the Western Military Frontier* (Norman: University of Oklahoma Press, 1988), 36–38, 50.
4. Utley, 107–8; Mathey, Col. E. G. Interview by Walter M. Camp, 19 October 1910, Box 6, Folder 5, Camp Papers, Harold B. Lee Library, Brigham Young University, Provo, Utah.
5. William T. Sherman to Elizabeth B. Custer, 4 January 1889, Elizabeth Bacon Custer Collection, Microfilm Roll 3, Little Bighorn Battlefield National Monument, Crow Agency, Montana.
6. Theodore Roosevelt to Honorable H. A. Conant, 16 January 1907, Michigan Custer Memorial Association Minutes, quoted by Lawrence Frost, *General Custer's Libbie* (Seattle: Superior Publishing Co., 1976), 292.

INTRODUCTION

By Jane R. Stewart

AFTER HER HUSBAND WAS KILLED at the Battle of the Little Big Horn on June 25, 1876, Mrs. George Armstrong Custer turned to what had been her solace at the other times of separation from him—writing. Only now, instead of writing letters to "Autie" about events at home, she was writing to the American public about the everyday occurrences of the life she and her husband had shared during the twelve years she had followed him from post to post as an army wife. *"Boots and Saddles,"* published in 1885, had met with such popular acclaim, if not great financial success, that when Mrs. Custer found herself in financial difficulties she again took up her pen.

Apparently most of the $4,750 received from a policy with the New York Life Insurance Company and over $1,000 from a widows' relief fund, organized by the *Army and Navy Journal* in co-operation with several newspapers, had been used to satisfy her husband's creditors and to take care of her own living expenses. When Russell Alger, who had served in the Civil War under General Custer, was governor of Michigan, Mrs. Custer wrote him and asked his assistance in selling her home in Monroe, Michigan, "converting it into money which would do me so much good if I had it nowadays." She added that he, along with other friends in Michigan, had noted "the successful sale and newspaper recommendation" of her book, but de-

clared that her hope that it would prove a money-maker
had been disappointed, for "bookmaking is only a source
of profit to the publishers and brings but a few hundred
dollars to the author,"[1] a sentiment that has been shared by
authors before and since.

Tenting on the Plains, published on December 13, 1887,
was issued not by Harper and Brothers who had published
"Boots and Saddles," but by C. L. Webster and Company,
also of New York, possibly because of Mrs. Custer's financial disappointment over the first book. The original edition of *Tenting on the Plains* was printed in large type and
contained 702 outsize pages. It was published in London
in the same format in 1888 and in the next year, 1889, was
reprinted by Webster. In 1893, Webster issued the work
in a smaller format with 403 pages, some chapters being
omitted. In that same year the abridged edition was also
published in London.

In 1895 the shorter version was reprinted by Harper
and Brothers. The Harpers reprint is identical with the
1893 edition except for the title page and the deletion of
several unnumbered pages of book advertising at the end
of the volume. In 1890, Harpers had published Mrs. Custer's
Following the Guidon, the third volume of the trilogy, and
it may have been considered advantageous to have all
three books issued by the same house. New printings of
Tenting on the Plains were made at intervals until January
19, 1915, the year the original copyright expired. The
present edition is a reprint of the 1895 edition (abridged)
published by Harpers.

Chronologically *Tenting on the Plains* is the first of the
three volumes, though it was the second book published. It
covers the earliest incidents recorded by Mrs. Custer, from
the Custers' marriage in 1864 until the court-martial in
1867, an event which Mrs. Custer does not mention at all.
Following the Guidon, published last, is concerned with
the period of greatest activity against the Indians, from

1867 to 1869. "*Boots and Saddles*," published first, tells of the Custers' last years together, ending when the army wives waiting at Fort Lincoln, North Dakota, received word of the tragedy at the Little Big Horn.

In addition to these books, Mrs. Custer wrote several articles. "Out of the Way Outing" appeared in *Harper's Weekly* for July 18, 1891; "Woman's Life on the Frontier" in *Lippincott's* for February, 1900; and in September, 1900, "Home Making in the American Army" in *Harper's Bazaar*.

Tenting on the Plains deals with the period immediately following the Civil War, when General Custer was stationed first in Texas and later on the Kansas frontier and covers a period of relative calm in his fighting career. Mrs. Custer had many letters and other written sources which she could use for reference; yet to a considerable extent she had to depend on her memory, and we may be sure that General Custer's reputation did not suffer thereby.

In writing about the summer expedition of 1867, Mrs. Custer relies almost entirely on extracts from letters written to her by Custer. She states that out of the many letters received she used only those "pertaining to the chase, the march, and the camp life after the tents were pitched at night." The first letter, dated March 27, 1867, was written at the first night's encampment on Chapman Creek, about a three-hour march from Fort Riley. The last letter, dated June 22, 1867, was from a campsite near the forks of the Republican River, about twenty-five miles from Fort Wallace, in which Custer says, "Tell me when you can be at [Fort] Wallace and I will send a squadron there for you. Our marching will not be hard for you, although we sometimes make thirty-five miles a day, it is not usual."

Throughout these extracts—which comprise three chapters—we read of Custer's concern for his wife's welfare and his great desire that she join him. A fourth chapter, devoted to extracts from some of Mrs. Custer's letters to

Custer, throws considerable light upon her personality and disposition: she was not always the understanding and uncomplaining wife which she seemed to have been.

As in all of her books, Mrs. Custer refers to her husband as "the General" regardless of his actual rank at any particular time. In doing so, she was perfectly correct, since under army regulations an officer was entitled to be addressed or referred to by the title of the highest rank he had held, whether actual or brevet. This practice of calling an officer "Colonel," for example, when his real or current rank was captain is often confusing to present-day readers and seems an affectation, but it was usual and permissible. Custer is mentioned on almost every page of the book, and if at times the title is almost an intrusion, it must be remembered that Mrs. Custer's greatest interest and desire was to keep Autie's name before the public. She apparently felt that everyone else would be as much interested in the General and his activities as she was herself.

Mrs. Custer's narrative begins as the Civil War was drawing to a close. At the end of the war, while Custer's command was encamped at Arlington, Virginia, General Sheridan asked Custer if he would like to take command of a division of cavalry on the Red River in Louisiana and lead a march into Texas. He believed it would be necessary to police the former Confederate states of Louisiana and especially Texas, which had been rather isolated and harbored many lawless men within its borders. Later Sheridan's idea was reinforced by General Sherman, who indicated that an expedition might be ordered into Texas against Kirby Smith, the leader of a rebel army which was still defying the United States government.

The primary reason for the proposed expedition, however, was French intervention in Mexico. Taking advantage of the fact that the attention of the United States government was centered on the Civil War and domestic problems arising from it, French Emperor Napoleon III had installed the Archduke Maximilian of Hapsburg as Emperor of

Mexico in 1864 and supported him with a French army. When the Civil War was over, a United States army was concentrated along the Río Grande, and Napoleon was notified to either withdraw his troops or have them thrown out of Mexico.

Custer accepted the assignment with alacrity and received his official orders the day before the Grand Review, which was held in Washington the twenty-third and twenty-fourth of May, 1865. Jay Monaghan gives a graphic account of the review in his *Custer—the Life of General George Armstrong Custer* (Boston, 1959). At the review, General Custer, according to his wife, "was permitted to doff his hat and bow low, as he proudly led that superb body of men, the Third Division of Cavalry, in front of the grand stand." But she makes no mention of the runaway, when Custer's horse, Don Juan, bolted and carried his rider past the reviewing stand in a wild dash. Custer quickly brought his steed under control, rode back to his place in the column, and passed the reviewing stand again, this time in a more decorous manner. It was difficult for some persons to believe that Custer, a master horseman, had lost control of his mount on such an occasion, and they put it down as simply a grand-stand play designed to attract attention. Immediately after the review, Custer took sad leave of his division at their encampment on the outskirts of Washington.

The early chapters of *Tenting on the Plains* which describe the journey by train from Washington, D.C., to Louisville, Kentucky, and thence by steamer to New Orleans, Louisiana, give us a colorful account of conditions existing at the time of the journey and so are interesting as social history, for by the time the book appeared in print, many customs were rapidly fading into the past.

On this trip, General and Mrs. Custer were accompanied by members of the General's staff, for whose services he had applied when he became a brigadier general, and by Eliza, a former slave set free by the Civil War. She had been Custer's cook during the last three years of the war, and although taken prisoner twice by the Confederates, had managed to escape and return to Custer both times. She had accompanied his command on many raids and winter marches, and was present at most of the important battles of the Army of the Potomac. There is an account of her courage under fire, when she would mutter about the bothersome shells bursting around her, take up her pots, start a fire in a new location, and continue cooking.

At one of the eating stops along the way to Louisiana, the proprietor of a lunchroom tried to banish Eliza from the dining table because of her color; but General Custer insisted that since no other table had been provided for servants, she should remain. The staff backed the General, and the proprietor was forced to give in, though he did so somewhat ungraciously. General Custer, who had real affection for Eliza whatever his feelings may have been toward the Negro race, says that she was a great favorite with most of the officers and soldiers in the cavalry and that "few had not at some time or other cause to remember her kindness."[2]

Traveling on the same train as the Custer party were many discharged officers and soldiers, happy to be going home at last, full of fun and mischief. One trick which they pulled was an old one, and has been described often with slight variations. The idea was for a pair of soldiers who wanted an entire coach seat to themselves to pretend that the coats which they were wearing had recently belonged to smallpox victims. As they discussed this in loud voices, the original occupants of the car would leave in haste. And, of course, if the soldiers felt they were dispossessing civilians who had profited by the war, it just made a good joke better.

Mrs. Custer says that at every station stop en route, the debarking soldiers were greeted with great enthusiasm and festivities which often included a parade and a brass band. Occasionally a sad note was sounded when a wounded soldier was carried out of a railroad car on a stretcher, at which time the crowd stood by quietly and respectfully.

In describing these homecoming celebrations, Mrs. Custer expresses regret that the General, in choosing to serve his country further, received none of the fanfare. She speaks of the lucrative political appointments that were going to other returning heroes, while her husband's only reward was her adulation. She failed to consider the fact that, during the summer months the Custers had spent in Monroe after the General was mustered out of the army, he had declined several business opportunities and even the possibility of a consular post; he was not quite as neglected as she implies.

The railroad journey terminated at Louisville, Kentucky, and from there the trip continued on one of the largest and most luxurious Mississippi River steamboats, the *Ruth.* At New Orleans the Custers and staff left this steamer with real regret.

Orders detained them at New Orleans for days, and they took full advantage of the delay. They were intrigued with the foreign flavor of the city, especially the French restaurants and the open markets with their colorful displays of fruits and vegetables. They spent a good part of their time sight-seeing in the horse-drawn cars, attending the theaters, and shopping in the exclusive stores. General Custer succeeded in getting Eliza to wear the colorful turban which was so much a part of the costume of the local servants. One of the popular fads of the day for the great and near-great was to have a miniature portrait painted on a porcelain vase, and Custer took advantage of an opportunity to have his picture painted by Mr. R. T. Lux, one of the popular artists of the city.[3]

The Custers dined with General Sheridan in his mansion, where, according to Mrs. Custer, he was living most handsomely. Later in the evening, leaving Mrs. Custer to be entertained by other guests and relatives, the two generals withdrew for a discussion of the problems of the army which Sheridan was organizing for the possible campaign across the border. Pontoon trains had been sent up the Red River to Alexandria, where troops were being concentrated, and Custer was expected to organize these regiments for a march into Texas. If an invasion of Mexico proved to be unnecessary, as it eventually did, the troops were to stay in Texas and maintain order in that rebellious state.

After Custer joined the cavalry division at Alexandria, he experienced severe disciplinary problems which closely approached mutiny. The problem was not peculiar to Custer's command, however; the troops which Colonels Samuel Walker and Nelson Cole led into the Powder River country in 1866 as part of the Connor expedition came close to mutiny, and their actions were partly responsible for this great campaign's turning into a grand fiasco. Several factors caused the crisis at Alexandria—for one thing, the volunteers who had joined the army to fight the Civil War felt that they should be discharged and sent home since the conflict was over. In addition, Custer was something of a martinet, having little patience with green troops, and some of his disciplinary measures seem to have been unduly harsh.

Eventually, if not inevitably, the problem came to a climax, with an episode involving the Third Michigan. It started with a rather trivial incident which went too far and led to the court-martial of a sergeant who was one of the ringleaders. He was convicted and sentenced to be shot. This sentence in turn led to threats that if it were carried out, General Custer would be shot in retaliation. In the ensuing confrontation Custer called his command's bluff, and won. Mrs. Custer gives us a very dramatic version, possibly somewhat exaggerated, of the whole affair. And she later discovered that the revolver Custer kept by his side at her request during this incident was never loaded.

Custer had other problems in Alexandria with both the former Confederate soldiers and the Negroes. Many Confederates still showed a rebellious spirit, and many of the Negroes, reveling in their new freedom, seemed to think that it was no longer necessary for them to work to support themselves. Custer finally issued an order that no freedmen were to be allowed in the vicinity of the camps unless they were employed.

From Alexandria the column first moved to Hempstead, Texas, where a semipermanent camp was established to recruit men and horses. General Custer's brother Tom, who was to serve as forage agent, and his father, Emanuel, joined the Custers there, having come from Galveston by boat. A short time later, the wives of two of the staff officers arrived in camp; one of them, Mrs. Jacob Greene, the wife of Custer's assistant adjutant general, was the former Nettie Humphrey of Monroe and a good friend of Mrs. Custer.

To break the monotony of camp life, the little community organized hunting parties and horse races, activities which the senior Custer enjoyed as much as his sons. He was an excellent judge of horseflesh and devised a plan to even the score with his sons for the many practical and somewhat rough jokes they had played on him. He inveigled them into a horse-judging contest with Mrs. Custer, which was made more interesting by a good-sized side bet. Then on the sly he supplied her with all the correct answers, so that she easily won the contest, the horse, and the side bet, the proceeds of which went for a new dress.

In November, orders came to move on to Austin, the state capital, for the winter. Mrs. Custer complained of the lawlessness in Texas—many of the returned Confederate soldiers were unemployed and, like countless other southerners, reluctant to admit that the war was over. They were also unwilling to accept the Emancipation Proclamation, and in the northern part of the state slaves were still being bought and sold. These difficulties were partially offset by the fact that Texas was one Southern state which had not been devastated by the war, and gradually civil authorities were better able to enforce the laws. This fact, along with the growing belief in the North that the South should be allowed to work out its own problems, was responsible for the decision that a cavalry division was no longer needed there. On January 31, 1866, General Custer received the order mustering him out of service as major general of volunteers and sending him north to await a new assignment.

The Custers headed home by way of Galveston and New Orleans. Arriving in Monroe, Michigan, they were warmly welcomed by their respective families, and moved into the home of Judge Bacon, Mrs. Custer's father.

It was a time of readjustment, and, probably in an attempt to learn what plans the War Department had for him, General Custer went to Washington and New York City. In the national capital he talked with Secretary of War Stanton and also with General Grant. Then, on May 18, 1866, Judge Bacon died, and Custer promptly returned to Monroe to be with his wife. Judge Bacon left all of his estate to his only child, with the provision that enough property be sold to raise the sum of $5,000, which was to be lent out, the interest accruing to be paid to her stepmother for life.

Although with the demobilization of the Union armies he reverted to the rank of captain, Custer after some months of indecision decided to keep his army commission. He had considered, and ultimately rejected, the possibility of serving under Juárez, leader of the republican forces in Mexico which were attempting to drive Maximilian out of the country now that he no longer had French support. The Army Reorganization Bill of 1866 created the post of Inspector General of Cavalry, to which Custer apparently hoped to be appointed. Failing this, he accepted the lieutenant-colonelcy of one of the four cavalry regiments, two of them Negro, also created by this bill. He probably chose the Seventh Cavalry instead of the Ninth because of the belief then common among army officers that Negroes did not make good soldiers; the appointment as lieutenant colonel of the Ninth went to Wesley Merritt, who had graduated from West Point ahead of Custer and was one step ahead of him in the list of lieutenant colonels. Appointment to a Negro regiment, however, was not a disadvantage—both Ranald Mackenzie, who had graduated from the military academy after Custer, and Nelson Miles, who had gone into the army directly from civilian life at the beginning of the Civil War, became colonels of Negro infantry regiments. Both were later transferred to white regiments, Miles to the Fifth Infantry and Mackenzie to the Fourth Cavalry, without any loss of rank or privileges.

Custer was first ordered to report for duty to Fort Garland, Colorado, but the increasing opposition of the Sioux to the construction of the Kansas Pacific Railroad led to a change of orders. He was sent instead to Fort Riley, Kansas, and it was here that the new regiment, the Seventh Cavalry, came into being. Fort Riley was in the Department of Missouri, one of four departments composing the Division of the Missouri, all under the command of General William Tecumseh Sherman.

Mrs. Custer felt the change in orders was an improvement—it was much easier to locate Fort Riley on the map, and the Kansas Pacific Railroad had been laid to within ten miles of the fort. It was completed to Fort Riley and beyond while the Custers were stationed there. Indeed, the railroad from Fort Harker to Fort Riley was to be partly responsible for the indiscretion that led to Custer's subsequent court-martial.

The things which Mrs. Custer does not tell us are often as interesting as those she does relate. This was the period of reconstruction, highlighted by the unfortunate and bitter quarrel between President Andrew Johnson and a radical Congress determined that the states of the former Confederacy must be punished. Custer was a Democrat. He shared the Southern point of view on many subjects and had many friends among the officers of the Confederate forces; moreover, his residence in Louisiana and Texas had given him an understanding of the problems faced by the people of the South in restoring a normal way of life and in taking their proper place in the life of the nation. He regarded the granting of immediate suffrage to the former slaves as an absurdity, and he did not hesitate to say so, basing his objections on his own observations of Southern field hands. He accompanied the President on the famous "swing around the circle," but soon became the subject of considerable criticism and was astute enough to realize that he was trying to move against the current of American public opinion. Compared with the cutthroat competition of politics, a military career was peaceful and secure. Thus he abruptly abandoned the political scene and headed for the "wide open spaces" of the western plains where he was to establish his greatest reputation.

Furnishings for the Custers' quarters at Fort Riley were to be purchased at Fort Leavenworth to shorten the hauling distance and decrease the expense. However, in order to "beautify their army quarters," they did take a companion for Mrs. Custer from Monroe, a Miss Diana. Mrs. Custer frequently mentions the girl, always by her given name or simply as "our young friend." Her surname is not given. In a cavalry post where there were few young attractive, unmarried women, Diana became very popular and much sought after.

A week was spent in St. Louis, Missouri, where the Custers and their party had arrived in a private railroad car, the guests of friends. A highlight of their stay was attending the new play, *Rosedale*, starring Lawrence Barrett. According to Mrs. Custer, on finding that Mr. Barrett was staying at their hotel, General Custer was able to entice him to a reception to meet their friends. Barrett's version was that Custer came backstage and knocked on the door of his dressing room. In any case, the two men were mutually attracted, and a life-long friendship developed.

From St. Louis, the Custers went to Fort Leavenworth, Kansas. This fort, which has been maintained as an army post since it was established in 1827, was to be the basic supply depot for Custer's command. From there they traveled by rail to the end of the line, ten miles from Fort Riley. Laborers were laying track for the line which was to extend to Denver, Colorado, and part of the Seventh Cavalry's duty would be to guard them from Indian attacks. As she admits, Mrs. Custer's first reaction to Fort Riley was one of extreme disappointment. She had expected something much more elaborate than this bare parade ground surrounded by small buildings, without a tree in sight. This was probably the typical reaction of army wives from the East, who thought of a fort as a set of neat, well-kept brick or frame buildings surrounding an attractive tree-shaded parade ground.

But Mrs. Custer also mentions the warm hospitality extended by Mrs. Alfred Gibbs, the wife of the senior major of the Seventh Cavalry who had been commanding at the post. As the regular Seventh Cavalry officers reported for duty, the officers from other regiments who had been on temporary or detached service started to move out. When Andrew J. Smith, the regiment's colonel, arrived, the Custers were "ranked out" of their quarters. This old army custom of assigning quarters according to rank was new to Mrs. Custer, but she soon became accustomed to the practice and even somewhat amused by it.

Colonel Smith was a veteran of the Mexican War and like Custer had been a major general during the Civil War. He had also spent considerable time on the western frontier in the 1850's. But his active years were largely behind him, and he was perfectly willing to let the real task of getting the regiment into shape fall on the shoulders of its lieutenant colonel. A great deal of drill and discipline was necessary to make the regiment an effective fighting force; and although Custer did not like this task, he did not shirk it. Desertions, which were a serious problem throughout the army at this time, were extremely heavy in regiments on the western frontier, including the Seventh Cavalry.

Custer also had problems with his officers, a motley and dissentious group composed of West Point graduates, political appointees, and men who had come up through the ranks. While there were some men of excellent character and ability, others were seeking the easy life which they mistakenly believed the peacetime army would afford. A few of the officers were simply incompetent, and some found it impossible to adjust to the hard realities of service at a frontier post. A number, like Custer, had held higher rank during the Civil War, and they resented not only their reduction in rank but also the necessity of serving under a commanding officer who was considerably their junior in years.

Mrs. Custer says she watched with some apprehension as General Custer worked with his new officers; noting the lack of harmony, she felt sure that a "less persevering man would have been discouraged." Her misgivings were not without foundation, as the regiment soon divided into pro- and anti-Custer factions. Not identifying any by name, Mrs. Custer mentions that there were several Irish officers, one of whom had served in the Papal army; this must have been Captain Myles Keogh, who lost his life at the Battle of the Little Big Horn. Another officer she mentions, a descendant of Alexander Hamilton, was Captain Louis McLane Hamilton, who was killed at the Battle of the Washita. Some of the other officers were Captain George Yates, an old Monroe friend, Myles Moylan, and Lieutenant William Cook, who had received his lieutenant-colonelcy in the closing days of the Civil War and had been made adjutant to the Seventh by Custer.

Elizabeth Bacon Custer could make a house a home wherever the General was stationed, but she was somewhat deficient in housekeeping skills, possibly because of the overindulgence of her stepmother. General Custer did not like his wife to be burdened with housekeeping duties, especially the primitive ones of the frontier. He wanted a wife who was ready to drop everything to go for a gallop with him or to join him in the library to read the newest issues of *Harper's Weekly* or *Harper's Bazaar*. He was demanding of her time and attention and saw no reason for her to do tasks which could be turned over to others, so in addition to the ever faithful Eliza other help was added whenever possible.

The spring months of 1867 saw the expedition against the Indians materialize. It came as no surprise to the regiment; they knew that with the resumption of construction on the Kansas Pacific Railroad, the Indians would be on the warpath. The expedition, one of the most elaborate ever planned against the Indians of the Great Plains, was under the command of General Winfield Scott Hancock, commander of the Department of Missouri, who left Fort Leavenworth on March 1, 1867, with seven companies of infantry and a battery of artillery. At Fort Riley they were joined by the Seventh Cavalry, with Colonel Smith and Lieutenant Colonel Custer commanding. Beset with troubles almost from the start, the expedition was far from a success. It had been given much publicity and was even accompanied by two journalists, Henry Morton Stanley of the *New York Herald* and the *Missouri Democrat* and Theodore R. Davis of *Harper's*. Pressures on the government had been increasing, and General Sherman had hoped to clear out the unfriendly Indians in the area between the Arkansas and the Platte rivers with the cavalry under Custer's command.[4]

Hancock had attempted to hold a council with the hostile Indians, but they managed to elude him by abandoning their village, leaving most of the tipis standing. Custer was sent in pursuit with the cavalry. Six companies of the Seventh Cavalry were ordered to leave the Smoky Hill River and ride toward the Platte. They were to scout to Fort McPherson on the Platte, describe a small semicircle southward, touching the headwaters of the Republican

River, and then travel toward Fort Sedgwick on the Platte. Here supplies would be replenished, and afterward they would move south to Fort Wallace on the Smoky Hill (along the valley of which ran the overland stage route) and thence to the starting point at Fort Hays—about one thousand miles in all.[5]

At Riverside station, some fifty miles west of Fort Sedgwick, Custer sent a telegram to the fort to find out if there were any instructions from General Sherman. Upon learning that he had missed the orders which Lieutenant Lyman S. Kidder with a guide and ten soldiers was trying to deliver to him, Custer ordered a forced march to try to locate Kidder and his party.

Among some of the officers as well as the troopers there was considerable resentment to the many forced marches. Desertions by this time had become an almost nightly occurrence despite all efforts to prevent them, and the situation was further aggravated by the fact that the men were campaigning in a region on the main-traveled road to the Colorado mines.

While the group was preparing to march at dawn, about forty more men deserted, but because of the need for haste no attempt was made to pursue them. After a fifteen-mile march, the command halted at noon to rest and graze the horses. While the group was repacking to continue the march, thirteen soldiers started out across the plains, six dismounted and seven on government horses.[6]

Custer ordered the officer of the guard to mount his command and try to overtake the deserters. The officer of the day, Lieutenant Jackson, was not prepared to move immediately, but Major Elliot, Adjutant Cook, and Tom Custer started in pursuit. Shots were heard, and shortly six prisoners were brought in, three of them wounded. The others had made good their escape. Custer was later accused of having ordered the doctor not to treat these wounded men, but some of the officers testified that out of hearing of the men he did request treatment for them.

On the next day's march, Custer again forced the pace, knowing that unless Lieutenant Kidder and his party were found soon, it might be too late. His apprehension proved to be right when the column located the men's bodies, stripped and badly mutilated.[7]

After giving proper military burial to Kidder and his men, Custer's command moved on to Fort Wallace, which was on the road from Fort Riley to Denver. On arriving there, they found the fort suffering from the cholera then spreading through the western settlements, and the problem of moldy and substandard rations was intensified by the fact that Indians had virtually cut off all supply lines. In the absence of further specific orders, Custer devised a plan to take one hundred of the best mounted men and travel the most dangerous stretch, the 150 miles to Fort Hays, in a body. From there he and a small escort would push on to Fort Harker and have wagons with supplies ready to return to Fort Wallace when the slower-moving main body arrived.

On July 15 at sunset, Custer left Fort Wallace for Forts Hays and Harker. The marching was done at night, the column stopping at the stations on the stagecoach line. At one of these stops, Downer's Station, Custer was advised that a small group of soldiers who had loitered at the rear of the column had been cut off and attacked by Indians and two cavalrymen killed. He decided to leave their burial to the troops at the station, and pushed on. Failure to aid the detachment, recover the bodies, and try to retaliate against the Indians were among the specifications leveled against Custer by the prosecution at his court-martial.[8]

Custer arrived at Fort Hays at 3:00 A.M. on July 18, having marched the 150 miles in just fifty-five hours, including all halts and rest stops. He continued his ride to Fort Harker, accompanied by Lieutenant Cook, Tom Custer, and two troopers, reaching the post at 2:00 A.M. on July 19. Custer made his report to Colonel A. J. Smith, who was commanding the District of the Lower Arkansas with headquarters at Fort Harker, and, after requesting permission of Colonel Smith, left an hour later on the train for Fort Riley and in a few hours was home with Mrs. Custer. Whether or not he believed that permission had been given is a moot point. Mrs. Custer says that "he [Custer] knew well that nothing we might encounter could equal the desolation and suspense of the days that I was enduring at Fort Riley." She refers to a long, perfect day and concludes her narrative with these lines: "It was mine and blessed be our memory, which preserves to us the joys as well as the sadness of life!—it is still mine, for time and eternity."

Shortly after Custer's arrival at Fort Riley, he received a telegram from Colonel Smith ordering him to return to his command at once. Custer knew that he was in serious trouble, but was unable to get a return train until July 21. When he reported to Colonel Smith, he was placed under arrest. Smith liked Custer and, since he was accompanied by Mrs. Custer, ordered him to return to Fort Riley and stay there under arrest until he received court-martial charges.[9]

Several charges were preferred against Custer—leaving his command at Fort Wallace without authority; excessive cruelty and illegal conduct in ordering his officers to shoot deserters; abandoning the two soldiers who were killed near Downer's Station; and ordering his men on excessively long marches.

The court-martial convened at Fort Leavenworth, Kansas, at 11:00 A.M. on September 15, 1867. Approximately a month later a verdict of guilty was delivered, and Brevet Major General George A. Custer, lieutenant colonel of the Seventh United States Cavalry, was suspended from rank and command for one year, forfeiting his pay proper for the same time. The trial is a matter of official record, and in his book, *The Court-Martial of General George Armstrong Custer* (Norman, 1968), Lawrence Frost gives a detailed explanation of the trial and its background.

During this period Mrs. Custer corresponded frequently

with her cousin and good friend, Rebecca Richmond. Commenting on the unfairness of the sentence in one of her letters, she added that at least she and her husband could be together for a whole year and he would not be participating in any Indian campaigns. Perhaps it was just bravado, but she concluded her letter by saying that she and Autie were in high spirits, much to the amazement of their friends at the post.

Undoubtedly both of the Custers were deeply hurt and bitter over the trial, but the appearance they tried to maintain was light and debonair. Custer referred to his sentence as a vacation and said that it would give him the time and leisure to do some writing. He even claimed to be contemplating foreign travel, which he well knew would not be possible without specific permission from the War Department.

Court-martial at that time was not considered the disgrace that it is today, and the Custers had the freedom of the post. General Sheridan, who apparently had a distinct liking for Custer, allowed him to occupy the Sheridans' quarters at Fort Leavenworth during the winter; in the spring the Custers returned to Monroe. At Sheridan's request, Custer was recalled to duty to help in the Indian campaigns before the end of his year's sentence.

Mrs. Custer never criticized Autie in any way, nor allowed anyone else to do so without a prompt rebuttal, usually in print. It has been said many times that she was the best press agent a man could have. Thus it is fitting that a brief account of Mrs. Custer be included here.

She was born Elizabeth Clift Bacon on April 8, 1842, in Monroe, Michigan, the daughter of Judge and Mrs. Daniel Bacon. Her mother, the former Sophia Page of Grand Rapids, Michigan, had married Daniel Bacon in September,

1837. Mrs. Bacon died in August, 1854, and the judge moved to a boarding house, placing his daughter in a boarding school. Several years later he married Mrs. Rhoda Pitts, the widow of a Congregational minister, thus providing a home life once again for Elizabeth.

Called "Libbie" by her friends, who seem to have been numerous, Elizabeth enjoyed a busy round of social activities. She attended a female seminary in Monroe, which had been established by her father and several other leading citizens who were interested in education.

One winter (probably in November, 1862) while Captain George Armstrong Custer was spending his leave in Monroe at the home of his half sister, Mrs. David Reed, he was introduced to Elizabeth Bacon. From their first meeting he was greatly attracted to Elizabeth, and she in turn was not immune to the attentions of the dashing young Captain Custer. Although Judge Bacon admired Custer for his record in the Civil War, he did not approve of the army as a career, feeling that the life of an army officer's wife would be much too difficult for his daughter. Several letters were exchanged between Custer and Elizabeth's good friend Nettie Humphrey, all pertaining to the subject close to the former's heart—Libbie Bacon. Custer finally became impatient and, taking matters into his own hands, wrote directly to Judge Bacon asking for the privilege of corresponding with Elizabeth. (Social custom would not allow such correspondence without the consent of her parents.) Permission was granted, and, assuming that it also implied the right of courtship, Custer lost no time in trying to persuade Elizabeth to be his wife. They wrote many, many letters to each other, a habit which continued after they were married, and Elizabeth saved every letter that she ever received from Armstrong. Their wedding took place on February 9, 1864, in the Presbyterian church in Monroe, only a year and a few months after their first meeting.

Small, slender, and delicate in appearance almost to the

point of fragility, Elizabeth Bacon Custer did not look the type to share a life of privation and hardship.[10] Yet she did just that, giving up friends and a comfortable home to be the wife of a man whose career would lead her to many varied, temporary homes—she was the only army wife who always followed her husband wherever he was stationed. Undoubtedly, Mrs. Custer exaggerated some of the dangers which she faced at these various army posts. She was perhaps a little bit of a coward and had a tendency to over-emphasize the hardships which she endured. What she did not exaggerate, however, was the love and admiration that she had for her husband.

She was two days short of her ninety-first birthday when she died on the fourth of April, 1933, in the New York City apartment where she had lived quietly for several years. Her fifty-seven years of widowhood were devoted to memorializing her husband. It was almost an axiom among students of the Battle of the Little Big Horn that the full truth about the battle would never be known as long as Mrs. Custer lived; the officers and men who survived held their tongues out of deference to her, and she outlived all her husband's critics. At her death the only surviving officer was Charles Varnum, who had been a second lieutenant in charge of Indian scouts. Thus, through determination, persistence, and longevity, the final triumph was hers.

Notes to Introduction

1. This letter, dated June 15 (no year is given, but it was probably 1885 or 1886) and from 148 East Eighteenth Street, is now in the William L. Clements Library at the University of Michigan and is quoted by permission. Alger was elected governor of Michigan in 1884.

2. General George Armstrong Custer, *My Life on the Plains*, edited by Edgar I. Stewart (Norman, University of Oklahoma Press, 1962), 69.

3. A copy of this, which is now in possession of the J. C.

Custer family, is reproduced in Lawrence J. Frost, *The Court-Martial of General George Armstrong Custer* (Norman, University of Oklahoma Press, 1968), 48.

4. Frost, *Court-Martial*, 36.

5. G. A. Custer, *My Life on the Plains*, 53, 66.

6. *Ibid.*, 100–104; Also see Frost, *Court-Martial*, 69–71.

7. G. A. Custer, *My Life on the Plains*, 111–12; Also see Frost, *Court-Martial*, 24.

8. G. A. Custer, *My Life on the Plains*, 113–18; Also see Frost, *Court-Martial*, for a very detailed account of the proceedings of the trial.

9. Frost, *Court-Martial*, 85–86.

10. *Philadelphia Inquirer* "Army & Navy Journal," December 6, 1890.

CONTENTS

ILLUSTRATIONS

TENTING ON THE PLAINS.

CHAPTER I.

GOOD-BY TO THE ARMY OF THE POTOMAC.

GENERAL CUSTER was given scant time, after the last gun of the war was fired, to realize the blessings of peace. While others hastened to discard the well-worn uniforms, and don again the dress of civilians, hurrying to the cars, and groaning over the slowness of the fast-flying trains that bore them to their homes, my husband was almost breathlessly preparing for a long journey to Texas. He did not even see the last of that grand review of the 23d and 24th of May, 1865. On the first day he was permitted to doff his hat and bow low, as he proudly led that superb body of men, the Third Division of Cavalry, in front of the grand stand, where sat the "powers that be." Along the line of the division, each soldier straightened himself in the saddle, and felt the proud blood fill his veins, as he realized that he was one of those who, in six months, had taken 111 of the enemy's guns, sixty-five battle-flags, and upward of 10,000 prisoners of war, while they had never lost a flag, or failed to capture a gun for which they fought.

In the afternoon of that memorable day General Custer and his staff rode to the outskirts of Washington, where his beloved Third Cavalry Division had encamped after returning from taking part in the review. The trumpet was sounded, and the call brought these war-worn veterans out once more, not for a charge, not for duty, but to say that word which we, who have been compelled to live in its mournful sound so many years, dread even to write. Down the line rode their yellow-haired " boy general," waving his hat, but setting his teeth and trying to hold with iron nerve the quivering muscles of his speaking face; keeping his eyes wide open,'that the moisture dimming their vision might not gather and fall. Cheer after cheer rose on that soft spring air. Some enthusiastic voice started up afresh, before the hurrahs were done, " A tiger for old Curley!" Off came the hats again, and up went hundreds of arms, waving the good-by and wafting innumerable blessings after the man who was sending them home in a blaze of glory, with a record of which they might boast around their firesides. I began to realize, as I watched this sad parting, the truth of what the General had been telling me; he held that no friendship was like that cemented by mutual danger on the battle-field.

The soldiers, accustomed to suppression through strict military discipline, now vehemently expressed their feelings; and though it gladdened the General's heart, it was still the hardest sort of work to endure it all without show of emotion. As he rode up to where I was waiting, he could not, dared not, trust himself to speak to me. To those intrepid men he was indebted for his success. Their unfailing trust in his judgment, their willingness to follow where he led— ah! he knew well that one looks upon such men but once in a lifetime. Some of the soldiers called out for the General's wife. The staff urged me to ride forward to the troops, as it was but a little thing thus to respond to their good-by. I tried to do so, but after a few steps, I begged those beside whom I rode to take me back to where we had been standing. I was too overcome, from having seen the suffering on my husband's face, to endure any more sorrow.

As the officers gathered about the General and wrung his hand in parting, to my surprise the soldiers gave me a cheer. Though very grateful for the tribute to me as their acknowledged comrade, I did not feel that I deserved it. Hardships

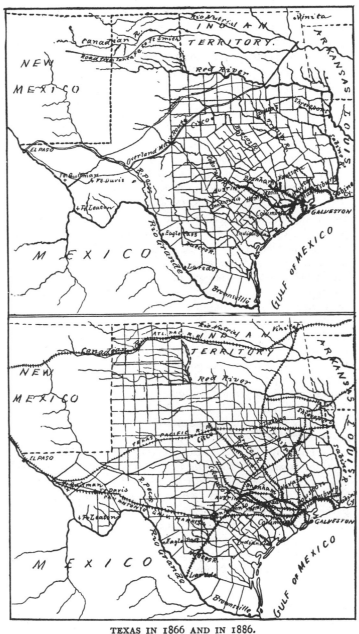

TEXAS IN 1866 AND IN 1886.

such as they had suffered for a principle require a far higher
order of character than the same hardships endured when the
motive is devotion individualized.

Once more the General leaped into the saddle, and we rode
rapidly out of sight. How glad I was, as I watched the set
features of my husband's face, saw his eyes fixed immovably
in front of him, listened in vain for one word from his over-
burdened heart, that I, being a woman, need not tax every
nerve to suppress emotion, but could let the tears stream
down my face, on all our silent way back to the city.

Then began the gathering of our "traps," a hasty collection of a few suitable things for a Southern climate, orders
about shipping the horses, a wild tearing around of the im-
provident, thoughtless staff—good fighters, but poor provid-
ers for themselves. Most of them were young men, for
whom my husband had applied when he was made a brigadier. His first step after his promotion was to write home
for his schoolmates, or select aides from his early friends then
in service. It was a comfort, when I found myself grieving
over the parting with my husband's Division, that our military family were to go with us. At dark we were on the
cars, with our faces turned southward. To General Custer
this move had been unexpected. General Sheridan knew
that he needed little time to decide, so he sent for him as
soon as we encamped at Arlington, after our march up from
Richmond, and asked if he would like to take command of
a division of cavalry on the Red River in Louisiana, and
march throughout Texas, with the possibility of eventually entering Mexico. Our Government was just then
thinking it was high time the French knew that if there was
any invasion of Mexico, with an idea of a complete "gob-
bling up" of that country, the one to do the seizure and
gather in the spoils was Brother Jonathan. Very wisely,
General Custer kept this latter part of the understanding why
he was sent South from the "weepy" part of his family.
He preferred transportation by steamer, rather than to be
floated southward by floods of feminine tears. All I knew

was, that Texas, having been so outside of the limit where the armies marched and fought, was unhappily unaware that the war was over, and continued a career of bushwhacking and lawlessness that was only tolerated from necessity before the surrender, and must now cease. It was considered expedient to fit out two detachments of cavalry, and start them on a march through the northern and southern portions of Texas, as a means of informing that isolated State that depredations and raids might come to an end. In my mind, Texas then seemed the stepping-off place; but I was indifferent to the points of the compass, so long as I was not left behind.

The train in which we set out was crowded with a joyous, rollicking, irrepressible throng of discharged officers and soldiers, going home to make their swords into ploughshares. Everybody talked with everybody, and all spoke at once. The Babel was unceasing night and day; there was not a vein that was not bursting with joy. The swift blood rushed into the heart and out again, laden with one glad thought, "The war is over!" At the stations, soldiers tumbled out and rushed into some woman's waiting arms, while bands tooted excited welcomes, no one instrument according with another, because of throats overcharged already with bursting notes of patriotism that would not be set music. The customary train of street gamins, who imitate all parades and promptly copy the pomp of the circus and other processions, stepped off in a mimic march, following the conquering heroes as they were lost to our sight down the street, going home.

Sometimes the voices of the hilarious crowd at the station were stilled, and a hush of reverent silence preceded the careful lifting from the car of a stretcher bearing a form broken and bleeding from wounds, willingly borne, that the home to which he was coming might be unharmed. Tender women received and hovered lovingly over the precious freight, strong arms carried him away; and we contrasted the devoted care, the love that would teach new ways to heal, with the condition of the poor fellows we had left in the crowded

Washington hospitals, attended only by strangers. Some of
the broken-to-pieces soldiers were on our train, so deftly
mended that they stumped their way down the platform, and
began their one-legged tramp through life, amidst the loud
huzzas that a maimed hero then received. They even joked
about their misfortunes. I remember one undaunted fellow,
with the fresh color of buoyant youth beginning again to dye
his cheek, even after the amputation of a leg, which so de-
pletes the system. He said some grave words of wisdom to
me in such a roguish way, and followed up his counsel by
adding, " You ought to heed such advice from a man with
one foot in the grave."

We missed all the home-coming, all the glorification award-
ed to the hero. General Custer said no word of regret. He
had accepted the offer for further active service, and grate-
fully thanked his chief for giving him the opportunity. I,
however, should have liked to have him get some of the celebrations that our country was then showering on its defenders. I missed the bonfires, the processions, the public meeting of distinguished citizens, who eloquently thanked the
veterans, the editorials that lauded each townsman's deed,
the poetry in the corner of the newspaper that was dedicated
to a hero, the overflow of a woman's heart singing praise to
her military idol. But the cannon were fired, the drums beat,
the music sounded for all but us. Offices of trust were offered at once to men coming home to private life, and towns
and cities felt themselves honored because some one of their
number had gone out and made himself so glorious a name
that his very home became celebrated. He was made the
mayor, or the Congressman, and given a home which it
would have taken him many years of hard work to earn.
Song, story and history have long recounted what a hero is
to a woman. Imagination pictured to my eye troops of
beautiful women gathering around each gallant soldier on
his return. The adoring eyes spoke admiration, while the
tongue subtly wove, in many a sentence, its meed of praise.
The General and his staff of boys, loving and reverencing

women, missed what men wisely count the sweetest of adulation. One weather-beaten slip of a girl had to do all their banqueting, cannonading, bonfiring, brass-banding, and general hallelujahs all the way to Texas, and—yes, even after we got there; for the Southern women, true to their idea òf patriotism, turned their pretty faces away from our handsome fellows, and resisted, for a long time, even the mildest flirtation.

The drawing-room car was then unthought of in the minds of those who plan new luxuries as our race demand more ease and elegance. There was a ladies' car, to which no men unaccompanied by women were admitted. It was never so full as the other coaches, and was much cleaner and better ventilated.

This was at first a damper to the enjoyment of a military family, who lost no opportunity of being together, for it compelled the men to remain in the other cars. The scamp among us devised a plan to outwit the brakemen; he borrowed my bag just before we were obliged to change cars, and after waiting till the General and I were safely seated, boldly walked up and demanded entrance, on the plea that he had a lady inside. This scheme worked so well that the others took up the cue, and my cloak, bag, umbrella, lunch-basket, and parcel of books and papers were distributed among the rest before we stopped, and were used to obtain entrance into the better car. Even our faithful servant, Eliza, was unexpectedly overwhelmed with urgent offers of assistance; for she always went with us, and sat by the door. This plan was a great success, in so far as it kept our party together, but it proved disastrous to me, as the scamp forgot my bag at some station, and I was minus all those hundred-and-one articles that seem indispensable to a traveler's comfort. In that plight I had to journey until, in some merciful detention, we had an hour in which to seek out a shop, and hastily make the necessary purchases.

At one of our stops for dinner we all made the usual rush for the dining-hall, as in the confusion of over-laden trains at that excited time it was necessary to hurry, and, besides,

as there were delays and irregularities in traveling, on account
of the home-coming of the troops, we never knew how long
it might be before the next eating-house was reached.   The
General insisted upon Eliza's going right with us, as no other
table was provided.   The proprietor, already rendered indifferent to people's comfort by his extraordinary gains, said
there was no table for servants.   Eliza, the best-bred of maids,
begged to go back dinnerless into the car, but the General
insisted on her sitting down between us at the crowded table.
A position so unusual, and to her so totally out of place,
made her appetite waver, and it vanished entirely when the
proprietor came, and told the General that no colored folks
could be allowed at his table.   My husband quietly replied
that he had been obliged to give the woman that place, as
the house had provided no other.   The determined man still
stood threateningly over us, demanding her removal, and
Eliza uneasily and nervously tried to go.   I trembled, and
the fork failed to carry the food, owing to a very wobbly arm.
The General firmly refused, the staff rose about us, and all
along the table up sprang men we had supposed to be citizens,
as they were in the dress of civilians.   "General, stand your
ground; we'll back you; the woman shall have food."   How
little we realize in these piping times of peace, how great a
flame a little fire kindled in those agitating days.   The proprietor slunk back to his desk; the General and his hungry
staff went on eating as calmly as ever; Eliza hung her embarrassed head, and her mistress idly twirled her useless fork
—while the proprietor made $1.50 clear gain on two women
that were too frightened to swallow a mouthful.   I spread a
sandwich for Eliza, while the General, mindful of the returning hunger of the terrified woman, and perfectly indifferent
as to making himself ridiculous with parcels, marched by the
infuriated but subdued bully, with either a whole pie or some
such modest capture in his hand.   We had put some hours
of travel between ourselves and the "twenty-minutes-for-din-
ner" place which came so near being a battle-ground, before
Eliza could eat what we had brought for her.

I wonder if any one is waiting for me to say that this incident happened south of the Mason and Dixon line. It did not. It was in Ohio—I don't remember the place. After all, the memory over which one complains, when he finds how little he can recall, has its advantages. It hopelessly buries the names of persons and places, when one starts to tell tales out of school. It is like extracting the fangs from a rattlesnake; the reptile, like the story, may be very disagreeable, but I can only hope that a tale unadorned with names or places is as harmless as a snake with its poison withdrawn.

I must stop a moment and give our Eliza, on whom this battle was waged, a little space in this story, for she occupied no small part in the events of the six years after; and when she left us and took an upward step in life by marrying a colored lawyer, I could not reconcile myself to the loss; and though she has lived through all the grandeur of a union with a man "who gets a heap of money for his speeches in politics, and brass bands to meet him at the stations, Miss Libbie," she came to my little home not long since with tears of joy illuminating the bright bronze of her expressive face. It reminded me so of the first time I knew that the negro race regarded shades of color as a distinctive feature, a beauty or a blemish, as it might be. Eliza stood in front of a bronze medallion of my husband when it was first sent from the artist's in 1865, and amused him hugely, by saying, in that partnership manner she had in our affairs, "Why, Ginnel, it's jest my color." After that, I noticed that she referred to her race according to the deepness of tint, telling me, with scorn, of one of her numerous suitors: "Why, Miss Libbie, he needent think to shine up to me; he's nothing but a black African." I am thus introducing Eliza, color and all, that she may not seem the vague character of other days; and whoever chances to meet her will find in her a good war historian, a modest chronicler of a really self-dying and courageous life. It was rather a surprise to me that she was not an old woman when I saw her again this autumn, after so many years, but she is not yet fifty. I imagine she did so much mothering in those days when she comforted me in my loneliness, and quieted me in my frights, that I counted her old even then.

Eliza requests that she be permitted to make her little bow to the reader, and repeat a wish of hers that I take great pains in quoting her, and not represent her as saying, "like field-hands, *whar* and *thar*." She says her people in Virginia, whom she reverences and loves, always taught her not to say "them words; and if they should see what I have told you they'd feel bad to think I forgot." If *whar* and *thar* appear occasionally in my efforts to transfer her literally to these pages, it is only a *lapsus linguæ* on her part. Besides, she has lived North so long now, there is not that distinctive dialect peculiar to the Southern servant. In her excitement, narrating our scenes of danger or pleasure or merriment, she occasionally drops into expressions that belonged to her early life. It is the fault of her historian if these phrases get into print. To me they are charming, for they are Eliza in undress uniform—Eliza without her company manners.

She describes her leaving the old plantation during war times: "I jined the Ginnel at Amosville, Rappahannock County, in August, 1863. Everybody was excited over freedom, and I wanted to see how it was. Everybody keeps asking me why I left. I can't see why they can't recollect what war was for, and that we was all bound to try and see for ourselves how it was. After the 'Mancipation, everybody was a-standin' up for liberty, and I wasent goin' to stay home when everybody else was a-goin'. The day I came into camp, there was a good many other darkeys from all about our place. We was a-standin' round waitin' when I first seed the Ginnel.

"He and Captain Lyon cum up to me, and the Ginnel says, 'Well, what's *your* name!' I told him Eliza; and he says, looking me all over fust, 'Well, Eliza, would you like to cum and live with me?' I waited a minute, Miss Libbie. I looked *him* all over, too, and finally I sez, 'I reckon I would.' So the bargain was fixed up. But, oh, how awful lonesome I was at fust, and I was afraid of everything in the

shape of war. I used to wish myself back on the old plantation with my mother. I was mighty glad when you cum,
Miss Libbie. Why, sometimes I never sot eyes on a woman
for weeks at a time."

Eliza's story of her war life is too long for these pages; but
in spite of her confession of being so " 'fraid," she was a marvel of courage. She was captured by the enemy, escaped,
and found her way back after sunset to the General's camp.
She had strange and narrow escapes. She says, quaintly :
" Well, Miss Libbie, I set in to see the war, beginning and
end. There was many niggers that cut into cities and huddled up thar, and laid around and saw hard times; but I went
to see the end, and I stuck it out. I allus thought this, that
I didn't set down to wait to have 'em all free *me*. I helped
to free myself. I was all ready to step to the front whenever
I was called upon, even if I didn't shoulder the musket.
Well, I went to the end, and there's many folks says that a
woman can't follow the army without throwing themselves
away, but I know better. I went in, and I cum out with the
respect of the men and the officers."

Eliza often cooked under fire, and only lately one of the
General's staff, recounting war days, described her as she was
preparing the General's dinner in the field. A shell would
burst near her; she would turn her head in anger at being
disturbed, unconscious that she was observed, begin to growl
to herself about being obliged to move, but take up her kettle and frying-pan, march farther away, make a new fire, and
begin cooking as unperturbed as if it were an ordinary disturbance instead of a sky filled with bits of falling shell. I
do not repeat that polite fiction of having been on the spot,
as neither the artist nor I had Eliza's grit or pluck; but we
arranged the camp-kettle, and Eliza fell into the exact expression, as she volubly began telling the tale of " how mad
those busting shells used to make her." It is an excellent
likeness, even though Eliza objects to the bandana, which
she has abandoned in her new position; and I must not forget that I found her one day turning her head critically from

ELIZA COOKING UNDER FIRE.

side to side looking at her picture; and, out of regard to her, will mention that her nose, of which she is very proud, is, she fears, a touch too flat in the sketch. She speaks of her dress as "completely whittled out with bullets," but she would like me to mention that "she don't wear them rags now."

When Eliza reached New York this past autumn, she told me, when I asked her to choose where she would go, as my time was to be entirely given to her, that she wanted first to go to the Fifth Avenue Hotel and see if it looked just the same as it did "when you was a bride, Miss Libbie, and the Ginnel took you and me there on leave of absence." We went through the halls and drawing-rooms, narrowly watched by the major-domo, who stands guard over tramps, but fortified by my voice, she "oh'd" and "ah'd" over its grandeur to her heart's content. One day I left her in Madison Square, to go on a business errand, and cautioned her not to stray away. When I returned I asked anxiously, "Did any one speak to you, Eliza?" "*Every*body, Miss Libbie," as nonchalant and as complacent as if it were her idea of New York hospitality. Then she begged me to go round the Square, "to hunt a lady from Avenue A, who see'd you pass with me, Miss Libbie, and said she knowed you was a lady, though I reckon she couldn't 'count for me and you bein' together." We found the Avenue A lady, and I was presented, and, to her satisfaction, admired the baby that had been brought over to that blessed breathing-place of our city.

The Elevated railroad was a surprise to Eliza. She "didn't believe it would be so high." At that celebrated curve on the Sixth Avenue line, where Monsieur de Lesseps, even, exclaimed, "Mon Dieu ! but the Americans are a brave people," the poor, frightened woman clung to me and whispered, "Miss Libbie, couldn't we get down anyway? Miss Libbie, I'se seed enough. I can tell the folks at home all about it *now*. Oh, I never did 'spect to be so near heaven till I went up for good."

At the Brooklyn Bridge she demurred. She is so intelligent that I wanted to have her see the shipping, the wharves, the harbor, and the statue of Liberty; but nothing kept her from flight save her desire to tell her townspeople that she had seen the place where the crank jumped off. The policeman, in answer to my inquiry, commanded us in martial tones to stay still till he said the word; and when the wagon crossing passed the spot, and the maintainer of the peace said "Now!" Eliza shivered and whispered, "*Now*, let's go home, Miss Libbie. I dun took the cullud part of the town fo' I come; the white folks hain't seen what I has, and they'll be took when I tell 'em;" and off she toddled, for Eliza is not the slender woman I once knew her.

Her description of the Wild West exhibition was most droll. I sent her down because we had lived through so many of the scenes depicted, and I felt sure that nothing would recall so vividly the life on the frontier as that most realistic and faithful representation of a Western life that has ceased to be, with advancing civilization. She went to Mr. Cody's tent after the exhibition, to present my card of introduction, for he had served as General Custer's scout after Eliza left us, and she was, therefore, unknown to him except by hearsay. They had twenty subjects in common; for Eliza, in her way, was as deserving of praise as was the courageous Cody. She was delighted with all she saw, and on her return her description of it, mingled with imitations of the voices of the hawkers and the performers, was so incoherent that it presented only a confused jumble to my ears. The buffalo were a surprise, a wonderful revival to her of those hunting-days when our plains were darkened by the herds. "When the buffalo cum in, I was ready to leap up and holler, Miss Libbie; it 'minded me of ole times. They made me think of the fifteen the Ginnel fust struck in Kansas. He jest pushed down his ole hat, and went after 'em linkety-clink. Well, Miss Libbie, when Mr. Cody come up, I see at once his back and hips was built precisely like the Ginnel, and when I come on to his tent, I jest said to him: ' Mr. Buffalo Bill, when you cum up to the stand and wheeled round, I said to myself,

" *Well*, if he ain't the 'spress image of Ginnel Custer in battle I never seed any one that was!" ' I jest wish he'd come to
my town and give a show ! He could have the hull fair-
ground there.   My ! he could raise money so fast 'twouldn't
take him long to *pay* for a church.   And the shootin' and
ridin' ! why, Miss Libbie, when I seed one of them ponies
brought out, I know'd he was one of the hatefulest, sulki-
est ponies that ever lived.   He was a-prancin' and curvin',
and he jest stretched his ole neck and throwed the men as
fast as ever they got on."

After we had strolled through the streets for many days,
Eliza always amusing me by her droll comments, she said to
me one day: "Miss Libbie, you don't take notice, when me
and you's walking on, a-lookin' into shop-windows and
a-gazin' at the new things I never see before, how the folks
does stare at us.   But I see 'em a-gazin', and I can see 'em
a-ponderin' and sayin' to theirsel's, ' Well, I do declar'! that's
a lady, there ain't no manner of doubt.   She's one of the
bong tong; but whatever she's a-doin' with that old scrub
nigger, I can't make out.' "   I can hardly express what a recreation and delight it was to go about with this humorous
woman and listen to her comments, her unique criticisms,
her grateful delight, when she turned on the street to say:
"Oh, *what* a good time me and you is having, Miss Libbie,
and *how* I will 'stonish them people at home !"   The best of
it all was the manner in which she brought back our past,
and the hundred small events we recalled, which were made
more vivid by the imitation of voice, walk, gesture she gave
in speaking of those we followed in the old marching days.

On this journey to Texas some accident happened to our
engine, and detained us all night.   We campaigners, accustomed to all sorts of unexpected inconveniences, had learned
not to mind discomforts.   Each officer sank out of sight into
his great-coat collar, and slept on by the hour, while I slum-
bered till morning, curled up in a heap, thankful to have the
luxury of one seat to myself.   We rather gloried over the
citizens who tramped up and down the aisle, groaning and

becoming more emphatic in their language as the night advanced, indulging in the belief that the women were too sound asleep to hear them.   I wakened enough to hear one old man say, fretfully, and with many adjectives: " Just see how those army folks sleep; they can tumble down anywhere, while I am so lame and sore, from the cramped-up place I am in, I can't even doze."   As morning came we noticed our scamp at the other end of the car, with his legs stretched comfortably on the seat turned over in front of him.   All this unusual luxury he accounted for afterward, by telling us the trick that his ingenuity had suggested to obtain more room.   " You see," the wag said, " two old codgers sat down in front of my pal and me, late last night, and went on counting up their gains in the rise of corn, owing to the war, which, to say the least, was harrowing to us poor devils who had fought the battles that had made them rich and left us without a ' red.'   I concluded, if that was all they had done for their country, two of its brave defenders had more of a right to the seat than they had.   I just turned to H—— and began solemnly to talk about what store I set by my old army coat, then on the seat they occupied; said I couldn't give it up, though I had been obliged to cover a comrade who had died of small-pox, I not being afraid of contagion, having had varioloid.   Well, I got that far when the eyes of the old galoots started out of their heads, and they vamoosed the ranche, I can tell you, and I saw them peering through the window at the end of the next car, the horror still in their faces."   The General exploded with merriment.   How strange it seems, to contrast those noisy, boisterous times, when everybody shouted with laughter, called loudly from one end of the car to the other, told stories for the whole public to hear, and sang war-songs, with the quiet, orderly travelers of nowadays, who, even in the tremor of meeting or parting, speak below their breath, and, ashamed of emotion, quickly wink back to its source the prehistoric tear.

We bade good-by to railroads at Louisville, and the jouneying south was then made by steamer.   How peculiar it seemed to us, accustomed as we were to lake craft with deep hulls, to see for the first time those flat-bottomed boats drawing so little water, with several stories, and upper decks loaded with freight. I could hardly rid myself of the fear that, being so top-heavy, we would blow over. The tempests of our western lakes were then my only idea of sailing weather. Then the long, sloping levees, the preparations for the rise of water, the strange sensation, when the river was high, of looking over the embankment, down upon the earth ! It is a novel feeling to be for the first time on a great river, with such a current as the Mississippi flowing on above the level of the plantations, hemmed in by an embankment on either side. Though we saw the manner of its construction at one point where the levee was being repaired, and found how firmly and substantially the earth was fortified with stone and logs against the river, it still seemed to me an unnatural sort of voyaging to be above the level of the ground; and my tremors on the subject, and other novel experiences, were instantly made use of as a new and fruitful source of practical jokes. For instance, the steamer bumped into the shore anywhere it happened to be wooded, and an army of negroes appeared, running over the gang-plank like ants. Sometimes at night the pine torches, and the resinous knots burning in iron baskets slung over the side of the boat, made a weird and gruesome sight, the shadows were so black, the streams of light so intense, while the hurrying negroes loaded on the wood, under the brutal voice of a steamer's mate. Once a negro fell in. They made a pretense of rescuing him, gave it up soon, and up hurried our scamp to the upper deck to tell me the horrible tale. He had good command of language, and allowed no scruples to spoil a story. After that I imagined, at every night wood-lading, some poor soul was swept down under the boat and off into eternity. The General was sorry for me, and sometimes, when I imagined the calls of the crew to be the despairing wail of a dying man, he made pilgrimages, for my sake, to the lower deck to make sure that no one was drowned. My imaginings were not always so respected, for the occasion gave too good an opportunity for a joke, to be passed quietly by. The scamp and my husband put their heads together soon after this, and prepared a talc for the "old lady," as they called me. As we were about to make a landing, they ran to me and said, "Come, Libbie, hurry up! hurry up! You'll miss the fun if you don't scrabble." "Miss what?" was my very natural question, and exactly the reply they wanted me to make. "Why, they're going to bury a dead man when we land." I exclaimed in horror, "Another man drowned? how can you speak so irreverently of death?" With a "do you suppose the mate cares for one darkey more or less?" they dragged me to the deck. There I saw the great cable which was used to tie us up, fastened to a strong spar, the two ends of which were buried in the bank. The ground was hollowed out underneath the centre, and the rope slipped under to fasten it around the log. After I had watched this process of securing our boat to the shore, these irrepressibles said, solemnly, "The sad ceremony is now ended, and no other will take place till we tie up at the next stop." When it dawned upon me that "tying up" was called, in steamer vernacular, "burying a dead man," my eyes returned to their proper place in the sockets, breath came back, and indignation filled my soul. Language deserts us at such moments, and I resorted to force.

The *Ruth* was accounted one of the largest and most beautiful steamers that had ever been on the Mississippi River, her expenses being $1,000 a day. The decorations were sumptuous, and we enjoyed every luxury. We ate our dinners to very good music, which the boat furnished. We had been on plain fare too long not to watch with eagerness the arrival of the procession of white-coated negro waiters, who each day came in from the pastry-cook with some new device in cake, ices, or confectionery. There was a beautiful Ruth gleaning in a field, in a painting that filled the semicircle over the entrance of the cabin. Ruths with sheaves held up the branches of the chandeliers, while the pretty gleaner looked out from the glass of the stateroom doors. The captain being very patient as well as polite, we pervaded every corner of the great boat. The General and his boy-soldiers were too accustomed to activity to be quiet in the cabin. Even that unapproachable man at the wheel yielded to our longing eyes, and let us into his round tower. Oh, how good he was to me ! The General took me up there, and the pilot made a place for us, where, with my bit of work, I listened for hours to his stories. My husband made fifty trips up and down, sometimes detained when we were nearing an interesting point, to hear the story of the crevasse. Such tales were thrilling enough even for him, accustomed as he then was to the most exciting scenes. The pilot pointed out places where the river, wild with the rush and fury of spring freshets, had burst its way through the levees, and, sweeping over a peninsula, returned to the channel beyond, utterly annihilating and sinking out of sight forever the ground where happy people had lived on their plantations. It was a sad time to take that journey, and even in the midst of our intense enjoyment of the novelty of the trip, the freedom from anxiety, and the absence of responsibility of any kind, I recall how the General grieved over the destruction of plantations by the breaks in the levee. The work on these embankments was done by assessment, I think. They were cared for as our roads and bridges are kept in order, and when men were absent in the war, only the negroes were left to attend to the repairing. But the inundations then were slight, compared with many from which the State has since suffered. In 1874 thirty parishes were either wholly or partly overflowed by an extraordinary rise in the river. On our trip we saw one plantation after another submerged, the grand old houses abandoned, and standing in lakes of water, while the negro quarters and barns were almost out of sight. Sometimes the cattle huddled on a little rise of ground, helpless and pitiful. We wished, as we used to do in that beautiful Shenandoah Valley, that if wars must come, the devastation of homes might be avoided; and I usually added, with one of the totally impracticable suggestions conjured up by a woman, that battles might be fought in desert places.

A Southern woman, who afterward entertained us, described, in the graphic and varied language which is their gift, the breaking of the levee on their own plantation. How stealthily the small stream of water crept on and on, until their first warning was its serpent-like progress past their house. Then the excitement and rush of all the household to the crevasse, the hasty gathering in of the field-hands, and the homely devices for stopping the break until more substantial materials could be gathered. It was a race for life on all sides. Each one, old or young, knew that his safety depended on the superhuman effort of the first hour of danger. In our safe homes we scarcely realize what it would be to look out from our windows upon, what seemed to me, a small and insufficient mound of earth stretching along the frontage of an estate, and know that it was our only rampart against a rushing flood, which seemed human in its revengeful desire to engulf us.

The General was intensely interested in those portions of the country where both naval and land warfare had been carried on. At Island No. 10, and Fort Pillow especially, there seemed, even then, no evidence that fighting had gone on so lately. The luxuriant vegetation of the South had covered the fortifications; nature seemed hastening to throw a mantle over soil that had so lately been reddened with such a precious dye. The fighting had been so desperate at the latter point, it is reported the Confederate General Forrest said: "The river was dyed with the blood of the slaughtered for two hundred yards."

At one of our stops on the route, the Confederate General Hood came on board, to go to a town a short distance below, and my husband, hearing he was on the boat, hastened to seek him out and introduce himself. Such reunions have now become common, I am thankful to say, but I confess to watching curiously every expression of those men, as it seemed very early, in those times of excited and vehement conduct, to begin such overtures. And yet I did not forget that my husband sent messages of friendship to his classmates on the other side throughout the war. As I watched this meeting, they looked, while they grasped each other's hand, as if they were old-time friends happily united. After they had carried on an animated conversation for a while, my husband, always thinking how to share his enjoyment, hurried to bring me into the group. General Custer had already taught me, even in those bitter times, that he knew his classmates fought from their convictions of right, and that, now the war was over, I must not be adding fuel to a fire that both sides should strive to smother.

General Hood was tall, fair, dignified and soldierly. He used his crutch with difficulty, and it was an effort for him to rise when I was presented. We three instantly resumed the war talk that my coming had interrupted. The men plied each other with questions as to the situation of troops at certain engagements, and the General fairly bombarded General Hood with inquiries about the action on their side in different campaigns. At that time nothing had been written for Northern papers and magazines by the South. All we knew was from the brief accounts in the Southern newspapers that our pickets exchanged, and from papers captured or received from Europe by way of blockade-runners. We were greatly amused by the comical manner in which General Hood described his efforts to suit himself to an artificial leg, after he had contributed his own to his beloved cause. In his campaigns he was obliged to carry an extra one, in case of accident to the one he wore, which was strapped to his led horse. He asked me to picture the surprise of the troops who captured all the reserve horses at one time, and found this false leg of his suspended from the saddle. He said he had tried five, at different times, to see which of the inventions was lightest and easiest to wear; "and I am obliged to confess, Mrs. Custer, much as you may imagine it goes against me to do so, that of the five—English, German, French, Yankee and Confed-

erate—the Yankee leg was the best of all." When General Custer carefully helped the maimed hero down the
cabin stairs and over the gangway, we bade him good-by
with real regret— so quickly do soldiers make and cement a
friendship when both find the same qualities to admire in
each other.

The novelty of Mississippi travel kept even our active,
restless party interested.   One of our number played guitar ac-
companiments, and we sang choruses on deck at night, forgetting that the war-songs might grate on the ears of some of the
people about us.   The captain and steamer's crew allowed
us to roam up and down the boat at will, and when we found,
by the map or crew, that we were about to touch the bank
in a hitherto unvisited State, we were the first to run over
the gang-plank and caper up and down the soil, to add a new
State to our fast-swelling list of those in which we had been.
We rather wondered, though, what we would do if asked
questions by our elders at home as to what we thought of
Arkansas, Mississippi and Tennessee, as we had only scampered on and off the river bank of those States while the
wooding went on.   We were like children let out of school,
and everything interested us.   Even the low water was an
event.   The sudden stop of our great steamer, which, large
as it was, drew but a few feet of water, made the timbers
groan and the machinery creak.   Then we took ourselves to
the bow, where the captain, mate and deck-hands were preparing for a siege, as the force of the engines had ploughed
us deep into a sand-bar.   There was wrenching, veering and
struggling of the huge boat; and at last a resort to those two
spars which seem to be so uselessly attached to each side of
the forward deck of the river steamers.   These were swung
out and plunged into the bank, the rope and tackle put into
use, and with the aid of these stilts we were skipped over the
sand-bar into the deeper water.   It was on that journey that
I first heard the name Mr. Clemens took as his *nom de plume*.
The droning voice of the sailor taking soundings, as we
slowly crept through low water, called out, " Mark twain !"

and the pilot answered by steering the boat according to the story of the plumb-line.

The trip on a Mississippi steamer, as we knew it, is now one of the things of the past. It was accounted then, and before the war, our most luxurious mode of travel. Every one was sociable, and in the constant association of the long trip some warm friendships sprung up. We had then our first acquaintance with Bostonians as well as with Southerners. Of course, it was too soon for Southern women, robbed of home, and even the necessities of life, by the cruelty of war, to be wholly cordial. We were more and more amazed at the ignorance in the South concerning the North. A young girl, otherwise intelligent, thawed out enough to confess to me that she had really no idea that Yankee soldiers were like their own physically. She imagined they would be as widely different as black from white, and a sort of combination of gorilla and chimpanzee. Gunboats had but a short time before moored at the levee that bounded her grandmother's plantation, and the negroes ran into the house crying the terrible news of the approach of the enemy. The very thought of a Yankee was abhorrent; but the girl, more absorbed with curiosity than fear, slipped out of the house to where a view of the walk from the landing was to be had, and, seeing a naval officer approaching, raced back to her grandmother, crying out in surprise at finding a being like unto her own people, "Why, it's a man!"

As we approached New Orleans the plantations grew richer. The palmetto and the orange, by which we are "twice blessed" in its simultaneous blossom and fruit; the oleander, treasured in conservatories at home, here growing to tree size along the country roads, all charmed us. The wide galleries around the two stories of the houses were a delight. The course of our boat was often near enough the shore for us to see the family gathered around the supper-table spread on the upper gallery, which was protected from the sun by blinds or shades of matting.

We left the steamer at New Orleans with regret. It seems,

even now, that it is rather too bad we have grown into so
hurried a race that we cannot spare the time to travel as leisurely or luxuriously as we did then.   Even pleasure-seekers
going off for a tour, when they are not restricted by time nor
mode of journeying, study the time-tables closely, to see by
which route the quickest passage can be made.

CHAPTER II.

NEW ORLEANS AFTER THE WAR.

WE were detained, by orders, for a little time in New Orleans, and the General was enthusiastic over the city. All day we strolled through the streets, visiting the French quarter, contrasting the foreign shopkeepers—who were never too hurried to be polite—with our brusque, business-like Northern clerk; dined in the charming French restaurants, where we saw eating made a fine art. The sea-food was then new to me, and I hovered over the crabs, lobsters and shrimps, but remember how amused the General was by my quick retreat from a huge live green turtle, whose locomotion was suspended by his being turned upon his back. He was unconsciously bearing his own epitaph fastened upon his shell: "I will be served up for dinner at 5 P. M." We of course spent hours, even matutinal hours, at the market, and the General drank so much coffee that the old mammy who served him said many a " Mon Dieu ! " in surprise at his capacity, and volubly described in French to her neighbors what marvels a Yankee man could do in coffee-sipping. For years after, when very good coffee was praised, or even Eliza's strongly commended, his *ne plus ultra* was, " Almost equal to the French market." We here learned what artistic effects could be produced with prosaic carrots, beets, onions and turnips. The General looked with wonder upon the leisurely creole grandee who came to order his own dinner. After his epicurean selection he showed the interest and skill that a Northern man might in the buying of a picture or a horse, when the servant bearing the basket was entrusted with what was to be enjoyed at night.   We had never known men that took time to market, except as our hurried Northern fathers of families sometimes made sudden raids upon the butcher, on the way to business, and called off an order as they ran for a car.

The wide-terraced Canal Street, with its throng of leisurely promenaders, was our daily resort.   The stands of Parma violets on the street corners perfumed the whole block, and the war seemed not even to have cast a cloud over the first foreign pleasure-loving people we had seen.   The General was so pleased with the picturesque costumes of the servants that Eliza was put into a turban at his entreaty.   In vain we tried for a glimpse of the creole beauties.   The duenna that guarded them in their rare promenades, as they glided by, wearing gracefully the lace mantilla, bonnetless, and shaded by a French parasol, whisked the pretty things out of sight, quick as we were to discover and respectfully follow them. The effects of General Butler's reign were still visible in the marvelous cleanliness of the city.   We drove on the shell road, spent hours in the horse-cars, went to the theatres, and even penetrated the rooms of the most exclusive milliners, for General Custer liked the shops as much as I did.   Indeed, we had a grand play-day, and were not in the least troubled at our detention.

General Scott was then in our hotel, about to set out for the North.   He remembered Lieutenant Custer, who had reported to him in 1861, and was the bearer of despatches sent by him to the front, and he congratulated my husband on his career in terms that, coming from such a veteran, made his boy-heart leap for joy.   General Scott was then very infirm, and, expressing a wish to see me, with old-time gallantry begged my husband to explain to me that he would be compelled to claim the privilege of sitting.   But it was too much for his etiquettical instincts, and, weak as he was, he feebly drew his tall form to a half-standing position, leaning against the lounge as I entered.   Pictures of General Scott, in my father's home, belonged to my earliest recollections.

He was a colossal figure on a fiery steed, whose prancing forefeet never touched the earth. The Mexican War had hung a halo about him, and my childish explanation of the clouds of dust that the artist sought to represent was the smoke of battle, in which I supposed the hero lived perpetually. And now this decrepit, tottering man—I was almost sorry to have seen him at all, except for the praise that he bestowed upon my husband, which, coming from so old a soldier, I deeply appreciated.

General Sheridan had assumed command of the Department of the Mississippi, and the Government had hired a beautiful mansion for headquarters, where he was at last living handsomely after all his rough campaigning. When we dined with him, we could but contrast the food prepared over a Virginia camp-fire, with the dainty French cookery of the old colored Mary, who served him afterward so many years. General Custer was, of course, glad to be under his chief again, and after dinner, while I was given over to some of the military family to entertain, the two men, sitting on the wide gallery, talked of what it was then believed would be a campaign across the border. I was left in complete ignorance, and did not even know that an army of 70,000 men was being organized under General Sheridan's masterly hand. My husband read the Eastern papers to me, and took the liberty of reserving such articles as might prove incendiary in his family. If our incorrigible scamp spoke of the expected wealth he intended to acquire from the sacking of palaces and the spoils of churches, he was frowned upon, not only because the General tried to teach him that there were some subjects too sacred to be touched by his irreverent tongue, but because he did not wish my anxieties to be aroused by the prospect of another campaign. As much of my story must be of the hardships my husband endured, I have here lingered a little over the holiday that our journey and the detention in New Orleans gave him. I hardly think any one can recall a complaint of his in those fourteen years of tent-life; but he was taught, through deprivations, how to enjoy every moment of such days as that charming journey and city experience gave us.

The steamer chartered to take troops up the Red River was finally ready, and we sailed the last week in June. There were horses and Government freight on board. The captain was well named Greathouse, as he greeted us with hospitality and put his little steamer at our disposal. Besides the fact that this contract for transportation would line his pockets well, he really seemed glad to have us. He was a Yankee, and gave us his native State (Indiana) in copious and inexhaustible supplies, as his contribution to the talks on deck. Long residence in the South had not dimmed his patriotism; and in the rapid transits from deck to pilot-house, of this tall Hoosier, I almost saw the straps fastening down the trousers of Brother Jonathan, as well as the coat-tails cut from the American flag, so entirely did he personate in his figure our emblematic Uncle Sam. It is customary for the Government to defray the expenses of officers and soldiers when traveling under orders; but so much red-tape is involved that they often pay their own way at the time, and the quartermaster reimburses them at the journey's end. The captain knew this, and thought he would give himself the pleasure of having us as his guests. Accordingly, he took the General one side, and imparted this very pleasing information. Even with the provident ones this would be a relief; while we had come on board almost wrecked in our finances by the theatre, the tempting flowers, the fascinating restaurants, and finally, a disastrous lingering one day in the beguiling shop of Madam Olympe, the reigning milliner. The General had bought some folly for me, in spite of the heroic protest that I made about its inappropriateness for Texas, and it left us just enough to pay for our food on our journey, provided we ordered nothing extra, and had no delays. Captain Greathouse little knew to what paupers he was extending his hospitality. No one can comprehend how carelessly and enjoyably army people can walk about with empty pockets, knowing that it is but a matter of thirty days' waiting till Richard shall be himself again. My husband made haste to impart the news quietly to the staff, that the captain was going to invite them all to be his guests, and so relieve their anxiety about financial embarrassment. The scamp saw a chance for a joke, and when the captain again appeared he knew that he was going to receive the invitation, and anticipated it. In our presence he jingled the last twenty-six cents he had in the world against the knife in his almost empty pockets, assumed a Crœsus-like air, and begged to know the cost of the journey, as he loftily said he made it a rule always to pay in advance. At this, the General, unable to smother his laughter, precipitated himself out of the cabin-door, nearly over the narrow guard, to avoid having his merriment seen. When the captain said blandly that he was about to invite our party to partake of his hospitality, our scamp bowed, and accepted the courtesy as if it were condescension on his part, and proceeded to take possession, and almost command, of the steamer.

It was a curious trip, that journey up the Red River. We saw the dull brownish-red water from the clay bed and banks mingling with the clearer current of the Mississippi long before we entered the mouth of the Red River. We had a delightful journey; but I don't know why, except that youth, health and buoyant spirits rise superior to everything. The river was ugliness itself. The tree trunks, far up, were gray and slimy with the late freshet, the hanging moss adding a dismal feature to the scene. The waters still covered the low, muddy banks strewn with fallen trees and underbrush. The river was very narrow in places, and in our way there were precursors of the Red River raft above. At one time, before Government work was begun, the raft extended forty-five miles beyond Shreveport, and closed the channel to steamers. Sometimes the pilot wound us round just such obstructions—logs and driftwood jammed in so firmly, and so immovable, they looked like solid ground, while rank vegetation sprung up through the thick moss that covered the decaying tree trunks. The river was very crooked. The

whistle screeched when approaching a turn; but so sudden
were some of these, that a steamer coming down, not slack-
ening speed, almost ran into us at one sharp bend. It shaved
our sides and set our boat a-quivering, while the vituperations of the boat's crew, and the loud, angry voices of the
captain and pilot, with a prompt return of such civilities
from the other steamer, made us aware that emergencies
brought forth a special and extensive set of invectives, reserved for careless navigation on the Red River of the South.
We grew to have an increasing respect for the skill of the
pilot, as he steered us around sharp turns, across low water
filled with branching upturned tree trunks, and skillfully took
a narrow path between the shore and a snag that menacingly
ran its black point out of the water. A steamer in advance
of us, carrying troops, had encountered a snag, while going
at great speed, and the obstructing tree ran entirely through
the boat, coming out at the pilot-house. The troops were
unloaded and taken up afterward by another steamer. Sometimes the roots of great forest trees, swept down by a freshet,
become imbedded in the river, and the whole length of the
trunk is under water, swaying up and down, but not visible
below the turbid surface. The forest is dense at some points,
and we could see but a short distance as we made our circuitous, dangerous way.

The sand-bars, and the soft red clay of the river-banks,
were a fitting home for the alligators that lay sunning themselves, or sluggishly crawled into the stream as the General
aimed at them with his rifle from the steamer's guards.
They were new game, and gave some fresh excitement to the
long, idle days. He never gave up trying, in his determined
way, for the vulnerable spot in their hide just behind the eye.
I thought the sand-hill crane must have first acquired its
tiresome habit of standing on one leg, from its disgust at
letting down the reserve foot into such thick, noisome water.
It seemed a pity that some of those shots from the steamer's
deck had not ended its melancholy existence. Through all
this mournful river-way the guitar twanged, and the dense

forest resounded to war choruses or old college glees that we sent out in happy notes as we sat on deck. I believe Captain Greathouse bade us good-by with regret, as he seemed to enjoy the jolly party, and when we landed at Alexandria he gave us a hogshead of ice, the last we were to see for a year.

A house abandoned by its owners, and used by General Banks for headquarters during the war, was selected for our temporary home. As we stepped upon the levee, a tall Southerner came toward me and extended his hand. At that time the citizens were not wont to welcome the Yankee in that manner. He had to tell me who he was, as unfortunately I had forgotten, and I began to realize the truth of the saying, that "there are but two hundred and fifty people in the world," when I found an acquaintance in this isolated town. He proved to be the only Southerner I had ever known in my native town in Michigan, who came there when a lad to visit kinsfolk. In those days his long black hair, large dark eyes and languishing manner, added to the smooth, soft-flowing, flattering speeches, made sad havoc in our school-girl ranks. I suppose the youthful and probably susceptible hearts of our circle were all set fluttering, for the boy seemed to find pleasure in a chat with any one of us that fell to him in our walks to and from school. The captivating part of it all was the lines written on the pages of my arithmetic, otherwise so odious to me—" Come with me to my distant home, where, under soft Southern skies, we'll breathe the odor of orange groves." None of us had answered to his " Come," possibly because of the infantile state of our existence, possibly because the invitation was too general. And here stood our youthful hero, worn prematurely old and shabby after his four years of fighting for " the cause." The boasted " halls of his ancestors," the same to which we had been so ardently invited, were a plain white cottage. No orange groves, but a few lime-trees sparsely scattered over the prescribed lawn. In the pleasant visit that we all had, there was discreet avoidance of the poetic license he had taken in early years, when describing his home under the southern sky.

Alexandria had been partly burned during the war, and was built up mostly with one-story cottages. Indeed, it was always the popular mode of building there. We found everything a hundred years behind the times. The houses of our mechanics at home had more conveniences and modern improvements. I suppose the retinue of servants before the war rendered the inhabitants indifferent to what we think absolutely necessary for comfort. The house we used as headquarters had large, lofty rooms separated by a wide hall, while in addition there were two wings. A family occupied one-half of the house, caring for it in the absence of the owners. In the six weeks we were there, we never saw them, and naturally concluded they were not filled with joy at our presence. The house was delightfully airy; but we took up the Southern custom of living on the gallery. The library was still intact, in spite of its having been headquarters for our army; and evidently the people had lived in what was considered luxury for the South in its former days, yet every-thing was primitive enough. This great house, filled as it once was with servants, had its sole water supply from two tanks or cisterns above ground at the rear. The rich and the poor were alike dependent upon these receptacles for water; and it was not a result of the war, for this was the only kind of reservoir provided, even in prosperous times. But one well was dug in Alexandria, as the water was brack-ish and impure. Each house, no matter how small, had cis-terns, sometimes as high as the smaller cottages themselves. The water in those where we lived was very low, the tops were uncovered, and dust, leaves, bugs and flies were blown in, while the cats strolled around the upper rim during their midnight orchestral overtures. We found it necessary to husband the fast lowering water, as the rains were over for the summer. The servants were enjoined to draw out the home-made plug (there was not even a Yankee faucet) with the ut-most care, while some one was to keep vigilant watch on a cow, very advanced in cunning, that used to come and hook at the plug till it was loosened and fell out.   The sound of flowing water was our first warning of the precious wasting. No one could drink the river-water, and even in our ablutions we turned our eyes away as we poured the water from the pitcher into the bowl.   Our rain-water was so full of gallinip-pers and pollywogs, that a glass stood by the plate untouched until the sediment and natural history united at the bottom, while heaven knows what a microscope, had we possessed one, would have revealed!

Eliza was well primed with stories of alligators by the negroes and soldiers, who loved to frighten her.   One meas-uring thirteen feet eight inches was killed on the river-bank, they said, as he was about to partake of his favorite supper, a negro sleeping on the sand.   It was enough for Eliza when she heard of this preference for those of her color, and she duly stampeded.   She was not well up in the habits of ani-mals, and having seen the alligators crawling over the mud of the river banks, she believed they were so constituted that at night they could take long tramps over the country.   She used to assure me that she nightly heard them crawling around the house.   One night, when some fearful sounds issued from the cavernous depths of the old cistern, she ran to one of the old negroes of the place, her carefully braided wool rising from her head in consternation, and called out, " Jest listen! jest listen!"   The old mammy quieted her by, " Oh la, honey, don't you be skeart; nothin's goin' to hurt you; them's only bull-toads."   This information, though it quieted Eliza's fears, did not make the cistern-water any more enjoyable to us.

The houses along Red River were raised from the ground on piles, as the soil was too soft and porous for cellars.   Before the fences were destroyed and the place fell into dilapidation, there might have been a lattice around the base of the build-ing, but now it was gone.   Though this open space under the house gave vent for what air was stirring, it also offered free circulation to pigs, that ran grunting and squealing back and forth, and even the calves sought its grateful shelter from the sun and flies. And, oh, the mosquitoes! Others have exhausted adjectives in trying to describe them, and until I came to know those of the Missouri River at Fort Lincoln, Dakota, I joined in the general testimony, that the Red River of the South could not be outdone. The bayous about us, filled with decaying vegetable matter, and surrounded with marshy ground, and the frequent rapid fall of the river, leaving banks of mud, all bred mosquitoes, or gallinippers, as the darkies called them. Eliza took counsel as to the best mode of extermination, and brought old kettles with raw cotton into our room, from which proceeded such smudges and such odors as would soon have wilted a Northern mosquito; but it only resulted in making us feel like a piece of dried meat hanging in a smoke-house, while the undisturbed insect winged its way about our heads, singing as it swirled and dipped and plunged its javelin into our defenseless flesh. There were days there, as at Fort Lincoln, when the wind, blowing in a certain direction, brought such myriads of them that I was obliged to beat a retreat under the netting that enveloped the high, broad bed, which is a specialty of the extreme South, and with my book, writing or sewing, listened triumphantly to the clamoring army beating on the outside of the bars. The General made fun of me thus enthroned, when he returned from office work; but I used to reply that he could afford to remain unprotected, if the greedy creatures could draw their sustenance from his veins without leaving a sting.

At the rear of our house were two rows of negro quarters, which Eliza soon penetrated, and afterward begged me to visit. Only the very old and worthless servants remained. The owners of the place on which we were living had three other sugar plantations in the valley, from one of which alone 2,300 hogsheads of sugar were shipped in one season, and at the approach of the army 500 able-bodied negroes were sent into Texas. Eliza described the decamping of the owner of the plantation thus, "Oh, Miss Libbie, the war made a mighty scatter." The poor creatures left were in desperate straits. One, a bed-ridden woman, having been a house-servant, was intelligent for one of her race. After Eliza had taken me the rounds, I piloted the General, and he found that, though the very old woman did not know her exact age, she could tell him of events that she remembered when she was in New Orleans with her mistress, which enabled him to calculate her years to be almost a hundred. Three old people claimed to remember " Washington's war." I look back to our visit to her little cabin, where we sat beside her bed, as one of vivid interest. The old woman knew little of the war, and no one had told her of the proclamation until our arrival. We were both much moved when, after asking us questions, she said to me, " And, Missey, is it really true that I is free?" Then she raised her eyes to heaven, and blessed the Lord for letting her live to see the day. The General, who had to expostulate with Eliza sometimes for her habit of feeding every one out of our supplies, whether needy or not, had no word to say now. Our kitchen could be full of grizzly, tottering old wrecks, and he only smiled on the generous dispenser of her master's substance. Indeed, he had them fed all the time we stayed there, and they dragged their tattered caps from their old heads, and blessed him as we left, for what he had done, and for the food that he provided for them after we were gone.

It was at Alexandria that I first visited a negro prayer-meeting. As we sat on the gallery one evening, we heard the shouting and singing, and quietly crept round to the cabin where the exhorting and groaning were going on. My husband stood with uncovered head, reverencing their sincerity, and not a muscle of his face moved, though it was rather difficult to keep back a smile at the grotesqueness of the scene. The language and the absorbed manner in which these old slaves held communion with their Lord, as if He were there in person, and told Him in simple but powerful language their thanks that the day of Jubilee had come, that their lives had been spared to see freedom come to His peo-

ple, made us sure that a faith that brought their Saviour
down in their midst was superior to that of the more civilized,
who send petitions to a throne that they themselves surround
with clouds of doctrine and doubt. Though they were so
poor and helpless, and seemingly without anything to inspire
gratitude, evidently there were reasons in their own minds
for heartfelt thanks, as there was no mistaking the genuine-
ness of feeling when they sang:

> " Bless the Lord that I can rise and tell
> That Jesus has done all things well."

Old as some of these people were, their religion took a
very energetic form. They swayed back and forth as they
sat about the dimly lighted cabin, clapped their hands spas-
modically, and raised their eyes to heaven in moments of
absorption. There were those among the younger people
who jumped up and down as the "power" possessed them,
and the very feeblest uttered groans, and quavered out the
chorus of the old tunes, in place of the more active demonstrations for which their rheumatic old limbs now unfitted
them. When, afterward, my husband read to me newspaper
accounts of negro camp-meetings or prayer-meetings graph-
ically written, no description seemed exaggerated to us ; and
he used to say that nothing compared with that night when
we first listened to those serious, earnest old centenarians,
whose feeble voices still quavered out a tune of gratitude, as,
with bent forms and bowed heads, they stood leaning on
their canes and crutches.

As the heat became more overpowering, I began to make
excuses for the slip-shod manner of living of the Red River
people. Active as was my temperament, climatic influences
told, and I felt that I should have merited the denunciation
of the antique woman in "Uncle Tom's Cabin," of "Heow
shiftless!" It was hard to move about in the heat of the
day, but at evening we all went for a ride. It seemed to me
a land of enchantment. We had never known such luxuriance of vegetation. The valley of the river extended several

miles inland, the foliage was varied and abundant, and the sunsets had deeper, richer colors than any at the North. The General, getting such constant pleasure out of nature, and not in the least minding to express it, was glad to hear even the prosaic one of our number, who rarely cared for color or scenery, go into raptures over the gorgeous orange and red of that Southern sky. We sometimes rode for miles along the country roads, between hedges of osage-orange on one side, and a double white rose on the other, growing fifteen feet high. The dew enhanced the fragrance, and a lavish profusion was displayed by nature in that valley, which was a constant delight to us. Sometimes my husband and I remained out very late, loth to come back to the prosy, uninteresting town, with its streets flecked with bits of cotton, evidences of the traffic of the world, as the levee was now piled up with bales ready for shipment. Once the staff crossed with us to the other side of the river, and rode out through more beautiful country roads, to what was still called Sherman Institute. General Sherman had been at the head of this military school before the war, but it was subsequently converted into a hospital. It was in a lonely and deserted district, and the great empty stone building, with its turreted corners and modern architecture, seemed utterly incongruous in the wild pine forest that surrounded it. We returned to the river, and visited two forts on the bank opposite Alexandria. They were built by a Confederate officer who used his Federal prisoners for workmen. The General took in at once the admirable situation selected, which commanded the river for many miles. He thoroughly appreciated, and endeavored carefully to explain to me, how cleverly the few materials at the disposal of the impoverished South had been utilized. The moat about the forts was the deepest our officers had ever seen. Closely as my husband studied the plan and formation, he said it would have added greatly to his appreciation, had he then known, what he afterward learned, that the Confederate engineer who planned this admirable fortification was one of his classmates at West Point,

of whom he was very fond.   In 1864 an immense expedition
of our forces was sent up the Red River, to capture Shreveport and open up the great cotton districts of Texas. It was
unsuccessful, and the retreat was rendered impossible by low
water, while much damage was done to our fleet by the very
Confederate forts we were now visiting.   A dam was constructed near Alexandria, and the squadron was saved from
capture or annihilation by this timely conception of a quick-
witted Western man, Colonel Joseph Bailey.   The dam was
visible from the walls of the forts, where we climbed for a
view.

As we resumed our ride to the steamer, the General, who
was usually an admirable pathfinder, proposed a new and
shorter road ; and liking variety too much to wish to travel
the same country twice over, all gladly assented. Everything
went very well for a time. We were absorbed in talking,
noting new scenes on the route, or, as was our custom when
riding off from the public highway, we sang some chorus ;
and thus laughing, singing, joking, we galloped over the
ground thoughtlessly into the very midst of serious danger.
Apparently, nothing before us impeded our way. We knew
very little of the nature of the soil in that country, but had
become somewhat accustomed to the bayous that either
start from the river or appear suddenly inland, quite disconnected from any stream.   On that day we dashed heedlessly
to the bank of a wide bayou that poured its waters into the
Red River.   Instead of thinking twice, and taking the precaution to follow its course farther up into the country, where
the mud was dryer and the space to cross much narrower,
we determined not to delay, and prepared to go over. The
most venturesome dashed first on to this bit of dried slough,
and though the crust swayed and sunk under the horses' flying feet, it still seemed caked hard enough to bear every
weight.   There were seams and fissures in portions of the
bayou, through which the moist mud oozed ; but these were
not sufficient warning to impetuous people.   Another and
another sprang over the undulating soil. Having reached

the other side, they rode up and down the opposite bank, shouting to us where they thought it the safest to cross, and of course interlarded their directions with good-natured scoffing about hesitation, timidity, and so on. The General, never second in anything when he could help it, remained behind to fortify my sinking heart and urge me to undertake the crossing with him. He reminded me how carefully Custis Lee had learned to follow and to trust to him, and he would doubtless plant his hoofs in the very tracks of his own horse. Another of our party tried to bolster up my courage, assuring me that if the heavy one among us was safely on the other bank, my light weight might be trusted. I dreaded making the party wait until we had gone further up the bayou, and might have mustered up the required pluck had I not met with trepidation on the part of my horse. His fine, delicate ears told me, as plainly as if he could speak, that I was asking a great deal of him. We had encountered quicksands together in the bed of a Virginia stream, and both horse and rider were recalling the fearful sensation when the animal's hindlegs sank, leaving his body engulfed in the soil. With powerful struggles with his forefeet and muscular shoulders, we plunged to the right and left, and found at last firm soil on which to escape. With such a recollection still fresh, as memory is sure to retain terrors like that, it was hardly a wonder that we shrank from the next step. His trembling flanks shook as much as the unsteady hand that held his bridle. He quivered from head to foot, and held back. I urged, and patted his neck, while we both continued to shiver on the brink. The General laughed at the two cowards we really were, but still gave us time to get our courage up to the mark. The officer remaining with us continued to encourage me with assurances that there was " not an atom of danger," and finally, with a bound, shouting out, " Look how well I shall go over ! " sprang upon the vibrating crust. In an instant, with a crack like a pistol, the thin layer of solid mud broke, and down went the gay, handsomely caparisoned fellow, engulfed to his waist in the foul black crust.

There was at once a commotion. With no ropes, it was hard to effect his release. His horse helped him most, struggling frantically for the bank, while the officers, having flung themselves off from their animals to rush to his rescue, brought poles and tree branches, which the imbedded man was not slow to grasp and drag himself from the perilous spot when only superhuman strength could deliver him, as the mud of a bayou sucks under its surface with great rapidity anything with which it comes in contact. As soon as the officer was dragged safely on to firm earth, a shout went up that rent the air with its merriment. Scarcely any one spoke while they labored to save the man's life, but once he was out of peril, the rescuers felt their hour had come. They called out to him, in tones of derision, the vaunting air with which he said just before his engulfment, " Look at me ; see how I go over ! " He was indeed a sorry sight, plastered from head to foot with black mud. Frightened as I was—for the trembling had advanced to shivering, and my chattering teeth and breathless voice were past my control—I still felt that little internal tremor of laughter that somehow pervades one who has a sense of the ludicrous in very dangerous surroundings.

I had certainly made a very narrow escape, for it would have been doubly hard to extricate me. The riding habits in those days were very long, and loaded so with lead to keep them down in high winds—and, I may add, in furious riding—that it was about all I could do to lift my skirt when I put it on.

I held my horse with a snaffle, to get good, smooth going out of him, and my wrists became pretty strong; but in that slough I would have found them of little avail, I fear. There remained no opposition to seeking a narrower part of the bayou, above where I had made such an escape, and there was still another good result of this severe lesson after that: when we came to such ominous-looking soil, Custis Lee and his mistress were allowed all the shivering on the brink that their cowardice produced, while the party scattered to investigate the sort of foundation we were likely to find, before we attempted to plunge over a Louisiana quagmire.

The bayous were a strange feature of that country. Often without inlet or outlet, a strip of water appeared, black and sluggish, filled with logs, snags, masses of underbrush and leaves. The banks, covered with weeds, noisome plants and rank tangled vegetation, seemed the dankest, darkest, most weird and mournful spots imaginable, a fit home for ghouls and bogies. There could be no more appropriate place for a sensational novelist to locate a murder. After a time I became accustomed to these frequently occurring water-ways, but it took me a good while to enjoy going fishing on them. The men were glad to vary their days by dropping a line in that vile water, and I could not escape their urging to go, though I was excused from fishing.

On one occasion we went down the river on a steamer, the sailors dragging the small boats over the strip of land between the river and the bayou, and all went fishing or hunting. This excursion was one that I am likely to remember forever. The officers, intent on their fishing, were rowed slowly through the thick water, while I was wondering to myself if there could be, anywhere, such a wild jungle of vines and moss as hung from the trees and entangled itself in the mass of weeds and water-plants below. We followed little indentations of the stream, and the boat was rowed into small bays and near dark pools, where the fish are known to stay, and finally we floated. The very limbs of the trees and the gnarled trunks took on human shape, while the drooping moss swayed as if it might be the drapery of a lamia, evolved out of the noisome vapors and floating above us. These fears and imaginings, which would have been put to flight by the assurances of the General, had he not been so intent on his line, proved to be not wholly spectres of the imagination. A mass of logs in front of us seemed to move. They did move, and the alligator, that looked so like a tree-trunk, established his identity by separating himself from the floating timber and making off. It was my scream, for the officers themselves did not enjoy the proximity of the beast, that caused the instant use of the oars and a quick retreat.

I went fishing after that, of course; I couldn't get out of it; indeed I was supported through my tremors by a pleasure to which a woman cannot be indifferent—that of being wanted on all sorts of excursions. But logs in the water never looked like logs after that; to my distended vision they appeared to writhe with the slow contortions of loathsome animals.

A soldier captured a baby-alligator one day, and the General, thinking to quiet my terror of them by letting me see the reptile "close to," as the children say, took me down to camp, where the delighted soldier told me how he had caught it, holding on to the tail, which is its weapon. The animal was all head and tail; there seemed to be no intermediate anatomy. He flung the latter member at a hat in so vicious and violent a way, that I believed instantly the story, which I had first received with doubt, of his rapping over a puppy and swallowing him before rescue could come. This pet was in a long tank of water the owner had built, and it gave the soldiers much amusement.

The General was greatly interested in alligator-hunting. It was said that the scales were as thick as a china plate, except on the head, and he began to believe so when he found his balls glancing off the impenetrable hide as if from the side of an ironclad. I suppose it was very exciting, after the officers had yelped and barked like a dog, to see the great monster decoyed from some dark retreat by the sound of his favorite tidbit. The wary game came slowly down the bayou, under fire of the kneeling huntsmen concealed in the underbrush, and was soon despatched. For myself, I should have preferred, had I been consulted, a post of observation in the top of some tree, instead of the boat in which I was being rowed.

CHAPTER III.

THERE was a great deal to do in those weeks of our detention at Alexandria, during the working hours of the day, in organizing the division of cavalry for the march. Troops that had been serving in the West during the war were brought together at that point from all directions, and an effort was made to form them into a disciplined body. This herculean task gave my husband great perplexity. He wrote to my father that he did not entirely blame the men for the restlessness and insubordination they exhibited, as their comrades, who had enlisted only for the war, had gone home, and, of course, wrote back letters to their friends of the pleasures of reunion with their families and kindred, and the welcome given them by their townspeople. The troops with us had not served out the time of their enlistment, and the Government, according to the strict letter of the law, had a right to the unexpired time for which the men were pledged. Some of the regiments had not known the smell of gunpowder during the entire war, having been stationed in and near Southern cities, and that duty is generally demoralizing. In the reorganizing of this material, every order issued was met with growls and grumbling. It seemed that it had been the custom with some of their officers to issue an order, and then go out and make a speech, explaining the whys and wherefores. One of the colonels came to the General one day at his own quarters, thinking it a better place than the office to make his request. He was a spectacle, and though General Custer was never in after years incautious enough to mention his name, he could not, with his keen sense of the ludicrous, resist a laughing description of the interview. The man was large and bulky in build. Over the breast of a long, loose, untidy linen duster he had spread the crimson sash, as he was officer of the day. A military sword-belt gathered in the voluminous folds of the coat, and from his side hung a parade sword. A slouch hat was crowded down on a shock of bushy hair. One trouser-leg was tucked into his boot, as if to represent one foot in the cavalry; the other, true to the infantry, was down in its proper place. He began his interview by praising his regiment, gave an account of the success with which he was drilling his men, and, leaning confidentially on the General's knee, told him he "would make them so —— near like regglers you couldn't tell 'em apart." Two officers of the regular army were then in command of the two brigades, to one of which this man's regiment was assigned. But the object of the visit was not solely to praise his regiment; he went on to say that an order had been issued which the men did not like, and he had come up to expostulate. He did not ask to have the order rescinded, but told the General he would like to have him come down and give the reasons to the troops. He added that this was what they expected, and when he issued any command he went out and got upon a barrel and explained it to the boys. My husband listened patiently, but declined, as that manner of issuing orders was hardly in accordance with his ideas of discipline.

The soldiers did not confine their maledictions to the regular officers in command; they openly refused to obey their own officers. One of the colonels (I am glad I have forgotten his name) made a social call at our house. He was in great perturbation of mind, and evidently terrified, as in the preceding night his dissatisfied soldiers had riddled his tent with bullets, and but for his "lying low" he would have been perforated like a sieve. The men supposed they had ended his military career; but at daylight he crept out. The soldiers were punished; but there seemed to be little to expect in the way of obedience if, after four years, they ignored their superiors and took affairs into their own hands.

Threats began to make their way to our house. The staff had their tents on the lawn in front of us, and even they tried to persuade the General to lock the doors and bolt the windows, which were left wide open day and night. Failing to gain his consent to take any precautions, they asked me to use my influence; but in such affairs I had little success in persuasion. The servants, and even the orderlies, came to me and solemnly warned me of the threats and the danger that menaced the General. Thoroughly frightened in his behalf, they prefaced their warnings with the old-fashioned sensational language : "This night, at 12 o'clock," etc. The fixing of the hour for the arrival of the assassin completely unnerved me, as I had not then escaped from the influence that the melodramatic has upon youth. I ran to the General the moment he came from his office duties, to tell him, with tears and agitation, of his peril. As usual, he soothed my fears, but, on this occasion, only temporarily. Still, seeing what I suffered from anxiety, he made one concession, and consented, after much imploring, to put a pistol under his pillow. A complete battery of artillery round our house could not have secured to me more peace of mind than that pistol; for I knew the accuracy of his aim, and I had known too much of his cool, resolute action, in moments of peril, not to be sure that the small weapon would do its work. Peace was restored to the head of our house; he had a respite from the whimpering and begging. I even grew so courageous as to be able to repeat to Eliza, when she came next morning to put the room in order, what the General had said to me, that " barking dogs do not bite." The mattress was proudly lifted, and the pistol, of which I stood in awe, in spite of my faith in its efficacy, was exhibited to her in triumph. I made wide détours around that side of the bed the rest of the time we remained at Alexandria, afraid of the very weapon to which I was indebted for tranquil hours. The cats, pigs and calves might charge at will under the house. If I mistook them for the approaching adversary I remembered the revolver and was calmed.

Long afterward, during our winter in Texas, my husband
began one day to appear mysterious, and assume the suppressed air that invariably prefaced a season of tormenting,
when a siege of questions only brought out deeper and ob-
scurer answers to me. Pouting, tossing of the head, and
reiterated announcements that I didn't care a rap, I didn't
want to know, etc., were met by chuckles of triumph and
wild juba patting and dancing around the victim, unrestrained
by my saying that such was the custom of the savage while
torturing his prisoner. Still, he persisted that he had such a
good joke on me. And it certainly was: there had not been
a round of ammunition in the house that we occupied at
Alexandria, neither had that old pistol been loaded during
the entire summer !

The soldiers became bolder in their rebellion; insubordination reached a point where it was almost uncontrollable.
Reports were sent to General Sheridan, in command of the
Department, and he replied to my husband, "Use such sum-
mary measures as you deem proper to overcome the mutinous
disposition of the individuals in your command." A Western
officer, a stranger to us up to that time, published an account of one of the regiments, which explains what was not
clear to us then, as we had come directly from the Army of
the Potomac:

"One regiment had suffered somewhat from indifferent
field officers, but more from the bad fortune that overtook so
many Western regiments in the shape of garrison duty in
small squads or squadrons, so scattered as to make each a
sort of independent command, which in the end resulted in
a loss of discipline, and the ruin of those bonds of sympathy
that bound most regiments together. To lead such a regiment into a hotly contested fight would be a blessing, and
would effectually set at rest all such trouble; but their fighting had been altogether of the guerrilla kind, and there was
no regimental pride of character, simply because there had
been no regimental deed of valor. Tired out with the long
service, weary with an uncomfortable journey by river from

Memphis, sweltering under a Gulf-coast sun, under orders to go farther and farther from home when the war was over, the one desire was to be mustered out and released from a service that became irksome and baleful when a prospect of crushing the enemy no longer existed. All these, added to the dissatisfaction among the officers, rendered the situation truly deplorable. The command had hardly pitched their tents at Alexandria before the spirit of reckless disregard of authority began to manifest itself. The men, singly or in squads, began to go on extemporaneous raids through the adjoining country, robbing and plundering indiscriminately in every direction. They seemed to have no idea that a conquered and subdued people could possibly have any rights that the conquerors were bound to respect. But General Custer was under orders to treat the people kindly and considerately, and he obeyed orders with the same punctiliousness with which he exacted obedience from his command." The anger and hatred of these troops toward one especial officer culminated in their peremptory demand that he should resign. They drew up a paper, and signed their names. He had not a friend, and sought the commanding officer for protection. This was too pronounced a case of mutiny to be treated with any but the promptest, severest measures, and all who had put their names to the document were placed under arrest. The paper was in reality but a small part of the incessant persecution, which included threats of all kinds against the life of the hated man; but it was written proof that his statements regarding his danger were true.

All but one of those that were implicated apologized, and were restored to duty. A sergeant held out, and refused to acknowledge himself in the wrong. A court-martial tried him and he was sentenced to death. Those who had been associated in the rebellion against their officer were thoroughly frightened, and seriously grieved at the fate to which their comrade had been consigned by their uncontrollable rage, and began to speak among themselves of the wife and children at home. The wife was unconscious that the heart-

breaking revelations were on their way; that the saddest of
woman's sorrows, widowhood, was hers to endure, and
that her children must bear a tainted name. It came to be
whispered about that the doomed man wore on his heart a
curl of baby's hair, that had been cut from his child's head
when he went out to serve his imperiled country. Finally,
the wretched, conscience-stricken soldiers sued for pardon
for their condemned companion, and the very man against
whom the enmity had been cherished, and who owed his life
to an accident, busied himself in collecting the name of every
man in the command, begging clemency for the imperiled
sergeant. Six days passed, and there was increased misery
among the men, who felt themselves responsible for their
comrade's life. The prayer for pardon, with its long roll of
names, had been met by the General with the reply that the
matter would be considered.

The men now prepared for vengeance. They lay around
the camp-fires, or grouped themselves in tents, saying that
the commanding officer would not dare to execute the sentence of the court-martial, while messages of this kind reached
my husband in cowardly, roundabout ways, and threats and
menaces seemed to fill the air. The preparation for the sergeant's execution was ordered, and directions given that a
deserter, tried by court-martial and condemned, should be
shot on the same day. This man, a vagabond and criminal
before his enlistment, had deserted three or four times, and
his sentence drew little pity from his comrades. At last
dawned in the lovely valley that dreadful day, which I recall
now with a shudder. It was impossible to keep me from
knowing that an execution was to occur. There was no place
to send me. The subterfuges by which my husband had
kept me from knowing the tragic or the sorrowful in our military life heretofore, were of no avail now. Fortunately, I
knew nothing of the petition for pardon ; nothing, thank
God! of the wife at her home, or of the curl of baby's hair
that was rising and falling over the throbbing, agonized
heart of the condemned father. And how the capacity we

may have for embracing the sorrows of the whole world disappears when our selfish terrors concentrate on the safety of our own loved ones !

The sergeant's life was precious as a life; but the threats, the ominous and quiet watching, the malignant, revengeful faces of the troops about us, told me plainly that another day might darken my life forever, and I was consumed by my own torturing suspense. Rumors of the proposed murder of my husband reached me through the kitchen, the orderlies about our quarters, and at last through the staff. They had fallen into the fashion of my husband, and spared me anything that was agitating or alarming; but this was a time, they felt, when all possible measures should be taken to protect the General, and they implored me to induce him to take precautions for his safety. My pleading was of no avail. He had ordered the staff to follow him unarmed to the execution. They begged him to wear his side-arms, or at least permit them the privilege, in order that they might defend him; but he resolutely refused. How trivial seem all attempts to describe the agonies of mind that filled that black hour when the General and his staff rode from our lawn toward the dreaded field !

Eliza, ever thoughtful of me, hovered round the bed, where I had buried my head in the pillows to deaden the sound of the expected volley. With terms of endearment and soothing, she sought to assure me that nothing would happen to the General. " Nothin' ever does, you know, Miss Libbie," she said, her voice full of the mother in us all when we seek to console. And yet that woman knew all the plans for the General's death, all the venom in the hearts of those who surrounded us, and she felt no hope for his safety.

Pomp and circumstance are not alone for "glorious war," but in army life must also be observed in times of peace. There are good reasons for it, I suppose. The more form and solemnity, the deeper the impression; and as this day was to be a crucial one, in proving to the insubordinate that order must eventually prevail, nothing was hurried, none of the usual customs were omitted. Five thousand soldiers formed a hollow square in a field near the town. The staff, accustomed to take a position and remain with their General near the opening left by the division, followed with wonder and alarm as he rode slowly around the entire line, so near the troops that a hand might have been stretched out to deal a fatal blow. The wagon, drawn by four horses, bearing the criminals sitting on their coffins, followed at a slow pace, escorted by the guard and the firing-party, with reversed arms. The coffins were placed in the centre of the square, and the men seated upon them at the foot of their open graves. Eight men, with livid countenances and vehemently beating hearts, took their places in front of their comrades, and looked upon the blanched, despairing faces of those whom they were ordered to kill. The provost-marshal carried their carbines off to a distance, loaded seven, and placed a blank cartridge in the eighth, thus giving the merciful boon of permanent uncertainty as to whose was the fatal shot. The eyes of the poor victims were then bandaged, while thousands of men held their breath as the tragedy went on. The still, Southern air of that garden on earth was unmoved by any sound, save the unceasing notes of the mocking-birds that sang night and day in the hedges. Preparations had been so accurately made that there was but one word to be spoken after the reading of the warrant for execution, and that the last that those most miserable and hopeless of God's creatures should hear on earth.

There was still one more duty for the provost-marshal before the fatal word, "Fire!" was sounded. But one person understood his movements as he stealthily drew near the sergeant, took his arm, and led him aside. In an instant his voice rang out the fatal word, and the deserter fell back dead, in blessed ignorance that he went into eternity alone; while the sergeant swooned in the arms of the provost-marshal. When he was revived, it was explained to him that the General believed him to have been the victim of undue influence, and had long since determined upon the pardon; but some punishment he thought necessary, and he was also determined that the soldiers should not feel that he had been intimidated from performing his duty because his own life was in peril. It was ascertained afterward that the sergeant's regiment had gone out that day with loaded carbines and forty rounds besides; but the knowledge of this would have altered no plan, nor would it have induced the commanding officer to reveal to any but his provost-marshal the final decision.

Let us hope that in these blessed days of peace some other tiny curls are nestling in a grandfather's neck, instead of lying over his heart, as did the son's in those days, when memories and mementos were all we had of those we loved.

General Custer not only had his own Division to organize and discipline, but was constantly occupied in trying to establish some sort of harmony between the Confederate soldiers, the citizens, and his command. The blood of everyone was at boiling-point then. The soldiers had not the grief of returning to homes desolated by war, because Louisiana escaped much and Texas all of the devastation of campaigns; but they came home obliged to begin the world again. The negroes of the Red River country were not an easy class to manage in days of slavery. We heard that all desperate characters in the border States had been sold into Louisiana, because of its comparative isolation, and that the most ungovernable cases were congregated in the valley of the Red River. However that may have been, it certainly was difficult to make them conform to the new state of affairs. The master, unaccustomed to freedom, still treated the negro as a slave. The colored man, inflated with freedom and reveling in idleness, would not accept common directions in labor. How even the South tolerates a name that it once hated, in the prosperity of the new régime, and in the prospect of their splendid future ! How fresh the enthusiasm in the present day, at any mention of the liberator of the slaves !

But when we consider through what bungling errors we groped blindly in those early days of emancipation, we might well wish that Abraham Lincoln could have been spared to bring his justice and gentle humanity to bear upon the adjusting of that great transition from slavery to freedom.

At the least intimation of a "show" or a funeral—which is a festivity to them, on account of the crowds that congregate—off went the entire body of men, even if the crops were in danger of spoiling for want of harvesting. It was a time in our history that one does not like to look back upon. The excitement into which the land was thrown, not only by war, but by the puzzling question of how to reconcile master to servant and servant to master—for the colored people were an element most difficult to manage, owing to their ignorance and the sudden change of relations to their former owners—all this created new and perplexing problems, which were the order of each day.

The Confederate soldiers had to get their blood down from fever heat. Some took advantage of the fact that the war was over and the Government was ordering its soldiers into the State, not as invaders but as pacifiers, to drag their sabres through the street and talk loudly on the corners in belligerent language, without fear of the imprisonment that in war-times had so quickly followed.

The General was obliged to issue simultaneous orders to his own men, demanding their observance of every right of the citizen, and to the returned Confederate soldiers, assuring them that the Government had not sent troops into their country as belligerents, but insisting upon certain obligations, as citizens, from them.

In an order to the Division, he said: "Numerous complaints having reached these headquarters, of depredations having been committed by persons belonging to this command, all officers and soldiers are hereby urged to use every exertion to prevent the committal of acts of lawlessness, which, if permitted to pass unpunished, will bring discredit upon the command. Now that the war is virtually ended, the rebellion put down, and peace about to be restored to our entire country, let not the lustre of the past four years be dimmed by a single act of misconduct toward the persons or property of those with whom we may be brought in contact. In the future, and particularly on the march, the utmost care will be exercised to save the inhabitants of the country in which we may be located from any molestation whatever. Every violation of order regarding foraging will be punished. The Commanding-General is well aware that the number of those upon whom the enforcement of this order will be necessary will be small, and he trusts that in no case will it be necessary. All officers and soldiers of this command are earnestly reminded to treat the inhabitants of this Department with conciliation and kindness, and particularly is this injunction necessary when we are brought in contact with those who lately were in arms against us. You can well afford to be generous and magnanimous."

In another order, addressed to the Confederate soldiers, he said: " It is expected, and it will be required, that those who were once our enemies, but are now to be treated as friends, will in return refrain from idle boasts, which can only result in harm to themselves. If there still be any who, blind to the events of the past four years, continue to indulge in seditious harangues, all such disturbers of the peace will be arrested, and brought to these headquarters."

Between the troublesome negroes, the unsubdued Confederates, and the lawless among our own soldiers, life was by no means an easy problem to solve. A boy of twenty-five was then expected to act the subtle part of statesman and patriot, and conciliate and soothe the citizen; the part of stern and unrelenting soldier, punishing evidences of unsuppressed rebellion on the part of the conquered; and at the same time the vigilant commanding officer, exacting obedience from his own disaffected soldiery.

As for the positions he filled toward the negro, they were varied — counseling these duties to those who employed them, warning them from idleness, and urging them to work, feeding and clothing the impoverished and the old. It seems to me it was a position combining in one man doctor, lawyer,

taskmaster, father and provider. The town and camp
swarmed with the colored people, lazily lying around waiting
for the Government to take care of them, and it was necessary to issue a long order to the negroes, from which I make
an extract:

" Since the recent advent of the United States forces into
this vicinity, many of the freedmen of the surrounding country seem to have imbibed the idea that they will no longer be
required to labor for their own support and the support of
those depending upon them. Such ideas cannot be tolerated,
being alike injurious to the interests and welfare of the freedmen and their employers. Freedmen must not look upon
military posts as places of idle resort, from which they can
draw their means of support. Their proper course is to obtain employment, if possible, upon the same plantations
where they were previously employed. General Order No.
23, Headquarters Department of the Gulf, March 11, 1865,
prescribes the rules of contract in the case of these persons.
The coming crops, already maturing, require cultivation, and
will furnish employment for all who are disposed to be indus-
trious. Hereafter, no freedmen will be permitted to remain
in the vicinity of the camps who are not engaged in some
proper employment."

Standing alone in the midst of all this confusion, and endeavoring to administer justice on all sides, General Custer
had by no means an enviable task. I do not wonder now
that he kept his perplexities as much as possible from me.
He wished to spare me anxiety, and the romp or the gallop
over the fragrant field, which he asked for as soon as office-
hours were over, was probably more enjoyable with a woman
with uncorrugated brow. Still, I see now the puzzled shake
of the head as he said, " A man may do everything to keep
a woman from knowledge of official matters, and then she
gets so confounded keen in putting little trifles together, the
first thing you know she is reading a man's very thoughts."
Yet it does not strike me as remarkable keenness on the part
of a woman if, after the experience she gains in following the

bugle a time, and with her wits sharpened by affection, she decides that a move is about to take place. The General used to turn quickly, almost suspiciously, to me and say, as if I had been told by the staff, " How did you find out we were ordered to move ? "—when he had been sending for the quartermaster and the commissary, and looking at his maps, for ever so long before ! It was not much of a mystery to solve when the quartermaster meant transportation, the commissary food, and the maps a new route.

After determined efforts to establish discipline, order began to be evolved out of the chaos, and the men resigned themselves to their hard fate. Much as I feared them, and greatly as I had resented their attempt to lay all their present detention and compulsory service to my husband, I could not but agree with him when he argued for them that it was pretty hard not to be allowed to go home, when the other soldiers had returned to receive the rewards of the victorious. They wrote home abusive newspaper articles, which were promptly mailed to the General by unknown hands, but of which he took no notice. I recollect only once, after that, knowing of an absolutely disagreeable encounter. During the following winter in Texas, my husband came quickly into our room one morning, took my riding-whip and returned across the hall to his office. In a short time he as quickly returned, and restored it to its place, and I extracted from him an explanation. Among the newspaper articles sent him from the North, there was an attack on his dear, quiet, un-offending father and mother. He sent for the officer who was credited with the authorship, and, after his denial of the article, told him what he had intended to do had he been guilty of such an assault; that he was prepared for any attack on himself, but nothing would make him submit to seeing his gray-haired parents assailed. Then he bade him good-morning, and bowed him out.

The effect of the weeks of discipline on the Division was visible on our march into Texas. The General had believed that the men would eventually conform to the restrictions, and he was heartily relieved and glad to find that they did. The Texans were amazed at the absence of the lawlessness they had expected from our army, and thankful to find that the Yankee column was neither devastating nor even injuring their hitherto unmolested State, for the war on land had not reached Texas. The troops were not permitted to live on the country, as is the usage of war, and only one instance occurred, during the entire march, of a soldier's simply helping himself to a farmer's grain. Every pound of food and forage was bought by the quartermaster. It was hard to realize that the column marching in a methodical and orderly manner was, so short a time before, a lawless and mutinous command.

They hated us, I suppose. That is the penalty the commanding officer generally pays for what still seems to me the questionable privilege of rank and power. Whatever they thought, it did not deter us from commending, among ourselves, the good material in those Western men, which so soon made them orderly and obedient soldiers.

But I have anticipated somewhat, and must go back and say good-by to that rich, flower-scented valley. It had been a strange experience to me. I had no woman but Eliza to whom I could speak. The country and all its customs seemed like another world, into which I had unexpectedly entered. I had spent many hours of anxiety about my husband's safety. But the anxiety, heat, mosquitoes, poor water, alligators, mutiny, all combined, failed to extract a complaint. There was not an atom of heroism in this; it was undeniably the shrewd cunning of which women are accused, for I lived in hourly dread of being sent to Texas by the other route, via New Orleans and the Gulf of Mexico. The General had been advised by letters from home to send me that way, on the ground that I could not endure a march at that season. Officers took on a tone of superiority, and said that they would not think of taking *their* wives into such a wilderness. My fate hung in the balance, and under such circumstances it was not strange that the inconveniences of our stay on

Red River were not even so much as acknowledged. It is true that I was not then a veteran campaigner, and the very newness of the hardships would, doubtless, have called forth a few sighs, had not the fear of another separation haunted me. It is astonishing how much grumbling is suppressed by the fear of something worse awaiting you. In the decision which direction I was to take, I won; my husband's scruples were overcome by my unanswerable arguments and his own inclination.

I prepared to leave Alexandria with regret, for the pleasures of our stay had outnumbered the drawbacks. It was our first knowledge that the earth could be so lovely and so lavishly laden with what began to be tropical luxuriance. I do not recall the names of all the birds, but the throats of all of them seemed to be filled with song. In a semicircle on the lawn in front of our house, grew a thick hedge of crape myrtle, covered with fragrant blossoms. Here the mocking-birds fearlessly built their nests, and the stillest hour of the night was made melodious with the song that twilight had been too short to complete. Really, the summer day there was too brief to tell all that these birds had to say to their mates.

To the General, who would have had an aviary had it been just the thing for a mounted regiment, all this song, day and night, was enchanting. In after years he never forgot those midnight serenades, and in 1873 he took a mocking-bird into the bleak climate of Dakota. Eliza mildly growled at " sich nonsense " as " toting round a bird, when 'twas all folks like us could do to get transportation for a cooking-kit." Nevertheless, she took excellent care of the feathered tribe that we owned.

Among the fruits we first ate in Louisiana were fresh figs, which we picked from the tree. It was something to write home about, but at the same time we wished that instead we might have a Northern apple.

The time came to bid farewell to birds, fruits, jasmine and rose, and prepare for a plunge into the wilderness—much talked of with foreboding prophecies by the citizens, but a hundred times worse in reality than the gloomiest predictions.

It was known that the country through which we were to travel, having been inaccessible to merchants, and being even then infested with guerrillas, had large accumulations of cotton stored at intervals along the route that was marked out for our journey. Speculators arrived from New Orleans, and solicited the privilege of following with wagons that they intended to load with cotton. They asked no favors, desiring only the protection that the cavalry column would afford, and expected to make their way in our wake until the seaboard was reached and they could ship their purchases by the Gulf of Mexico. But their request was refused, as the General hardly thought it a fitting use to which to put the army. Then they assailed the quartermaster, offering twenty-five thousand dollars to the General and him, as a bribe. But both men laughed to scorn that manner of getting rich, and returned to their homes the year after as poor as when they had left there five years before. As I think of the instances that came under my knowledge, when quartermasters could have made fortunes, it is a marvel to me that they so often resisted all manner of temptation. The old tale, perhaps dating back to the War of 1812, still applies, as it is a constantly recurring experience. There was once a wag in the quartermaster's department, and even when weighted down with grave responsibility of a portion of the Government treasury, he still retained a glimmer of fun. Contractors lay in wait for him with bribes, which his spirit of humor allowed to increase, even though the offers were insults to his honor. Finally, reaching a very large sum, in sheer desperation he wrote to the War Department: "In the name of all the gods, relieve me from this Department; they've almost got up to my price." Civilians hardly realize that, even in times of peace like this, when the disbursements will not compare with the money spent in years of war, between eight and nine millions of dollars are yearly paid out by the quartermaster's department alone. Since the war the embezzlements have been hardly worthy of so serious a name, amounting to but a few hundred dollars, all told.

The General had an ambulance fitted up as a traveling-wagon for me; the seats so arranged that the leather backs could be unstrapped at the sides and laid down so as to form a bed, if I wished to rest during the march. There was a pocket for my needlework and book, and a box for luncheon, while my traveling-bag and shawl were strapped at the side, convenient, but out of the way. It was quite a complete little house of itself. One of the soldiers, who was interested in the preparations for my comfort, covered a canteen with leather, adding of his own accord, in fine stitchery in the yellow silk used by the saddlers, "Lady Custer." Each day of our journey this lofty distinction became more and more incongruous and amusing, as I realized the increasing ugliness, for which the rough life was, in a measure, responsible. By the time we reached the end of our march there was a yawning gulf between the soldier's title and the appearance of the owner of the canteen. The guide that had been employed was well up in all the devices for securing what little measure of comfort was to be found in overland travel. I followed his suggestion, and after the canteen was filled in the morning, it was covered with a piece of wet blanket and hung, with the cork left out, to the roof of the wagon, in order to catch all the air that might be stirring. Under this damp treatment the yellow letters of "Lady Custer" faded out as effectually as did all semblance of whatever delicacy of coloring the owner once possessed.

A short time after we set out, we left the valley of the Red River, with its fertile plantations, and entered a pine forest on the table-land, through which our route lay for a hundred and fifty miles. A great portion of the higher ground was sterile, and the forest much of the way was thinly inhabited. We had expected to hire a room in any farm-house at which we halted at the end of each day's journey, and have the privilege of sleeping in a bed. Camping on the ground was an old story to me after our long march in Virginia; but,

with the prospect of using the bosom of mother Earth as a
resting-place for the coming thirty years, we were willing to
improve any opportunity to be comfortable when we could.
The cabins that we passed on the first day discouraged us.
Small, low, log huts, consisting of one room each, entirely
separated and having a floored open space between them,
were the customary architecture. The windows and doors
were filled with the vacant faces of the untidy children of the
poor white trash and negroes. The men and women slouched
and skulked around the cabins out of sight, and every sign
of abject, loathsome poverty was visible, even in the gaunt
and famished pigs that rooted around the doorway. I determined to camp out until we came to more inviting habitations, which, I regret to say, we did not find on that march.
We had not brought the thin mattress and pillows that had
been made for our traveling-wagon in Virginia; but the hardest sort of resting-place was preferable to braving the squalor
of the huts along our way.

My husband rolled his overcoat for my pillow, telling me
that a soldier slept like a top with such an one, and it was
much better than a saddle, in the hollow of which he had
often laid his flaxen top-knot. But a woman cannot make
herself into a good soldier all in a minute. If one takes hold
of the thick, unwieldy material that Uncle Sam puts into the
army overcoat, some idea can be gained of the rocky roll it
makes when doing duty as a resting-place; and anyone whose
neck has made the steep incline from head to shoulder that
this substitute for a pillow necessitates, is apt to waken less
patriotic than when he retired. After repeated efforts to get
accustomed to this, buoyed up by my husband's praise of my
veteran-like behavior, I confided to Eliza that I should not
be ungrateful for any device she might think out for my relief, if she would promise not to tell that I had spoken to
her. The next day she gathered moss from the trees along
the stream, and I felt that I could serve my country just as
well by resting on this soft bed. I had begged off from using
a tent in that country, as there seemed to be no insect that

was not poisonous, and even many of the vines and under-brush were dangerous to touch. My husband had the wagon placed in front of the tent every night when our march was ended, and lifted me in and out of the high sleeping-room, where I felt that nothing venomous could climb up and sting. The moss, though very comfortable, often held in its meshes the horned toad, a harmless little mottled creature that had two tiny horns, which it turned from side to side in the gravest, most knowing sort of way. The officers sent these little creatures home by mail as curiosities, and, true to their well-known indifference to air, they jumped out of the box at the journey's end in just the same active manner that they had hopped about under our feet. Still, harmless as they were held to be, they were not exactly my choice as bed-fellows, any more than the lizards the Texans call swifts, which also haunted the tangles of the moss. Eliza tried to shake out and beat it thoroughly, in order to dislodge any inhabitants, before making my bed. One night I found that hay had been substituted, and felt myself rich in luxury. I remembered gladly that hay was so clean, so free from all natural history, and closed my eyes in gratitude. And then it smelt so good, so much better than the damp, vegetable odor of the moss. A smudge at the end of the wagon was rising about me to drive away mosquitoes, and though the smoke scalds the eyes in this heroic remedy, I still comforted myself with the fresh odor of the hay, and quietly thought that life in a manger was not the worst fate that could come to one. All this pervading sense of comfort was slightly dis-turbed in the night, when I was awakened by a munching and crunching at my ear. Wisps of hay were lying over the side of the wagon, as it was too warm to leave the curtains down, and the attraction proved too much for a stray mule, which was quietly eating the pillow from under my head. It was well our tent and wagon were placed to one side, quite off by themselves, for the General would have waked the camp with his peals of laughter at my indignation and mo-mentary fright. It did not need much persuasion to rout the mule after all the hubbub my husband made with his merriment, but I found that I inclined to the moss bed after that.

As we advanced farther into the forest, Eliza received further whispered confidences about my neck, stiff and sore from the roll of patriotic blue that was still the rest for my tired head, and she resolved to make an attempt to get a feather pillow. One day she discovered, near our camp, a house that was cleaner than the rest we had seen, and began

A MULE LUNCHING FROM A PILLOW.

negotiations with the mistress. She offered a "greenback," as we had no silver then; but they had never seen one, and would not believe that it was legal money. Finally, the woman said that, if we had any calico or muslin for sale, she would exchange her pillows for either the one or the other. Eliza forgot her diplomacy, and rather indignantly explained that we were not traveling peddlers. At last, after several trips to and from our camp, in which I was secretly interested, she made what she thought a successful trade by exchanging some blankets. Like the wag's description of the first Pullman-car pillows, which he said he lost in his ear, they were diminutive excuses for our idea of what one should be, but I cannot remember anything that ever impressed me as such a luxury; and I was glad to see that, when the pillows were installed in their place, the faith in my patriotism and in my willingness to endure privations was not shaken.

The General was satisfied with his soldiers, and admired the manner in which they endured the trials of that hard experience. His perplexities departed when they took everything so bravely. He tried to arrange our marches every day so that we might not travel over fifteen miles. So far as I can remember, there was no one whose temper and strength were not tried to the uttermost, except my husband. His seeming indifference to excessive heat, his having long before conquered thirst, his apparent unconsciousness of the stings or bites of insects, were powerful aids in encountering those suffocating days. Frequently after a long march, when we all gasped for breath, and in our exhaustion flung ourselves down "anywhere to die," as we laughingly said, a fresh horse was saddled, and off went the General for a hunt, or to look up the prospects for water in our next day's journey. If this stifling atmosphere, to which we were daily subjected, disturbed him, we did not know it. He held that grumbling did not mend matters; but I differed with him. I still think a little complaining, when the patience is sorely taxed, eases the troubled soul, though at that time I took good care not to put my theory into practice, for reasons I have explained when the question of my joining the march hung in the balance.

My life in a wagon soon became such an old story that I could hardly believe I had ever had a room. It constantly reminded me of my father. He had opposed my marrying in the army, as I suppose most fond fathers do. His opposition caused me great suspense, and I thought, as all the very young are apt to, that it was hopeless misery. Now that the struggle was ended, I began to recall the arguments of my parents. Father's principal one, mindful of the deprivations he had seen officers' wives endure in Michigan's early days, was that, after the charm and dazzle of the epaulet had passed, I might have to travel " in a covered wagon like an emigrant." I told this reason of my father's to my husband, and he often laughed over it. When I was lifted from my rather lofty apartment, and set down in the tent in the dark —and before dawn in a pine forest it *is* dark—the candle revealed a twinkle in the eye of a man who could joke before breakfast. " I wonder what your father would say now," was the oft-repeated remark, while the silent partner scrabbled around to get ready for the day. There was always a pervading terror of being late, and I could not believe but that it might happen, some day, that thousands of men would be kept waiting because a woman had lost her hair-pins. Imaging the ignominy of any of the little trifles that delay us in getting ourselves together, being the cause of detaining an expedition in its morning start on the march. Fortunately, the soldiers would have been kept in merciful ignorance of the cause of the detention, as a commanding officer is not obliged to explain why he orders the trumpeter to delay the call of " boots and saddles; " but the chagrin would have been just as great on the part of the " camp-follower," and it would have given the color of truth to the General's occasional declaration that " it is easier to command a whole division of cavalry than one woman." I made no protest to this declaration, as I had observed, even in those early days of my married life, that, in matrimonial experiences, the men that make open statements of their wrongs in rather a pompous, boastful way, are not the real sufferers. Pride teaches subtlety in hiding genuine injuries.

Though I had a continued succession of frights, while prowling around the tent before day hunting my things, believing them lost sometimes, and thus being thrown into wild stampedes, I escaped the mortification of detaining the command. The Frenchman's weariness of a life that was given over to buttoning and unbuttoning, was mine, and in the short time between reveillé and breakfast, I lived through much perturbation of mind, fearing I was behind time, and devoutly wished that women who followed the drum could have been clothed like the feathered tribe, and ready for the wing at a moment's notice. On this expedition I brought down the art of dressing in a hurry to so fine a point that I could take my bath and dress entirely in seven minutes. My husband timed me one day, without my knowledge, and I had the honor of having this added to a very brief list of my attributes as a soldier. There was a second recommendation, which did duty as a mild plaudit for years afterward. When faithful soldiers are discharged after their term of service has expired, they have papers given them by the Government, with statements of their ability and trustworthiness. Mine consisted in the words usually used in presenting me to a friend. Instead of referring to a few meagre accomplishments which my teachers had struggled to implant, as is the fashion of some exuberant husbands, who proudly introduce their wives to intimate friends, the General usually said, " Oh, I want you to know my wife; she slept four months in a wagon."

Perhaps some people in the States may not realize that army women have a hard time even in saying their prayers. The closet that the New Testament tells us to frequent is seldom ours, for rarely does our frugal Government allow us one in army quarters large enough to crowd in our few gowns, much less to "enter in and shut the door "; while on a march like that in Texas, devotions would be somewhat disturbed when one kneeled down in a tent, uncertain whether it would be on a centipede or a horned toad. To say a prayer undisturbed, it was necessary to wait until one went to bed. Fortunately, mine were brief, since I had nothing to ask for, as I believed the best of everything on earth had already been given to me. If I was tired, and fell asleep in the midst of my thanks, I could only hope the Heavenly Father would forgive me. I was often so exhausted at night, that it was hard to keep my eyes open after my head had touched the pillow, especially after the acquisition of the blessed feather pillow. An army woman I love, the most consistent and honorable of her sex, was once so worn out after a day of danger and fatigue on a march, that she fell asleep while kneeling beside the bed in the room she occupied, saying her prayers; and there she found herself, still on her knees, when the sun wakened her in the morning.

CHAPTER IV.

MARCHES THROUGH PINE FORESTS.

For exasperating heat, commend me to a pine forest.

Those tall and almost branchless Southern pines were simply smothering. In the fringed tops the wind swayed the delicate limbs, while not a breath descended to us below. We fumed and fussed, but not ill-naturedly, when trying to find a spot in which to take a nap. If we put ourselves in n narrow strip of shadow made by the slender trunk of a tree, remorseless Sol followed persistently, and we drowsily dragged ourselves to another, to be pursued in the same determined manner and stared into instant wakefulness by the burning rays.

The General had reveillé sounded at 2 o'clock in the morning, causing our scamp to remark, *sotto voce*, that if we were to be routed out in the night, he thought he would eat his breakfast the evening before, in order to save time. It was absolutely necessary to move before dawn, as the moment the sun came in sight the heat was suffocating. It was so dark when we set out that it was with difficulty we reached the main road, from our night's camp, in safety. My husband tossed me into the saddle, and cautioned me to follow as close as my horse could walk, as we picked our way over logs and through ditches or underbrush. Custis Lee * was doglike in his behavior at these times. He seemed to aim to put his hoof exactly in the footprint of the General's horse.

---

* My horse was captured from a staff-officer of General Custis Lee during the war, purchased by my husband from the Government, and named for the Confederate general.

In times of difficulty or moments of peril, he evidently considered that he was following the commanding officer rather than carrying me. I scarcely blamed him, much as I liked to control my own horse, and gladly let the bridle slacken on his neck as he cautiously picked his circuitous way; but once on the main road, the intelligent animal allowed me to take control again. Out of the dark my husband's voice came cheerily, as if he were riding in a path of sunshine: "Are you all right?" "Give Lee his head." "Trust that old plug of yours to bring you out ship-shape." This insult to my splendid, spirited, high-stepping F. F. V.—for he was that among horses, as well as by birth—was received calmly by his owner, especially as the sagacious animal was taking better care of me than I could possibly take of myself, and I spent a brief time in calling out a defense of him through the gloom of the forest. This little diversion was indulged in now and again by the General to provoke an argument, and thus assure himself that I was safe and closely following; and so it went on, before day and after dark; there was no hour or circumstance out of which we did not extract some amusement.

The nights, fortunately, were cool; but such dews fell, and it was so chilly that we were obliged to begin our morning march in thick coats, which were tossed off as soon as the sun rose. The dews drenched the bedding. I was sometimes sure that it was raining in the night, and woke my husband to ask to have the ambulance curtains of our bed lowered; but it was always a false alarm; not a drop of rain fell in that blistering August. I soon learned to shut our clothes in a little valise at night, after undressing in the tent, to ensure dry linen in the penetrating dampness of the morning. My husband lifted me out of the wagon, when reveillé sounded, into the tent, and by the light of a tallow candle I had my bath and got into my clothes, combing my hair straight back, as it was too dark to part it. Then, to keep my shoes from being soaked with the wet grass, I was carried to the dining-tent, and lifted upon my horse afterward.

One of my hurried toilets was stopped short one morning by the loss of the body of my riding-habit. In vain I tossed our few traps about to find it. and finally remembered that I had exchanged the waist for a jacket, and left it under a tree where we had been taking a siesta the day before. Eliza had brought in the blanket, books, and hats, but alas for my dress body! it was hopelessly lost. In a pine forest, dark and thick with fallen trees, what good did one tallow dip do in the hasty search we made? A column of thousands of men could not be detained for a woman's gown. My husband had asked me to braid the sleeves like his own velvet jacket. Five rows of gilt braid in five loops made a dash of color that he liked, which, though entirely out of place in a thoroughfare, was admissible in our frontier life. He regretted the loss, but insisted on sending for more gilt braid as soon as we were out of the wilderness, and then began to laugh to himself and wonder if the traveler that came after us, not knowing who had preceded him, might not think he had come upon a part of the wardrobe of a circus troupe. It would have been rather serious joking if in the small outfit in my valise I had not brought a jacket, for which, though it rendered me more of a fright than sun and wind had made me, I still was very thankful; for without the happy accident that brought it along, I should have been huddled inside the closed ambulance, waistless and alone. Our looks did not enter into the question very much. All we thought of was how to keep from being prostrated by the heat, and how to get rested after the march for the next day's task.

We had a unique character for a guide. He was a citizen of Texas, who boasted that not a road or a trail in the State was unfamiliar to him. His mule, Betty, was a trial; she walked so fast that no one could keep up with her, but not faster did she travel than her master's tongue. As we rode at the head of the column, the sun pouring down upon our heads, we would call out to him, " In heaven's name, Stillman, how much longer is this to keep up?" meaning, When shall we find a creek on which to camp? " Oh, three miles further you're sure to find a bold-flowin' stream," was his confident reply; and, sure enough, the grass began to look greener, the moss hung from the trees, the pines were varied by beautiful cypress, or some low-branched tree, and hope sprang up in our hearts. The very horses showed, by quickening step, they knew what awaited us. Our scorched and parched throats began to taste, in imagination, what was our idea of a bold-flowing stream—it was cool and limpid, dancing over pebbles on its merry way. We found ourselves in reality in the bed of a dried creek, nothing but pools of muddy water, with a coating of green mold on the surface. The Custers made use of this expression the rest of their lives. If ever we came to a puny, crawling driblet of water, they said, "This must be one of Stillman's bold-flowing streams." On we went again, with that fabricator calling out from Betty's back, "Sho' to find finest water in the land five miles on!" Whenever he had "been in these parts afore, he had always found at all seasons a roaring torrent." One day we dragged through forty miles of arid land, and after passing the dried beds of three streams, the General was obliged to camp at last, on account of the exhausted horses, on a creek with pools of muddy, standing water, which Stillman, coming back to the column, described as "rather low." This was our worst day, and we felt the heat intensely, as we usually finished our march and were in camp before the sun was very high. I do not remember one good drink of water on that march. When it was not muddy or stagnant, it tasted of the roots of the trees. Some one had given my husband some claret for me when we set out, and but for that, I don't really know how the thirst of the midsummer days could have been endured. The General had already taught himself not to drink between meals, and I was trying to do so. All he drank was his mug of coffee in the early morning and at dinner, and cold tea or coffee, which Eliza kept in a bottle, for luncheon.

The privations did not quench the buoyancy of those gay young fellows. The General and his staff told stories and

GENERAL CUSTER AS A CADET.

sang, and a man with good descriptive powers recounted the
bills of fare of good dinners and choice viands he had enjoyed, while we knew we had nothing to anticipate in this
wilderness but army fare. Sometimes, as we marched along,
almost melted with heat, and our throats parched for water,
the odor of cucumbers was wafted toward us. Stillman, the
guide, being called on for an explanation, as we wondered if
we were nearing a farm, slackened Betty, waited for us, and
took down our hopes by explaining that it was a certain spe-
cies of snake, which infested that part of the country. The
scorpions, centipedes and tarantulas were daily encountered.
I not only grew more and more unwilling to take my nap,
after the march was over, under a tree, but made life a burden to my husband till he gave up flinging himself down
anywhere to sleep, and induced him to take his rest in the
traveling wagon. I had been indolently lying outstretched
in a little grateful shade one day, when I was hurriedly roused
by some one, and moved to avoid what seemed to me a small,
dried twig. It was the most venomous of snakes, called the
pine-tree rattlesnake. It was very strange that we all escaped being stung or bitten in the midst of thousands of
those poisonous reptiles and insects. One teamster died
from a scorpion's bite, and, unfortunately, I saw his bloated,
disfigured body as we marched by. It lay on a wagon, ready
for burial, without even a coffin, as we had no lumber.

What was most aggravating were two pests of that region,
the seed-tick and the chigger. The latter bury their heads
under the skin, and when they are swollen with blood, it is
almost impossible to extract them without leaving the head
imbedded. This festers, and the irritation is almost unbearable. If they see fit to locate on neck, face or arms, it is
possible to outwit them in their progress; but they generally
choose that unattainable spot between the shoulders, and the
surgical operation of taking them out with a needle or knife-
point, must devolve upon some one else. To ride thus with
the skin on fire, and know that it must be endured till the
march was ended, caused some grumbling, but it did not last

long. The enemy being routed, out trilled a song or laugh from young and happy throats. If we came to a sandy stretch of ground, loud groans from the staff began, and a cry, " We're in for the chiggers! " was an immediate warning. We all grew very wary of lying down to rest in such a locality, but were thankful that the little pests were not venomous. There's nothing like being where something dangerous lies in wait for you, to teach submission to what is only an irritating inconvenience.

One of the small incidents out of which we invariably extracted fun, was our march at dawn past the cabins of the few inhabitants. On the open platform, sometimes covered, but often with no roof, which connects the two log huts, the family are wont to sleep in hot weather. There they lay on rude cots, and were only awakened by the actual presence of the cavalry, of whose approach they were unaware. The children sat up in bed, in wide-gaping wonder; the grown people raised their heads, but instantly ducked under the covers again, thinking they would get up in a moment, as soon as the cavalcade had passed, From time to time a head was cautiously raised, hoping to see the end of the column. Then such a shout from the soldiers, a fusillade of the wittiest comments, such as only soldiers can make—for I never expect to hear brighter speeches than issue from a marching column—and down went the venturesome head, compelled to obey an unspoken military mandate and remain "under cover." There these people lay till the sun was scorching them, imprisoned under their bed-clothes by modesty, while the several thousand men filed by, two by two, and the long wagon-train in the rear had passed the house.

There came a day when I could not laugh and joke with the rest. I was mortified to find myself ill—I, who had been pluming myself on being such a good campaigner, my desire to keep well being heightened by overhearing the General boasting to Tom that "nothing makes the old lady ill." We did not know that sleeping in the sun in that climate brings on a chill, and I had been frightened away from the snake-

infested ground, where there might be shade, to the wagon
for my afternoon sleep.   It was embarrassing in the extreme.
I could neither be sent back, nor remain in that wilderness,
which was infested by guerrillas.   The surgeon compelled me
to lie down on the march.   It was very lonely, for I missed
the laughter and story at the head of the column, which had
lightened the privations of the journey.   The soil was so
shallow that the wagon was kept on a continual joggle by
the roots of the trees over which we passed.   This uneven-
ness was of course not noticeable on horseback, but now it
was painfully so at every revolution of the wheels.   The General and Tom came back to comfort me every now and again,
while Eliza "mammied" and nursed me, and rode in the
seat by the driver.   It was "break-bone fever."   No one
knowing about it can read these words and not feel a shudder.   I believe it is not dangerous, but the patient is introduced, in the most painful manner, to every bone in his body.
Incredible as it used to seem when, in school, we repeated
the number of bones, it now became no longer a wonder,
and the only marvel was, how some of the smallest on the
list could contain so large an ache.   I used to lie and specu-
late how one slender woman could possibly conceal so many
bones under the skin.   Anatomy had been on the list of
hated books in school; but I began then to study it from life,
in a manner that made it likely to be remembered.   The surgeon, as is the custom of the admirable men of that profession in the army, paid me the strictest attention, and I swal-
lowed quinine, it seemed to me, by the spoonful.   As I had
never taken any medicine to speak of, it did its duty quickly,
and in a few days I was lifted into the saddle, tottering and
light-headed, but partly relieved from the pain, and very glad to
get back to our military family, who welcomed me so warmly
that I was aglow with gratitude.   I wished to ignore the fact
that I had fallen by the way, and was kept in lively fear that
they would all vote me a bother.   After that, my husband
had the soldiers who were detailed for duty at headquarters,
when they cut the wood for camp-fires, build a rough shade

of pine branches over the wagon, when we reached camp. Even that troubled me, though the kind-hearted fellows did not seem to mind it; but the General quieted me by explaining that the men, being excused from night duty as sentinels, would not mind building the shade as much as losing their sleep, and, besides, we were soon afterward out of the pine forest and on the prairie.

Our officers suffered dreadfully on that march, though they made light of it, and were soon merry after a trial or hardship was over. The drenching dews chilled the air that was encountered just at daybreak. They were then plunged into a steam bath from the overpowering sun, and the impure water told frightfully on their health. I have seen them turn pale and almost reel in the saddle, as we marched on. They kept quinine in their vest-pockets, and horrified me by taking large quantities at any hour when they began to feel a chill coming on, or were especially faint. Our brother Tom did not become quite strong, after his attack of fever, for a long time, and had inflammatory rheumatism at Fort Riley a year or more afterward, which the surgeons attributed to his Texas exposure. I used to see the haggard face of the adjutant-general, Colonel Jacob Greene, grow drawn and gray with the inward fever that filled his veins and racked his bones with pain. The very hue of his skin comes back to me after all these years, for we grieved over his suffering, as we had all just welcomed him back from the starvation of Libby Prison.

I rode in their midst, month after month, ever revolving in my mind the question, whence came the inexhaustible supply of pluck that seemed at their command, to meet all trials and privations, just as their unfaltering courage had enabled them to go through the battles of the war? And yet, how much harder it was to face such trials, unsupported by the excitement of the trumpet-call and the charge. There was no wild clamor of war to enable them to forget the absence of the commonest necessities of existence. In Texas and Kansas, the life was often for months unattended by excitement

of any description. It was only to be endured by a grim
shutting of the teeth, and an iron will. The mother of one
of the fallen heroes of the Seventh Cavalry, who passed uncomplainingly through the privations of the frontier, and
gave up his life at last, writes to me in a recent letter that
she considers "those late experiences of hardship and suffering, so gallantly borne, by far the most interesting of General
Custer's life, and the least known." For my part I was constantly mystified as I considered how our officers, coming
from all the wild enthusiasm of their Virginia life, could, as
they expressed it, "buckle down" to the dull, exhausting
days of a monotonous march.

Young as I then was, I thought that to endure, to fight for
and inflexibly pursue a purpose or general principle like
patriotism, seemed to require far more patience and courage
than when it is individualized. I did not venture to put my
thoughts into words, for two reasons : I was too wary to let
them think I acknowledged there were hardships, lest they
might think I repented having come ; for I knew then, as I
know now, but feared they did not, that I would go through
it all a hundred times over, if inspired by the reasons that
actuated me. In the second place, I had already found what
a habit it is to ridicule and make light of misfortune or vicissi-
tude. It cut me to the quick at first, and I thought the officers and soldiers lacking in sympathy. But I learned to
know what splendid, loyal friends they really were, if misfortune came and help was needed ; how they denied themselves to loan money, if it is the financial difficulty of a
friend ; how they nursed one another in illness or accident ;
how they quietly fought the battles of the absent ; and one
occasion I remember, that an officer, being ill, was unable to
help himself when a soldier behaved in a most insolent manner, and his brother officer knocked him down, but immediately apologized to the captain for taking the matter out of
his hands. A hundred ways of showing the most unswerving
fidelity taught me, as years went on, to submit to what I still
think the deplorable habit, if not of ridicule, of suppressed

sympathy. I used to think that even if a misfortune was not serious, it ought to be recognized, and none were afraid of showing that they possessed truly tender, gentle, sympathetic natures, with me or with any woman that came among them.

The rivers, and even the small streams, in Texas have high banks. It is a land of freshets, and the most innocent little rill can rise to a roaring torrent in no time. Anticipating these crossings, we had in our train a pontoon bridge. We had to make long halts while this bridge was being laid, and then, oh ! the getting down to it. If the sun was high, and the surgeon had consigned me to the traveling-wagon, I looked down the deep gulley with more than inward quaking. My trembling hands clutched wildly at the seat and my head was out at the side to see my husband's face, as he directed the descent, cautioned the driver, and encouraged me. The brake was frequently not enough, and the soldiers had to man the wheels, for the soil was wet and slippery from the constant passing of the pioneer force, who had laid the bridge. The heavy wagons, carrying the boats and lumber for the bridge, had made the side-hill a difficult bit of ground to traverse. The four faithful mules apparently sat down and slid to the water's edge ; but the driver, so patient with my quiet imploring to go slowly, kept his strong foot on the brake and knotted the reins in his powerful hands. I blessed him for his caution, and then at every turn of the wheel I implored him again to be careful. Finally, when I poured out my thanks at the safe transit, the color mounted in his brown face, as if he had led a successful charge. In talking at night to Eliza, of my tremors as we plunged down the bank and were bounced upon the pontoon, which descended to the water's edge under the sudden rush with which we came, I added my praise of the driver's skill, which she carefully repeated as she slipped him, on the sly, the mug of coffee and hot biscuits with which she invariably rewarded merit, whether in officers or men. When I could, I made these descents on horseback, and climbed up the opposite bank with my hands wound in Custis Lee's abundant mane.

Eliza, in spite of her constant lookout for some variety for our table, could seldom find any vegetables, even at the huts we passed. Corn pone and chine were the principal food of these shiftless citizens, butternut-colored in clothing and complexion, indifferent alike to food and to drink. At the Sabine River the water was somewhat clearer. The soldiers, leading their horses, crossed carefully, as it was dangerous to stop here, lest the weight should carry the bridge under ; but they are too quick-witted not to watch every chance to procure a comfort, and they tied strings to their canteens and dragged them beside the bridge, getting, even in that short progress, one tolerably good drink. The wagon-train was of course a long time in crossing, and dinner looked dubious to our staff. Our faithful Eliza, as we talk over that march, will prove in her own language, better than I can portray, how she constantly bore our comfort on her mind:

"Miss Libbie, do you mind, after we crossed the Sabine River, we went into camp? Well, we hadn't much supplies, and the wagons wasn't up ; so, as I was a-waitin' for you all, I says to the boys, ' Now, you make a fire, and I'll go a-fishin'.' The first thing, I got a fish—well, as long as my arm. It was big, and jumped so it scart me, and I let the line go, but one of the men caught hold and jumped for me and I had him, and went to work on him right away. I cleaned him, salted him, rolled him in flour, and fried him ; and, Miss Libbie, we had a nice platter of fish, and the General was just delighted when he came up, and he was surprised, too, and he found his dinner—for I had some cold biscuit and a bottle of tea in the lunch-box—while the rest was a-waitin' for the supplies to come up. For while all the rest was a-waitin', I went fishin', mind you !"

CHAPTER V.

OUT OF THE WILDERNESS.

As we came out of the forest, the country improved somewhat. The farm-houses began to show a little look of comfort, and it occurred to us that we might now vary the monotony of our fare by marketing. My husband and I sometimes rode on in advance of the command, and approached the houses with our best manners, soliciting the privilege of buying butter and eggs. The farmer's wife was taking her first look at Yankees, but she found that we neither wore horns nor were cloven-footed, and she even so far unbent as to apologize for not having butter, adding, what seemed then so flimsy an excuse, that "I don't make more than enough butter for our own use, as we are only milking seven cows now." We had yet to learn that what makes a respectable dairy at home was nothing in a country where the cows give a cupful of milk and all run to horns. It was a great relief to get out of the wilderness, but though our hardships were great, I do not want them to appear to outnumber the pleasures. The absence of creature comforts is easily itemized. We are either too warm or too cold, we sleep uncomfortably, we have poor food, we are wet by storms, we are made ill by exposure. Happiness cannot be itemized so readily ; it is hard to define what goes to round and complete a perfect day. We remember hours of pleasure as bathed in a mist that blends all shades into a roseate hue ; but it is impossible to take one tint from colors so perfectly mingled, and define how it adds to the perfect whole.

The days now seemed to grow shorter and brighter. In place of the monotonous pines, we had magnolia, mulberry, pecan, persimmon and live-oak, as well as many of our own Northern trees, that grew along the streams. The cactus, often four feet high, was covered with rich red blossoms, and made spots of gorgeous color in the prairie grass. I had not then seen the enormous cacti of old Mexico, and four feet of that plant seemed immense, as at home we labored to get one to grow six inches. The wild-flowers were charming in color, variety and luxuriance. The air, even then beginning to taste of the sea, blew softly about us. Stillman no longer blackened his soul with prophecies about the streams on which we nightly pitched our tents. The water did flow in them, and though they were then low, so that the thousands of horses were scattered far up and down when watering-time came, the green scum of sluggish pools was a thing of the past.

A few days before we reached what was to be a permanent camp, a staff-officer rode out to meet us, and brought some mail. It was a strange sensation to feel ourselves restored by these letters to the outside world. General Custer received a great surprise. He was brevetted major, lieutenant-colonel and brigadier-general in the regular army. The officers went off one side to read their sweethearts' letters ; and some of our number renewed their youth, sacrificed in that dreadful forest to fever, when they read the good news of the coming of their wives by sea. At Hempstead we halted, and the General made a permanent camp, in order to recruit men and horses after their exhausting march. Here General Sheridan and some of his staff came, by way of Galveston, and brought with them our father Custer, whom the General had sent for to pay us a visit. General Sheridan expressed great pleasure at the appearance of the men and horses, and heard with relief and satisfaction of the orderly manner in which they had marched through the enemy's country, of how few horses had perished from the heat, and how seldom sunstroke had occurred. He commended the General—as he knew how to do so splendidly—and placed him in command of all the cavalry in the State. Our own Division then numbered four thousand men.

I was again mortified to have to be compelled to lie down for a day or two, as so many weeks in the saddle had brought me to the first discovery of a spinal column. It was nothing but sheer fatigue, for I was perfectly well, and could laugh and talk with the rest, though not quite equal to the effort of sitting upright, especially as we had nothing but camp-stools, on which it is impossible to rest. Indisposition, or even actual illness, has less terrors in army life than in the States. We were not condemned to a gloomy upper chamber in a house, and shut in alone with a nurse whom we had never before seen. In our old life, ailing people lay on a lounge in the midst of all the garrison, who were coming and going a dozen times a day, asking, "How does it go now?" and if you had studied up anything that they could do for you? I principally recall being laid up by fatigue, because of the impetuous assault that my vehement father Custer made on his son for allowing me to share the discomforts; and when I defended my husband by explaining how I had insisted upon coming, he only replied, "Can't help it if you did. Armstrong, you had no right to put her through such a jaunt." It was amusing to see the old man's horror when our staff told him what we had been through. It would have appeared that I was his own daughter, and the General a son-in-law, by the manner in which he renewed his attack on the innocent man. Several years afterward it cost Lieutenant James Calhoun long pleading, and a probationary state of two years, before the old man would consent to his taking his daughter Margaret into the army. He shook his gray head determinedly, and said, "Oh, no; you don't get me to say she shall go through what Libbie has." But the old gentleman was soon too busy with his own affairs, defending himself against not only the ingenious attacks of his two incorrigible boys, but the staff, some of whom had known him in Monroe. His eyes twinkled, and his face wrinkled itself into comical smiles, as he came every morning with fresh tales of what a "night of it he had put in." He had a collection of mild vituperations for the boys, gath-

ered from Maryland, Ohio and Michigan, where he had
lived, which, extensive as the list was, did not, in my mind,
half meet the situation.

The stream on which we had encamped was wide and
deep, and had a current. Our tents were on the bank, which
gently sloped to the water. We had one open at both ends,
over which was built a shade of pine boughs, which was extended in front far enough for a porch. Some lumber from
a pontoon bridge was made into the unusual luxury of a floor.
My husband still indulged my desire to have the traveling-
wagon at the rear, so that I might take up a safe position at
night, when sleep interrupted my vigils over the insects and
reptiles that were about us constantly. The cook-tent, with
another shade over it, was near us, where Eliza flourished a
skillet as usual. The staff were at some distance down the
bank, while the Division was stretched along the stream,
having, at last, plenty of water. Beyond us, fifty miles of
prairie stretched out to the sea. We encamped on an unused
part of the plantation of the oldest resident of Texas, who
came forth with a welcome and offers of hospitality, which
we declined, as our camp was comfortable. His wife sent me
over a few things to make our tent habitable, as I suppose
her husband told her that our furniture consisted of a bucket
and two camp-stools. There's no denying that I sank down
into one of the chairs, which had a back, with a sense of enjoyment of what seemed to me the greatest luxury I had ever
known. The milk, vegetables, roast of mutton, jelly, and
other things which she also sent, were not enough to tempt
me out of the delightful hollow, from which I thought I never
could emerge again. But military despots pick up their
families and carry them out to their dinner, if they refuse to
walk. The new neighbors offered us a room with them, but
the General never left his men, and it is superfluous to say
that I thought our clean, new hospital tent, as large again
as a wall-tent, and much higher, was palatial after the trials
of the pine forests.

The old neighbor continued his kindness, which was returned by sending him game after the General's hunt, and protecting his estate. He had owned 130 slaves, with forty in his house. He gave us dogs and sent us vegetables, and spent many hours under our shade. He had lived under eight governments in his Texas experience, and, possibly, the habit of "speeding the parting and welcoming the coming guest" had something to do with his hospitality. I did not realize how Texas had been tossed about in a game of battle-door and shuttle-cock till he told me of his life under Mexican rule, the Confederacy, and the United States.

I find mention, in an old letter to my parents, of a great luxury that here appeared, and quote the words of the exuberant and much-underlined girl missive: " I rejoice to tell you that I am the happy possessor of a mattress. It is made of the moss which festoons the branches of all the trees at the South. The moss is prepared by boiling it, then burying it in the ground for a long time, till only the small thread inside is left, and this looks like horse-hair. An old darkey furnished the moss for three dollars, and the whole thing only cost seven dollars—very cheap for this country. We are living finely now; we get plenty of eggs, butter, lard and chickens. Eliza cooks better than ever, by a few logs, with camp-kettles and stew-pans. She has been washing this past week, and drying her things on a line tied to the tent-poles and on bushes, and ironing on the ground, with her ironing-sheet held down by a stone on each corner. To-day we are dressed in white. She invites us to mark Sunday by the luxury of wearing white. Her ' ole miss used to.' We are regulated by the doings of that ' ole miss,' and I am glad that among the characteristics of my venerable predecessor, which we are expected to follow, wearing white gowns is included."

Eliza, sitting here beside me to-day, has just reminded me of that week, as it was marked in her memory by a catastrophe. Eliza's misfortunes were usually within the confines of domestic routine. I quote her words: " It was on the Gros Creek, Miss Libbie, that I had out that big wash, and all your

lace-trimmed things, and all the Ginnel's white linen pants
and coats. I didn't know nothin' 'bout the high winds then,
but I ain't like to forget 'em ever again. The first thing I
I knew, the line was jest lifted up, and the clothes jest spread
in every direction, and I jest stood still and looked at 'em,
and I says, ' Is *this* Texas ? How long am I to contend with
this ? ' [With hands uplifted and a camp-meeting roll in her
eyes.] But I had to go to work and pick 'em all up. Some
fell in the sand, and some on the grass. I gathered 'em all,
with the sun boiling down hot enough to cook an egg.
While I was a-pickin' 'em up, the Ginnel was a-standin' in
the tent entrance, wipin' down his moustache, like he did
when he didn't want us to see him laughin'. Well, Miss
Libbie, I was *that* mad when he hollered out to me, ' Well,
Eliza, you've got a spread-eagle thar.' Oh, I was so mad and
hot, but he jest bust right out laughin'. But there wasn't
anything to do but rinse and hang 'em up again."

We had been in camp but a short time when the daughter
of the newly appointed collector of the port came from their
plantation near to see us. She invited me to make my home
with them while we remained, but I was quite sure there was
nothing on earth equal to our camp. The girl's father had
been a Union man during the war, and was hopelessly invalided by a long political imprisonment. I remember nothing
bitter, or even gloomy, about that hospitable, delightful family. The young girl's visit was the precursor of many more,
and our young officers were in clover. There were three
young women in the family, and they came to our camp and
rode and drove with us, while we made our first acquaintance
with Southern home life. The house was always full of
guests. The large dining-table was not long enough, however, unless placed diagonally across the dining-room, and it
was sometimes laid three times before all had dined. The
upper part of the house was divided by a hall running the
length of the house. On one side the women and their guests
—usually a lot of rollicking girls—were quartered, while the
men visitors had rooms opposite; and then I first saw the

manner in which a Southern gallant comes as a suitor or a
friend.   He rode up to the house with his servant on another horse, carrying a portmanteau. They came to stay several
weeks.   I wondered that there was ever an uncongenial marriage in the South, when a man had such a chance to see his
sweetheart.   This was one of 'the usages of the country that
our Northern men adopted when they could get leave to be
absent from camp, and delightful visits we all had.

It seemed a great privilege to be again with women, after
the long season in which I had only Eliza to represent the
sex.   But I lost my presence of mind when I went into a
room for the first time and caught a glimpse of myself in a
mirror. The only glass I had brought from the East was
broken early in the march, and I had made my toilet by feeling.   The shock of the apparition comes back to me afresh,
and the memory is emphasized by my fastidious mother's
horror when she saw me afterward. I had nothing but a nar-
row-brimmed hat with which to contend against a Texas sun.
My face was almost parboiled and swollen with sunburn,
while my hair was faded and rough.   Of course, when I
caught the first glimpse of myself in the glass I instantly hurried to the General and Tom, and cried out indignantly,
"Why didn't you tell me how horridly I looked?"—the inconsistent woman in me forgetting that it would not have
made my ugliness any easier to endure.   My husband hung
his head in assumed humility when he returned me to my
mother, six months later, my complexion seemingly hopelessly thickened and darkened; for, though happily it improved after living in a house, it never again looked as it did
before the Texas life.   My indignant mother looked as if her
son-in-law was guilty of an unpardonable crime.   I told her,
rather flippantly, that it had been offered up on the altar of
my country, and she ought to be glad to have so patriotic a
family; but she withered the General with a look that spoke
volumes.   He took the first opportunity to whisper conde-
scendingly that, though my mother was ready to disown me,
and quite prepared to annihilate him, he would endeavor not

to cast me off, if I was black, and would try to like me, " notwithstanding all."

The planters about the country began to seek out the General, and invite him to go hunting; and, as there was but little to do while the command was recruiting from the march, he took his father and the staff and went to the different plantations where the meet was planned. The start was made long before day, and breakfast was served at the house where the hunters assembled, dinner being enjoyed at the same hospitable board on the return at night. Each planter brought his hounds, and I remember the General's delight at his first sight of the different packs—thirty-seven dogs in all—and his enthusiasm at finding that every dog responded to his master's horn. He thereupon purchased a horn, and practiced in camp until he nearly split his cheeks in twain, not to mention the spasms into which we were driven; for his five hounds, presents from the farmers, ranged themselves in an admiring and sympathetic semicircle, accompanying all his practicing by tuning their voices until they reached the same key. I had no idea it was such a difficult thing to learn to sound notes on a horn. When we begged off sometimes from the impromptu serenades of the hunter and his dogs, the answer was, " I am obliged to practice, for if anyone thinks it is an easy thing to blow on a horn, just let him try it." Of course Tom caught the fever, and came in one day with the polished horn of a Texas steer ready for action. The two were impervious to ridicule. No detailed description of their red, distended cheeks, bulging eyes, bent and laborious forms, as they struggled, suspended the operation. The early stages of this horn music gave little idea of the gay picture of these debonair and spirited athletes, as they afterward appeared. When their musical education was completed, they were wont to leap into the saddle, lift the horn in unconscious grace to their lips, curbing their excited and rearing horses with the free hand, and dash away amidst the frantic leaping, barking and joyous demonstration of their dogs.

At the first hunt, when one of our number killed a deer, the farmers made known to our officers, on the sly, the old established custom of the chase. While Captain Lyon stood over his game, volubly narrating, in excited tones, how the shot had been sent and where it had entered, a signal, which he was too absorbed to notice, was given, and the crowd rushed upon him and so plastered him with blood from the deer that scarcely an inch of his hair, hands and face was spared, while his garments were red from neck to toes. After this baptism of gore, they dragged him to our tent on their return, to exhibit him, and it was well that he was one of the finest-hearted fellows in the world, for day and night these pestering fellows kept up the joke. Notwithstanding he had been subjected to the custom of the country, which demands that the blood of the first deer killed in the chase shall anoint the hunter, he had glory enough through his success to enable him to submit to the penalty.

Tom also shot a deer that day, but his glory was dimmed by a misfortune, of which he seemed fated never to hear the last. The custom was to place one or two men at stated intervals in different parts of the country where the deer were pretty sure to run, and Tom was on stand watching through the woods in the direction from which the sound of the dogs came. As the deer bounded toward him, he was so excited that when he fired, the shot went harmlessly by the buck and landed in one of the General's dogs, killing the poor hound instantly. Though this was a loss keenly felt, there was no resisting the chance to guy the hunter. Even after Tom had come to be one of the best shots in the Seventh Cavalry, and when the General never went hunting without him, if he could help it, he continued to say, "Oh, Tom's a good shot, a sure aim—he's sure to hit something !" Tom was very apt, also, to find newspaper clippings laid around, with apparent carelessness by his brother, where he would see them. For example, like this one, which I have kept among some old letters, as a reminder of those merry days: " An editor went hunting the other day, for the first time in twenty-two years, and he was lucky enough to bring down an old farmer by a shot in the leg. The distance was sixty-six yards."

We had long and delightful rides over the level country. Sometimes my husband and I, riding quietly along at twilight, for the days were still too warm for much exercise at noon-time, came upon as many as three coveys of quail scurrying to the underbrush. In a short walk from camp he could bag a dozen birds, and we had plenty of duck in the creek near us. The bird dog was a perpetual pleasure. She was the dearest, chummiest sort of house-dog, and when we took her out she still visited with us perpetually, running to us every now and again to utter a little whine, or to have us witness her tail, which, in her excitement in rushing through the underbrush, cacti and weeds, was usually scratched, torn and bleeding. The country was so dry that we could roam at will, regardless of roads. Our horses were accustomed to fording streams, pushing their way through thickets and brambles, and becoming so interested in making a route through them that my habit sometimes caught in the briars, and my hat was lifted off by the low-hanging moss and branches; and if I was not very watchful, the horse would go through a passage between two trees just wide enough for himself, and rub me off, unless I scrambled to the pommel. The greater the obstacles my husband encountered, even in his sports, the more pleasure it was to him. His own horses were so trained that he shot from their backs without their moving. Mine would also stand fire, and at the report of a gun, behaved much better than his mistress.

Eliza, instead of finding the General wearing his white linen to celebrate Sunday, according to her observances, was apt to get it on week-days after office-hours, far too often to suit her. On the Sabbath, she was immensely puffed up to see him emerge from the tent, speckless and spotless, because she said to me, "Whilst the rest of the officers is only too glad to get a white shirt, the Ginnel walks out among 'em all, in linen from top to toe." She has been sitting beside

me, talking over a day at that time: "Do you mind, Miss
Libbie, that while we was down in Texas the Ginnel was
startin' off on a deer-hunt, I jest went up to him and tole
him, 'Now, Ginnel, you go take off them there white pants.'
He said so quiet, sassy, cool, roguish-like, 'The deer always
like something white'—telling me that jest 'cause he wanted
to keep 'em on. Well, he went, all the same, and when he
came back, I says, 'I don't think the deer saw you in those
pants.' He was covered with grass-stains and mud, and a
young fawn swinging across the saddle. But them pants
was mud and blood, and green and yellow blotches, from
hem to bindin'. But he jest laughed at me because I was
a-scoldin', and brought the deer out to me, and I skinned it
the fust time I ever did, and cooked it next day, and we had
a nice dinner."

At that time Eliza was a famous belle. Our colored coach-
man, Henry, was a permanent fixture at the foot of her
throne, while the darkeys on the neighboring plantations
came nightly to worship. She bore her honors becomingly,
as well as the fact that she was the proud possessor of a
showy outfit, including silk dresses. The soldiers to whom
Eliza had been kind in Virginia had given her clothes that
they had found in the caches where the farmers endeavored
to hide their valuables during the war. Eliza had made one
of these very receptacles for her "ole miss" before she left
the plantation, and while her conscience allowed her to take
the silken finery of some other woman whom she did not
know, she kept the secret of the hiding-place of her own people's valuables until after the war, when the General sent her
home in charge of one of his sergeants to pay a visit. Even
the old mistress did not know the spot that Eliza had chosen,
which had been for years a secret, and she describes the joy
at sight of her, and her going to the place in the field and
digging up the property "with right smart of money, too,
Miss Libbie—enough, with that the Ginnel gave me to take
home, to keep 'em till the crops could be harvested."

This finery of Eliza's drove a woman servant at the next

place to plan a miserable revenge, which came near sending us all into another world. We were taking our breakfast one morning, with the table spread under the awning in front of our tent. The air, not yet heated by the sun, came over the prairie from the sea. The little green swift and the chameleon, which the General had found in the arbor roof and tamed as pets, looked down upon as reposeful and pretty a scene as one could wish, when we suddenly discovered a blaze in the cook-tent, where we had now a stove—but Eliza shall tell the story; " When I fust saw the fire, Miss Libbie, I was a-waitin' on you at breakfast. Then the first thought was the Ginnel's powder-can, and I jest dropped everythin' and ran and found the blaze was a-runnin' up the canvas of my tent, nearly reachin' the powder. The can had two handles, and I ketched it up and ran outside. When I first got in the tent, it had burnt clar up to the ridge-pole on one side. Some things in my trunk was scorched mightily, and one side of it was pretty well burnt. The fire was started right behind my trunk, not very near the cook-stove. The Ginnel said to me how cool and deliberate I was, and he told me right away that if my things had been destroyed, I would have everythin' replaced, for he was bound I wasn't going to lose nothin'."

My husband, in this emergency, was as cool as he always was. He followed Eliza as she ran for the powder-can, and saved the tent and its contents from destruction, and, without doubt, saved our lives. The noble part that I bore in the moment of peril was to take a safe position in our tent, wring my hands and cry. If there was no one else to rush forward in moments of danger, courage came unexpectedly, but I do not recall much brave volunteering on my part.

Eliza put such a broad interpretation upon the General's oft-repeated instruction not to let any needy person go away from our tent or quarters hungry, that occasionally we had to protest. She describes to me now his telling her she was carrying her benevolence rather too far, and her replying, "Yes, Ginnel, I do take in some one *once* and a *while*, *off* and *on.*" "Yes," he replied to me, "more on than off, I should say." "One chile I had to hide in the weeds a week, Miss Libbie. The Ginnel used to come out to the cook-tent and stand there kinder careless like, and he would spy a little path running out into the weeds. Well, he used to carry me high and dry about them little roads leading off to folks he said I was a-feedin.' I would say, when I saw him lookin' at the little path in the weeds, 'Well, what is it, Ginnel?' He would look at me so keen-like out of his eyes, and say, 'That's what *I* say.' Then he'd say he was goin' to get a couple of bloodhounds, and run 'em through the bushes to find out just how many I was a-feedin'. Then, Miss Libbie, we never did come to a brush or a thicket but that he would look around at me so kinder sly like, and tell me that would be a fust-rate ranch for me. Then I would say, 'Well, it's a good thing I do have somebody sometimes, 'cause my cook-tent is allus stuck way off by itself, and it's lonesome, and sometimes I'm so scart.' "But, you know, Miss Libbie," she added, afraid I might think she reflected on one whose memory she reveres, "my tent was obliged to be a good bit off, 'cause the smell of the cookin' took away the Ginnel's appetite; he was so uncertain like in his eatin', you remember."

In Texas, two wretched little ragamuffins—one, of the poor white trash, and another a negro—were kept skulking about the cook-tent, making long, circuitous détours to the creek for water, for fear we would see them, as they said "Miss Lize tole us you'd make a scatter if you knew 'no 'count' chillern was a-bein' fed at the cook-tent." They slipped into the underbrush at our approach, and lay low in the grass at the rear of the tent if they heard our voices. The General at first thought that, after Eliza had thoroughly stuffed them and made them fetch and carry for her, they would disappear, and so chose to ignore their presence, pretending he had not seen them. But at last they appeared to be a permanent addition, and we concluded that the best plan would be to acknowledge their presence and make the best of the infliction; so we named one Texas, and the other Jeff. Eliza beamed, and told the orphans, who capered out boldly in sight for the first time, and ran after Miss "Lize" to do her

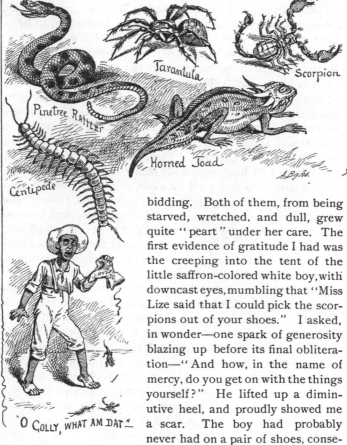

Pinetree Rattler

Tarantula

Scorpion

Horned Toad

Centipede

"O Golly, what am dat"

bidding. Both of them, from being starved, wretched, and dull, grew quite "peart" under her care. The first evidence of gratitude I had was the creeping into the tent of the little saffron-colored white boy, with downcast eyes, mumbling that "Miss Lize said that I could pick the scorpions out of your shoes." I asked, in wonder—one spark of generosity blazing up before its final obliteration—"And how, in the name of mercy, do you get on with the things yourself?" He lifted up a diminutive heel, and proudly showed me a scar. The boy had probably never had on a pair of shoes, consequently this part of his pedal extremity was absolutely so callous, so evidently obdurate to any object less penetrating than a sharpened spike driven in with a hammer, I found myself wondering how a scorpion's little spear could have effected an entrance through the seemingly impervious outer cuticle. Finally, I concluded that at a more tender age that "too solid flesh" may have been susceptible to an "honorable wound." It turned out that this cowed and apparently life-less little midget was perfectly indifferent to scorpions. By this time I no longer pretended to courage of any sort; I had found one in my trunk, and if, after that, I was compelled to go to it, I flung up the lid, ran to the other side of the tent, and "shoo-shooed" with that eminently senseless feminine call which is used alike for cows, geese, or any of these acknowl-edged foes. Doubtless a bear would be greeted with the same word, until the supposed occupants had run off. Night and morning my husband shook and beat my clothes while he helped me to dress. The officers daily came in with stories of the trick, so common to the venomous reptiles, of hiding between the sheets, and the General then even shook the bedding in our eyrie room in the wagon. Of all this he was re-lieved by the boy that Eliza called "poor little picked spar-row," who was appointed as my maid. Night and morning the yellow dot ran his hands into shoes, stockings, night-gown, and dress-sleeves, in all the places where the scorpions love to lurk; and I bravely and generously gathered myself into the armchair while the search went on.

Eliza has been reminding me of our daily terror of the creeping, venomous enemy of those hot lands. She says, "One day, Miss Libbie, I got a bite, and I squalled out to the Ginnel, 'Somethin's bit me!' The Ginnel, he said, 'Bit you! bit you whar?' I says, 'On my arm;' and, Miss Lib-bie, it was pizen, for my arm it just swelled enormous and got all up in lumps. Then it pained me so the Ginnel stopped a-laughin' and sent for the doctor, and he giv' me a drink of whiskey. Then what do you think! when I got better, didn't he go and say I was playin' off on him, just to get a big drink of whiskey? But I 'clar' to you, Miss Libbie, I was bad off that night. The centipede had crept into my bedclothes, and got a good chance at me, I can tell you."

Our surgeon was a naturalist, and studied up the vipers
and venomous insects of that almost tropical land. He
showed me a captured scorpion one day, and, to make me
more vigilant, infuriated the loathsome creature till it flung
its javelin of a tail over on its back and stung itself to death.

Legends of what had happened to army women who had
disregarded the injunctions for safety were handed down
from elder to subaltern, and a plebe fell heir to these stories
as much as to the tactics imparted by his superiors, or the
campaigning lore. I hardly know when I first heard of the
unfortunate woman who lingered too far behind the cavalcade, in riding for pleasure or marching, and was captured
by the Indians, but for ten years her story was related to me
by officers of all ages and all branches of the service as a
warning. In Texas, the lady who had been frightfully stung
by a centipede pointed every moral. The sting was inflicted
before the war, and in the far back days of "angel sleeves,"
which fell away from the arm to the shoulder. Though this
misfortune dated back from such a distant period, the young
officers, in citing her as a warning to us to be careful, described the red marks all the way up the arm, with as much
fidelity as if they had seen them. No one would have
dreamed that the story had filtered through so many chan-
nels. But surely one needed little warning of the centipede.
Once seen, it made as red stains on the memory as on the
beautiful historic arm that was used to frighten us. The
Arabs call it the mother of forty-four, alluding to the legs;
and the swift manner in which it propels itself over the
ground, aided by eight or nine times as many feet as are
allotted to ordinary reptiles, makes one habitually place himself in a position for a quick jump or flight while campaigning in Texas. We had to be watchful all the time we were
in the South. Even in winter, when wood was brought in
and laid down beside the fireplace, the scorpions, torpid
with cold at first, crawled out of knots and crevices, and
made a scattering till they were captured, One of my friends
was stationed at a post where the quarters were old and of

adobe, and had been used during the war for stables by the Confederates. It was of no use to try to exterminate these reptiles; they run so swiftly it takes a deft hand and a sure stroke to finish them up. Our officers grew expert in devising means to protect themselves, and, in this instance, a box of moist mud, with a shingle all ready, was kept in the quarters. When a tarantula showed himself, he was plastered on the wall. It is impossible to describe how loathsome that great spider is. The round body and long, far-reaching legs are covered with hairs, each particular hair visible; and the satanic eyes bulge out as they come on in your direction, making a feature of every nightmare for a long time after they are first seen. The wife of an officer, to keep these horrors from dropping on her bed as they ran over the ceiling, had a sheet fastened at the four corners and let down from the rough rafters to catch all invaders, and thus insured herself undisturbed sleep.

Officers all watch and guard the women who share their hardships. Even the young, unmarried men—the bachelor officers, as they are called — patterning after their elders, soon fall into a sort of fatherly fashion of looking out for the comfort and safety of the women they are with, whether old or young, pretty or ugly. It often happens that a comrade, going on a scout, gives his wife into their charge. I think of a hundred kindly deeds shown to all of us on the frontier; and I have known of acts so delicate that I can hardly refer to them with sufficient tact, and wish I might write with a tuft of thistle-down. In the instance of some very young women—with hearts so pure and souls so spotless they could not for one moment imagine there lived on earth people depraved enough to question all acts, no matter how harmless in themselves—I have known a little word of caution to be spoken regarding some exuberance of conduct that arose from the excess of a thoughtless, joyous heart. The husband who returned to his wife could thank the friend who had watched over his interests no more deeply than the wife who owed her escape from criticism to his timely word. And sometimes, when we went into the States, or were at a post with strange officers, it would not occur to us, gay and thoughtless as we were, that we must consider that we were not among those with whom we had "summered and wintered;" and the freedom and absolute naturalness of manner that arose from our long and intimate relationship in isolated posts, ought perhaps to give way to more formal conduct. If the women said to the men, " Now we are among strangers, do you not think they would misunderstand our dancing or driving or walking together just as fearlessly as at home?" That was sufficient. The men said, "Sure enough! It never occurred to me. By Jove! I wish we were back where a fellow need not be hampered by having every act questioned;" and then no one sought harder or more carefully so to act that we might satisfy the exactions of that censorious group of elderly women who sat in hotel parlors, looking on and remarking, "We did not do so when we were girls," or even some old frump in a garrison we visited, who, having squeezed dry her orange of life, was determined that others should get no good out of theirs if she could insert one drop of gall.

Occasionally the young officers, perhaps too timid to venture on a personal suggestion, sent us word by roundabout ways that they did not want us to continue to cultivate someone of whom we knew nothing save that he was agreeable. How my husband thanked them! He walked the floor with his hands behind him, moved so that his voice was unsteady, and said his say about what he owed to men who would not let a woman they valued be even associated with any one who might reflect on them. He was a home-lover, and not being with those who daily congregated at the sutler's store, the real "gossip-mill" of a garrison, he heard but little of what was going on. A man is supposed to be the custodian of his own household in civil life; but it must be remembered that in our life a husband had often to leave a young and inexperienced bride to the care of his comrades while he went off for months of field duty. The grateful tears rise now in my eyes at the recollection of men who guarded us from the very semblance of evil as if we had been their sisters.

CHAPTER VI.

A TEXAS NORTHER.

WE had not been long in our camp at Hempstead, before the wives of two of the staff arrived by way of Galveston. Their tents were put on a line with or near ours, and arbors built over them. One of these women, Mrs. Greene, had been one of my dearest girlhood friends, and every pleasure of my happy life was enhanced by the presence of this lovely woman. We all went out, after the heat of the day, on long rides about the country. Our father Custer was a fine rider, and not only sat his horse well, but it was almost impossible to unseat him. He grew more wary and watchful of his tormenting sons every day. If they halted, apparently only to say a casual word or so to their paternal, that keen old man spurred his horse to one side with the agility of a circus-rider, just in time to avoid the flying heels of the horse of his offspring in front of him, which had been taught to fling his hoofs up when touched just back of the saddle. If both boys came together and rode one on each side of him, he looked uneasily from one to the other, suspicious of this sudden exhibition of friendship; and well he might, for while one fixed his attention by some question that provoked an answer, usually about politics, the other gave a quick rap on the back of the horse, and the next thing, the father was grasping the pommel to keep from being flung forward of the animal as he threw up his heels and plunged his head down, making the angle of an incline plane. Even when, after a concerted plan, one rode up and pulled the cape of the elder man's overcoat over his head and held it there a moment, while the other gave the horse a cut, he sat like a centaur, and no surprise unseated him or loosened his grip on the reins. They knew his horsemanship well, as he had ridden after the hounds in Maryland and Virginia in his younger days, and had taught them to sit a horse bareback, when their little fat legs were too short to describe a curve on the animal's side. Of course I was always begging to have them spare father, but it was needless championship. He enjoyed their pranks with all his fun-loving soul.

It was very hard to get postage, and he was unwary enough one day—on account of the color being the same as the issue of that year—to buy a dollar's worth of his eldest scion, only to find them old ones, such as were used before the war. Whether he considered the joke worth a dollar, I could not decipher, for he was silent; but soon afterward he showed me an envelope marked in the writing of his son Armstrong, "Conscience-money," containing the $1 unlawfully obtained.

We were invited one night to go to a coon-hunt, conducted in the real old Southern style. The officers wanted us to see some hunting, but were obliged to leave us behind hitherto when they crossed the Brazos River on deer-hunts, and were the guests of the planters in the chase, that began before dawn and lasted all day. We had thickets, underbrush and ditches to encounter, before the dogs treed the coon; then a little darkey, brought along for the climbing, went up into the branches and dislodged the game, which fell among our and the neighbors' dogs. No voice excited them more wildly than the "Whoop-la!" of our old father, and when we came home at 2 A. M., carrying a coon and a possum, he was as fresh as the youngest of us.

The citizens surrounding us were so relieved to find that our troops left them unmolested, they frankly contrasted the disciplined conduct with the lawlessness to which they had been witness in States where the Confederate army was stationed. But they scarcely realized that an army in time of peace is much more restricted. They could hardly say enough about the order that was carried out, preventing the negroes from joining the column as it marched into Texas.

There was no way of taking care of them, and the General directed that none should follow, so they went back, contented to work where they would be fed and clothed.

One reason that our life seemed to me the very perfection of all that is ever attained on earth was, that the rumors of trouble with Mexico had ceased. The demands of our Government had been complied with; but it was thought best to keep the troops in the field the rest of the year, though there was to be no war.

Our first experience with a Texas norther surprised and startled us. It came on in the night, preceded by the usual heavy, suffocating air which renders breathing an effort. After this prelude, the wild blast of wind swept down on us with a fury indescribable. We heard the roar as it approached over the stretch of prairie between us and the sea. Our tent, though it was guyed by ropes stretched from the ridge-pole to a strong post driven far into the ground, both in front and at the rear, shook, rattled, and flapped as if with the rage of some human creature. It was twisted and wrenched from side to side; the arbor overhead seemed to toss to and fro, and the wagon rocked in a crazy effort to spill us out. Though the ropes stretched and cracked like cordage at sea, and the canvas flapped like loosened sails, we did not go down. Indeed, rocked in this improvised "cradle of the deep," it was hard to tell whether one was at sea or on land. I begged to get up and dress for the final collapse that I was sure was coming, but my husband quieted me and calmed my fears, believing that the approaching rain would still the wind, as it eventually did. Next morning a scene of havoc was visible. Our neighbors crept out of their tents, and we women, in a little whispered aside, exchanged our opinions upon the climate of the "Sunny South."

They also had passed a night of terror, but fortunately their tents did not go down. Mrs. Lyon had just come from the North, and expected to join her husband; meanwhile she was our guest, and the General and I had endeavored to give her as cordial a welcome as we could, feeling that all must be

so strange to her after the security and seclusion of her girlhood's home. The night preceding the norther we took her
to her tent near ours, and helped her arrange for the night,
assuring her that we were so near that we could hear her
voice, if she was in the least afraid. We, being novices in
the experience of that climate and its gales, had no idea the
wind would rise to such concert pitch that no voice could be
distinguished. She said that when we fastened her in from
the outside world with two straps, she felt very uncertain
about her courage holding out. We kept on assuring her
not to be afraid, but on bidding her good-night and saying
again not to be in the least disturbed, that the sentinel walked
his beat in front of her tent all night, she dared not own up
that this assurance did not tend to soothe her anxious fears,
for she thought she would be more afraid of the guard than
of anything else. And as I think of it, such a good-night
from us was rather unsatisfactory. My husband, soldier-like,
put the utmost faith in the guard, and I, though only so
short a time before mortally afraid of the stern, unswerving
warrior myself, had soon forgotten that there were many
timid women in the world who knew nothing of sleeping
without locks or bolts, and thought, perhaps, that at the
slightest ignorance or dereliction of duty the sentinel would
fire on an offender, whether man or woman. Added to this
fear of the sentinel, the storm took what remnant of nerve
she had left; and though she laughed next morning about
her initiation into the service of the Government, there were
subsequent confessions to the horror of that unending night.
In talking with Major and Mrs. Lyon nowadays, when it is
my privilege to see them, there seemed to be no memories
but pleasant ones of our Texas life. They might well cherish
two reminiscences as somewhat disturbing, for Mrs. Lyon's
reception by the hurricane, and the Major's baptism of gore
when he killed his first deer, were not scenes that would bear
frequent repetition and only leave pleasant memories.

The staff-officers had caused a long shade to be built, instead of shorter ones, which would have stood the storms

better. Under this all of their tents were pitched in two rows facing each other; and protected by this arbor, they daily took the siesta which is almost compulsory there in the heat of the noontide. Now the shade was lifted off one side and tilted over, and some of the tents were also flat. Among them was that of our father Custer. He had extricated himself with difficulty from under the canvas, and described his sensations so quaintly that his woes were greeted with roars of laughter from us all. After narrating the downfall of his "rag house," he dryly remarked that it would seem, owing to the climate and other causes, he was not going to have much uninterrupted sleep, and, looking slyly at the staff, he added that his neighborhood was not the quietest he had ever known.

The letters home at that time, in spite of their description of trivial events, and the exuberant underlined expressions of girlish pleasure over nothings, my father enjoyed and preserved. I find that our idle Sundays were almost blanks in life, as we had no service and the hunting and riding were suspended. I marked the day by writing home, and a few extracts will perhaps present a clearer idea of the life there than anything that could be written now:

"Every Sunday I wake up with the thought of home, and wish that we might be there and go to church with you. I can imagine how pleasant home is now. Among other luxuries, I see with my 'mind's eye,' a large plate of your nice apples on the dining-room table. I miss apples here; none grow in this country; and a man living near here told our Henry that he hadn't seen one for five years. Father Custer bought me some small, withered-looking ones for fifty cents apiece. It seems so strange that in this State, where many planters live who are rich enough to build a church individually, there is such a scarcity of churches. Why, at the North, the first knowledge one has of the proximity of a village is by seeing a spire, and a church is almost the first building put up when a town is laid out. Here in this country it is the last to be thought of. Cotton is indeed king.

The cake you sent to me by Nettie Greene, dear mother, was a perfect godsend. Oh, anything you make does taste so good!

"Our orderly has perfected a trade for a beautiful little horse for me, so that when Custis Lee's corns trouble him, I am not obliged to take the choice of staying at home or riding one of Armstrong's prancers. The new horse has cunning tricks, getting down on his knees to let me get on and off, if I tell him to do so. He is very affectionate, and he racks a mile inside of three minutes. We talk 'horse' a great deal here, dear father, and my letters may be like our talk; but any man who has kept in his stable, for months at a time, a famous race-horse worth $9,000, as you have kept Don Juan,* ought not to object to a little account of other people's animals. We had an offer of $500 for Custis Lee at Alexandria."

.   .   .   .

"I sometimes have uninvited guests in my tent. Friday, Nettie saw something on the tray that Eliza was carrying. It had a long tail, and proved to be a stinging scorpion. The citizens pooh-pooh at our fear of scorpions, and insist that they are not so very dangerous; but I was glad to have that particular one killed by Armstrong planting his gun on it. I feel much pleased, and Armstrong is quite proud, that I made myself a riding-habit. You know I lost the waist of mine in the forest. It took me weeks to finish it, being my first attempt. I ripped an old waist, and copied it by drawing lines with a pencil, pinning and basting; but it fits very well. I remember how you both wanted me to learn when I was at home, and I almost wished I had, when I found it took me such ages to do what ought to have been short work.

"Our letters take twenty days in coming, and longer if

---

* Don Juan was a horse captured by our soldiers during the war, and bought, as was the custom, by the General, for the appraised value of a contract horse. It was the horse that ran away with him at the grand review, and it afterward died in Michigan.

there are storms in the Gulf. The papers are stale enough,
but Armstrong goes through them all. I feel so rich, and am
luxuriating in four splint-bottom chairs that we hired an old
darkey to make for us. I want to sit in all four at once, it
seems so good to get anything in which to rest that has a
back.

"Our dogs give us such pleasure, though it took me some
time to get used to the din they set up when Armstrong
practiced on the horn. They call it ' giving tongue ' here,
but I call that too mild a word. Their whole bodies seem
hollow, they bring forth such wild cries and cavernous howls.
We call them Byron, Brandy, Jupiter, Rattler, Sultan, and
Tyler."

.   .   .   .

"Something awful is constantly occurring among the citizens. It is a lawless country. A relative of one of our old
army officers, a prominent planter living near here, was shot
dead in Houston by a man bearing an old grudge against
him. It is a common occurrence to shoot down men here
for any offense whatever. Armstrong never goes anywhere
except for hunting, and as we have plenty of books and our
evening rides, we enjoy life thoroughly. Nettie fell from her
horse, and we were frightened for a time, but she was only
lamed. Though she weighs 165 pounds, Autie* picked her
up as if she were a baby, and carried her into their tent."

.   .   .   .

"Besides visiting at the house of the collector of the port,
where there is a houseful of young girls, we have been hos-
pitably treated by some people to whom Armstrong was able
to be of use. One day, a gentle well-bred Southern woman
came into our tent to see Armstrong, and asked his protection for her boy, telling him that for some childish carelessness the neighboring colored people had threatened his life.

---

* An abbreviation of the General's second name, Armstrong,
given him by his elder sister's children, when they were too young
to pronounce the full name Armstrong.

Armstrong believed her, and melted.   He afterward inquired elsewhere into the matter, and was convinced that the boy had not intentionally erred.   The child himself was proof, by his frank manner and his straightforward story, of his innocence.

"I suppose we were the first Yankees these people had ever known, and doubtless nothing but gratitude induced them even to speak with us; yet they conquered prejudice, and asked us to dinner.   They had been so well dressed when they called—and were accounted rich, I believe, by the neighbors—that I could scarcely believe we had reached the right house when we halted.   It was like 'the cabins of the 'poor white trash' in the forest, only larger.   I thought we had mistaken the negro quarters for the master's.   Two large rooms, with extensions at the rear, were divided by an open space roofed over, under which the table was spread.   The house was of rough logs, and unpainted.   Unless the Texans built with home materials, their houses cost as much as palaces abroad, for the dressed lumber had to be hauled from the seacoast.

"The inside of this queer home was in marked contrast with the exterior.   The furniture was modern and handsome, and the piano, on which the accomplished mother, as well as her little son, gave us music, was from one of our best Northern manufactories.   The china, glass and linen on the dinner-table were still another surprise.

"They never broached politics, gave us an excellent dinner, and got on Armstrong's blind side forever by giving him a valuable full-blooded pointer, called Ginnie, short for Virginia.   With four game chickens, a Virginia cured ham (as that was their former State), and two turkeys, we were sent on our way rejoicing."

.   .   .   .

"Our Henry has gone home, and we miss him, for he is fidelity itself.   He expects to move his entire family of negroes from Virginia to Monroe, because he says, father, you are the finest man he ever *did* see.   Prepare, then, for the dark cloud that is moving toward you, and you may have the privilege of contributing to their support for a time, if he follows Eliza's plan of billeting the orphan upon us.

"We have a new cook called Uncle Charley, who has heretofore been a preacher, but now condescends to get up good dinners for us. We had eleven to dine to-day, and borrowed dishes of our Southern neighbors. We had a soup made out of an immense turtle that Armstrong killed in the stream yesterday. Then followed turkeys, boiled ham—and roast beef, of course, for Armstrong thinks no dinner quite perfect without his beef. We are living well, and on so little. Armstrong's pay as a major-general will soon cease, and we are trying now to get accustomed to living on less.

"I listen to the citizens talking over the prospects of this State, and I think it promises wonders. There are chances for money-making all the time thrown in Armstrong's way; but he seems to think that while he is on duty he had better not enter into business schemes.

"Armstrong has such good success in hunting and fishing that he sends to the other officers' messes turtle, deer, duck, quail, squirrels, doves and prairie chickens. The possums are accepted with many a scrape and flourish by the 'nigs.' I forgot to tell you that our nine dogs sleep round our wagon at night, quarreling, growling, snoring, but I sleep too soundly to be kept awake by them."

The very ants in Texas, though not poisonous, were provided with such sharp nippers that they made me jump from my chair with a bound, if, after going out of sight in the neck or sleeves of my dress, they attempted to cut their way out. They clipped one's flesh with sharp little cuts that were not pleasant, especially when there remained a doubt as to whether it might be a scorpion. We had to guard our linen carefully, for they cut it up with ugly little slits that were hard to mend. Besides, we had to be careful, as we were so cut off that we could not well replace our few clothes, and it costs a ruinous sum to send North, or even to New Orleans, for anything. I found this out when the General paid an express bill on a gown from New York—ordered before we left the East—far larger than the cost of the material and the dressmaker's bill together.   The ants besieged the cook-tent and set Uncle Charley and Eliza to growling; but an old settler told them to surround the place with tan-bark, and they were thus freed. It was all I could do to keep the General from digging down into the ant-mounds, as he was anxious to see into their mechanism.   The colored people and citizens told us what fighters they were, and what injuries they inflicted on people who molested them.   We watched them curiously day by day, and wanted to see if the residents had told us stories about their stripping the trees of foliage just to guy us.   (It has long been the favorite pastime of old residents to impose all sorts of improbable tales on the new-comer.)   Whether this occurrence happens often or not I cannot say, but it certainly took place once while we were there.   One morning my husband ran into the tent and asked me to hurry up with my dressing; he had something strange to show me, and helped me scramble into my clothes.

The carriage-road in front of our tents cut rather deep ruts, over which the ants found a difficult passage, so they had laid a causeway of bits of cut leaves, over which they journeyed between a tree and their ant-hills, not far from our tents on the other side of the road.   They were still traveling back and forth, each bearing a bit of leaf bigger than itself; and a half-grown tree near us, which had been full of foliage the day before, was entirely bare.

For some reason unexplainable, malarial fever broke out among our staff.   It was, I suppose, the acclimation to which we were being subjected.   My father Custer was ill, and came forth from the siege whitened out, while the officers disappeared to mourn over the number of their bones for a few days, and then crept out of the tents as soon as they could move. My husband all this time had never even changed color. His powers of endurance amazed me.   He seemed to have set his strong will against yielding to climatic influences; but after two days of this fighting he gave in and tossed himself on our borrowed lounge, a vanquished man. He was very sick. Break-bone fever had waited to do its worst with its last victim. Everything looked very gloomy to me. We had not even a wide bed, on which it is a little comfort if a fever-tossed patient can fling himself from side to side. We had no ice, no fruit, indeed nothing but quinine. The supplies of that drug to the hospital department of Texas must be sent by the barrel, it seemed to me, from the manner in which it was consumed.

Our devoted surgeon came, of his own accord, over and over again, and was untiring in his patience in coming when I sent for him in-between-times, to please me in my anxiety. My husband was so racked and tormented by pain, and burnt up with fiery heat, that he hardly made the feeblest fight about the medicine, after having attained the satisfaction of my tasting it, to be sure that I knew how bitter it was. As the fever abated every hour, I resorted to new modes of bribery and corruption to get him to swallow the huge pill. My stepmother's cake had come in the very best time, for I extracted the raisins and hid the quinine in them, as my father had done when giving me medicine as a child. It seemed to me an interminable time before the disease began to yield to the remedies. In reality, it was not long, as the General was unaccustomed to medicine, and its effect was more quickly realized on that account. Even when my husband began to crawl about again, the doctor continued the medicine, and I as nurse remorselessly carried out his directions, though I had by no means a tractable patient, as with returning health came restored combative powers. My husband noticed the rapid disappearance of the pills from the table when he lay and watched the hated things with relief, as he discovered that he was being aided in the consumption by some unknown friend. One morning we found the plate on which the doctor had placed thirty the night before, empty. Of course I accused the General of being the cause of the strange disappearance, and prepared to send for more, inexorable in my temporary reign over a weak man. He attempted a mild

kicking celebration and clapping accompaniment over the
departure of his hated medicine, as much as his rather unsteady feet and arms would allow, but stoutly denied having
done away with the offending pills. The next night we kept
watch over the fresh supply, and soon after dark the ants began their migrations up the loose tent-wall on the table-cover
that fell against the canvas, and while one grasped the flour-
mixed pill with his long nippers, the partner pushed, steered
and helped roll the plunder down the side of the tent on to
the ground.

The triumph of the citizens was complete. Their tales
were outdone by our actual experience. After that there was
no story they told us which we did not take in immediately
without question.

The hunting included alligators also. In the stream below us there were occasional deep pools, darkened by the
overhanging trees. As we women walked on the banks, we
kept a respectful distance from the places where the bend in
the creek widened into a pond, with still water near the high
banks. In one of these dark pools lived an ancient alligator,
well known to the neighbors, on which they had been unsuc-
cessfully firing for years. The darkeys kept aloof from his
fastness, and even Eliza, whose Monday-morning soul longed
for the running water of the stream, for she had struggled
with muddy water so long, trembled at the tales of this monster. She reminds me now "what a lovely place to wash
that Gros wash-house was, down by the creek. But it was
near the old alligator's pool, and I know I hurried up my
wash awfully, for I was afraid he might come up; for you know,
Miss Libbie, it was reckoned that they was mighty fond of
children and colored people."

One of the young officers was determined to get this veteran, and day after day went up and down the creek, coming
home at night to meet the jeers of the others, who did not
believe that alligator-hunting in a hot country paid. One
night he stopped at our tent, radiant and jubilant. He had
shot the old disturber of the peace, the intimidator of the

neighborhood, and was going for help to haul him up to the tents. He was a monster, and it cost the men tough pulling to get him up the bank, and then to drag him down near our tent. There he was left for us women to see. We walked around and around him, very brave, and quite relieved to think that we were rid of so dangerous a neighbor, with a real old Jonah-and-the-whale mouth. The General congratulated the young officer heartily, and wished it had been his successful shot that had ended him. Part of the jaw had

MEASURING AN ALLIGATOR.

been shot away, evidently years ago, as it was then calloused over. It was distended to its utmost capacity, and propped open with a stick. Nettie brought out a broom from her tent, with which to get a rough estimate of his length, as we knew well that if we did not give some idea of his size in our letters home, they would think the climate, which enervates so quickly, had produced a total collapse in our power to tell the truth. The broom did not begin to answer, so we pieced out the measure with something else, in order to arrive at some kind of accuracy. Then we thought we would like to see how the beast looked with his mouth closed, and the of-

ficers, patient in humoring our whims, pulled out the props.
There was a sudden commotion.   The next thing visible was
three sets of flying petticoats making for the tent, as the
alligator, revived by the sudden let-down of his upper jaw,
sprawled out his feet and began to walk over the grass.   The
crack of the rifle a moment after brought the heads of three
cowards from their tents, but after that no woman hovered
over even his dead hide.   The General was convulsed over
our retreat.   The drying skin of his majesty, the lord of the
pool, flung and flapped in the wind, suspended to the pole of
the officers' arbor for weeks, and it was well tanned by the
air long before they ceased to make sly allusions to women's
curiosity.

At last, in November, the sealed proposals from citizens to
the quartermaster for the contract for transporting the camp
equipage and baggage, forage, etc., over the country, were
all in, and the most reasonable of the propositions was accepted.   Orders had come to move on to Austin, the capital,
where we were to winter.   It was with real regret that I saw
our traps packed, the tents of our pretty encampment taken
down, the arbors thrown over, and our faces turned toward
the interior of the State.   The General, too buoyant not to
think that every move would better us, felt nothing but pleasure to be on the march again.   The journey was very pleasant through the day, and we were not compelled to rise before dawn, for the sun was by no means unbearable, as it had
been in August.   It was cold at night, and the wind blew
around the wagon, flapping the curtains, under which it
penetrated, and lifting the covers unless they were strongly
secured.   As to trying to keep warm by a camp-fire in November, I rather incline to the belief that it is impossible.
Instead of heat coming into the tent where I put on my habit
with benumbed fingers, the wind blew the smoke in.   Sometimes the mornings were so cold I begged to be left in bed,
and argued that the mules could be attached and I could go
straight on to camp, warm all the way.   But my husband
woke my drowsy pride by saying "the officers will surely

think you a 'feather-bed soldier,'" which term of derision
was applied to a man who sought soft places for duty and
avoided hardships, driving when he ought to ride.

If we all huddled around one of my husband's splendid
camp-fires, I came in for the smoke. The officers' pretty little gallantries about "smoke always following beauty," did
not keep my eyes from being blistered and blinded. It was,
after all, not a very great hardship, as during the day we had
the royal sun of that Southern winter.

My husband rode on in advance every day to select a camp.
He gave the choice into my hands sometimes, but it was
hard to keep wood, water and suitable ground uppermost ; I
wanted always the sheltered, pretty spots. We enjoyed every
mile of our march. It rained sometimes, pouring down so
suddenly that a retreat to the traveling wagons was impossible. One day I was wet to the skin three times, and my
husband wondered what the anxious father and mother, who
used frantically to call "rubbers" after me, as a girl, when I
tried to slip out unnoticed, would say to him then ; but it
did not hurt me in the least. The General actually seemed
unconscious of the shower. He wore a soldier's overcoat,
pulled his broad hat down to shed the rain, and encouraged
me by saying I was getting to be a tough veteran, which
among us was very high praise. Indeed, we were all then so
well, we snapped our fingers at the once-dreaded break-bone
fever. If we broke the ice in the bucket for our early ablutions, it became a matter to joke over when the sun was up
and we all rode together, laughing and singing, at the head
of the column.

Our march was usually twenty-five miles, sometimes thirty,
in a day. The General and I foraged at the farms we passed,
and bought good butter, eggs and poultry. He began to
collect turkeys for the winter, until we had enough for a
year. Uncle Charley was doing his best to awe Eliza with
his numerous new dishes. Though he was a preacher,
he put on that profession on Sundays as he did his best
coat ; and if during the week the fire smoked, or a dog

stole some prepared dish that was standing one side to cool, he expressed himself in tones not loud but deep, and had as extensive a collection of negro oaths as Texas afforded, which, I believe, is saying a good deal. My husband, observant as he always was, wondered what possessed the old fellow when preparing poultry for dinner. We used slyly to watch him go one side, seize the chicken, and, while swiftly wringing its neck, mumble some unintelligible words to himself, then throw down the fowl in a matter-of-fact way, and sit down to pluck it. We were mystified, and had to get Eliza to explain this peculiar proceeding that went on day after day. She said that "though Uncle Charley does swear so powerful, he has a kind of superstition that poultry has a hereafter." Evidently he thought it was not right to send them to their last home without what he intended for a funeral oration. Sometimes he said, as fast as his nimble old tongue could clatter :

> " Hark, from the tombs a doleful sound,
>   Mine ears attend the cry !
> Ye living hens, come view the ground
>   Where you must shortly die."

Once after this my husband, by hiding, contrived to be present, though unseen, at one of these funeral ceremonies :

> " Princes, this clay must be your bed,
>   In spite of all your towers,
> The tall, the wise, the reverend head,
>   Must lie as low as yours."

He so timed his verses that with one wrench he gave the final turn to the poor chicken's head as he jerked out the last line. My husband, perfectly convulsed himself, was in terror for fear Uncle Charley would have his feelings hurt by seeing us, and hearing my giggling, and I nearly smothered myself in the attempt to get back to our tent, where the General threw himself down with shrieks of laughter.

We varied our march by many an exciting race after jack-rabbits. The chapparral bushes defeated us frequently by making such good hiding-places for the hare.* If we came to a long stretch of open prairie, and a rabbit lifted his doe-like head above the grass, the General uttered a wild whoop to his dog, a "Come on!" to me, and off we dashed. Some of the staff occasionally joined, while our father Custer bent over his old roan horse, mildly struck him with a spur, and was in at the death. The ground was excellent for a run— level and grassy. We had a superb greyhound called Byron, that was devoted to the General, and after a successful chase it was rewarded with many a demonstration of affection. He was the most lordly dog, I think, I ever saw—powerful, with deep chest, and carrying his head in a royal way. When he started for a run, with his nostrils distended and his delicate ears laid back on his noble head, each bound sent him flying through the air. He hardly touched the elastic cushions of his feet to earth, before he again was spread out like a dark, straight thread. This gathering and leaping must be seen, to realize how marvelous is the rapidity and how the motion seems flying, almost, as the ground is scorned except at a sort of spring bound. He trotted back to the General, if he happened to be in advance, with the rabbit in his mouth, and, holding back his proud head, delivered the game only to his chief. The tribute that a woman pays to beauty in any form, I gave to Byron, but I never cared much for him. A greyhound's heart could be put into a thimble. Byron cared for the General as much as his cold soul could for any one, but it was not to be compared with the dear Ginnie : she was all love, she was almost human.

The dog was in an injured state with me much of the time. In quarters he resented all my rights. My husband had a great fashion of flinging himself on the bed, or even on the floor, if it was carpeted. He told me he believed he must

---

* I never liked hunting when the game was killed, and I was relieved to find how often the hare rabbit escaped into the thickets.

unconsciously have acquired the habit at West Point, where the zeal of the cadet seems divided between his studies and an effort to keep the wrinkles out of the regulation white pantaloons, which, being of duck, are easily creased. What punishment Government sees fit to inflict for each separate crease, I don't know, but certainly its embryo soldiers have implanted in them a fear of consequences, even regarding rumpled linen. As soon as the General tossed himself on the bed, Byron walked to him and was invited to share the luxury. "Certainly," my husband used to say, sarcastically ; "walk right up here on this clean white spread, without troubling yourself to care whether your feet are covered with mud or not. Your Aunt Eliza wants you to lie on nice white counterpanes ; she washes them on purpose for you." Byron answered this invitation by licking his host's hand, and turning in the most scornful manner on me, as I uttered a mild protest regarding his muddy paws. The General quickly remarked that I made invidious distinctions, as no spread seemed too fine or white for Ginnie, in my mind, while if Eliza happened to enter, a pair of blazing eyes and an energetically expressed opinion of Byron ensued, and he retorted by lifting his upper lip over some of the whitest fangs I ever saw. The General, still aiding and abetting, asked the dog to let Aunt Eliza see what an intelligent, knowing animal he was—how soon he distinguished his friends from his foes. Such an exasperating brute, and such a tormenting master, were best left alone. But I was tired, and wanted to lie down, so I told Eliza that if she would stand there, I would try the broom, a woman's weapon, on his royal highness. Byron wouldn't move, and growled even at me. Then I quite meekly took what little place was left, the General's sense of mischief, and his peculiar fondness for not interfering in a fight, now coming in to keep him silent. The dog rolled over, and shammed sleep, but soon planting his feet against my back, which was turned in high dudgeon, he pushed and pushed, seemingly without premeditation, his dreadful eyes shut, until I was nearly shoved off. I was conquered, and

rose, afraid of the dog and momentarily irritated at my de-
feat and his tyranny, while Eliza read a lesson to the General. She said, "*Now* see what you've done. You keer
more for that *pesky*, *sassy* old hound than you does for Miss
Libbie. Ginnel, I'd be 'shamed, if I was you. What would
your mother Custer think of you now?" But my feelings
were not seriously hurt, and the General, having watched to
the last to see how far the brute would carry his jealousy,
gave him a kick that sent him sprawling on the floor, springing up to restore me to my place and close the colored ha-
rangue that was going on at the foot of the bed. Eliza
rarely dignified me with the honor of being referee in any
disputed question. She used to say, "No matter whether
it's right or wrong, Miss Libbie's sho' to side with the Ginnel." Her droll way of treating him like a big boy away
from home for the first time, always amused him. She threatened to tell his mother, and brought up that sainted woman
in all our encounters, as she did in the dog episode just mentioned, as if the very name would restore order at once, and
give Eliza her own way in regulating us. But dear mother
Custer had been in the midst of too many happy scuffles, and
the centre of too many friendly fisticuffs among her active,
irrepressible boys, in the old farm-days, for the mention of
her name to restore order in our turbulent household.

CHAPTER VII.

LIFE IN A TEXAS TOWN.

ONE day we heard shout upon shout from many a soldier's throat in camp. The headquarters guard and officers' servants, even the officers themselves, joined in the hallooing, and we ran out to see what could be the matter. It was our lordly Byron. Stately and superb as he usually was, he had another side to his character, and now he was racing up from camp, a huge piece of meat in his jaws, which he had stolen from the camp-kettle where it was boiling for the soldiers' dinner. His retreat was accompanied with every sort of missile—sticks, boots and rocks—but this dog, that made himself into a "greased streak of lightning," as a colored woman described him, bounded on, untouched by the flying hail of the soldiers' wrath. The General did not dare to shout and dance in sight of the men, over what he thought so cunning in this hateful dog, as he was not protected by the friendly walls of our tent ; but he chuckled, and his eyes danced, for the brute dropped the hot meat when he had looked about to discover how close his pursuers were, and then, seeing the enemy nearing him, picked it up and distanced them all. The General went back to his tent, and called Eliza, to torment her with an account of what "her favorite" had done all by himself. She spared no words to express her opinion of the hated hound, for Byron was no respecter of persons when the sly side of his character was uppermost. He stole his master's dinner just as readily as the neighbors'. Eliza said no one could tell how many times he had made off with a part of her dinner, just dished up to be served, and then gone off on a prowl, "after he'd gorged hissel," as she expressed it, "hidin' from the other dogs, and burying it in jest such a stingy way you might 'spect from such a worthless, plunderin' old villain."

The march to Austin was varied by fording. All the streams and rivers were crossed in that manner, except one, where we used the pontoon bridge. The Colorado we found too high to ford, and so made a détour of some miles. The citizens were not unfriendly, while there was a total cessation of work on the part of the negroes until our column went by. They sat on the fences like a row of black crows, and with their usual politeness made an attempt to answer questions the troops put to them, which were unanswerable, even in the ingenious brain of the propounder. "Well, uncle, how far is it ten miles down the road from here?" If their feelings were hurt by such irrepressible fun, they were soon healed by the lively trade they kept up in chickens, eggs and butter.

The citizens sometimes answered the General's salute, and his interested questions about the horse they rode, by joining us for a short distance on the march. The horseflesh of Texas was a delight to him; but I could not be so interested in the fine points as to forget the disfiguring brands that were often upon the foreshoulder, as well as the flank. They spoke volumes for the country where a man has to sear a thoroughbred with a hot iron, to ensure his keeping possession. Father Custer used to say, "What sort of country is this, anyhow, when a man, in order to keep his property, has got to print the whole constitution of the United States on his horse?" The whole get-up of the Texans was rather cumbersome, it seemed to me, though they rode perfectly. They frequently had a Mexican saddle, heavily ornamented with silver on the high pommel, and everywhere else that it could be added. Even the design of the stamped leather, for which Mexico is famous, was embroidered with silver bullion. The stirrup had handsome leather covers, while a fringe of thongs fell almost to the ground, to aid in pushing their way through the tall prairie grass. Sometimes

the saddle-cloth, extending to the crupper, was of fur. The
bridle and bit were rich with silver also.   On the massive silver pommel hung an incongruous coil of horse-hair rope,
disfiguring and ugly.   There was an iron picket-pin attached
to the lariat, which we soon learned was of inestimable value
in the long rides that the Texans took. If a man made a
halt, he encircled himself with this prickly lariat and lay
down securely, knowing that no snake could cross that bar-
rier.   In a land of venomous serpents, it behooved a man to
carry his own abatis everywhere.   The saddle was also secured by a cinch or girth of cow's-hair, which hard riders found
a great help in keeping the saddle firm.   The Texan himself,
though not often wearing the high-crowned, silver-embroid-
ered Mexican sombrero, wore usually a wide-brimmed felt
hat, on which the General afterward doted, as the felt was
of superior quality.   If the term " dude " had been invented
then, it would often have applied to a Texan horseman.
The hair was frequently long, and they wore no waistcoat,
I concluded because they could better display the vast expanse of shirt-front.   While the General and his casual companion in our march talked horse, too absorbed to notice
anything else, I used to lose myself in the contemplation of
the maze of tucks, puffs and embroidery of this cambric finery, ornamented with three old-fashioned bosom-pins.   The
wearer seemed to me to represent two epochs: the fine linen,
side-saddle and blooded horse belonged to " befo' the war; "
while the ragged elbows of the coat-sleeves, and the worn
boots, were decidedly "since the war."   If the shirt-front
was intricate in its workmanship, the boots were ignored by
the placid owner.
    They usually had the Mexican serape strapped to the back
of the saddle, or, if it was cold, as it was in our late November march, they put their head through the opening in the
middle, so woven for that purpose, and flung the end across
their breast and over one shoulder in a picturesque manner.
The bright hues of the blanket, dyed by the Indians from the
juice of the prickly pear, its soft, flexible folds having been

woven in a hand-loom, made a graceful and attractive bit of
color, which was not at all out of place in that country.
These blankets were valuable possessions. They were so
pliable and perfectly water-proof, that they protected one
from every storm. We had a pair, which we used through
every subsequent campaign, and when the cold in Kansas
and Dakota became almost unbearable, sometimes, after the
long trial of a journey in the wagon, my husband used to
say, "We will resort to extreme measures, Libbie, and wrap
you in the Mexican blankets." They were the warmest of
all our wraps. Nothing seemed to fade them, and even when
burnt with Tom's cigarette ashes, or stuck through with the
General's spurs, they did not ravel, as do other fabrics. They
have hung as portières in my little home, and the design and
coloring are so like the Persian rug on the floor, that it seems
to be an argument to prove that Mr. Ignatius Donnelly, in
his theory of Atlantis, is right, and that we once had a land
highway between the East and Mexico, and that the reason
the Aztec now uses the designs on his pottery and in his
weaving is, that his ancestors brought over the first sketches
on papyrus.*

A Texan travels for comfort and safety rather than for
style. If a norther overtakes him, he dismounts and drives
the picket-pin into the ground, thus tethering his horse,
which turns his back, the better to withstand the oncoming
wind. The master throws himself, face down, in the long

---

* In a town of Mexico last year I saw these small looms with
blankets in them, in various stages of progress, in many cottages.
Among the Indians the rude loom is carried about in the mountain villages, and with some tribes there is a superstition about
finishing the blankets in the same place where they were begun.
A squaw will sometimes have one half done, and if an order is
given her she will not break over her rule to finish it if a move is
made in the midst of her work. She waits until the next year,
when her people return to the same camp, as is the custom when
the Indian seeks certain game or grazing, or to cut longer poles.

grass, buried in his blanket, and thus awaits the termination
of the fury with which the storm sweeps a Texas prairie.

Sometimes one of the planters, after riding a distance with
us, talking the county over, and taking in every point of our
horses as he rode, made his adieus and said he was now at
his own place, where he turned in. The General followed
his fine thoroughbred with longing eyes, and was more than
astonished to find in what stables they kept these valuable
and delicate animals. No matter if the house was habitable, the stable was usually in a state of careless dilapidation.
Doors swung on one hinge, and clapboards were torn off
here and there, while the warped roof was far from weather-
proof. Even though Texas is in the "Sunny South," the
first sharp norther awakens one to the knowledge that it is not
always summer. Sometimes these storms are quickly over,
but frequently they last three days. This carelessness about
stabling stock was not owing to the depredations of an invad-
ing army. We were the first "Yankees" they had seen. It
was the general shiftlessness that creeps into one's veins.
We were not long there ourselves before climatic influence
had its effect on even the most active among us.

Before we reached Austin, several citizens sent out invitations for us to come to their houses; but I knew the General
would not accept, and, cold as the nights were, I felt unwilling to lose a day of camp life. We pitched our tents on
rolling ground in the vicinity of Austin, where we overlooked
a pretty town of stuccoed houses that appeared summery in
the midst of the live-oak's perennial green. The State
House, Land Office, and governor's mansion looked regal to us
so long bivouacking in the forest and on uncultivated prairies.
The governor offered for our headquarters the Blind Asylum,
which had been closed during the war. This possessed one
advantage that we were glad to improve: there was room
enough for all the staff, and a long saloon parlor and dining-
room for our hops during the winter. By this time two pretty, agreeable women, wives of staff-officers, were added to our
circle. Still, I went into the building with regret. The

wagon in which the wind had rocked me to sleep so often, and which had proved such a stronghold against the crawling foes of the country, was consigned to the stable with a sigh. Camp life had more pleasures than hardships.

There were three windows in our room, which we opened at night; but, notwithstanding the air that circulated, the feeling, after having been so long out of doors, was suffocating. The ceiling seemed descending to smother us. There was one joy —reveillé could ring out on the dawning day and there was no longer imperative necessity to spring from a warm bed and make ablutions in ice-water. There is a good deal of that sort of mental snapping of the fingers on the part of campaigners when they are again stationary and need not prepare for a march. Civilization and a looking-glass must now be assumed, as it would no longer do to rough it and ignore appearances, after we had moved into a house, and were to live like "folks." Besides, we soon began to be invited by the townspeople to visit them. Refined, agreeable and well-dressed women came to see us, and, womanlike, we ran our eyes over their dresses. They were embroidered and trimmed richly with lace—"befo' the war" finery or from the cargo of a blockade runner; but it was all strange enough in such an isolated State. Almost everything was then brought from the terminus of the Brenham Railroad to Austin, 150 miles, by ox-team. We had been anxiously expected for some time, and there was no manner of doubt that the arrival of the Division was a great relief to the reputable of both sides. They said so frankly—the returned Confederate officers and the "stay-at-home rangers," as well as the newly appointed Union governor.

Texas was then a "go-as-you-please" State, and the lawlessness was terrible. The returned Confederate soldiers were poor, and did not know how to set themselves to work, and in many instances preferred the life of a freebooter. It was so easy, if a crime was committed, to slip into Mexico, for though it was inaccessible except by stage or on horseback, a Texan would not mind a forced march over the country to the Rio Grande. There were then but one or two short railroads in operation. The one from Galveston to Brenham was the principal one, while telegraph lines were not in use. The stage to Brenham was our one means of communication with the outside world.

It was hard for the citizens who had remained at home to realize that war was over, and some were unwilling to believe there ever had been an emancipation proclamation. In the northern part of the State they were still buying and selling slaves. The lives of the newly appointed United States officers were threatened daily, and it was an uneasy head that wore the gubernatorial crown. I thought them braver men than many who had faced the enemy in battle. The unseen, lurking foe that hides under cover of darkness was their terror. They held themselves valiantly; but one wife and daughter were on my mind night after night, as from dark till dawn they slept uneasily, and started from their rooms out into the halls at every strange sound. The General and I thought the courageous daughter had enough brave, devoted blood in her veins to distill a portion into the heart of many a soldier who led a forlorn hope. They told us that in the early part of the war the girl had known of a Union flag in the State House, held in derision and scornfully treated by the extremists. She and her younger brother climbed upon the roof of a wing of the building, after dark, entered a window of the Capitol, found the flag, concealed it in the girl's clothing, and made their perilous descent safely. The father of such a daughter might well prize her watchfulness of his safety, as she vigilantly kept it up during our stay, and was equal to a squadron of soldiers. She won our admiration; and our bachelor officers paid the tribute that brave men always pay to courageous, unselfish women, for she danced, rode and walked with them, and when she was not so engaged, their orderlies held their horses before the official door, while they improved every hour allowed them within the hospitable portal.

It was a great relief to find a Southern State that was not

devastated by the war. The homes destroyed in Virginia could not fail to move a woman's heart, as it was women and children that suffered from such destruction. In Texas nothing seemed to have been altered. I suppose some profited, for blockade-running could be carried on from the ports of that great State, and there was always Mexico from which to draw supplies.

In our daily rides we found the country about Austin delightful. The roads were smooth and the surface rolling. Indeed, there was one high hill, called Mount Brunnel, where we had picnics and enjoyed the fine view, far and near, taking one of the bands of the regular regiments from the North that joined us soon after our arrival. Mount Brunnel was so steep we had to dismount and climb a part of the distance. The band played the "Anvil Chorus," and the sound descended through the valley grandly. The river, filled with sand-bars and ugly on close examination, looked like a silver ribbon. At that height, the ripened cotton, at certain seasons of the year, looked like fields of foam. The thermometer was over eighty before we left the lowlands; but at the altitude to which we climbed the air was cool. We even went once to the State Insane Asylum, taking the band, when the attendants asked if dance music might be played, and we watched with wonder the quadrille of an insane eight.

The favorite ride for my husband was across the Colorado to the Deaf and Dumb Asylum. There seemed to be a fascination for him in the children, who were equally charmed with the young soldier that silently watched their pretty, pathetic exhibitions of intelligent speech by gesture. My husband riveted his gaze on their speaking eyes, and as their instructor spelt the passions of love, hatred, remorse and reverence on his fingers, one little girl represented them by singularly graceful gestures, charming him, and filling his eyes with tears, which he did not seek to hide. The pupils were from ten to sixteen years of age. Their supple wrists were a delight to us, and the tiny hands of a child of the matron, whom the General held, talked in a cunning way to its playmates, who, it knew, could not comprehend its speech. It was well that the Professor was hospitality itself, and did not mind a cavalcade dashing up the road to his house. My husband, when he did not openly suggest going, used some subterfuge as trivial as going for water-cress, that grew in a pond near the Asylum. The children knew him, and welcomed him with lustrous, eloquent eyes, and went untiringly through their little exhibitions, learning to bring him their compositions, examples and maps, for his commendation. How little we thought then that the lessons he was taking, in order to talk with the children he learned to love, would soon come into use while sitting round a camp-fire and making himself understood by Indians. Of course, their sign-language is wholly their own, but it is the same method of using the simplest signs as expressive of thought. It was a long, pleasant ride; its only drawback to me being the fording of the river, which had quicksands and a rapid current. The Colorado was low, but the river-bed was wide and filled with sand-bars. The mad torrent that the citizens told us of in freshets, we did not see. If I followed my husband, as Custis Lee had learned to do, I found myself guided safely, but it sometimes happened that our party entered the river, laughing and talking so earnestly, noisily and excitedly that we forgot caution. One lesson was enough; the sensation of the sinking of the horse's hindlegs in quicksands is not to be forgotten. The loud cry of the General to "saw on the bit" or whip my horse, excited, frightened directions from the staff to turn to the right or the left, Custis Lee trembling and snorting with fear, but responding to a sharp cut of my whip (for I rarely struck him), and we plunged on to a firmer soil, wiser for all the future on account of that moment of serious peril.

We seldom rode through the town, as my husband disliked the publicity that a group of cavalrymen must necessarily cause in a city street. If we were compelled to, the staff and Tom pointed out one after another of the loungers about the stores, or the horseman, who had killed his man. It seemed to be thought the necessary thing, to establish the Texan's idea of courage, to have either fought in duels, or, by waylaying the enemy, to have killed from one to five men. The Southern climate seems to keep alive a feud that our cold Northern winters freeze out. Bad blood was never kept in abeyance; they had out their bursts of temper when the attack of rage came on. Each man, even the boys of twelve, went armed. I used to wonder at the humped-up coats, until a norther, before which we were one day scudding for safety, lifted the coats of men making a similar dash, and the pistol was revealed.

It was the favorite pastime of our men (having concocted the scheme with the General) to ride near some of the outskirts, and, when we reached some lone tree, tell me that from that limb a murdered man had lately swung. This grim joke was often practiced on me, in order that the shuddering horror and the start Custis Lee and I made, to skim over the country away from such a hated spot, might be enjoyed. I came to think the Texas trees bore that human fruit a little too often for truth; but some of the citizens gloated over these scenes of horror, and added a lamp-post in town to the list of localities from which, in future, I must turn away my head.

The negroes in Texas and Louisiana were the worst in all the South. The border States had commonly sold their most insubordinate slaves into these two distant States.* For-

---

* In order to gain some idea of the immense territory in which our troops were attempting to restore order, I have only to remind the reader that Texas is larger than either the German or the Austrian Empire. The area of the State is 274,356 square miles. It is as large as France, Belgium, England and Wales all combined. If we could place the northwestern corner of Texas at Chicago, its most southerly point would be at Jacksonville, Fla., its most easterly at Petersburg, Va., and its most westerly in the interior of Missouri. It would thus cover the entire States

tunately, our now well-disciplined Division and the regular cavalry kept everything in a better condition; but there were constantly individual cases of outrageous conduct, and often of crime, among whites and blacks, high and 'low. Texas had so long been looked upon as a sort of "city of refuge" by outlaws, that those whom the other States refused to harbor came to that locality. A country reached only by sea from the south or by a wagon-train from the north, and through which no telegraph lines ran until after we came, would certainly offer an admirable hiding-place for those who leave their country for their country's good. I have read somewhere that Texas derived its name from a group of rascals, who, sitting around a fire on their arrival on the soil that was to protect them, composed this couplet:

> " If every other land forsakes us,
>   This is the land that freely takes us (Texas)."

As story after story reached us, I began to think the State was well named. There were a great many excellent, law-abiding citizens, but not enough to leaven the lump at that chaotic period. Even the women learned to defend themselves, as the war had deprived them of their natural protectors, who had gone either in the Northern or Southern army—for Texas had a cavalry regiment of refugees in our service. One woman, while we were there, found a teamster getting into her window, and shot him fatally. Fire-arms were so constantly about—for the men did not dress without a pistol in their belts—that women grew accustomed to the sight of weapons. There was a woman of whom I constantly heard, rich and refined, but living out of town on a plantation that seemed to be fit only for negroes. She

---

of Indiana, Kentucky and the two Carolinas, and nearly all of Tennessee, with one-third of Ohio, two-thirds of Virginia, half of Georgia, and portions of Florida, Alabama, Illinois and Missouri. The cities of Chicago, Toledo, Cincinnati, Washington, Richmond, Charleston, Atlanta and Nashville would all be included within its borders.

rode fearlessly, and diverted her monotonous life by hunting. The planters frequently met her with game slung upon her saddle, and once she lassoed and brought in a wolf alone. Finally, this woman came to see me, but curiosity made me hardly civil for a few moments, as I was trying to reconcile myself to the knowledge that the quiet, graceful person before me, with rich dress, jewels and a French hat, could take her gun and dogs, mount a fiery horse, and go hunting alone. We found, on returning the visit, that, though they were rich, owning blooded horses, a plantation and a mill, their domicile was anything but what we at the North would call comfortable. It was a long, one-storied, log building, consisting of a parlor, dining-room, bedroom and two small "no-'count" rooms, as the servants said, all opening into one another and upon the porch. The first surprise on entering was, that the roof did not fit down snugly on the side wall. A strip of the blue sky was visible on three sides, while the partition of the dining-room only came up part way. There seemed to be no sort of provision for "Caudle lectures." The walls were roughly plastered, but this space just under the roof was for ventilation, and I fancied they would get enough of it during a norther.

I am reminded of a story that one of the witty Southern women told me, after repeating some very good comic verses, in which they excel. She said the house I described was not uncommon in Texas, and that once she was traveling over a portion of the State, on a journey of great suffering, as she was accompanying her husband's remains to a family burial-ground. They assisted her from her carriage into one of the rooms of a long log house, used as a wayside inn, and the landlady kindly helped her into bed, as she was prostrated with suffering and fatigue. After she left her, the landlady seemed to forget that the partition did not extend to the rafters, and began questioning her servant as to what was the matter, etc. Hearing that the lady had lost her husband, the old dame exclaimed, sympathetically, "Poor thing! Poor thing! I know how it is; I've lost three of 'em."

The General and his staff got a good deal of sport out of the manner in which they exaggerated the tales of bloodshed to me, and aroused the anger, grief and horror that I could not suppress. I must defend myself from the supposition that I may have been chronicling their absurd and highly colored tales. All that I have written I have either seen or have reliable authority for. Their astounding stories, composed among themselves, began with a concocted plan by which one casually started a story, the others met it with surprise, and with an " Is it possible?" and the next led up to some improbable narrative of the General's—I growing more and more shivery as the wicked tormentors advanced. Always rather gullible, I suppose, I must confess the torn and distracted state of society in Texas made everything they said seem probable. I don't know how long I kept up a fashion of starting and shuddering over the frequent crack of a rifle or pistol, as we rode through the woods about the town. My husband and his attendant scamps did all they could to confirm my belief that the woods were full of assassins, and I rode on after these sharp reports, expecting to come upon the lifeless remains of a murdered man. They all said, with well-assumed feeling, that Texas was an awful country in which to live, where a man's life was not safe an hour, and excitedly exclaimed at each shot, " There goes some other poor fellow !" I have reason to believe it was a serious disappointment to the whole confederation of jokers, to have me actually see a Mexican driver (a greaser) crack his whip over the heads of his oxen, as they crawled along in front of us one day when we were riding. There is no sound like the snap of the lash of a "bull-whacker," as they are called, and perhaps brighter women than I am might have been taken in by it, and thought it a pistol-shot. This ended my taking it as the signal of a death.

The lawlessness of the State was much diminished by the troops scattered through the country. General Custer was much occupied in answering communications that came from distant parts of Texas, describing the demoralized state of the country, and asking for troops. These appeals were from all sides. It was felt more and more that the presence of the troops was absolutely necessary, and it was certainly agreeable to us that we were not looked upon as invaders. The General then had thirteen regiments of infantry and as many of cavalry, scattered in every part of the State comprised in his district. The regular troops arriving brought their wives and daughters, and it was a great addition, as we had constant entertainments, in which the civilians, so long cut off from all gayety, were glad to participate. The staff assisted me greatly in my preparations. We dressed the long parlors in evergreens, made canopies of flags, arranged waxlights in impromptu wooden sconces, and with the waxed floor it was tempting enough to those who cared for dancing. The soldiers soon organized a string band, and a sergeant called off the quadrilles. Sometimes my husband planned and arranged the suppers alone, but usually the staff divided the duty of preparing the refreshments. Occasionally we attempted a dinner, and, as we wanted to invite our own ladies as well as some from the regular regiments, the table was a subject of study; for when twenty came, the dishes gave out. The staff dined early, so that we could have theirs, and the Southern woman who occupied two rooms in the building lent everything she had. Uncle Charley, our cook, who now had found a colored church in which to preach on Sunday, did up all his religion on that day, and swore all the week, but the cellar-kitchen was distant, and, besides, my husband used to argue that it was just as well to endure placidly the evils right about us, but not to seek for more. The swearing did not interfere with the cooking, and Charley thought it necessary to thus clear the kitchen, as our yard at that time was black with the colored race. Each officer's servant had his circle of friends, and they hovered round us like a dark cloud. The dishes that Uncle Charley sent up were excellent. The Texas beef and poultry were of superior quality, and we even had a respite from condensed milk, as a citizen had lent us a cow.

At one of these dinners Eliza had enlisted a colored boy to help her wait on the table. I had tried to borrow enough dishes, and thought the table was provided. But the glory of the occasion departed when, after soup, roast game, etc., all served with the great luxury, at that place, of separate plates, Uncle Charley bethought himself that he would add, as a surprise, a dessert. It is almost unnecessary to say that a dessert at that time was an event. Uncle Charley said his "best holt" was on meats, and his attempts at pastry would not only have ruined the remnant of his temper, but, I am afraid, if often indulged in, would have effectually finished our digestion. For this I had not counted, and, to my dismay, after the pudding had been deposited with great salaam and ceremony before the General, the colored boy rushed around and gathered everybody's coffee-saucer. Until he returned them washed, and placed them at the head of the table, I did not imagine what he was doing; I simply waited, in that uncertain frame of mind that a hostess well knows. My husband looked at the array of cups down the long table, standing bereft of their partners, laid his head back and shouted. Then everybody else laughed, and, very red and very mortified, I concluded to admit that I had not arranged for this last course, and that on that table were the united contents of all our mess-chests, and there were no saucers or dessert-plates nearer than town. We were aware that our stay in the South was limited, and made no effort to keep enough crockery for dinners of twenty.

Afrer many enjoyable parties in our parlor, we received a pathetic and carefully worded hint from Eliza, who was now a great belle, that she would like to return some of the hospitality shown her by the colored people of the town, and my husband was only too glad to prove to Eliza how we valued her faithful, self-denying life in our service. We composed an invitation, in which Miss Eliza Brown presented her compliments to Mr. Washington or Mr. Jefferson, as the case might be, and would be happy to see him on such an evening, with the word "dancing" in the left-hand corner. A gathering of the darkeys seemed equally jubilant, whether it was a funeral, a camp-meeting or a dance; but it seemed they made a difference in dress for these occasions, if not in manners. So it was best, Eliza thought, to add "dancing," though it was only at first a mirthful suggestion of the General's fertile brain. He gave the copying to the office clerk, who, being a professional penman, put as many tails to his capitals and flourishes to his words as he did for the white folks, Eliza's critical eye watching for any less elaborate embellishment.

The lower part of the house was given over to the negroes, who polished the floor, trimmed the windows, columns and chimney with garlands of live-oak, and lavished candles on the scene, while at the supper they had a heterogeneous jumble of just what they asked for, including coon, the dish garnished with watercress and bits of boiled beet. I think we were not asked; but as the fiddle started the jigs, the General's feet began to keep time, and he executed some *pas seul* around our room, and then, extracting, as usual, a promise from me not to laugh, he dragged me down the steps, and we hid where we saw it all. The quadrille ended, the order of ceremonies seemed to consist in the company going down to one end of the room in response to an order from Uncle Charley to "cl'ar the flo'." Then the old man of sixty, a grandfather, now dressed in white tie, vest and gloves, with shining black clothes, took the floor. He knew himself to be the cynosure of all eyes, and bore himself accordingly He had previously said to me, " To-night, I expects, Miss Libbie, to put down some steps those colored folks has never seen befo'." And surely he did. He ambled out, as lithe as a youngster, cut some pigeon-wings, and then skipped and flung himself about with the agility of a boy, stopping not only for breath, but to watch the expressions, envious and admiring, of the spectators at the end of the room. When his last breath was exhausted, Aunt Ann, our old laundress, came tripping down the polished floor, and executed a shuffle, most decorous at first, and then, reviving her youth, she struck into a hoydenish jig, her son encouraging her by patting time. More quadrilles, then another clearing of the floor, and a young yellow woman pirouetted down the room, in bright green tarlatan petticoats, very short and airy. She executed a hornpipe and a reel, and, like Uncle Charley, improvised some steps for the occasion. This black sylph was surrounded with a cloud of diaphanous drapery; she wreathed her arms about her head, kept on the smirk of the ballet-girl, and coquetted and skipped about, with manners that brought down the house. The fattest darkey of all waddled down next and did a breakdown, at which all the assembly patted juba, and with their woolly heads kept time to the violin. My husband never moved from his hiding-place, but chuckled and shook over the sight, novel to us, till Eliza found us out and forgave the " peeking."

The clothes worn looked as if the property-room of a third-rate theatre had been rifled—faded finery, fag ends of old lace, tumbled flowers that had done duty at many a "white folks'" ball, on the pretty costume of the missus, old feathers set up in the wool, where what was left of the plume bobbed and quavered, as the head of the owner moved to the time of the music, or nodded and swayed back and forth while conversation was kept up. The braiding, oiling and smoothing had gone on for days previous, to straighten the wool and make it lie flat; but the activity in the pursuit of pleasure soon set the little kinks free, and each hair stood on tiptoe, joining in a jig of its own. The powder begged from the toilet-table of the missus was soon swept away in the general shine; but the belles cared little for having suspended temporarily the breath of their rivals by the gorgeousness of their toilettes ; they forgot appearances and yielded to that absorption of excitement in which the colored soul is spellbound.

Eliza moved about, " queening it," as she knew how to do, and it was a proud hour of triumph to her, as she cast a complacent side glance at the tail of her gown, which she had wheedled out of me by cunning arguments, among which the most powerful was that " 'twas getting so mussed, and 'twasn't no sort of a dress for a Ginnel's wife, no how." The General lost nothing, for he sat in our hidden corner, shaking and throwing his head back in glee, but keeping a close and warning hold on my arm, as I was not so successful in smothering a titter as he was, having no mustache to deaden the sound. After Eliza discovered us, she let no one know of our perfidy, and the company, believing they were alone, abandoned themselves to complete enjoyment, as the fiddle played havoc with the heels of the entire assembly.

CHAPTER VIII.

LETTERS HOME.

THE trivial events of our daily life were chronicled in a weekly letter home, and from a number of these school-girl effusions I cull a few items, as they give an idea of my husband's recreations as well as his duties.

"We are quartered in the Blind Asylum, which is large and comfortable. The large rooms in the main part of the building we can use for entertaining, while the staff occupy the wings and the building in the yard, that was used for a schoolroom. Out there they can have all the 'walk-arounds' and 'high-jinks' they choose, without any one hearing them."

.   .   .   .

"Our room is large, and, mother, I have two bureaus and a wardrobe, and lose my things constantly, I am so unused to so much room. We women hardly knew what to make of the absence of looking-glasses, as the house is otherwise furnished, until it occurred to us that the former occupants wouldn't get much good out of a mirror. It isn't so necessary to have one, after all, as I got on all summer very well, after I learned to brush my hair straight back and not try to part it. I have a mirror now, and am wrestling with back hair again.

"I confess to you, mother, it is a comfort to get out of bed on to a carpet, and dress by a fire; but don't tell Armstrong I said so, as I never mentioned to him that dressing before day, my eyes streaming with tears from the camp-fire while I took an ice-water bath, was not the mode of serving my country that I could choose."

.   .   .   .

"Last Sunday it was uncomfortably warm. We wore thin summer clothes, and were languid from the heat. The thermometer was eighty-two in the shade. On Monday the weather changed from heat to cold in five minutes, in consequence of the sudden and violent winds which are called ' northers.'

"No one prepares for the cold in this country, but there was a general scattering when our first norther attacked us. Tom rushed for wood, and of course none was cut. He fished Tex out from the kitchen, borrowed an axe from one of the headquarters men, and soon appeared with an armful. As he took the sticks from Tex to build the fire, out dropped a scorpion to add to the excitement. It was torpid, but nevertheless it was a scorpion, and I took my usual safe position, in the middle of the bed, till there was an *auto da fe*. The loose windows rattled, and the wind howled around the corner of our room. I put a sack and shawl over my summer dress, and we shivered over Tom's fire. I rather wondered at Armstrong's huddling, as he is usually so warm, but each act of these boys needs investigating. By and by he went off to write, while father Custer took out his pipe, to calm the troubled scene into which the rush of Nova Zembla had thrown us. He sat 'way under the mantel to let the tobacco-smoke go up the chimney. Pretty soon Autie returned and threw some waste paper on the fire, and the next thing we all started violently back from a wild pyrotechnic display. With the papers went in a handful of blank cartridges, and these innocent-looking scamps faced their father and calmly asked him why he had jumped half-way across the room. They often repeat this Fourth-of-July exhibition with fire-crackers, either tied to his chair, or tossed carelessly on the burning logs, when his attention is attracted elsewhere. But don't pity him, mother. No matter what trick they play, he is never phased. He matches them too, and I help him, though I am obliged to confess I often join in the laugh, it is all so funny. This was not the last of the hullaba-loo. The wood gave out and Autie descended for more. Tex took this occasion, when everyone was hunting a fire and shelter from the cold, to right what he considered a

grievous wrong. Autie found him belaboring another colored boy, whom he had "downed." Autie investigated,
for if Tex was right he was bound to let the fight proceed.
You know in his West Point days he was arrested for allowing a fisticuff to go on, and because he said, 'Stand back,
boys, and let's have a fair fight.' But finding our boy in the
wrong, he arraigned him, and began, 'Did you strike Jake
with malice aforethought?' 'No sah! no sah! I dun struck
him with the back of the hatchet.' At this Autie found
himself no longer a 'most righteous judge.' This Daniel
beat a quick retreat, red with suppressed laughter, and made
Tom go down to do the punishing. Tom shut Tex in the
chicken-coop; but it was hard for me to see from my window
his shiny eyes looking out from between the slats, so they
made the sentence light, and he was set free in the afternoon.

"Now, mother, I have established the only Yankee wood-
pile in Texas. I don't mean to be caught again, and shrivel
up as we did this time. You don't know how these storms
deceive you. One hour we are so suffocated with the heavy,
oppressive air, we sit in the deep window-sills and pant for
breath. Along comes a roaring sound through the tree-tops,
and there's a scatter, I can tell you. We bang down the
windows, and shout for Texas to hunt the wood-pile, jump
into warm clothes, and before we are fairly prepared, the
hurricane is upon us. We really don't mind it a bit, as it
doesn't last long (once it lasted three days), besides, it is so
good to be in something that isn't going to blow down, as we
momentarily expected in a tent. Our Sundays pass so
slowly! The traveling-wagon holds a good many, and we
don't mind close quarters, so we all squeeze in, and the
bachelor officers ride with us to church. The Episcopal
church is still open, but as they have no fires we would be
glad if the rector warmed us up with his eloquence a little
more. However, it's church, and we begin to feel semi-
civilized.

.   .   .   .

"The citizens are constantly coming to pay their respects

to Armstrong. You see, we were welcomed instead of dreaded, as, Yankees or no Yankees, a man's life is just as good, preserved by a Federal soldier as by a Confederate, and everybody seems to be in a terrified state in this lawless land. Among the callers is one man that will interest you, father. I believe you are considered authority on the history of the fight that took place at Monroe, when the Kentucky regiment fought the British in 1812. Well, whom do you think we have found down here, but the old Colonel Groome who distinguished himself that day? He is a white-headed old soldier, and when Autie told him that we were right from Monroe, he was so affected the tears came to his eyes. It was he that set the barn on fire to prevent the British using it as a fortification for sharp-shooters. He crawled away from the burning building on his hands and knees, while their bullets cut his clothes and wounded him several times. Years afterward he met an old British officer, who told him, in their talk, that the man who fired the barn was killed by his own army, but Colonel Groome, in quite a dramatic way, said, 'No! I am the man.' He says that he would like to see you so much. Autie is greatly interested in this veteran, and we are going to call on him, and get two game chickens he is to give us.

" Now, father, don't wrinkle up your brows when I tell you that we race horses. Even I race with Mrs. L——, and much as you may disapprove, I know my father too well not to be sure he will be glad that his only daughter beat. But let me explain to you that racing among ourselves is not your idea of it. There is no money at stake, no rough crowd, none of the evils of which you may well disapprove, as we know horse-racing at home. Armstrong is considered the best judge of a horse here. The Texans supposed no one in the world could ride as well as themselves, and they do ride splendidly, but those who saw Armstrong keep his place in the saddle when Don Juan ran away with him at the grand review in Washington, concede that he does know how to ride, however mistaken his views on patriotism may be. We have now three running horses and a fast pony, none of which has beaten. Autie's bay pony beat a crack runner of which the town boasts, by three full lengths. The races are near our quarters, so we women can be in it all. Indeed, there is nothing they do not share with us.

" Our stable-boy is a tiny mulatto, a handsome little fellow, weighing about eighty pounds. Armstrong thinks he is the finest rider he has ever seen. I have just made him a tight-fitting red jacket and a red-white-and-blue skull cap, to ride in at races. We are running out to the stables half our time. Armstrong has the horses exercised on a quarter-of-a-mile track, holds the watch and times them, as we sit round and enjoy their speed."

.   .   .   .

"When I am so intent on my amateur dressmaking, and perplexed and tired, dear mother, you wouldn't wonder when I tell you that one dress, of which I am in actual need, I cut so that the figure ran one way on the skirt and another on the waist, and caused Armstrong to make some ridiculous remarks that I tried not to notice, but he was so funny, and the dress itself was so very queer when I put it on, I had to give in. Well, when I am so bothered, he comes in and throws my things all over the room, kicks over the lapboard, and picks me up for a tramp to the stable. Then he rubs down the horses' legs, and asks me to notice this or that fine point, which is all Greek to me. The truth is, that I would rather see a fine mane and tail than all the sinew, length of limb, etc. Then we sit down on kegs and boxes, and contemplate our wealth. Custis Lee greets me with a whinny. Dear mother, you would be simply horrified by our back yard. Autie and I march to the stables through a dark cloud of spectators. The negroes are upon us like the locusts of Egypt. It is rumored that our Uncle Charley keeps a flourishing colored boarding-house in the town, from what is decidedly more than the crumbs that fall from his master's table. After all, though, considering our house is filled with company, and we constantly give evening parties, I don't

think our mess-bills are very large.   Autie teases father Custer, by telling him he is going to brigade the colored troops
and make him chaplain.   You are well aware how father
Custer feels over the ' nigger ' question, and how he would
regard a chaplaincy.   I must not forget to tell you that the
wheel of time has rolled around, and among the regiments in
Armstrong's command is the Fourth Michigan Infantry.
Don't you remember that when he was a second lieutenant,
he crossed the Chickahominy with that regiment, and how,
having started before dawn, his comrades among whom he
had just come, did not know him, till, while they were lying
low, he would pop up his head and call out their first names,
or their nicknames at school in Monroe, and when it was
daylight, and they recognized him, how glad they were to
see him ? "

.   .   .   .

" We had a lovely Christmas.   I fared beautifully, as some
of our staff had been to San Antonio, where the stores have
a good many beautiful things from Mexico.   Here, we had
little opportunity to buy anything, but I managed to get up
some trifle for each of our circle.   We had a large Christmas-
tree, and Autie was Santa Claus, and handed down the presents, making side-splitting remarks as each person walked
up to receive his gift.   The tree was well lighted.   I don't
know how so many tapers were gotten together.   Of course
it would not be *us* if, with all the substantial gifts, some jokes
were not slipped in.   You know well father Custer's antip-
athy to the negro, and everybody gathered round to see him
open a box containing a nigger doll baby, while two of his
other parcels held a bunch of fire-crackers and a bunch of
cards.   Lately his sons have spent a good deal of time and
argument trying to induce him to play.   They, at last, taught
him some simple game, easy enough for even me to master.
The rogues let him beat at first, but finally he discovered his
luck was so persistently bad there must be a screw loose, and
those boys up to some rascality.   They had put him, with no
apparent intention, with his back to the mirror, and, of

course, saw his hand, which, like an amateur, he awkwardly
held just right to enable them to see all his cards. This ended his lessons, and we will return him to Monroe the same
good old Methodist that he left it. Everybody is fond of him,
and his real presents were a hat, handkerchief, necktie, pipe
and tobacco.

"One of our lieutenants, having just received his brevet as
major, had a huge pair of yellow leaves cut out of flannel, as
his insignia for the new rank.

"One of the staff, now a teetotaler, was reminded of his
past, which I hoped everyone would ignore, by the present
of a wooden faucet. No one escapes in such a crowd.

"Tom, who is always drumming on the piano, had a Jew's-
harp given him, with an explanatory line from Autie attached, 'to give the piano a rest.' Only our own military family
were here, and Armstrong gave us a nice supper, all of his
own getting up. We played games, sang songs, mostly for
the chorus, danced, and finally the merriest imitated the
darkeys by jigs and patting juba, and walk-arounds. The
rooms were prettily trimmed with evergreens, and over one
door a great branch of mistletoe, about which the officers
sang

> " Fair mistletoe !
> Love's opportunity !
> What trees that grow
> Give such sweet impunity ?"

"But it is too bad that, pretty as two or three of our
women are, they belong to some one else. So kissing begins
and ends with every man saluting his own wife.

"I wish you could see the waxen white berries and the
green leaves of the parasite on the naked branches of the
trees here, mother; and, oh ! to have you get one sniff of the
December roses, which rival the summer ones in richness of
color and perfume, would make my pleasure greater, I assure you. It is nearly spring here, and the grass on our lawn
is getting green, and the farmers began to plough in January.

"Nettie is such a nurse here! Her name is up for it, and she has even to go out to the servants' quarters if the little nigs burn their heels or toes. She is a great pleasure to us all, and enjoys every moment."

It seems that the general racing of which I wrote to my father, was too tempting for me to resist entirely, and our household was beguiled one day into a promise to bring my husband's war-horse, Jack Rucker, down to the citizens' track. Every one was confident of success, and no one took into consideration that the experiment of pitting gentlemen against turf roughs has never been successful. Our officers entered into all the preparations with high hopes, thinking that with one good whipping the civilians would cease to send bantering messages or drag presuming coat-tails before their eyes. They were accustomed to putting their steeds to their best speed when a party of equestrians from our headquarters were riding in their vicinity. Too fond of good horseflesh not to admire the pace at which their thoroughbreds sped over the smooth, firm roads about Austin, there was still a murmured word passed around that the owners of these fleet animals would hang their proud heads when "Jack" came into the field. We women were pressed into going. All of us liked the trial of speed on our own territory, but the hatred of a horse-track that was not conducted by gentlemen was imbedded deep in our minds. The officers did not ask us to go for good luck, as army women are so often told they bring it, but they simply said, "You could not miss seeing our Jack beat!" Off we went, a gay, boisterous party, till we reached the track; there we put on our quietest civilian manners and took our place to watch the coming triumph. The track was good, and the Texas men and women, more enthusiastic over a horse than over anything else in the world, cheered their blanketed favorite as he was led up and down before the judge's stand.

When the judge gave the final "Go!" our party were so excited, and our hearts so swelling with assured success, I would have climbed up on the saddle to see better, if it had not been that we were surrounded with strangers. Off went the beautiful Texas horse, like an arrow from a bow; but our Jack, in spite of the rider sticking the spur and cruelly cutting his silken neck with the whip, only lumbered around the first curve, and in this manner laboriously made his way the rest of the distance. Of course it was plain that we were frightfully beaten, and with loud and triumphant huzzas, the Texans welcomed their winning horse long before poor Jack dragged himself up to the stand. Our officers hurried out to look him over, and found the poor brute had been drugged by the contesting side. There was no serious injury, except to our pride. We were too disappointed, humiliated and infuriated to stand upon the order of our going. We all turned our backs upon the crowd and fled. The clatter of our horses' hoofs upon the hard road was the only sound, as none of us spoke.

My husband met that, as everything else, as nothing worthy of serious regret, and after the tempest of fury over our being so imposed upon, I rather rejoiced, because the speed of our horses, after that first and last essay, was confined to our own precincts. Nobody's pocket suffered, and the wounded spirits of those who race horses are more easily soothed if a wounded purse has not to be borne in addition.

There was one member of our family, to whom I have only referred, who was our daily joy. It was the pointer, Ginnie, whom the Virginia family in Hempstead had given us. My husband made her a bed in the hall near our room, and she did every cunning, intelligent act of which a dog is capable. She used to go hunting, walking and riding with us, and was *en rapport* with her master at all times. I often think, Who among our friends pleases us on all occasions? How few there are who do not rub us up the wrong way, or whom we ourselves are not conscious sometimes of boring, and of taxing their patience ! And do we not find that we sometimes approach those of whom we are fond, and discover intuitively that they are not in sympathy with our mood, and we must bide their time for responding to our overtures? With that dear Ginnie there was no question. She received us exactly in the spirit with which we approached her, responded, with measure pressed down and running over, to our affectionate demonstrations, and the blessed old girl never sulked if we dropped her to attend to something else. George Eliot says, "Animals are such agreeable friends! they ask no questions, they pass no criticisms."

A dog is so human to me, and dogs have been my husband's chosen friends so many years, I cannot look upon the commonest cur with indifference. Sometimes, as I stand now at my window, longing for the old pack that whined with delight, quarreled with jealousy for the best place near us, capered with excitement as we started off on a ride or walk, my eyes involuntarily follow each dog that passes on the street. I look at the master, to see if he realizes that all that is faithful and loving in this world is at his heels. If he stops to talk to a friend, and the dog leaps about him, licks his hand, rubs against him, and tries, in every way that his devoted heart teaches him, to attract the attention of the one who is all the world to him, all my sympathies are with the dog. I watch with jealous solicitude to see if the affectionate brute gets recognition. And if by instinct the master's hand goes out to the dog's head, I am quite as glad and grateful as the recipient. If the man is absorbed, and lets the animal sit patiently and adoringly watching his very expression, it seems to me I cannot refrain from calling his attention to the neglect.

My husband was as courteous in responding to his dogs' demonstrations, and as affectionate, as he would be to a person. If he sent them away, he explained, in dog talk, the reason, which might seem absurd if our canine family had not been our companions so constantly that they seemed to understand and accept his excuses as something unavoidable on his part. The men of our family so appreciated kindness to dogs that I have found myself this winter, involuntarily almost, calling to them to see an evidence of affection. One of my neighbors is a beer saloon, and though I am too busy

to look out of the window much, I have noticed occasionally
an old express horse waiting for his master to take " something warming." The blanket was humped up on his back
mysteriously. It turned out to be a dear little cur, which was
thus kept warm by a fond master. It recalls our men, and
the ways they devised for keeping their dogs warm, the times
innumerable when they shared their own blankets with them
when caught out in a cold snap, or divided short rations
with the dogs they loved.

Returning to Ginnie, I remember a day when there was a
strange disappearance ; she did not thump her tail on the
door for entrance, fetching our stockings in her mouth, as a
gentle hint that it was time to get up and have a fire, if the
morning was chilly. It did not take the General long to
scramble into his clothes and go to investigate, for he dearly
loved her, and missed the morning call. Soon afterward he
came bounding up the stairs, two steps at a time, to announce
that no harm had come to our favorite, but that seven other
little Ginnies were now taking the breakfast provided by their
mother, under the negro quarters at the rear of the house.
There was great rejoicing, and preparations to celebrate this
important event in our family. Eliza put our room in order,
and descended to the kitchen to tell what antics the General
was performing over the animal. When she was safely down-
stairs, where she could not intimidate us, my husband and I
departed to fetch the new family up near us. The General
would not trust any one with the responsibility of the removal.
He crawled under the building, which was set up on low
piles, and handed out the baby canines, one by one, to me.
Ginnie ran beside us, frantic with anxiety, but her eloquent
eyes full of love and trust in our intentions.

Her bed in the hall was hardly good enough for such an
epoch in her life, so the whole litter, with the proud mother
in their midst, was safely deposited in the middle of our bed,
where we paid court to this royalty. My husband went over
each little shapeless body, and called my special attention to
fine points, that, for the life of me, dog-lover as I was, I

could not discover in the pulpy, silken-skinned little rolls. As he took them up, one by one, Ginnie understood every word of praise he uttered. After all of these little blind atoms had been returned to their maternal, and the General had congratulated the mother on a restaurant where, he said, the advertisement of "warm meals at all hours" was for once true, he immediately set about tormenting Eliza. Her outraged spirit had suffered often, to see the kingly Byron reposing his head on the pillow, but the General said, "We must get her up-stairs, for there will be war in the camp now."

Eliza came peacefully up the stairs into our room, but her eyes blazed when she saw Ginnie. She asked her usual question, "Did I come way off down in this here no 'count country to wash white counterpanes for dogs?" At each speech the General said something to Ginnie in reply, to harrow her up more and more, and at last she had to give in and laugh at some of his drolleries. She recalls to me now her recollection: "Miss Libbie, do you mind how the Ginnel landed Ginnie and her whole brood of pups in the middle of the bed, and then had the 'dacity to send for me? But, oh! it was perfectly heartrendin', the way he would go on about his dogs when they was sick."

And we both remembered, when one of these little puppies of our beloved Ginnie was ill, how he walked the floor half the night, holding, rubbing, trying to soothe the suffering little beast. And in spite of his medical treatment—for he kept the dog-book on his desk, and ransacked it for remedies —and notwithstanding the anointing and the coddling, two died.

After Eliza had come down from her rampagious state, she was invited to take notice of what a splendid family Ginnie had. Then all the staff and the ladies came up to call. It was a great occasion for Ginnie, but she bore her honors meekly, and offered her paw, as was her old custom, to each new-comer, as if prepared for congratulations. When they were old enough to run about and bark, Ginnie took up her former habit of following at the General's heels ; and as he

crossed the yard to the stables there was so absurd a proces-
sion that I could not help laughing at the commanding officer, and question if he himself thought it added to the dignity
of his appearance, to see the court-like trail of mother and
five puppies in his wake. The independence of the chief was
too inborn to be laughed to scorn about appearances, and so
he continued to go about, as long as these wee toddlers followed their mother in quest of supplies. I believe there were
twenty-three dogs at this time about our house, most of them
ours. Even our father Custer accepted a bulky old cur as a
gift. There was no manner of doubt about the qualities that
had influenced our persecuted parent in selecting this one
from the numerous dogs offered him by his farmer friends.
His choice was made neither on account of breeding nor
speed. The cur was selected solely as a watch-dog. He was
all growl and bark, and as devotion is not confined, fortunately, to the canines of exalted paternity, the lumbering old
fellow was faithful. Nothing describes him better than some
lines from "The Outside Dog in the Fight;" for though he
could threaten with savage growls, and, I fancy, when aggravated, could have set savage teeth in the enemy of his master, he trotted beside our father's horse very peacefully, unmindful of the quarrelsome members of our canine family,
who bristled up to him, inviting an encounter merely to pass
the time.

> "You may sing of your dog, your bottom dog,
>   Or of any dog that you please ;
> I go for the dog, the wise old dog,
>   That knowingly takes his ease,
> And wagging his tail outside the ring,
>   Keeping always his bone in sight,
> Cares not a pin, in his wise old head,
>   For either dog in the fight.

> " Not his is the bone they are fighting for,
>   And why should my dog sail in,
> With nothing to gain but a certain chance
>   To lose his own precious skin ?

There may be a few, perhaps, who fail
   To see it in quite this light ;
But when the fur flies I had rather be
   The outside dog in the fight."

Affairs had come to such a pass that our father took his yellow cur into his bedroom at night. It was necessary to take prompt, precautionary measures to keep his sons from picking the lock of the door and descending on him in their marauding expeditions. The dog saw comparatively little of outside life, for, as time rounded, it became necessary for the old gentleman to shut up his body-guard daytimes also, as he found in his absence these same sons and their confederates had a fashion of dropping a little " nig " over the transom, with directions to fetch back to them anything he could lay his hands on. I have seen them at the door while our father was away, trying to soothe and cajole the old guardian of his master's effects into terms of peace. After all overtures were declined, and the little bedroom was filled up with bark and growl, the invaders contented themselves with tossing all sorts of missiles over the transom, which did not sweeten the enraged dog's temper. Nor did it render our father's bed as downy as it might have been.

I find myself recalling with a smile the perfectly satisfied manner in which this ungainly old dog was taken out by his venerable owner on our rides over the country. Father Custer had chosen him, not for his beauty, but as his companion, and finding him so successful in this one capacity, he was just as serene over his possession as ever his sons were with their high-bred hunters. The dog looked as if he were a make-up from all the rough clay that was discarded after modeling the sleek, high-stepping, springy, fleet-footed dogs of our pack. His legs were massive, while his cumbersome tail curled over his plebeian back in a tight coil, until he was tired—then, and only then, did it uncurl. The droop of his head was rendered even more ''loppy'' by the tongue, which dropped outside the sagging jaw. But for all that, he lumbered along, a blotch of ungainly yellow, beside our splendid

thoroughbreds ; he was never so tired that he could not understand the voice of a proud old man, who assured his retro-
grade sons that he "would match his Bowser 'gainst any of
their new-fangled, unreliable, highfalutin lot."

It was a strange sight, though, this one plebeian among
patricians. Our horses were fine, our father got good speed
and some style out of his nag, our dogs leaped over the country like deer, and there in the midst, panting and faithfully
struggling to keep up, was the rough, uncouth old fellow,
too absorbed in endeavoring not to be left behind to realize
that he was not all that a dog could finally become, after generations of training and breeding had done its refining work.

CHAPTER IX.

DISTURBED CONDITION OF TEXAS.

TEXAS was in a state of ferment from one end to the other. There was then no network of railroads running over its vast territory as there is now. Lawless acts might be perpetrated, and the inciters cross the Rio Grande into Mexico, before news of the depredations came to either military or civil headquarters. The regiments stationed at various points in the State had no easy duty. Jayhawkers, bandits and bushwhackers had everything their own way for a time. I now find, through official reports, what innumerable perplexities came up almost daily, and how difficult it was for an officer in command of a division to act in perfect justice to citizen, soldier and negro. It was the most natural result in the world that the restless throng let loose over the State from the Confederate service, should do what idle hands usually find to do. Consider what a land of tramps we were at the North, after the war ; and if, in our prosperous States and Territories, when so many business industries were at once resumed, we suffered from that class of men who refused to work and kept outside the pale of the law by a stealthy existence, what would naturally be the condition of affairs in a country like Texas, for many years the hiding-place of outlaws?

My own father was one of the most patriotic men I ever knew. He was too old to enter the service—an aged man even in my sight, for he had not married till he was forty; but in every way that he could serve his country at home he was foremost among the elderly patriots of the North. I remember how little war moved me. The clash of arms and glitter of the soldiery only appealed to me as it did to thoughtless, light-hearted young girls still without soldier lovers or brothers, who lived too far from the scenes of battle to know the tragic side. But my father impressed me by his sadness, his tears, his lamentations over our country's misfortunes. He was the first in town to get the news from the front, and so eager to hear the result of some awful day, when lives were being lost by thousands on a hotly contested field, that he walked a bleak, lonely mile to the telegraph station, waiting till midnight for the last despatches, and weeping over defeats as he wearily trod the long way homeward. I remember his striding up and down the floor, his grand head bent over his chest in grief, and saying, so solemnly as to arrest the attention of my stepmother, usually absorbed in domestic affairs, and even of me, too happy then with the very exuberance of living to think, while the sadness of his voice touched even our thoughtlessness: "Oh! the worst of this calamity will not be confined to war: our land, even after peace is restored, will be filled with cutthroats and villains."

The prediction came true immediately in Texas, and the troops had to be stationed over the extensive territory. Before the winter was over, the civil authorities began to be able to carry out the laws; they worked, as they were obliged to do, in connection with the military, and the rioting, oppressions and assassinations were becoming less common. It was considered unnecessary to retain the division of cavalry as an organization, since all anticipated trouble with Mexico was over, and the troops need no longer be massed in great numbers. The necessity for a special commander for the cavalry in the State was over, and the General was therefore mustered out of service as a major-general of volunteers, and ordered North to await his assignment to a new station.

We had very little to do in preparation, as our camp outfit was about all our earthly possessions at that time. It was a trial to part with the elderly dogs, which were hardly worth the experiment of transporting to the North, especially as we had no reason to suppose we should see another deer, except in zoölogical gardens. The hounds fell into good and appreciative hands, being given either to the planter who had presented them, or to the officers of the regular regiment that had just been stationed in Texas for a five-years' detail. The cow was returned to the generous planter who lent her to us. She was now a fat, sleek creature, compared with her appearance when she came from among the ranch cattle. The stables were emptied, and our brief enjoyment of an embryo blue-grass farm, with a diminutive private track of our own, was at an end. Jack Rucker, Custis Lee, Phil and the blooded mare were to go; but the great bargains in fast ponies had to be sacrificed.

My old father Custer had been as concerned about my horse education as his sons. He also tried, as well as his boys, to attract my attention from the flowing manes and tails, by which alone I judged the merits of a horse, to the shoulders, length of limb, withers, etc. One day there came an incentive for perfecting myself in horse lore, for my husband said that if I would select the best pony in a number we then owned, I should have him. I sat on a keg in the stable-yard, contemplating the heels of the horses, and wishing fervently I had listened to my former lessons in horse-flesh more attentively. All three men laughed at my perplexities, and even the soldiers who took care of the stable retired to a safe place to smile at the witticisms of their commanding officer, and were so deplorably susceptible to fun that even the wife of their chief was a subject for merriment. I was in imminent danger of losing my chance at owning a horse, and might to this day have remained ignorant of the peculiarly proud sensation one experiences over that possession, if my father Custer had not slyly and surreptitiously come over to my side. How he cunningly imparted the information I will not betray; but, since he was as good a judge of a horse as his sons, and had taught them their wisdom in that direction, it is needless to say that my final judgment, after repeated returns to the stable, was triumphant. Texas made

GENERAL CUSTER AT THE CLOSE OF THE WAR—AGED 25.

the old saw read, All is fair in love, war and horse-trades, so
I adapted myself to the customs of the country, and kept the
secret of my wise judgment until the money that the pony
brought—forty dollars in silver—was safely deposited in my
grasping palm.   I will not repeat the scoffing of the outwitted pair, after I had spent the money, at "Libbie's horse-
dress," but content myself with my father's praise at the
gown he had secured to me, when I enjoyed at the North the
serenity of mind that comes of silken attire.

The planters came to bid us good-by, and we parted from
them with reluctance. We had come into their State under trying circumstances, and the cordiality, generosity and genuine
good feeling that I know they felt, made our going a regret.
There was no reason why they should come from their distant
plantations to say good-by and wish us godspeed, except
from personal friendship, and we all appreciated the wish
they expressed that we might remain.

The journey from Austin to Hempstead was made much
more quickly than our march over. We had relays of horses,
the roads were good, and there was no detention. I only
remember one episode of any importance. At the little hotel at which we stopped in Brennan, we found loitering about
the doors and stoop and inner court a lounging, rough lot of
men, evidently the lower order of Confederate soldiers, the
lawless set that infest all armies, the tramp and the bummer.
They gathered in knots, to watch and talk of us. As we
passed them on our way to the dining-room, they muttered,
and even spoke audibly, words of spiteful insult. At every
such word I expected the fiery blood of the General and his
staff would be raised to fighting heat. But they would not
descend to altercation with fellows to whom even the presence
of a woman was no restraint.   It was a mystery, it still is,
to me, that hot-blooded men can control themselves if they
consider the foeman unworthy of the steel. My husband was
ever a marvel to me, in that he could in this respect carry
out his own oft-repeated counsel. I began very early with
that old maxim, "consider the source," as a subterfuge for

the lack of repartee, in choking senseless wrath; but it came
to be a family aphorism, and I was taught to live up to its
best meaning. The Confederates were only " barking," not
"biting," as the General said would be the case; but they
gave me a genuine scare, and I had serious objections to
traveling in Texas unaccompanied by a Division of cavalry.
I think the cold nights, smoky camp-fires, tarantulas, etc.,
that we encountered on our march over, would have been
gladly undertaken rather than run into the face of threatening men, unaccompanied by a single trooper, as we then
traveled.

    I wonder what the present tourist would think of the bit
of railroad over which we journeyed from Brennan to Galveston ! I scarcely think it had been touched, in the way of
repairs, during the war. The coaches were not as good as
our present emigrant cars. The rails were worn down thin,
and so loosely secured that they moved as we rolled slowly
over them. We were to be constantly in some sort of peril, it
seemed. There was a deep gully on the route, over which
was stretched a cobweb trestle, intended only as a temporary
bridge. There was no sort of question about its insecurity;
it quivered and menacingly swayed under us. The conductor
told us that each time he crossed he expected to go down. I
think he imagined there could be no better time than that,
when it would secure the effectual departure of a few Yankee
officers, not only from what he considered his invaded State,
but from the face of the earth. At any rate, he so graphic-
ally described to me our imminent peril that he put me
through all the preliminary stages of sudden death. Of
course, our officers, inured to risks of all sorts, took it all as
a matter of course, and the General slyly called the attention of our circle to the usual manner in which the " old lady "
met danger, namely, with her head buried in the folds of
a cloak.

    My husband knew what interest and admiration my father
Bacon had for " old Sam Houston," and he himself felt the delight that one soldier takes in the adventures and vicissitudes

of another. Consequently, we had listened all winter to the Texans' laudation of their hero, and many a story that never found its way into print was remembered for my father's sake. We were only too sorry that Houston's death, two years previous, had prevented our personal acquaintance. He was not, as I had supposed, an ignorant soldier of fortune, but had early scholarly tastes, and, even when a boy, could repeat nearly all of Pope's translation of the Iliad. Though a Virginian by birth, he early went with his widowed mother to Tennessee, and his roving spirit led him among the Indians, where he lived for years as the adopted son of a chief. He served as an enlisted man under Andrew Jackson in the war of 1812, and afterward became a lieutenant in the regular army. Then he assumed the office of Indian agent, and befriended those with whom he had lived.

From that he went into law in Nashville, and eventually became a Congressman. Some marital difficulties drove him back to barbarism, and he rejoined the Cherokees, who had been removed to Arkansas. He went to Washington to plead for the tribe, and returning, left his wigwam among the Indians after a time, and went to Texas. During the tumultuous history of that State, when it was being shifted from one government to another with such vehemence, no citizen could tell whether he would rise in the morning a Mexican, or a member of an independent republic, or a citizen of the United States.

With all that period Sam Houston was identified. He was evidently the man for the hour, and it is no wonder that our officers dwelt with delight upon his marvelous career. In the first revolutionary movement of Texas against Mexican rule, he began to be leader, and was soon commander-in-chief of the Texan army, and in the new Republic he was reëlected to that office. The dauntless man confronted Santa Anna and his force of 5,000 men with a handful of Texans—783 all told, undisciplined volunteers, ignorant of war. But he had that rare personal magnetism, which is equal to a reserve of armed battalions, in giving men confidence and inciting them to splendid deeds. Out of 1,600 regular Mexican soldiers, 600 were killed, and Santa Anna, disguised as a common soldier, was captured. Then Houston showed his magnanimous heart; for, after rebuking him for the massacres of Goliad and the Alamo, he protected him from the vengeance of the enraged Texans. A treaty made with the captive President resulted in the independence of Texas. When, after securing this to the State of his adoption, Houston was made President of Texas, he again showed his wonderful clemency—which I cannot help believing was early fostered and enhanced by his labors in behalf of the wronged Cherokees—in pardoning Santa Anna, and appointing his political rivals to offices of trust. If Mr. Lincoln gave every energy to promoting the perpetual annexation of California, by tethering that State to our Republic with an iron lariat crossing the continent, how quickly he would have seen, had he then been in office, what infinite peril we were in of losing that rich portion of our country.

The ambition of the soldier and conqueror was tempered by the most genuine patriotism, for Sam Houston used his whole influence to annex Texas to the Union, and the people in gratitude sent him to Washington as one of their first Senators. As President he had overcome immense difficulties, carried on Indian wars, cleared off an enormous debt, established trade with Mexico, made successful Indian treaties, and steadily stood at the helm, while the State was undergoing all sorts of upheavals. Finally he was made Governor of the State, and opposed secession, even resigning his office rather than take the oath required by the convention that assembled to separate Texas from the Union. Then, poor old man, he died before he was permitted to see the promised land, as the war was still in progress. His name is perpetuated in the town called for him, which, as the centre of large railroad interests, and as a leader in the march of improvement in that rapidly progressing State, will be a lasting monument to a great man who did so much to bring out of chaos a vast extent of our productive land, sure to become one of the richest of the luxuriant Southern States.

At Galveston we were detained by the non-arrival of the steamer in which we were to go to New Orleans. With a happy-go-lucky party like ours, it mattered little; no important interests were at stake, no business appointments awaiting us. We strolled the town over, and commented, as if we owned it, on the insecurity of its foundations. Indeed, for years after, we were surprised, on taking up the morning paper, not to find that Galveston had dropped down into China. The spongy soil is so porous that the water, on which rests the thin layer of earth, appears as soon as a shallow excavation is attempted. Of course there are no wells, and the ungainly cistern rises above the roof at the rear of the house. The hawkers of water through the town amused us vastly, especially as we were not obliged to pay a dollar a gallon, except as it swelled our hotel-bill. I remember how we all delighted in the oleanders that grew as shade-trees, whose white and red blossoms were charming. To the General, the best part of all our detention was the shell drive along the ocean. The island on which Galveston has its insecure footing is twenty-eight miles long, and the white, firm beach, glistening with the pulverized shells extending all the distance, was a delight to us as we spent hours out there on the shore.

It must surely have been this white and sparkling thread bordering the island, that drew the ships of the pirate Lafitte to moor in the harbor early in 1800. The rose-pink of the oleander, the blue of the sky, the luminous beach, with the long, ultramarine waves sweeping in over the shore, were fascinating; but on our return to the town, all the desire to remain was taken away by the tale of the citizens, of the frequent rising of the ocean, the submerging of certain portions, and the evidence they gave that the earth beneath them was honeycombed by the action of the water.

We paid little heed at first to the boat on which we embarked. It was a captured blockade-runner, built up with two stories of cabins and staterooms for passengers. In its original condition, the crew and passengers, as well as the freight, were down in the hull. The steamer was crowded. Our staterooms were tiny, and though they were on the upper deck, the odor of bilge water and the untidiness of the boat made us uncomfortable from the first. The day was sunny and clear as we departed, and we had hardly left the harbor before we struck a norther. Such a hurricane as it was at sea! We had thought ourselves versed in all the wind could do on land; but a norther in that maelstrom of a Gulf, makes a land storm mild in comparison. The Gulf of Mexico is almost always a tempest in a tea-pot. The waves seem to lash themselves from shore to shore, and after speeding with tornado fleetness toward the borders of Mexico, back they rush to the Florida peninsula. No one can be out in one of these tempests, without wondering why that thin jet of land which composes Florida has not long ago been swept out of existence. How many of our troops have suffered from the fury of that ungovernable Gulf, in the transit from New Orleans to Matamoras or Galveston! And officers have spoken, over and over again, of the sufferings of the cavalry horses, condemned to the hold of a Government transport. Ships have gone down there with soldiers and officers who have encountered, over and over again, the perils of battle. Transports have only been saved from being engulfed in those rapacious waves by unloading the ship of hundreds of horses; and to cavalrymen the throwing overboard of noble animals that have been untiring in years of campaigning, and by their fleetness and pluck have saved the lives of their masters, is like human sacrifice. Officers and soldiers alike bewail the loss, and for years after speak of it with sorrow.

Though the wind seems to blow in a circle much of the time on the Gulf, we found it dead against us as we proceeded. The captain was a resolute man, and would not turn back, though the ship was ill prepared to encounter such a gale. We labored slowly though the constantly increasing tempest, and the last glimpse of daylight lighted a sea that was lashed to white foam about us. At home, when the sun sets the wind abates; but one must look for an entire

change of programme where the norther reigns. There was
no use in remaining up, so I sought to forget my terror in
sleep, and crept onto one of the little shelves allotted to us.
The creaking and groaning of the ship's timbers filled me
with alarm, and I could not help calling up to my husband
to ask if it did not seem to him that all the new portion of
the steamer would be swept off into the sea. Though I was
comforted by assurances of its impossibility, I wished with all
my heart we were down in the hold. Sleep, my almost
never-failing friend, came to calm me, and I dreamed of the
strange days of the blockade-runner, when doubtless other
women's hearts were pounding against their ribs with more
alarming terrors than those that agitated me. For we well
knew what risks Confederate women took to join their husbands, in the stormy days on sea as well as on land.

In the night I was awakened suddenly by a fearful crash,
the quick veering of the boat, and her violent rolling from
side to side. At the same instant, the overturning of the
water-pitcher deluged me in my narrow berth. My husband,
hearing my cry of terror, descended from his berth and was
beside me in a moment. No one comprehended what had
happened. The crashing of timber, and the creaking, grind-
ing sounds rose above the storm. The machinery was stopped,
and we plunged back and forth in the trough of the sea, each
time seeming to go down deeper and deeper, until there appeared to be no doubt that the ship would be eventually engulfed. There seemed to be no question, as the breaking of
massive beams went on, that we were going to pieces. The
ship made a brave fight with the elements, and seemed to
writhe and struggle like something human.

In the midst of this, the shouts of the sailors, the trumpet
of the captain giving orders, went on, and was followed by
the creaking of chains, the strain of the cordage, and the mad
thrashing to and fro of the canvas, which we supposed had
been torn from the spars. Instant disorder took possession
of the cabin. Everything movable was in motion. The
trunks, which the crowded condition of the hold had com-

pelled us to put in the upper end of the cabin, slid down the
carpet, banging from side to side. The furniture broke from
its fastenings, and slipped to and fro; the smashing of lamps
in our cabin was followed by the crash of crockery in the adjoining dining-room; while above all these sounds rose the
cries and wails of the women. Some, kneeling in their
night-clothes, prayed loudly, while others sank in heaps on
the floor, moaning and weeping in their helpless condition.
The calls of frantic women, asking for some one to go and
find if we were going down, were unanswered by the terrified
men. Meanwhile my husband, having implored me to remain
in one spot, and not attempt to follow him, hastily threw on
his clothes and left me, begging that I would remember,
while he was absent, that the captain's wife and child were
with us, and if a man ever was nerved to do his best, that
brave husband and father would do so to-night.

It seemed an eternity to wait. I was obliged to cling to
the door to be kept from being dashed across the cabin.
While I wept and shivered, and endured double agony, knowing into what peril my husband had by that time struggled,
I felt warm, soft arms about me, and our faithful Eliza was
crooning over me, begging me to be comforted, that she was
there holding me. Awakened at the end of the cabin, where
she slept on a sofa, she thought of nothing but making her
way through the demolished furniture, to take me in her
protecting arms. Every one who knows the negro character
is aware what their terrors are at sea. How, then, can I recall the noble forgetfulness of self of that faithful soul, without tears of gratitude as fresh as those that flowed on her
tender breast when she held me? There was not a vestige
of the heroic about me. I simply cowered in a corner, and
let Eliza shelter me. Besides, I felt that I had a kind of
right to yield to selfish fright, for it was my husband, of all
the men on shipboard, who had climbed laboriously to the
deck to do what he could for our safety, and calm the agitated women below.

Some of the noble Southern women proved how deep was

their natural goodness of heart; for the very ones who had coldly looked me over and shrunk from a hated Yankee when we met the day before, crept slowly up to calm my terrors about my husband, and instruct Eliza what to do for me. At last—and oh, how interminable the time had seemed!—the General opened the cabin door, and struggled along to the weeping women. They all plied him with questions, and he was able to calm them, so the wailing and praying subsided somewhat. When he climbed up the companionway, the waves were dashing over the entire deck, and he was compelled to creep on his hands and knees, clinging to ropes and spars as best he could, till he reached the pilot-house. Only his superb strength kept him from being swept overboard. Every inch of his progress was a deadly peril. He found the calm captain willing to explain, and paid the tribute that one brave man gives another in moments of peril. The norther had broken in the wheel-house, and disabled the machinery, so that, but for the sails, which we who were below had heard raised, we must have drifted and tossed to shipwreck. If he could make any progress, we were comparatively safe, but with such a hurricane all was uncertain. This part of the captain's statement the General suppressed. We women were told, after the fashion of men who desire to comfort and calm our sex, only a portion of the truth.

The motion of the boat, as it rolled from side to side, made every one succumb except Eliza and me. The General, completely subdued and intensely wretched physically, crept into his berth, and though he was so miserable, I remember, toward morning, a faint thrust of ridicule at our adjoining neighbors, the Greenes, who were suffering also the tortures of seasickness. A sarcastic query as to the stability of their stomachs called forth a retort that he had better look to his own. Eliza held me untiringly, and though the terror of uncertainty had subsided somewhat, I could not get on without an assurance of our safety from that upper berth. My husband, in his helplessness, and abandoned as he was to physical misery, could scarcely turn to speak more than a word or two at a time, and even then Eliza would tell him, "Ginnel, you jest 'tend to your own self, and I'll 'tend to Miss Libbie."

It is difficult to explain what a shock it is to find one who never succumbs, entirely subjugated by suffering; all support seems to be removed. In all our vicissitudes, I had never before seen the General go under for an instant. He replied that he was intensely sorry for me; but such deadly nausea made him indifferent to life, and for his part he cared not whether he went up or down.

So the long night wore on. I thought no dawn ever seemed so grateful. The waves were mountains high, and we still plunged into what appeared to be solid banks of green, glittering crystal, only to drop down into seemingly hopeless gulfs. But daylight diminishes all terrors, and there was hope with the coming of light. A few crept out, and some even took courage for breakfast. The feeble notes disappeared from my husband's voice, and he began to cheer me up. Then he crept to our witty Mrs. Greene (the dear Nettie of our home days), to send more sly thrusts in her stateroom, regarding his opinion of one who yielded to seasickness; so she was badgered into making an appearance. While all were contributing experiences of the awful night, and commenting on their terrors, we were amazed to see the door of a stateroom open, and a German family walk out unconcernedly from what we all night supposed was an unoccupied room. The parents and three children showed wide-eyed and wide-mouthed wonder, when they heard of the night. Through all the din and danger they had peacefully slept, and doubtless would have gone down, had we been shipwrecked, unconscious in their lethargy that death had come to them.

Then the white, exhausted faces of our officers, who had slept in the other cabin, began to appear. Our father Custer came tottering in, and made his son shout out with merriment, even in the midst of all the wretched surroundings, when he laconically said to his boy, that " next time I follow you to Texas, it will be when this pond is bridged over."

Two of the officers had a stateroom next the pilot-house, and begged the General to bring me up there. My husband, feeling so deeply the terrible night of terror and entire wakefulness for me, picked me up, and carried me to the upper deck, where I was laid in the berth, and restored to some sort of calm by an opportune glass of champagne. The wine seemed to do my husband as much good as it did me, though he did not taste it; all vestige of his prostration of the preceding night disappeared, and no one escaped his comical recapitulation of how they conducted themselves when we were threatened with such peril. My terrors of the sea were too deep-rooted to be set aside, and even after we had left the hated Gulf, and were safely moving up the Mississippi to New Orleans, I felt no security. Nothing but the actual planting of our feet on *terra firma* restored my equanimity. Among the petitions of the Litany asking our Heavenly Father to protect us, none since that Gulf storm has ever been emphasized to me as the prayer for preservation from "perils by land and by sea."

New Orleans was again a pleasure to us, and this time we knew just where to go for recreation or for our dinner. Nearly a year in Texas had prepared us for gastronomic feats, and though the General was by no means a *bon-vivant*, any one so susceptible to surroundings as he would be tempted by the dainty serving of a French dinner. Our party had dined too often with Duke Humphrey in the pine forests of Louisiana and Texas, not to enjoy every delicacy served. All through the year it had been the custom to refer to the luxuries of the French market, and now, with our purses a little fuller than when we were on our way into Texas, we had some royal times—that is, for poor folks.

We took a steamer for Cairo, and though the novelty of river travel was over, it continued to be most enjoyable. And still the staff found the dinner-hour an event, as they were making up for our limited bill of fare the year past. A very good string band "charmed the savage" while he dined. It was the custom, now obsolete, to march the white coated

and aproned waiters in file from kitchen to dining-room, each
carrying aloft some feat of the cook, and as we had a table
to ourselves, there was no lack of witty comments on this
military serving of our food, and smacking of lips over edibles
we had almost forgotten in our year of semi-civilization.
The negroes were in a state of perpetual guffaws over the remarks made, *sotto voce*, by our merry table, and they soon
grew to be skillful confederates in all the pranks practiced on
our father Custer. For instance, he slowly read over the bill of
fare, or his sons read it, and he chose the viands as they were
repeated to him. Broiled ham on coals seemed to attract his
old-fashioned taste. Then my husband said, " Of course, of
course; what a good selection!" and gave the order, accompanied by a significant wink to the waiter. Presently our
parent, feeling an unnatural warmth near his ear, looked
around to find his order filled literally, and the ham sizzling
on red coals. He naturally did not know what to do with
the dish, fearing to set the boat on fire, and his sons were
preternaturally absorbed in talking with some one at the end
of the table, while the waiter slid back to the kitchen to have
his laugh out.

Our father Custer was of the most intensely argumentative
nature. He was the strongest sort of politician; he is now,
and grows excited and belligerent over his party affairs at
nearly eighty, as if he were a lad. He is beloved at home in
Monroe, but it is considered too good fun not to fling little
sneers at his candidate or party, just to witness the rapidity
with which the old gentleman plunges into a defense. Michigan's present Secretary of State, the Hon. Harry Conant, my
husband's, and now my father's, faithful friend, early took
his cue from the General, and loses no opportunity now to
get up a wordy war with our venerable Democrat, solely to
hear the defense. And then, too, our father Custer considers
it time well spent to " labor with that young man " over the
error he considers he has made in the choice of politics. As
the old gentleman drives or rides his son's war-horse, Dandy,
through the town, his progress is slow, for some voice is cer-

tain to be raised from the sidewalk calling out, " Well, father Custer, to-day's paper shows your side well whipped," or a like challenge to argument. Dandy is drawn up at once, and the flies can nip his sides at will, so far as his usually careful master is conscious of him, as he cannot proceed until the one who has good-naturedly agitated him has been struggled over, to convince him of the error of his belief.

I was driving with him in Monroe not long since, and as the train was passing through the town, Dandy was driven up to the cars. I expostulated, asking if he intended him to climb over or creep under; but he persisted, only explaining that he wished me to see how gentle Dandy could be. Suddenly the conductor swung himself from the platform, and called out some bantering words about politics. Our father was then for driving Dandy directly into the train. He fairly yelled some sort of imputation upon the other party, and then kept on talking, gesticulating with his whip and shaking it at the conductor, who laughed immoderately as he was being carried out of sight. I asked what was the matter— did he have any grudge or hatred for the man ? " Oh, no, daughter, he's a good enough fellow, only he's an onery scamp of a Republican."

His sons never lost a chance to enter into discussion with him. I have known the General to "bone up," as his West Point phrase expressed it, on the smallest details of some question at issue in the Republican party, for no other reason than to incite his parent to a defense. The discussion was so earnest, that even I would be deceived into thinking it something my husband was all on fire about. But the older man was never rasped or badgered into anger. He worked and struggled with his boy, and mourned that he should have a son who had so far strayed from the truth as he understood it. The General argued as vehemently as his father, and never undeceived him for days, but simply let the old gentleman think how misguided he really was. It served to pass many an hour of slow travel up the river. Tom connived with the General to deprive their father temporarily of his dinner. When the plate was well prepared, as was the old-time custom, the potato and vegetables seasoned, the meat cut, it was the signal for my husband to hurl a bomb of inflammable information at the whitening hairs of his parent. The old man would rather argue than eat, and, laying down his knife and fork, he fell to the discussion as eagerly as if he had not been hungry. As the argument grew energetic and more absorbing, Tom slipped away the father's plate, ate all the nicely prepared food, and returned it empty to its place. Then the General tapered off his aggravating threats, and said, "Well, come, come, come, father, why don't you eat your dinner?" Father Custer's blank face at the sight of the empty plate was a mirth-provoking sight to his offspring, and they took good care to tip the waiter and order a warm dinner for the still arguing man. In a quaint letter, a portion of which I give below, father Custer tells how, early in life, he began to teach his boys politics.

" TECUMSEH, Mich., Feb. 3, 1887.

"MY DEAR DAUGHTER ELIZABETH: I received your letter, requesting me to tell you something of our trip up the Mississippi with my dear boys, Autie and Tommy. Well, as I was always a boy with my boys, I will try and tell you of some of our jokes and tricks on each other. I want to tell you also of a little incident when Autie was about four years old. He had to have a tooth drawn, and he was very much afraid of blood. When I took him to the doctor to have the tooth pulled, it was in the night, and I told him if it bled well it would get well right away, and he must be a good soldier. When he got to the doctor he took his seat, and the pulling began. The forceps slipped off, and he had to make a second trial. He pulled it out, and Autie never even scrunched. Going home, I led him by the arm. He jumped and skipped, and said, ' Father, you and me can whip all the Whigs in Michigan.' I thought that was saying a good deal, but I did not contradict him.

" When we were in Texas, I was at Autie's headquarters one day, and something came up, I've forgotten what it was, but I said I would bet that it was not so, and he said, ' What will you

bet ?' I said, 'I'll bet my trunk.' I have forgotten the amount
he put up against it, but according to the rule of betting he won
my trunk.   I thought that was the end of it, as I took it just as a
joke, and I remained there with him for some time.   To my great
astonishment, here came an orderly with the trunk on his shoulder, and set it down before Autie.   Well, I hardly knew what to
think.   I hadn't been there long, and didn't know camp ways very
well.   I had always understood that the soldiers were a pretty
rough set of customers, and I wanted to know how to try and
take care of myself, so I thought I would go up to my tent and
see what had become of my goods and chattels.   When I got
there, all my things were on my bed.   Tom had taken them out,
and he had not been very particular in getting them out, so they
were scattered helter-skelter, for I suppose he was hurried and
thought I would catch him at it.   I began to think that I would
have to hunt quarters in some other direction.

  "The next trick Autie played me was on account of his knowing that I was very anxious to see an alligator.   He was out with
his gun one day, and I heard him shoot, and when he came up to
his tent I asked him what he had been firing at.   He said, an alligator, so I started off to see the animal, and when I found it,
what do you think it was, but an old Government mule that had
died because it was played out!   Well, he had a hearty laugh
over that trick.

  "Then, my daughter, I was going over my mess bill and some
of my accounts with Tommy, and to my great astonishment I
found I was out a hundred dollars.   I could not see how I
could have made such a mistake, but I just kept this to myself.
I didn't say a word about it until Autie and Tom could not stand
it any longer, so Autie asked me one day about my money matters.   I told him I was out a hundred dollars, and I could not
understand it.   Then he just told me that Tommy had hooked
that sum from me while he was pretending to help me straighten
up.   I went for Tom, and got my stolen money back.

  "The next outrage on me was about the mess bill.   There was
you, Libbie, Autie, Tom, Colonel and Mrs. Greene, Major and
Mrs. Lyon, and we divided up the amount spent each month, and
all took turns running the mess.   Somehow or other, my bill was
pretty big when Autie and Tom had the mess.   I just rebelled

against such extravagance, and rather than suffer myself to be robbed, I threatened to go and mess with the wagon-master or some other honest soldier, who wouldn't cheat an old man. That tickled the boys; it was just what they were aiming at. I wouldn't pay, so what do you think Tommy did, but borrow the amount of me to buy supplies, and when settling time came for mess bills, they said we came out about even in money matters!

"And so they were all the time playing tricks on me, and it pleased them so much to get off a good joke; besides, they knew I was just as good a boy with them as they were.

"Your affectionate father,

"E. H. CUSTER."

CHAPTER X.

ALL the smaller schemes to tease our father Custer gave
way to a grand one, concocted in the busy brains of his boys,
to rob their parent. While the patriarch sat in the cabin,
reading aloud to himself—as is still his custom—what he considered the soul-convincing editorial columns of a favorite
paper, his progeny were in some sheltered corner of the
guards, plotting the discomfiture of their father. The plans
were well laid; but the General was obliged to give as much
time to it, in a way, as when projecting a raid, for he knew
he had to encounter a wily foe who was always on guard. The
father, early in their childhood, playing all sorts of tricks on
his boys, was on the alert whenever he was with them, to
parry a return thrust. I believe several attempts had been
made to take the old gentleman's money, but he was too
wary. They knew that he had sewed some bills in his waistcoat, and that his steamer ticket and other money were in
his purse. These he carefully placed under his pillow at
night. He continues in his letter: " Tommy and I had a
stateroom together, and on one night in particular, all the
folks had gone to bed in the cabin, and Tom was hurrying
me to go to bed. I was not sleepy, and did not want to turn
in, but he hung round so, that at last I did go to our stateroom. He took the upper berth. I put my vest under the
pillow, and was pulling off my boots, when I felt sure I saw
something going out over the transom. I looked under the
pillow, and my vest was gone. Then I waked Tommy, who
was snoring already. I told him both my purse and vest
were gone, and, as the saying is, I ' smelt the rat.' I opened

the door, and felt sure that Autie had arranged to snatch the
vest and purse when it was thrown out.   I ran out in the
cabin to his stateroom, but he had the start of me, and was
locked in.   I did not know for sure which was his room, so
I hit and I thundered at his door.   The people stuck their
heads out of their staterooms, and over the transom came a
glass of water.   So I, being rather wet, concluded I would
give it up till the next morning.   And what do you think
those scamps did ? Tom, though I gave it to him well, wouldn't
own up to a thing, and just said ' it was too bad such rob-
beries went on in a ship like that;' he was very sorry for me,
and alluded to the fact that the door being unlocked was
proof that the thief had a skeleton key, and all that nonsense.   Next morning Autie met me, and asked what on
earth I had been about the night before.   Such a fracas ! all
the people had come out to look up the matter, and there I
was pounding at a young lady's door, a friend of Libbie's,
and a girl I liked (indeed, I had taken quite a shine to her).
They made out—those shameless rogues, and very solemn
Autie was about it, too—that it was not a very fine thing for
my reputation to be pounding on a young lady's door late at
night, frightening her half to death, and obliging her to. defend herself with a pitcher of water.   She thought I had
been trying to break in her door, and I had better go to her
at once and apologize, as the whole party were being com-
promised by such scandal.   They failed there; for I knew I
was not at her door, and I knew who it was that threw the
water on me.   I was bound to try and get even with them,
so one morning, while they were all at breakfast, I went to
Autie's stateroom; Eliza was making up the bed.   I looked
for Autie's pocket-book, and found it under the pillow.   I
kept out of the way, and did not come near them for some
days; but they got desperate, and were determined to beat
me; so they made it up that Tommy was to get round me,
seize me by my arms at the back, and Autie go through my
pockets.   Well, they left me without a dime, and I had to
travel without paying, and those outlaws of boys got the clerk

to come to me and demand my ticket. I told him I had none, that I had been robbed. He said he was sorry, but I would have to pay over again, as some one who stole the ticket would be likely to use it. I tried to tell him I would make it right before I left the boat, but I hadn't a penny then. Well, daughter, I came out best at the last, for Autie, having really all the money, though he wouldn't own up to it, had all the bills to pay, and when I got home I was so much the gainer, for it did not cost me anything from the time I left the boat, either, till we got home, and then Autie gave me up my pocket-book with all the money, and we all had a good langh, while the boys told their mother of the pranks they had played on me."

My father's story ceases without doing justice to himself; for the cunning manner in which he circumvented those mischievous fellows I remember, and it seems my husband had given a full account to our friend the Hon. Harry Conant. He writes to me, what is very true, that " it seems one must know the quaint and brave old man, to appreciate how exquisitely funny the incident, as told by the General, really was. The third day after the robbery the General and Tom, thinking their father engaged at a remote part of the boat, while talking over their escapade incautiously exhibited the pocket-book. Suddenly the hand that held it was seized in the strong grasp of the wronged father, who, lustily calling for aid, assured the passengers that were thronging up (and, being strangers, knew nothing of the relationship of the parties) that this purse was his, and that he had been robbed by these two scoundrels, and if they would assist in securing their arrest and restoring the purse, he would prove all he said. Seeing the crowd hesitate, he called out: ' For shame ! stand there, cowards, will you, and see an old man robbed ?' It was enough. The spectators rushed in, and the General was outwitted by his artful parent and obliged to explain the situation. But the consequent restoration of his property did not give him half the satisfaction that it did to turn the tables on the boys. Though they never acknowl-

"STAND THERE, COWARDS, WILL YOU, AND SEE AN OLD
MAN ROBBED?"

edged this robbery to their father, none were so proud of his victory as Tom and the General."

I must not leave to the imagination of the literal-minded people who may chance to read, the suspicion that my husband and Tom ever made their father in the least unhappy by their incessant joking. He met them half-way always, and I never knew them lack in reverence for his snowy head. He was wont to speak of his Texas life with his sons as his happiest year for many preceding, and used to say that, were it not for our mother's constantly increasing feebleness, he would go out to them in Kansas.

When he reached his own ground, he made Tom and the General pay for some of their plots and plans to render him uncomfortable, by coming to the foot of the stairs and roaring out (and he had a stentorian voice) that they had better be getting up, as it was late. Father Custer thought 6 o'clock A. M. was late. His sons differed. As soon as they found the clamor was to continue, assisted by the dogs, which he had released from the stable, leaping up-stairs and springing on our beds in excitement, they went to the head of the stairs, and shouted out for everything that the traveler calls for in a hotel—hot water, boot-black, cocktail, barber, morning paper, and none of these being forthcoming in the simple home, they vociferated in what the outsider might have thought angry voices, "What sort of hotel do you keep, any way?"

Father Custer had an answer for every question, and only by talking so fast and loud that they talked him down did they get the better of him. Our mother Custer almost invariably sided with her boys. It made no sort of difference if father Custer stood alone, he never seemed to expect a champion. He did seem to think that she was carrying her views to an advanced point, when she endeavored to decline a new cur that he had introduced into the house, on the strength of its having "no pedigree." Her sons talked dog to her so much that one would be very apt to be educated up to the demand for an authenticated grandfather. Besides, the

"Towsers" and "Rovers" and all that sort of mongrels, to which she had patiently submitted in all the childhood of her boys and their boyish father, entitled her to some choice in after years.

At Cairo our partings began, for there some of the staff left us for their homes. We dreaded to give them up. Our harmonious life, and the friendships welded by the sharing of hardships and dangers, made us feel that it would be well if, having tested one another, we might go on in our future together. At Detroit the rest of our military family disbanded. How the General regretted them! The men, scarce more than boys even then, had responded to every call to charge in his Michigan brigade, and afterward in the Third Cavalry Division. Some, wounded almost to death, had been carried from his side on the battle-field, as he feared, forever, and had returned with wounds still unhealed. One of those valiant men has just died, suffering all these twenty-three years from his wound ; but in writing, speaking in public when he could, talking to those who surrounded him when he was too weak to do more, one name ran through his whole anguished life, one hero hallowed his days, and that was his "boy-general." Still another of our military family, invalided by his eleven months' confinement in Libby Prison, set his wan, white face toward the uncertain future before him, and began his bread-winning, his soul undaunted by his disabled body. Another—oh, what a brave boy he was!—took my husband's proffered aid, and received an appointment in the regular army. He carried always, does now, a shattered arm, torn by a bullet while he was riding beside General Custer in Virginia. That did not keep him from giving his splendid energy, his best and truest patriotism, to his country down in Texas even after the war, for he rode on long, exhausting campaigns after the Indians, his wound bleeding, his life sapped, his vitality slipping away with the pain that never left him day or night. That summer when we were at home in Monroe, the General sent for him to come to us, and get his share of the pretty girls that Tom

and the Michigan staff, who lived near us, were appropriat-
ing. The handsome, dark-haired fellow carried off the favors ; for though the others had been wounded—Tom even
then bearing the scarlet spot on his cheek where the bullet
had penetrated—the last comer won, for he still wore his arm
in a sling. The bewitching girls had before them the evidence of his valor, and into what a garden he stepped ! He
was a modest fellow, and would not demand too much pity,
but made light of his wound, as is the custom of soldiers,
who, dreading effeminacy, carry the matter too far, and ignore what ought not to be looked upon slightingly. One
day he appeared without his sling, and a careless girl, dancing with him, grasped the arm in the forgetfulness of glee.
The waves of torture that swept over the young hero's face,
the alarm and pity of the girl, the instant biting of the lip
and quick smile of the man, dreading more to grieve the
pretty creature by him than to endure the physical agony—
oh, how proud the General was of him, and I think he felt
badly that a soldier cannot yield to impulse, and enfold his
comrade in his arms, as is our woman's sweet privilege with
one another.

Proudly the General followed the career of those young
fellows who had been so near him in his war-life. Of all
those in whom he continued always to retain an interest,
keeping up in some instances a desultory correspondence,
the most amazing evolution was that of the provost-marshal
into a Methodist minister. Whether he was at heart a stern,
unrelenting character, is a question I doubted, for he never
could have developed into a clergyman. But he had the
strangest, most implacable face, when sent on his thankless
duty by his commanding officer. He it was who conducted
the ceremonies that one awful day in Louisiana, when the
execution and pardon took place. I remember the General's
amazement when he received the letter in which the announcement of the new life-work was made. It took us both
some time to realize how he would set about evangelizing.
It was difficult to imagine him leading any one to the throne

of grace, except at the point of the bayonet, with a military band playing the Dead March in Saul. I know how pleased my husband was, though, how proud and glad to know that a splendid, brave soldier had given his talents, his courage— and oh, what courage for a man of the world to come out in youth on the side of one mighty Captain !—and taken up the life of poverty, self-denial, and something else that the General also felt a deprivation, the roving life that deprives a Methodist minister of the blessings of a permanent home.

The delightful letters we used to get from our military family when any epoch occurred in their lives, like the choice of a profession or business (for most of them went back to civil life), their marriage, the birth of a son – all gave my husband genuine pleasure ; and when their sorrows came he turned to me to write the letter—a heart-letter, which was his in all but the manipulation of the pen. His personal influence he gave, time and time again, when it was needed in their lives, and, best of all in my eyes, had patience with those who had a larger sowing of the wild-oat crop, which is the agricultural feature in the early life of most men.

Since I seek to make my story of others, I take the privilege of speaking of a class of heroes that I now seldom hear mentioned, and over whom, in instances of my husband's personal friends, we have grieved together. It is to those who, like his young staff-officer, bear unhealed and painful wounds to their life's end that I wish to beg our people to give thought. We felt it rather a blessing, in one way, when a man was visibly maimed ; for if a leg or an arm is gone, the empty sleeve or the halting gait keeps his country from forgetting that he has braved everything to protect her. The men we sorrowed for were those who suffered silently ; and there are more, North and South, than anyone dreams of, scattered all over our now fair and prosperous land. Sometimes, after they die, it transpires that at the approach of every storm they have been obliged to stop work, enter into the seclusion of their rooms, and endure the racking, torturing pain, that began on the battle-field so long ago. If any-

one finds this out in their lifetime, it is usually by accident;
and when asked why they suffer without claiming the sympathy that does help us all, they sometimes reply that the
war is too far back to tax anyone's memory or sympathy now.
Oftener, they attempt to ignore what they endure, and
change the subject instantly. People would be surprised to
know how many in the community, whom they daily touch
in the jostle of life, are silent sufferers from wounds or incur-
able disease contracted during the war for the Union. The
monuments, tablets, memorials which are strewn with flowers
and bathed with grateful tears, have often tribute that should
be partly given to the double hero who bears on his bruised
and broken body the torture of daily sacrifice for his country.
People, even if they know, forget the look, the word of ac-
knowledgment, that is due the maimed patriot.

I recall the chagrin I felt on the Plains one day, when one
of our Seventh Cavalry officers, with whom we had long been
intimately associated—one whom our people called "Fresh
Smith," or "Smithie," for short—came to his wife to get
her to put on his coat. I said something in bantering tones
of his Plains life making him look on his wife as the Indian
looks upon the squaw, and tried to rouse her to rebellion.
There was a small blaze, a sudden scintillation from a pair of
feminine eyes, that warned me of wrath to come. The captain accepted my banter, threw himself into the saddle,
laughed back the advantage of this new order of things,
where a man had a combination, in his wife, of servant and
companion, and tore out of sight, leaving me to settle accounts with the flushed madame. She told me, what I never
knew, and perhaps might not even now, but for the outburst
of the moment, that in the war "Smithie" had received a
wound that shattered his shoulder, and though his arm was
narrowly saved from amputation, he never raised it again,
except a few inches. As for putting on his coat, it was an
impossibility.

One day in New York my husband and I were paying our
usual homage to the shop windows and to the beautiful

women we passed, when he suddenly seized my arm and said, "There's Kiddoo! Let's catch up with him." I was skipped over gutters, and sped over pavements, the General unconscious that such a gait is not the usual movement of the New Yorker, until we came up panting each side of a tall, fine-looking man, apparently a specimen of physical perfection. The look of longing that he gave us as we ran up, flushed and happy, startled me, and I could scarcely wait until we separated, to know the meaning. It was this: General Joseph B. Kiddoo, shot in the leg during the war, had still the open wound, from which he endured daily pain and nightly torture, for he got only fragmentary sleep. To heal the hurt was to end his life, the surgeons said. When at last I heard he had been given release and slept the blessed sleep, what word of sorrow could be framed?

In the case of another friend, with whom we were staying in Tennessee, from whom my husband and I extracted the information by dint of questions and sympathy, when, late one night, we sat about the open fire, and were warmed into confidence by its friendly glow, we found that no single night for the twelve years after the war had such a boon as uninterrupted sleep been known to him. A body racked by pain was paying daily its loyal, uncomplaining tribute to his country. Few were aware that he had unremitting suffering as his constant companion. I remember that my husband urged him to marry, and get some good out of life and from the sympathy that wells perpetually in a tender woman's heart. But he denied himself the blessing of such companionship, from unselfish motives, declaring he could not ask a woman to link her fate with such a broken life as his. When we left his fireside, my husband counted him a hero of such rare mettle that few in his experience could equal him, and years afterward, when we sometimes read his name in print, he said, "Poor ——! I wonder if there's any let-up for the brave fellow."

Our home-coming was a great pleasure to us and to our two families. My own father was proud of the General's administration of civil as well as military affairs in Texas, and enjoyed the congratulatory letter of Governor Hamilton deeply. The temptations to induce General Custer to leave the service and enter civil life began at once, and were many and varied. He had not been subjected to such allurements the year after the war, when the country was offering posts of honor to returned soldiers, but this summer of our return from Texas, all sorts of suggestions were made. Business propositions, with enticing pictures of great wealth, came to him. He never cared for money for money's sake. No one that does, ever lets it slip through his fingers as he did. Still, his heart was set upon plans for his mother and father, and for his brothers' future, and I can scarcely see now how a man of twenty-five could have turned his back upon such alluring schemes for wealth as were held out to him. It was at that time much more customary than now, even, to establish corporations with an officer's name at the head who was known to have come through the war with irreproachable honor, proved possibly as much by his being as poor when he came out of service as when he went in, as by his conduct in battle. The country was so unsettled by the four years of strife that it was like beginning all over again, when old companies were started anew. Confidence had to be struggled for, and names of prominent men as associate partners or presidents were sought for persistently.

Politics offered another form of temptation. The people demanded for their representatives the soldiers under whom they had served, preferring to follow the same leaders in the political field that had led them in battle. The old soldiers, and civilians also, talked openly of General Custer for Congressman or Governor. It was a summer of excitement and uncertainty. How could it be otherwise to a boy who, five brief years before, was a beardless youth with no apparent future before him? I was too much of a girl to realize what a summer it was—indeed, we had little chance, so fast did one proposition for our future follow upon the other. When the General was offered the appointment of foreign Minister,

I kept silence as best I could, but it was desperately hard work. Honors, according to old saws, " were empty," but in that hey-day time they looked very different to me. I was inwardly very proud, and if I concealed the fact because my husband expressed such horror of inflated people, it was only after violent effort.

Among the first propositions was one for the General to take temporary service with Mexico. This scheme found no favor with me. It meant more fighting and further danger for my husband, and anxiety and separation for me. Besides, Texas association with Mexicans made me think their soldiery treacherous and unreliable. But even in the midst of the suspense pending the decision I was not insensible to this new honor that was offered.

Carvajal, who was then at the head of the Juarez military government, offered the post of Adjutant-General of Mexico to General Custer. The money inducements were, to give twice the salary in gold that a major-general in our army receives. As his salary had come down from a major-general's pay of $8,000 to $2,000, this might have been a temptation surely. There was a stipulation that one or two thousand men should be raised in the United States, any debts assumed in organizing this force to be paid by the Mexican Liberal Government. Señor Romero, the Mexican Minister, did what he could to further the application of Carvajal, and General Grant wrote his approval of General Custer's acceptance, in a letter in which he speaks of my husband in unusually flattering terms, as one " who rendered such distinguished service as a cavalry officer during the war," adding, " There was no officer in that branch of the service who had the confidence of General Sheridan to a greater degree than General Custer, and there is no officer in whose judgment I have greater faith than in Sheridan's. Please understand, then, that I mean to endorse General Custer in a high degree."

The stagnation of peace was being felt by those who had lived a breathless four years at the front. However much they might rejoice that carnage had ceased and no more broken hearts need be dreaded, it was very hard to quiet themselves into a life of inaction.   No wonder our officers went to the Khedive for service ! no wonder this promise of active duty was an inviting prospect for my husband ! It took a long time for civilians, even, to tone themselves down to the jog-trot of peace.

Everything looked, at that time, as if there was success awaiting any soldier who was resolute enough to lead troops against one they considered an invader.   Nothing nerves a soldier's arm like the wrong felt at the presence of foreigners on their own ground, and the prospect of destruction of their homes.   Maximilian was then uncertain in his hold on the Government he had established, and, as it soon proved, it would have been what General Custer then thought comparatively an easy matter to drive out the usurper.   The question was settled by the Government's refusing to grant the year's leave for which application was made, and the General was too fond of his country to take any but temporary service in another.

This decision made me very grateful, and when there was no longer danger of further exposure of life, I was also thankful for the expressions of confidence and admiration of my husband's ability as a soldier that this contemplated move had drawn out.   I was willing my husband should accept any offer he had received except the last.   I was tempted to beg him to resign; for this meant peace of mind and a long, tranquil life for me.   It was my father's counsel alone that kept me from urging each new proposition to take up the life of a civilian.   He advised me to forget myself.   He knew well what a difficult task it was to school myself to endure the life on which I had entered so thoughtlessly as a girl.   I had never been thrown with army people, and knew nothing before my marriage of the separations and anxieties of military life.   Indeed, I was so young that it never occurred to me that people could become so attached to each other that it would be misery to be separated.   And now that this

divided existence loomed up before me, father did not blame
me for longing for any life that would ensure our being
together. He had a keen sense of humor, and could not
help reminding me occasionally, when I told him despair-
ingly that I could not, I simply *would* not, live a life where I
could not be always with my husband, of days before I knew
the General, when I declared to my parents, if ever I did
marry it would not be a dentist, as our opposite neighbor appeared never to leave the house. It seemed to me then that
the wife had a great deal to endure in the constant presence
of her husband.

My father, strict in his sense of duty, constantly appealed
to me to consider only my husband's interests, and forget my
own selfish desires. In an old letter written at that time, I
quoted to the General something that father had said to me:
" Why, daughter, I would rather have the honor which grows
out of the way in which the battle of Waynesboro was fought,
than to have the wealth of the Indies. Armstrong's battle
is better to hand down to posterity than wealth." He used
in those days to walk the floor and say to me, " My child,
put no obstacles in the way to the fulfillment of his destiny.
He chose his profession. He is a born soldier. There he
must abide."

In the midst of this indecision, when the General was
obliged to be in New York and Washington on business, my
father was taken ill. The one whom I so sorely needed in
all those ten years that followed, when I was often alone in
the midst of the dangers and anxieties and vicissitudes attending our life, stepped into heaven as quietly and peacefully as
if going into another room. His last words were to urge me
to do my duty as a soldier's wife. He again begged me to
ignore self, and remember that my husband had chosen the
profession of a soldier; in that life he had made a name, and
there, where he was so eminently fitted to succeed, he should
remain.

My father's counsel and his dying words had great weight
with me, and enabled me to fight against the selfishness that

was such a temptation. Very few women, even the most
ambitious for their husbands' future, but would have confessed, at the close of the war, that glory came with too great
sacrifices, and they would rather gather the husbands, lovers
and brothers into the shelter of the humblest of homes, than
endure the suspense and loneliness of war times. I am sure
that my father was right, for over and over again, in after
years, my husband met his brother officers who had resigned,
only to have poured into his ear regrets that they had left
the service. I have known him to come to me often, saying
he could not be too thankful that he had not gone into civil
life. He believed that a business man or a politician should
have discipline in youth for the life and varied experience
with all kinds of people, to make a successful career. Officers, from the very nature of their life, are prescribed in
their associates. They are isolated so much at extreme posts
that they know little or nothing of the life of citizens. After
resigning, they found themselves robbed of the companionship so dear to military people, unable, from want of early
training, to cope successfully with business men, and lacking,
from inexperience, the untiring, plodding spirit that is requisite to the success of a civilian. An officer rarely gives a
note—his promise is his bond. It is seldom violated. It
would be impossible for me, even in my twelve years' experience, to enumerate the times I have known, when long-
standing debts, for which there was not a scrap of written
proof, were paid without solicitation on the part of the friend
who was the creditor. One of our New York hotels furnishes
proof of how an officer's word is considered. A few years
since, Congress failed to make the usual yearly appropriation
for the pay of the army. A hotel that had been for many
years the resort of military people, immediately sent far and
wide to notify the army that no bills would be presented until
the next Congress had passed the appropriation. To satisfy
myself, I have inquired if they lost by this, and been assured
that they did not.

Men reared to consider their word equal to the most bind-

ing legal contract ever made, would naturally find it difficult
to realize, when entering civil life, that something else is
considered necessary. The wary take advantage of the credulity of a military man, and usually the first experience is
financial loss to an officer who has confidingly allowed a
debt to be contracted without all the restrictive legal arrangements with which citizens have found it necessary to surround
money transactions. And so the world goes. The capital
with which an officer enters into business is lost by too much
confidence in his brother man, and when he becomes richer
by experience, he is so poor in pocket he cannot venture into
competition with the trained and skilled business men among
whom he had entered so sanguinely.

Politics also have often proved disastrous to army officers.
Allured by promises, they have accepted office, and been allowed a brief success; but who can be more completely done
for than an office-holder whose party goes out of power ? The
born politician, one who has grown wary in the great game,
provides for the season of temporary retirement which the
superseding of his party necessitates. His antagonist calls it
"feathering his nest," but a free-handed and sanguine military man has done no "feathering," and it is simply pitiful
to see to what obscurity and absolute poverty they are brought.
The men whose chestnuts the ingenuous, unsuspecting man
has pulled out of the fire, now pass him by unnoticed. Such
an existence to a proud man makes him wish he had died on
the field of battle, before any act of his had brought chagrin.

All these things I have heard my husband say, when we
have encountered some heartbroken man; and he worked
for nothing harder than that they might be reinstated in the
service, or lifted out of their perplexities by occupation of
some sort. There was an officer, a classmate at West Point,
who, he felt with all his heart, did right in resigning. If he
had lived he would have written his tribute, and I venture to
take up his pen to say, in my inadequate way, what he would
have said so well, moved by the eloquence of deep feeling.

My husband believed in what old-fashioned people term

a "calling," and he himself had felt a call to be a soldier, when he could scarcely speak plain. It was not the usual early love of boys for adventure. We realize how natural it is for a lad to enjoy tales of hotly contested fields, and to glory over bloodshed. The boy in the Sunday-school, when asked what part of the Bible he best liked, said promptly, "The fightenest part!" and another, when his saintly teacher questioned him as to whom he first wished to see when he reached heaven, vociferated loudly, "Goliath!" But the love of a soldier's life was not the fleeting desire of the child, in my husband; it became the steady purpose of his youth, the happy realization of his early manhood. For this reason he sympathized with all who felt themselves drawn to a certain place in the world. He thoroughly believed in a boy (if it was not a pernicious choice) having his "bent." And so it happened, when it was our good fortune to be stationed with his classmate, Colonel Charles C. Parsons, at Leavenworth, that he gave a ready ear when his old West Point chum poured out his longings for a different sphere in life. He used to come to me after these sessions, when the Colonel went over and over again his reasons for resigning, and wonder how he could wish to do so, but he respected his friend's belief that he had another "calling" too thoroughly to oppose him. He thought the place of captain of a battery of artillery the most independent in the service. He is detached from his regiment, he reports only to the commanding officer of the post, he is left so long at one station that he can make permanent arrangements for comfort, and, except in times of war, the work is garrison and guard duty. Besides this, the pay of a captain of a battery is good, and he is not subject to constant moves, which tax the finances of a cavalry officer so severely. After enumerating these advantages, he ended by saying, "There's nothing to be done, though, for if Parsons thinks he ought to go into an uncertainty, and leave what is a surety for life, why, he ought to follow his convictions."

The next time we saw the Colonel, he was the rector of a

small mission church on the outskirts of Memphis. We were with the party of the Grand Duke Alexis when he went by steamer to New Orleans. General Sheridan had asked General Custer to go on a buffalo hunt with the Duke in the Territory of Wyoming, and he in turn urged the General to remain with him afterward, until he left the country. At Memphis, the city gave a ball, and my husband begged his old comrade to be present. It was the first time since his resignation that the Colonel and his beautiful wife had been in society. Their parish was poor, and they had only a small and uncertain salary. Colonel Parsons was not in the least daunted; he was as hopeful and as enthusiastic as such earnest people alone can be, as certain he was right as if his duty had been revealed to him as divine messages were to the prophets of old. The General was touched by the fearless manner in which he faced poverty and obscurity.

It would be necessary for one to know, by actual observation, what a position of authority, of independence, of assured and sufficient income, he left, to sink his individuality in this life that he consecrated to his Master. When he entered our room, before we went to the ballroom, he held up his gloved hands to us and said: "Custer, I wish you to realize into what extravagance you have plunged me. Why, old fellow, this is my first indulgence in such frivolities since I came down here." Mrs. Parsons was a marvel to us. The General had no words that he thought high enough praise for her sacrifice. Hers was for her husband, and not a complaint did she utter.

Here, again, I should have to take my citizen reader into garrison before I could make clear what it was that she gave up. The vision of that pretty woman, as I remember her at Leavenworth, is fresh in my mind. She danced and rode charmingly, and was gracious and free from the spiteful envy that sometimes comes when a garrison belle is so attractive that the gossips say she absorbs all the devotion. Colonel Parsons, not caring much for dancing, used to stand and watch with pride and complete confidence when the men gathered round his wife at our hops. There were usually more than twice as many men as women, and the card of a good dancer and a favorite was frequently filled before she left her own house for the dancing-room. I find myself still wondering how any pretty woman ever kept her mental poise when queening it at those Western posts. My husband, who never failed to be the first to notice the least sacrifice that a woman made for her husband, looked upon Mrs. Parsons with more and more surprise and admiration, as he contrasted the life in which we found her with her former fascinating existence.

The Colonel, after making his concession and coming to our ball, asked us in turn to be present at his church on the following Sunday, and gave the General a little cheap printed card, which he used to find his way to the suburbs of the city. Colonel Parsons told me, next day, that when he entered the reading-desk and looked down upon the dignified, reverent head of my husband, a remembrance of the last time he had seen him in the chapel at West Point came like a flash of lightning into his mind, and he almost had a convulsion, in endeavoring to suppress the gurgles of laughter that struggled for expression. For an instant he thought, with desperate fright, that he would drop down behind the desk and have it out, and only by the most powerful effort did he rally. It seems that a cadet in their corps had fiery red hair, and during the stupid chapel sermon Cadet Custer had run his fingers into the boy's hair, who was in front of him, pretending to get them into white heat, and then, taking them out, pounded them as on an anvil. It was a simple thing, and a trick dating many years back, but the drollery and quickness of action made it something a man could not recall with calmness.

Colonel Parsons and his wife are receiving the rewards that only Heaven can give to lives of self-sacrifice. Mrs. Parsons, after they came North to a parish, only lived a short time to enjoy the comfort of an Eastern home. When the yellow fever raged so in the Mississippi Valley, in 1878, and volunteers came forward with all the splendid generosity of this part of the world, Colonel Parsons did not wait a second call from his conscience to enter the fever-scourged Memphis, and there he ended a martyr life: not only ready to go because in his Master's service, but because the best of his life, and one for whom he continually sorrowed, awaited him beyond the confines of eternity.

CHAPTER XI.

GENERAL CUSTER was the recipient of much kindness from the soldiers of his Michigan brigade while he remained in Michigan awaiting orders, and he went to several towns where his old comrades had prepared receptions for him. But when he returned from a reunion in Detroit to our saddened home, there was no grateful, proud father to listen to the accounts of the soldiers' enthusiasm. My husband missed his commendation, and his proud way of referring to his son. His own family were near us, and off he started, when he felt the absence of the noble parent who had so proudly followed his career, and, running through our stable to shorten the distance, danced up a lane through a back gate into his mother's garden, and thence into the midst of his father's noisy and happy household. His parents, the younger brother, Boston, sister Margaret, Colonel Tom, and often Eliza, made up the family, and the uproar that these boys and the elder boy, their father, made around the gentle mother and her daughters, was a marvel to me.

If the General went away to some soldiers' reunion, he tried on his return to give me a lucid account of the ceremonies, and how signally he failed in making a speech, of course, and his subterfuge for hiding his confusion and getting out of the scrape by proposing " Garry Owen " by the band, or three cheers for the old brigade. It was not that he had not enough to say: his heart was full of gratitude to his comrades, but the words came forth with such a rush, there was little chance of arriving at the meaning. I think nothing moved him in this coming together of his dear sol-

diers, like his pride at their naming babies after him. His
eyes danced with pleasure, when he told that they stopped
him in the street and held up a little George Armstrong Custer, and the shy wife was brought forward to be congratulated.
I dearly loved, when I chanced to be with him, to witness
their pride and hear their few words of praise.

Not long ago I was in a small town in Michigan, among
some of my husband's old soldiers. Our sister Margaret was
reciting for the benefit of the little church, and the veterans
asked for me afterward, and I shook hands with a long line
of bronzed heroes, now tillers of the soil. Their praise of
their "boy General" made my grateful tears flow, and many
of their eyes moistened as they held my hand and spoke of
war times. After all had filed by, they began to return one
by one and ask to bring their wives and children. One soldier, with already silvering head, said quaintly, "We have
often seen you riding around with our General in war days,"
and added, with a most flattering ignoring of time's treatment of me, "You look *just* the same, though you was a
young gal then; and now, tho' you followed your husband
and took your hardships with us, I want to show you an old
woman who was also a purty good soldier, for while I was
away at the front she run the farm." Such a welcome, such
honest tribute to his "old woman," recalled the times when
the General's old soldiers gathered about him, with unaffected words, and when I pitied him because he fidgeted
so, and bit his lips, and struggled to end what was the joy
of his life, for fear he would cry like a woman. Among
those who sought him out that summer was an officer who
had commanded a regiment of troops in the celebrated Michigan brigade—Colonel George Grey, a brave Irishman, with
as much enthusiasm in his friendships as in his fighting.
His wife and little son were introduced. The boy had very
light hair, and though taught to reverence and love the General by his gallant, impulsive father, the child had never realized until he saw him that his father's hero also had a yellow
head. Heretofore the boy had hated his hair, and implored

his mother to dye it dark.   But as soon as his interview with my husband was ended, he ran to his mother, and whispered in eager haste that she need not mind the dyeing now, he never would scold about his hair being light again, since he had seen that General Custer's was yellow.

As I look back and consider what a descent the major-generals of the war made, on returning to their lineal rank in the regular army after the surrender at Appomattox, I wonder how they took the new order of things so calmly, or that they so readily adapted themselves to the positions they had filled before the firing on Sumter in 1861.   General Custer held his commission as brevet major-general for nearly a year after the close of hostilities, and until relieved in Texas.   He did not go at once to his regiment, the Fifth Cavalry, and take up the command of sixty men in place of thousands, as other officers of the regular army were obliged to do, but was placed on waiting orders, and recommended to the lieuten-ant-colonelcy of one of the new regiments of cavalry, for five new ones had been formed that summer, making ten in all. In the autumn, the appointment to the Seventh Cavalry came, with orders to go to Fort Garland.   One would have imag-ined, by the jubilant manner in which this official document was unfolded and read to me, that it was the inheritance of a principality.   My husband instantly began to go over the "good sides" of the question.   He was so given to dwelling on the high lights of any picture his imagination painted, that the background, which might mean hardships and dep-rivations, became indefinite in outline, and obscure enough in detail to please the most modern impressionists.   Out of our camp luggage a map was produced, and Fort Garland was discovered, after long prowling about with the first fin-ger, in the space given to the Rocky Mountains.   Then he launched into visions of what unspeakable pleasure he would have, fishing for mountain trout and hunting deer.   As I cared nothing for fishing, and was afraid of a gun, I don't recall my veins bounding as his did over the prospect; but the embryo fisherman and Nimrod was so sanguine over his

future, it would have been a stolid soul indeed that did not
begin to think Fort Garland a sort of earthly paradise.   The
sober colors in this vivid picture meant a small, obscure post,
then several hundred miles from any railroad, not much more
than a handful of men to command, the most complete isolation, and no prospect of an active campaign, as it was far
from the range of the warlike Indians.   But Fort Garland
soon faded from our view, in the excitement and interest
over Fort Riley, as soon as our orders were changed to that
post.   We had no difficulty in finding it on the map, as it
was comparatively an old post, and the Kansas Pacific Railroad was within ten miles of the Government reservation.

We ascertained, by inquiry, that it was better to buy the
necessary household articles at Leavenworth, than to attempt
to carry along even a simple outfit from the East.   My attention had been so concentrated on the war, that I found the
map of Virginia had heretofore comprised the only important part of the United States to me, and it was difficult to
realize that Kansas had a city of 25,000 inhabitants, with
several daily papers.   Still, I was quite willing to trust to
Leavenworth for the purchase of household furniture, as it
seemed to me, what afterward proved true, that housekeeping in garrison quarters was a sort of camping out after all,
with one foot in a house and another in position to put into
the stirrup and spin " over the hills and far away."   We
packed the few traps that had been used in camping in Virginia and Texas, but most of our attention was given to the
selection of a pretty girl, who, it was held by both of us,
would do more toward furnishing and beautifying our army
quarters than any amount of speechless bric-à-brac or silent
tapestry.   It was difficult to obtain what seemed the one
thing needful for our new army home.   In the first place, the
mothers rose *en masse* and formed themselves into an anti-
frontier combination.   They looked right into my eyes, with
harassed expression, and said, " Why, Libbie, they might
marry an officer! " ignoring the fact that the happiest girl
among them had undergone that awful fate, and still laughed

back a denial of its being the bitterest lot that can come to a woman.   Then I argued that perhaps their daughters might escape matrimony entirely, under the fearful circumstances which they shuddered over, even in contemplation, but that it was only fair that the girls should have a chance to see the "bravest and the tenderest," and, I mentally added, the "livest" men, for our town had been forsaken by most of the ambitious, energetic boys as soon as their school-days ended. The "beau season" was very brief, lasting only during their summer vacations, when they came from wide-awake Western towns to make love in sleepy Monroe.   One mother at last listened to my arguments, and said, "I do want Laura to see what men of the world are, and she shall go." Now, this lovely mother had been almost a second one to me in all my lonely vacations, after my own mother died.   She took me from the seminary, and gave me treats with her own children, and has influenced my whole life by her noble, large way of looking at the world.   But, then, she has been East a great deal, and in Washington in President Pierce's days, and realized that the vision of the outside world, seen only from our Monroe, was narrow.   The dear Laura surprised me by asking to have over night to consider, and I could not account for it, as she had been so radiant over the prospect of military life.   Alas! next morning the riddle was solved, when she whispered in my ear that there was a youth who had already taken into his hands the disposal of her future, and "he" objected.   So we lost her.

Monroe was then thought to have more pretty girls than any place of its size in the country.   In my first experience of the misery of being paragraphed, it was announced that General Custer had taken to himself a wife, in a town where ninety-nine marriageable girls were left.   The fame of the town had gone abroad, though, and the ninety-nine were not without opportunities.   Widowers came from afar, with avant couriers in the shape of letters describing their wealth, their scholarly attainments, and their position in the community.   The "boys" grown to men halted in their race for wealth long enough to rush home and propose. Often we were all under inspection, and though demure and seemingly unconscious, I remember the after-tea walks when a knot of girls went off to " lovers' lane " to exchange experiences about some stranger from afar, who had been brought around by a solicitous match-maker to view the landscape o'er, and I am afraid we had some sly little congratulations when he, having shown signs of the conquering hero, was finally sent on his way, to seek in other towns, filled with girls, " fresh woods and pastures new." I cannot account for the beauty of the women of Monroe; the mothers were the softest, serenest, smoothest-faced women, even when white-haired. It is true it was a very quiet life, going to bed with the chickens, and up early enough to see the dew on the lawns. There was very little care, to plant furrows in the cheeks and those tell-tale radiating lines about the eyes. Nearly everybody was above want, and few had enough of this world's goods to incite envy in the hearts of the neighbors, which does its share in a younger face. I sometimes think the vicinity of Lake Erie, and the moist air that blew over the marsh, kept the complexions fresh. I used to feel actually sorry for my husband, when we approached Monroe after coming from the campaigns. He often said: " Shall we not stop in Detroit a day or two, Libbie, till you get the tired look out of your face ? I dread going among the Monroe women and seeing them cast reproachful looks at me, when your sunburned face is introduced among their fair complexions. When you are tired in addition, they seem to think I am a wretch unhung, and say, ' Why, General! what *have* you done with Libbie's transparent skin ? ' I am afraid it is hopelessly dark and irredeemably thickened!" In vain I argued that it wouldn't be too thick to let them all see the happy light shine through, and if his affection survived my altered looks, I felt able to endure the wailing over what they thought I had lost. After all, it was very dear and kind of them to care, and my husband appreciated their solicitude, even when he was supposed to be in disgrace for having sub-

jected me to such disfigurement. Still, these mothers were
neither going to run the risk of the peach-bloom and cream
of their precious girls all running riot into one broad sunburn up to the roots of the hair, and this was another reason, in addition to the paramount one that "the girls *might*
marry into the army." The vagrant life, the inability to
keep household gods, giving up the privileges of the church
and missionary societies, the loss of the simple village gayety, the anxiety and suspense of a soldier's wife, might well
make the mothers opposed to the life, but this latter reason
did not enter into all their minds. Some thought of the
loaves and fishes. One said, in trying to persuade me that
it was better to break my engagement with the General,
"Why, girl, you can't be a poor man's wife, and, besides, he
might lose a leg!" I thought, even then, gay and seemingly thoughtless as I was, that a short life with poverty and a
wooden leg was better than the career suggested to me. I
hope the dear old lady is not blushing as she reads this, and
I remind her how she took me up into a high mountain and
pointed out a house that might be mine, with so many dozen
spoons, "solid," so many sheets and pillow-slips, closets filled with jars of preserved fruit, all of which I could not hope
to have in the life in which I chose to cast my lot, where
peaches ripened on no garden-wall and bank-accounts were
unknown.

When we were ready to set out for the West, in October,
1866, our caravan summed up something like this list:
My husband's three horses—Jack Rucker, the thoroughbred
mare he had bought in Texas, a blooded colt from Virginia
named Phil Sheridan—and my own horse, a fast pacer named Custis Lee, the delight of my eyes and the envy of the
General's staff while we were in Virginia and Texas; several
hounds given to the General by the planters with whom he
had hunted deer in Texas; a superb greyhound, his head
carried so loftily as he walked his lordly way among the other
dogs, that I thought he would have asked to carry his family-
tree on his brass collar, could he have spoken for his rights.

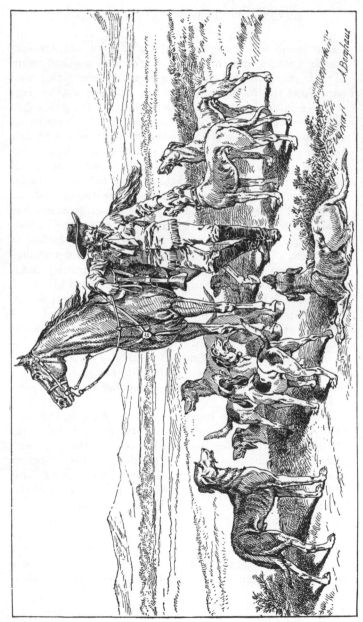

GENERAL CUSTER WITH HIS HORSE VIC, STAG HOUNDS AND DEER HOUNDS.

232

Last of all, some one had given us the ugliest white bull-dog I ever saw. But in time we came to think that the twist in his lumpy tail, the curve in his bow legs, the ambitious nose, which drew the upper lip above the heaviest of protruding jaws, were simply beauties, for the dog was so affectionate and loyal, that everything which at first seemed a draw-back leaned finally to virtue's side. He was well named "Turk," and a "set to" or so with Byron, the domineering greyhound established his rights, so that it only needed a deep growl and an uprising of the bristles on his back, to recall to the overbearing aristocrat some wholesome lessons given him when the acquaintance began. Turk was devoted to the colt Phil, and the intimacy of the two was comical; Phil repaid Turk's little playful nips at the legs by lifting him in his teeth as high as the feed-box, by the loose skin of his back. But nothing could get a whimper out of him, for he was the pluckiest of brutes. He curled himself up in Phil's stall when he slept, and in traveling was his close companion in the box car. If we took the dog to drive with us, he had to be in the buggy, as our time otherwise would have been constantly engaged in dragging him off from any dog that strutted around him and needed a lesson in humility. When Turk was returned to Phil, after any separation, they greeted each other in a most human way. Turk leaped around the colt, and in turn was rubbed and nosed about with speaking little snorts of welcome. When we came home to this ugly duckling, he usually made a spring and landed in my lap, as if he were the tiniest, silkiest little Skye in dogdom. He half closed his eyes, with that beatific expression peculiar to affectionate dogs, and did his little smile at my husband and me by raising what there was of his upper lip and showing his front teeth. All this with an ignoring of the other dogs and an air of exclusion, as if we three—his master, mistress, and himself—composed all there was of earth worth knowing.

We had two servants, one being Eliza, our faithful colored woman, who had been with us in Virginia and Texas, and

had come home with me to care for my father in his last illness. We had also a worthless colored boy, who had been
trained as a jockey in Texas and had returned with the
horses. What intellect he had was employed in devising
schemes to escape work. Eliza used her utmost persuasive
eloquence on him without effect, and failed equally with a
set of invectives that had been known heretofore to break
the most stubborn case of lethargy. My tender-hearted mother Custer screened him, for he had soon discovered her
amazing credulity, and had made out a story of abuses to
which he had been subjected that moved her to confide his
wrongs to me. Two years before, I too would have dropped
a tear over his history; but a life among horses had enlighten-
ed me somewhat. Every one knows that a negro will do almost anything to become a jockey. Their bitterest moment
is when they find that growing bone and muscle is making
avoirdupois and going to cut them off from all that makes
life worth living. To reduce their weight, so they can ride
at races, they are steamed, and parboiled if necessary. This
process our lazy servant described to our mother as having
been enforced on him as a torture and punishment, and such
a good story did he make out, that he did nothing but lie in
the sun and twang an old banjo all summer long, all owing
to mother's pity. We had to take him with us, to save her
from waiting on him and making reparation for what she
supposed had been a life of abuse before he came to us.

Last of all to describe in our party was Diana, the pretty
belle of Monroe. The excitement of anticipation gave added
brightness to her eyes, and the head, sunning over with a
hundred curls, danced and coquetted as she talked of our
future among the "brass buttons and epaulets."

My going out from home was not so hard as it had been,
for the dear father had gone home, saying in his last words,
"Daughter, continue to do as you have done; follow Armstrong everywhere." It had indeed been a temptation to
me to use all my influence to induce my husband to resign
and accept the places held out to him. I do not recollect

that ambition or a far look into his progress in the future
entered my mind.   I can only remember thinking with envy
of men surrounding us in civil life, who came home to their
wives, after every day's business.   Even now, I look upon a
laborer returning to his home at night with his tin dinner-
pail as a creature to be envied, and my imagination follows
the husband into his humble house.   The wife to whom he
returns may have lost much that ambition and success bring,
but she has secured for herself a lifetime of happy twilights,
when all she cares for is safe under her affectionate eyes.

Our father and mother Custer lived near us, and Sister
Margaret and the younger brother, "Bos," were then at
home and in school.   The parting with his mother, the only
sad hour to my blithe husband, tore his heart as it always
did, and he argued in vain with her, that, as he had come
home after five years of incessant battles, she might look for
his safe return again.   Each time seemed to be the last to
her, for she was so delicate she hardly expected to live to see
him again.

The summer had been one of such pleasure to her.   Her
beloved boy, dashing in and out in his restless manner, was
never too absorbed with whatever took up his active mind,
to be anything but gentle and thoughtful for her.   She found
our Eliza a mine of information, and just as willing as mother
herself to talk all day about the one topic in common—the
General and his war experiences.

Then the dogs and horses, and the stir and life produced
by the introduction of ourselves and our belongings into her
quiet existence, made her recall the old farm life when her
brood of children were all around her.   Brother Tom had
spent the summer skipping from flower to flower, tasting the
sweets of all the rosebud garden of girls in our pretty town.
I had already taken to myself a good deal of the mothering
of this wild boy, and began to worry, as is the custom of
mothers, over the advances of a venturesome woman who
was no longer young and playing for high stakes.   It was no
small matter to me, as I knew Tom would live with us always

if he could manage to do so, and my prospective sister-in-law
would be my nearest companion. Lad as he was, he escaped,
and preserved his heart in an unbroken condition during the
summer. Much to our regret, he was appointed to a lieu-
tenancy in a regiment stationed South, after he was mustered out of the volunteer service; but the General succeeded
in effecting his transfer to the Seventh Cavalry, and after a
short service in the South he joined us at Fort Riley that
year.

One of our Detroit friends invited us to go with a party of
pretty women, in a special car, to St. Louis; so we had a gay
send-off for our new home. I don't remember to have had
an anxiety as to the fnture; I was wholly given over to the
joy of realizing that the war was over, and, girl-like, now the
one great danger was passed, I felt as if all that sort of life
was forever ended. At any rate, the magnetic influence of
my husband's joyous temperament, which would not look on
the dark side, had such power over those around him that I
was impelled to look upon our future as he did. In St. Louis
we had a round of gayety. The great Fair was then at its
best, for every one was making haste to dispel the gloom
that our terrible war had cast over the land. There was not
a corner of the Fair-ground to which my husband did not
penetrate. He took me into all sorts of places to which our
pretty galaxy of belles, with their new conquests of St. Louis
beaux, had no interest in going—the stalls of the thoroughbred horses—when a chat with the jockeys was included; the
cattle, costing per head what, we whispered to each other,
would set us up in a handsome income for life and buy a
Blue-grass farm with blooded horses, etc., which was my husband's ideal home. And yet I do not remember that money
ever dwelt very long in our minds, we learned to have such a
royal time on so little.

There was something that always came before the Kentucky farm with its thoroughbreds. If ever he said, "If
I get rich, I'll tell you what I'll do," I knew as well before
he spoke just what was to follow—in all the twelve years he

never altered the first plan—"I'll buy a home for father and mother." They owned their home in Monroe then, but it was not good enough to please him ; nothing was good enough for his mother, but the dear woman, with her simple tastes, would have felt far from contented in the sort of home in which her son longed to place her.   All she asked was to gather her boys around her so that she could see them every day.

As we wandered round the Fair-grounds, side-shows with their monstrosities came into the General's programme, and the prize pigs were never neglected.   If we bent over the pens to see the huge things rolling in lazy contentment, my husband went back to his farm days, and explained what taught him to like swine, in which, I admit, I could not be especially interested.   His father had given each son a pig, with the promise exacted in return that they should be daily washed and combed.   When the General described the pink and white collection of pets that his father distributed among his sons, swine were no longer swine to me; they were "curled darlings," as he pictured them.   And now I recall, that long after he showed such true appreciation of his friend's stock on one of the Blue-grass farms in Kentucky where we visited, two pigs of royal birth, whose ancestors dated back many generations, were given to us, and we sent them home to our farmer brother to keep until we should possess a place of our own, which was one of the mild indulgences of our imagination, and which we hoped would be the diversion of our old age.   I think it rather strange that my husband looked so fearlessly into the future.   I hardly know how one so active could so calmly contemplate the days when his steps would be slow.   We never passed on the street an old man with gray curls lying over his coat-collar, but the General slackened his steps to say in a whisper, "There, Libbie, that's me, forty years from now."   And if there happened to be John Anderson's obese old wife by him, toddling painfully along, red and out of breath, he teasingly added, "And that's what you would *like* to be."   It was a never-ending source of argument

that I would be much more successful in the way of looks if
I were not so slender; and as my husband, even when a lad,
liked women who were slenderly formed, he loved to torment
me, by pointing out to what awful proportions a woman
weighing what was to me a requisite number of pounds sometimes arrived in old age.

A tournament was given in the great amphitheatre of the
Fair building in St. Louis, which was simply delightful to us.
The horsemanship so pleased my husband that he longed to
bound down into the arena, take a horse, and tilt with their
long lances at the rings.   Some of the Confederate officers
rode for the prizes, and their knights' costume and good
horses were objects of momentary envy, as they recalled the
riding academy exercises at West Point.   Finally, the pretty
ceremony of crowning the Queen of Love and Beauty by the
successful knight ended a real gala day to us.   At night a
ball at the hotel gave us an opportunity to be introduced to
the beautiful woman, who sat on a temporary throne in the
dancing-hall, and we thought her well worth tilting lances
for, and that nothing could encourage good horsemanship
like giving as a prize the temporary possession of a pretty
girl.

While in St. Louis we heard Mr. Lawrence Barrett for the
first time.   He was of nearly the same age as my husband,
and after three years' soldiering in our war, as a captain in
the Twenty-eighth Massachusetts Infantry, had returned to
his profession, full of ambition and the sort of "go" that
called out instant recognition from the General.

Mr. Barrett, in recalling lately the first time he met General Custer, spoke of the embarrassing predicament in which
he was placed by the impetuous determination of one whom
from that hour he cherished as his warmest friend.   He was
playing "Rosedale," and my husband was charmed with his
rendering of the hero's part.   He recalled for years the delicate
manner with which the lover allows his wounded hand to be
bound, and the subtle cunning with which he keeps the fair
minister of his hurts winding and unwinding the bandages.

Then Mr. Barrett sang a song in the play, which the General hummed for years afterward. I remember his going pell-mell into the subject whenever we met, even when Mr. Barrett was justifiably glowing with pride over his success in the legitimate drama, and interrupting him to ask why he no longer played " Rosedale." The invariable answer that the play required extreme youth in the hero, had no sort of power to stop the continued demand for his favorite melodrama. After we had seen the play—it was then acted for the first time—the General begged me to wait in the lobby until he had sought out Mr. Barrett to thank him, and on our return from the theatre we lay in wait, knowing that he stopped at our hotel. As he was going quietly to his room—reserved even then, boy that he was, with not a trace of the impetuous, ardent lover he had so lately represented before the footlights—off raced the General up the stairs, two steps at a time, to capture him. He demurred, saying his rough traveling suit of gray was hardly presentable in a drawing-room, but the General persisted, saying, " The old lady told me I must seize you, and go you must, for I don't propose to return without fulfilling her orders." Mr. Barrett submitted, and was presented to our party, who had accompanied us on the special car to St. Louis. The gray clothes were forgotten in a moment, in the reception we gave him; but music came out from the dining-room, and all rose to go, as Mr. Barrett supposed, to our rooms. The General took a lady on his arm, I, at my husband's suggestion, put my hand on Mr. Barrett's arm, and before he had realized it, he was being marched into the brilliantly lighted ballroom, and bowing from force of capture before the dais on which sat the Queen of Love and Beauty.

All this delighted the General. Unconventional himself, he nothing heeded the chagrin of Mr. Barrett over his inappropriate garb, and chuckled like a schoolboy over his successful raid. I think Mr. Barrett was not released until he pleaded the necessity for time to work. He was then reading and studying far into the night, to make up for the lapse in his profession that his army life had caused. He was not so absorbed in his literary pursuits, however, that he did not take in the charm of those beautitul St. Louis girls, and we three, in many a jolly evening since, have gone back to the beauty of the bewitching belles, as they floated by us in that ballroom or paused to capture the new *Richmonds* on their already crowded field. Mr. Barrett even remembers that the Queen of Love and Beauty vouchsafed him the eighth of a dance—for her royal highness dispensed favors by piecemeal to the waiting throng about her throne.

Our roving life brought us in contact with actors frequently. If the General found that Mr. Barrett was to play in any accessible city, he hurried me into my traveling-gown, flung his own dress-coat and my best bonnet in a crumpled mass into a little trunk, and off we started in pursuit. It is hard to speak fittingly of the meeting of those two men. They joyed in each other as women do, and I tried not to look when they met or parted, while they gazed with tears into each other's eyes, and held hands like exuberant girls. Each kept track of the other's movements, through the papers, and rejoiced at every success, while Mr. Barrett, with the voice my husband thought perfect in intonation and expression, always called to him the moment they met, " Well, old fellow, hard at work making history, are you ? "

A few evenings since I chanced to see Mr. Barrett's dresser, the Irish " Garry," who had charge of his costumes in those days when the General used to haunt the dressing-room in the last winter we were together in New York. As *Cassius* he entered the room in armor, and found his " old man Custer " waiting for him. Garry tells me that my husband leaped toward the mailed and helmeted soldier, and gave him some rousing bangs on the corseleted chest, for they sparred like boys. Mr. Barrett, parrying the thrust, said, " Custer, old man, you ought to have one of these suits of armor for your work." " Ye gods, no ! " said the General, in mimic alarm; " with that glistening breast-plate as a target, every arrow would be directed at me. I'd rather go naked than in that ! "

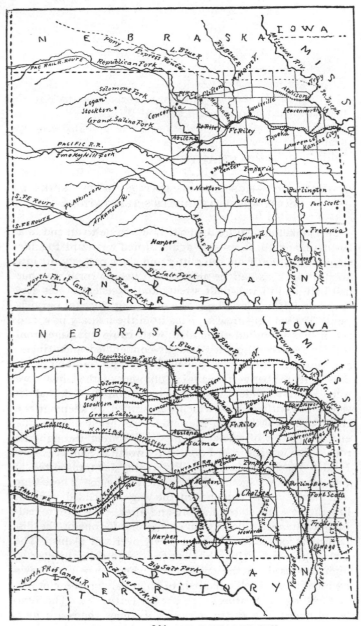

KANSAS IN 1866 AND KANSAS TO-DAY.

In 1866 there were three hundred miles of railroad; in 1886, six thousand one hundred and forty-four.

CHAPTER XII.

THE junketing and frolic at St. Louis came to an end in a few days, and our faces were again turned westward to a life about as different from the glitter and show of a gay city in a holiday week as can be imagined. Leavenworth was our first halt, and its well-built streets and excellent stores surprised us. It had long been the outfitting place for our officers. The soldiers drew supplies from the military post, and the officers furnished themselves with camp equipage from the city. Here also they bought condemned ambulances, and put them in order for traveling-carriages for their families. I remember getting a faint glimmer of the climate we were about to endure, by seeing a wagon floored, and its sides lined with canvas, which was stuffed to keep out the cold, while a little sheet-iron stove was firmly fixed at one end, with a bit of miniature pipe protruding through the roof. The journey from Fort Leavenworth to Santa Fé, New Mexico, then took six weeks. Everything was transported in the great army wagons called prairie-schooners. These were well named, as the two ends of the wagon inclined upward, like the bow and stern of a fore-and-after. It is hard to realize how strangely a long train of supplies for one of the distant posts looked, as it wound slowly over the plains. The blue wagon-beds, with white canvas covers rising up ever so high, disclosed, in the small circle where they were drawn together at the back, all kinds of material for the clothing and feeding of the army in the distant Territories. The number of mules to a wagon varies; sometimes there are four,

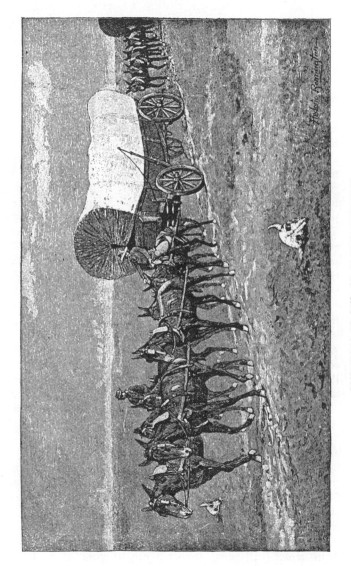

CONESTOGA WAGON, OR PRAIRIE-SCHOONER.

and again six. The driver rides the near-wheel mule. He holds in his hand a broad piece of leather, an inch and a half in width, which divides over the shoulders of the lead or pilot mule, and fastens to the bit on either side of his mouth. The leaders are widely separated. A small hickory stick, about five feet long, called the jockey-stick, not unlike a rake-handle, is stretched between a pilot and his mate. This has a little chain at either end, and is attached by a snap or hook to the bit of the other leader.

When the driver gives one pull on the heavy strap, the pilot mule veers to the left, and pulls his mate. Two quick, sudden jerks mean to the right, and he responds, and pushes his companion accordingly; and in this simple manner the ponderous vehicle and all the six animals are guided.   .   .   . The most spirited mules are selected from the train for leaders. They cannot be reached by the whip, and the driver must rely upon the emphasis he puts into his voice to incite them to effort. They know their names, and I have seen them respond to a call, even when not accompanied by the expletives that seem to be composed especially for this branch of charioteering. The driver of our mules naturally suppressed his invectives in my presence. The most profane soldier holds his tongue in a vise when he is in the presence of a woman, but he is sorely put to it to find a substitute for the only language he considers a mule will heed. I have seen our driver shake his head and move his jaws in an ominous manner, when the provoking leaders took a skittish leap on one side of the trail, or turned round and faced him with a protest against further progress. They were sometimes so afraid of buffalo, and always of Indians, they became rebellious to such a degree he was at his wits' end to get any further go out of them. It was in vain he called out, " You Bet, there !" "What are you about, Sal?" He plainly showed and said that he found "such 'ere tongue-lashing wouldn't work worth a rap with them vicious creeturs."

The driver, if he is not a stolid Mexican, takes much pride in his mules. By some unknown means, poor as he is, he possesses himself of fox or small coyote tails, which he fastens to their bridle, and the vagaries in the clipping of the poor beasts' tails, would set the fashion to a Paris hair-dresser. They are shaved a certain distance, and then a tuft is left, making a bushy ring. This is done twice, if Bet or Sal is vouchsafed an appendage long enough to admit of it; while the tuft on the end, though of little use to intimidate flies, is a marvel of mule-dudism. The coats of the beasts, so valued sometimes, shine like the fine hair of a good horse. Alas ! not when, in the final stages of a long march, the jaded, half-starved beasts dragged themselves over the trail. Driver and lead mules even, lose ambition under the scorching sun, and with the insufficient food and long water famines.

The old reliability of a mule-team is the off-wheeler. It is his leathery sides that can be most readily reached by the whip called a " black-snake," and when the descent is made into a stream with muddy bed, the cut is given to this faithful beast, and on his powerful muscles depends the wrench that jerks the old schooner out of a slough. The nigh or saddle mule does his part in such an emergency, but he soon reasons that, because he carries the driver, not much more is expected of him.

The General and I took great interest in the names given to the animals that pulled our traveling-wagon or hauled the supplies. As we rode by, the voice of the driver bringing out the name he had chosen, and sometimes affectionately, made us sure that the woman for whom the beast was christened was the sweetheart of the apparently prosaic teamster. I was avowedly romantic, and the General was equally so, though, after the fashion of men, he did not proclaim it. Our place at the head of the column was sometimes vacant, either because we were delayed for our luncheon, or because my husband remained behind to help the quartermaster or the head teamster get the train over a stream. It was then that we had the advantage of hearing the names conferred on the mules. They took in a wide range of female nomenclature, and we found it great fun to watch the family life of

one human being and his six beasts. My husband had the utmost respect for a mule's sense.   When I looked upon them
as dull, half-alive animals, he bade me watch how deceitful
were appearances, as they showed such cunning, and evinced
the wisdom of a quick-witted thoroughbred, when apparently they were unobserving, sleepy brutes.   It was the General
who made me notice the skill and rapidity with which a
group of six mules would straighten out what seemed to be a
hopeless tangle of chains and harness, into which they had
kicked themselves when there was a disturbance among them.
One crack of the whip from the driver who had tethered
them after a march, accompanied by a plain statement of his
opinion of such "fools," would send the whole collection
wide apart, and it was but a twinkling before they extricated
themselves from what I thought a hopeless mess. No chains
or straps were broken, and a meek, subdued look pervading
the group left not a trace of the active heels that a moment
before had filled the air.   " There," the General used to say,
" don't ever flatter yourself again that a mule hasn't sense.
He's got more wisdom than half the horses in the line."   It
took a good while to convince me, as a more logy-looking
animal can hardly be found than the army mule, which
never in his existence is expected to go off from a walk, or
to vary his life, from the day he is first harnessed until he
drops by the way, old or exhausted.

    At the time we were first on the Plains, many of the
teamsters were Mexicans, short, swarthy, dull, and hardly a
grade above the animal.   The only ambition of these creatures seemed to be to vie with one another as to who could
snap the huge " black-snake " the loudest.   They learned to
whisk the thong at the end around the ears of a shirking off
leader, and crack the lash with such an explosive sound that
I never got over jumping in my whole Plains life. I am sorry
to say my high-strung horse usually responded with a spring
that sent me into thin air anywhere between his ears and his
tail, with a good deal of uncertainty as to where I should alight.
I suspect it was an innocent little amusement of the drivers,

when occasionally we remained behind at nooning, and had to ride swiftly by the long train to reach the head of the column. The prairie-schooner disappeared with the advancing railroad ; but I am glad to see that General Meigs has perpetuated its memory, by causing this old means of transportation to be made one of the designs in the beautiful frieze carved around the outside of the Pension Office at Washington. Ungainly and cumbersome as these wagons were, they merit some such monument, as part of the history of the early days of frontier life in our country. We were in the West several years before the railroad was completed to Denver, and the overland trains became an every-day sight to us. Citizens used oxen a great deal for transportation, and there is no picture that represents the weariness and laggard progress of life like an ox-train bound for Santa Fé or Denver. The prairie-schooner might set out freshly painted, or perhaps washed in a creek, but it soon became gray with layer upon layer of alkali dust. The oxen—well, nothing save a snail can move more slowly, and the exhaustion of these beasts, after weeks of uninterrupted travel, was pitiful. Imagine, also, the unending vigil when the trains were insecurely guarded ; for in those days there was an immense unprotected frontier, and seemingly only a handful of cavalry. The regiments looked well on the roster, but there were in reality but few men. A regiment should number twelve hundred enlisted men ; but at no time, unless during the war, does the recruiting officer attempt to fill it to the maximum ; seventy men to a company is a large number. The desertions during the first years of the reorganization of the army after the war thinned the ranks constantly. Recruits could not be sent out fast enough to fill up the companies. The consequence was, that all those many hundred miles of trail where the Government undertook to protect citizens who carried supplies to settlements and the mines, as well as its own trains of material for building new posts, and commissary and quartermaster's stores for troops, were terribly exposed and very poorly protected.

"The Indians were, unfortunately, located on the great
highway of Western travel ; and commerce, not less than
emigration, demanded their removal." There are many
conflicting opinions as to the course pursued to clear the way ;
but I only wish to speak now of the impression the trains
made upon me, as we constantly saw the long, dusty, ex-
hausted-looking column wending its serpentine way over the
sun-baked earth. A group of cavalry, with their drooping
horses, rode in front and at the rear. The wagon-master was
usually the very quintessence of valor, It is true he formed
such a habit of shooting that he grew indiscriminate, and
should any of the lawless desperadoes whom he hired as
teamsters or trainmen ruffle his blood, kept up to boiling-
heat by suspense, physical exposure, and exasperating employees, he knew no way of settling troubles except the
effectual quietus that a bullet secures. I well remember my
husband and Tom, who dearly loved to raise my indignation,
and create signs of horror and detestation at their tales,
walking me down to the Government train to see a wagon-
master who had shot five men. He had emigrated from the
spot where he bade fair to establish a private cemetery with
his victims. No one needed a reason for his sudden appearance after the number of his slain was known. And yet no
questions were put as to his past. He made a capital wagon-
master ; he was obedient to his superiors, faithful, and on
time every morning, and the prestige of his past record answered so well with the citizen employees, that his pistol remained unused in the holster.

It seemed to be expected that the train-master would be a
villain. Whatever was their record as to the manner of ar-
ranging private disputes, a braver class of men never followed
a trail, and some of them were far superior to their chance
lot. Their tender care of women who crossed in these slow-
moving ox-trains, to join their husbands, ought to be com-
memorated. I have somewhere read one of their remarks
when a girl, going to her mother, had been secreted in a
private wagon and there was no knowledge of her presence

until the Indians were discovered to be near. "Tain't no time to be teamin' women folks over the trail with sech a fearsom sperit for Injuns as I be." He, like some of the bravest men I have known, spoke of himself as timid, while he knew no fear. It certainly unnerved the most valiant man when Indians were lurking near, to realize the fate that hung over women entrusted to their care. In a later portion of my story occurs an instance of an officer hiding the woman whose husband had asked him to take her into the States, even before firing a shot at the adversary, as he knew with what redoubled ferocity the savage would fight, at sight of the white face of a woman. It makes the heart beat, even to look at a picture of the old mode of traversing the highway of Western travel. The sight of the pictured train, seemingly so peacefully lumbering on its sleepy way, the scarcely revolving wheels, creaking out a protest against even that effort, recalls the agony, the suspense, the horror with which every inch of that long route has been made. The heaps of stones by the wayside, or the buffalo bones, collected to mark the spot where some man fell from an Indian arrow, are now disappearing. The hurricanes beating upon the hastily prepared memorials have scattered the bleached bones of the bison, and rolled into the tufted grass the few stones with which the train-men, at risk of their own lives, have delayed long enough to mark their comrade's grave.

The faded photographs or the old prints of those overland trains speak to me but one story. Instantly I recall the hourly vigilance, the restless eyes scanning the horizon, the breathless suspense, when the pioneers or soldiers knew from unmistakable signs that the Indian was lying in wait. In what contrast to the dull, logy, scarcely moving oxen were these keen-eyed heroes, with every nerve strained, every sense on the alert. And how they were maddened by the fate that consigned them, at such moments, to the mercy of "dull, driven cattle." When I have seen officers and soldiers lay their hands lovingly on the neck of their favorite horse, and perhaps, when no one was near to scoff at sentiment, say to me, "He saved my life," I knew well what a man felt when his horse took fire at knowledge of danger to his rider and sped on the wings of the wind, till he was lost to his pursuers, a tiny black speck on the horizon. The pathos of a soldier's parting with his horse moved us to quick sympathy. It often happens that a trooper retains the same animal through his entire enlistment, and it comes to be his most intimate friend. There is nothing he will not do to provide him with food ; if the forage runs low or the grazing is insufficient, stealing for his horse is reckoned a virtue among soldiers. Imagine, then, the anxiety, the real suffering, with which a soldier watches his faithful beast growing weaker day by day, from exhaustion or partial starvation. He walks beside him to spare his strength, and finally, when it is no longer possible to keep up with the column, and the soldier knows how fatal the least delay may be in an Indian country, it is more pitiful than almost any sight I recall, the sadness of his departure from the skeleton, whose eyes follow his master in wondering affection, as he walks away with the saddle and accoutrements. It is the most merciful farewell if a bullet is lodged in the brain of the famished or exhausted beast, but some one else than his sorrowing master has to do the trying deed.

This is not the last act in the harrowing scene. The soldier overtakes the column, loaded down with his saddle, if the train is too far away to deposit it in the company wagon. Then begins a tirade of annoying comments to this man, still grieving over the parting with his best friend. No one can conceive what sarcasm and wit can proceed from a column of cavalry. Many of the men are Irish, and their reputation for humor is world-wide. "Hullo, there ! joined the doeboys, eh ?" "How do you like hoofing it ?" are tame specimens of the remarks from these tormenting tongues ; such a fusillade of sneers is followed not long after by perhaps the one most gibing of all flinging himself off from his horse, and giving his mount to the one he has done his best to stir into wrath. A cavalryman hates, beyond any telling, enforced pedestrianism, and " Share and share alike " is a motto that our Western soldiers keep in use.

If the wagons held merchandise only, by which the pioneer hoped to grow rich, the risk and suspense attending these endless marches were not worth commemorating ; but the bulk of the freight was the actual necessities of life. Conceive, if you can, how these brave men felt themselves chained, as they drove or guarded the food for those living far in advance. There were not enough to admit of a charge on the enemy, and the defensive is an exasperating position for a soldier or frontiersman. He longs to advance on the foe ; but no such privilege was allowed them, for in these toilsome journeys they had often to use precautions to hide themselves. If Indians were discovered to be roaming near, the camp was established, trains corralled, animals secured inside a temporary stockade ; the fires for coffee were forbidden, for smoke rises like a funnel, and hangs out an instant signal in that clear air. Even the consoling pipe was smoked under a sage-bush or in a hollow, if there happened to be a depression of the ground. Few words were spoken, the loud oaths sank into low mutterings, and the bray of a hungry mule, the clank of wagon-chains, or the stamping of cattle on the baked earth, sounded like thunder in the ears of the anxious, expectant men.

Fortunately, our journey in these trains was not at once forced upon us at Leavenworth. The Kansas Pacific Railroad, projected to Denver, was built within ten miles of Fort Riley, and it was to be the future duty of the Seventh Cavalry to guard the engineers in building the remainder of the road out to the Rocky Mountains. It did not take us long to purchase an outfit in the shops, for, as usual, our finances were low, and consequently our wants were curtailed. We had the sense to listen to a hint from some practical officer who had been far beyond railroads, and buy a cook-stove the first thing, and this proved to be the most important of our possessions when we reached our post, so far from the land of shops. Not many hours after we left Leavenworth, the settlements became farther and farther apart, and we began to realize that we were actual pioneers. Kansas City was then but a small town, seemingly with a hopeless future, as the bluffs rose so steeply from the river, and even when the summit was reached, the ups and downs of the streets were discouraging. It seemed, then, as if it would never be worth while to use it as a site for a town; there would be a lifetime of grading. It is very easy to become a city forefather in such a town, for in the twenty-one years since then, it has grown into a city of over 132,000 inhabitants—but they are still grading. The lots which we could have had almost for the asking, sell now for $1,000 a front foot. Topeka, the capital, showed no evidence of its importance, except the little circle of stars that surrounded it on our atlas. There were but three towns beyond Fort Riley then, and those were built, if I may so express it, of canvas and dug-outs.

Our railroad journey came to an end about ten miles from Fort Riley. The laborers were laying track from that point. It had been a sort of gala day, for General Sherman, on one of his tours of inspection of the frontier posts, had been asked by railroad officials to drive the final spike of the division of the road then finished. We found a wagon waiting for our luggage, and an ambulance to carry us the rest of the journey. These vehicles are not uncomfortable when the long seats on either side are so arranged that they make a bed for the ill or wounded by spreading them out, but as traveling conveyances I could not call them a success. The seats are narrow, with no back to speak of, and covered with carriage-cloth, which can keep you occupied, if the country is rough, in regaining the slippery surface for any number of miles at a stretch. Fort Riley came in sight when we were pretty well tired out. It was my first view of a frontier post. I had either been afraid to confess my ignorance, or so assured there was but one variety of fort, and the subject needed no investigation, that Fort Riley came upon me as a great surprise. I supposed, of course, it would be exactly like Fortress Monroe, with stone walls, turrets for the sentinels, and a deep moat. As I had heard more and more about Indians since reaching Kansas, a vision of the enclosure where we would eventually live was a great comfort to me. I could scarcely believe that the buildings, a story and a half high, placed around a parade-ground, were all there was of Fort Riley. The sutler's store, the quartermaster and commissary storehouses, and the stables for the cavalry horses, were outside the square, near the post, and that was all. No trees, and hardly any signs of vegetation except the buffalo-grass that curled its sweet blades close to the ground, as if to protect the nourishment it held from the blazing sun. The post was beautifully situated on a wide plateau, at the junction of the Republican and Smoky Hill rivers. The Plains, as they waved away on all sides of us, like the surface of a vast ocean, had the charm of great novelty, and the absence of trees was at first forgotten in the fascination of seeing such an immense stretch of country, with the soft undulations of green turf rolling on, seemingly, to the setting sun. The eye was relieved by the fringe of cottonwood that bordered the rivers below us.

Though we came afterward to know, on toilsome marches under the sweltering sun, when that orb was sometimes not even hidden for one moment in the day by a grateful cloud, but the sky was spread over as a vast canopy of dazzling blue, that enthusiasm would not outlast such trials, still, a rarely exultant feeling takes possession of one in the gallops over the Plains, when in early spring they are a trackless sea of soft verdure. And the enthusiasm returns when the campaign for the summer is over, and riding is taken up for pleasure. My husband was full of delight over the exquisite haze that covered the land with a faint purple light, and exclaimed, "Now I begin to realize what all that transparent veil of faint color means in Bierstadt's paintings of the Rocky Mountains and the West." But we had little time to take in atmospheric effects, as evening was coming on and we were yet to be housed, while servants, horses, dogs and all of us were hungry after our long drive. The General halted the

wagon outside the post, and left us to go and report to the
commanding officer.

At that time I knew nothing of the hospitality of a frontier
post, and I begged to remain in the wagon until our quarters
were assigned us in the garrison. Up to this time we had
all been in splendid spirits; the novelty, the lovely day and
exhilarating air, and all the possibilities of a future with a
house of our own, or, rather, one lent to us by Uncle Sam,
seemed to fill up a delightful cup to the brim. We sat outside the post so long—at least it seemed so to us—and grew
hungrier and thirstier, that there were evident signs of mutiny. The truth is, whenever the General was with us, with
his determination of thinking that nothing could exceed his
surroundings, it was almost impossible to look upon anything
except in the light that he did. He gave color to everything,
with his hopeful views. Eliza sat on the seat with the driver,
and both muttered occasional hungry words, but our Diana
and I had the worst of it. We had bumped over the country, sometimes violently jammed against the framework of
the canvas cover, and most of the time sliding off from the
slippery cushions upon the insulted dogs—for of course the
General had begged a place for two of them. He had kept
them in order all the way from the termination of the railroad; but now that he was absent, Turk and Byron renewed
hostilities, and in the narrow space they scrambled and
snarled and sprang at each other. When the General came
back he found the little hands of our curly-headed girl
clenched over the collar of Byron at one end of the ambulance, while Turk sat on my lap, swelling with rage because
my fingers were twisted in the chain that held him, as I sat
at the door shaking with terror. It was quick work to jerk
the burly brute out of the door, and end our troubles for the
time; but the General, after quieting our panic, threw us into
a new one by saying we must make up our minds to be the
guests of the commanding officer. Tired, travel-stained, and
unaccustomed to what afterward became comparatively easy,
we were driven to one of the quarters and made our entrance

among strangers. I then realized, for the first time, that we had reached a spot where the comforts of life could not be had for love or money.

It is a strange sensation to arrive at a place where money is of little use in providing shelter, and here we were beyond even the commonest railroad hotel. Mrs. Gibbs, who received us, was put to a severe test that night. Already a room in her small house had been prepared for General Sherman, who had arrived earlier in the day, and now there were five of us bearing down upon her. I told her how I had begged to be allowed to go into quarters, even though there were no preparations, not even a fireplace where Eliza could have cooked us food enough over the coals to stay hunger; but she assured me that, having been on the Plains before the war, she was quite accustomed to a state of affairs where there was nothing to do but quarter yourself upon strangers; and then gave up her own room to our use. From that night—which was a real trial to me, because I felt so keenly the trouble we caused them all—dates the beginning of a friendship that has lasted through the darkest as well as the brightest hours of my life. I used to try to remember afterward, when for nine years we received and entertained strangers who had nowhere else to go, the example of undisturbed hospitality shown me by my first friend on the frontier.

The next day my husband assumed command of the garrison, and our few effects were moved into a large double house built for the commanding officer. There were parlors on one side, whose huge folding doors were flung open, and made our few articles of furniture look lonely and meagre. We had but six wooden chairs to begin with, and when, a few miles more of the railroad being completed, a party of one hundred and fifty excursionists arrived, I seated six of them—yes, seven, for one was tired enough to sit on a trunk —and then concluded I would own up that in the larger rooms of the house, into which they looked significantly, there were no more chairs concealed. I had done my best, and tried to make up for not seating or feeding them, by very busy talking. Meanwhile there were incessant inquiries for the General. It seems that he had begun that little trick of hiding from strangers, even then. He had seen the advancing column of tourists, and fled. One of the servants finally unearthed him, and after they had gone and he found that I had been so troubled to think I could do nothing for the citizens, and so worried because he was *non est*, he did not leave me in such strait again until I had learned to adapt myself to the customs of the country where the maxim that "every man's house is his castle" is a fallacy.

The officers who had garrisoned the post began to move out as our own Seventh Cavalry officers reported for duty. The colonel of the regiment arrived, and ranked us out of our quarters, in this instance much to our relief, as the barrack of a building would never fill up from the slow rate at which our belongings increased. This army regulation, to which I have elsewhere referred, was then new to me. The manner in which the Government sees fit to arrange quarters is still amusing to me, but I suppose no better plan has ever been thought out. In the beginning of a well-built post, there is but little choice. It is the aim to make the houses, except that of the commanding officer, exactly alike. From time to time new quarters are built. The original plan is not followed; possibly a few improvements are added to the newer houses. Ah! then the disturbance ensues! Fort Vancouver, in Washington Territory, is one of the old posts, quite interesting from the heterogeneous collection of quarters added through fifty years. I was spending a day or two, in 1875, with my husband's niece, whose husband was some distance down on the list, and consequently occupied a low log building, that dated back no one knows how far. Even in that little cabin they were insecure, for in reply to my question, "Surely you are permanently fixed, and won't be moved," they pathetically answered: "Not by any means! We live from hour to hour in uncertainty, and there are worse quarters than these, which we walk by daily with dread, as ———— ranks us, and he is going to be married, so out we go!"

Assigning quarters according to rank goes on smoothly for a time, but occasionally an officer reports for duty who ranks everyone. Not long ago this happened at a distant post, and the whole line went down like a row of bricks, as eight officers' families were ousted by his arrival, the lowest in rank having to move out one of the non-commissioned officers who had lived in a little cabin with two rooms. If possible, in choosing a time to visit our frontier posts, let this climax of affairs be avoided. Where there is little to vary life the monotony is apt to be deeply stirred by private rages, which would blow away in smoke if there was anything else to think of. It is rather harrowing to know that some one has an eye on the home you have furnished with your own means. I could hardly blame a man I knew, who, in an outburst of wrath concerning an officer who had at last uprooted him, secretly rejoiced that a small room that had been the object of envy, having been built at the impoverished post of refuse lumber from the stables, was unendurable on a warm day; and the new possessor was left to find it out when he had settled himself in the coveted house.

After our quarters were chosen by the Colonel, we took another house, of moderate size, bought a few pieces of furniture of an officer leaving the post, and began to live our first homelike life. The arrival of the new officers was for a time our only excitement. Most of them had been in the volunteer service, and knew nothing of the regular army. There was no one to play practical jokes on the first comers; but they had made some ridiculous errors in dress and deportment, when reporting at first, and they longed to take out their mortification at these harmless mistakes, by laying pitfalls for the verdant ones who were constantly arriving. The discipline of the regular army, and the punctilious observance compelling the wearing of the uniform, was something totally new to men who had known little of parades in their fighting days in the tented field. If it was possible to intimidate a new officer by tales of the strictness of the commanding officer regarding the personal appearance of his

regiment, they did so.   One by one, those who had preceded
the last comer called in to pay their compliments; but by
previous agreement they one and all dwelt upon the necessity of his making a careful toilet before he approached the
august presence of the Lieutenant-colonel.   Then one or
two offered carelessly to help him get himself up for the occasion.   Our brother Tom had arrived by this time, but there
was nothing to be made out of him, for he had served a few
months with a regular regiment before being transferred to
ours.   He was therefore sent one day to prepare me for the
call of an officer who had been assisted into his new uniform
by the mischievous knot of men who had been longest with
us.   If I had known to what test I was to be put to keep my
face straight, or had dreamed what a gullible creature had
come into their roguish hands, I would not have consented
to receive him.   But it was one of the imperative roles that
each officer, after reporting for duty, must pay a formal visit
to the commanding officer and his family.   I went into the
parlor to find a large, and at that time awkward, man, in full
uniform, which was undeniably a tight fit for his rather portly
figure.   He wore cavalry boots, the first singularity I noticed,
for they had such expanse of top I could not help seeing
them.   They are of course out of order with a dress coat.
The red sash, which was then *en règle* for all officers, was
spread from up under his arms to as far below the waist line
as its elastic silk could be stretched.   The sword-belt, with
sabre attached, surrounded this; and, folded over the wide
red front, were his large hands, encased in white cotton
gloves.   He never moved them; nor did he move an eyelash,
so far as I could discover, though it seems he was full of internal tremors, for the officers had told him on no account to
remove his regulation hat.   At this he demurred, and told
them I would surely think he was no gentleman; but they
assured him I placed military etiquette far above any ordinary rule for manners in the presence of ladies, while the truth
was I was rather indifferent as to military rules of dress.   As
this poor man sat there, I could think of nothing but a child

THE OFFICER'S DRESS—A NEW-COMER FOR A CALL.

who is so carefully dressed in new furbelows that it sits as if
it were carved out of wood, for fear of disarranging the finished toilet. Diana made an almost instant excuse to leave
the room. The General's mustache quivered, and he moved
restlessly around, even coming again to shake hands with the
automaton and bid him welcome to the regiment; but finally
he dashed out of the door to enjoy the outburst of mirth
that he could no longer control. I was thus left to meet the
situation as best I could, but was not as fortunate as the General, who had a friendly mustache to curtain the quiver in
his mouth. The poor victim apparently recalled to himself
the martial attitude of Washington crossing the Delaware, or
Napoleon at Waterloo, and did not alter the first position he
had assumed. In trying to prevent him from seeing my confusion, I redoubled my efforts to entertain him, and succeeded only too well, for when he slowly moved out of the door
I found myself tired out, and full of wrath toward my returning family. I never could remember that these little spurts
of rage were the primest fun for my people. The poor officer who had been so guyed did not gratify his tormentors by
getting angry, but fell to planning new mischief for the next
arrival. He lost no time in begging my pardon for the hat,
and though I never saw much of him afterward, he left only
pleasant impressions on my mind of a kind-hearted man, and
one of those rare beings who knew how to take a joke.

We derived great pleasure from our horses and dogs during
the autumn. A very pretty sorrel horse was selected for
Diana, but we had little opportunity to have her for a companion. The young officers engaged her a week in advance,
and about all we saw of her riding was an avalanche of flying
curls as she galloped off beside some dashing cavalier. I remember once, when she was engaged otherwise, and my
horse temporarily disabled, I took hers, and my husband kept
begging me to guide the animal better, for it was nettling his
fiery beast by insisting upon too close proximity. It finally
dawned upon us that the little horse was a constitutional
snuggler, and we gave up trying to teach him new tricks.

But how the General shouted, and bent himself forward and back in his saddle, after the horse had almost crushed his leg and nothing would keep him at a distance. He could hardly wait to get back to garrison, and when we did, he walked into the midst of a collection of the beaux and told the whole story of how dreadfully demoralized a cavalry horse in good and regular standing could become, in the hands of a belle. The girl blushed, and the officers joined in the laughter, and yet every one of them had doubtless been busy in teaching that little telltale animal this new development of character.

It was deiightful ground to ride over about Fort Riley. Ah! what happy days they were, for at that time I had not the slightest realization of what Indian warfare was, and consequently no dread. We knew that the country they infested was many miles away, and we could ride in any direction we chose. The dogs would be aroused from the deepest sleep at the very sight of our riding costumes, and by the time we were well into them and whip in hand, they leaped and sprang about the room, tore out on the gallery, and tumbled over one another and the furniture in racing back, and such a din of barking and joyful whining as they set up —the noisier the better for my husband. He snapped his whip to incite them, and bounded around crying out, "Whoop 'em up! whoop 'em up!" adding to the mêlée by a toot on the dog-horn he had brought from the Texas deerhunts. All this excited the horses, and when I was tossed into the saddle amidst this turmoil, with the dogs leaping around the horses' heads, I hardly knew whether I was myself or the venturesome young woman who spends her life in taking airy flights through paper-covered circles in a sawdust ring. It took some years for me to accustom myself to the wild din and hubbub of our starting for a ride or a hunt. As I have said before, I had lived quietly at home, and my decorous, suppressed father and mother never even spoke above a certain tone. The General's father, on the contrary, had rallied his sons with a hallo and resounding shouts from their childhood. So the hullabaloo of all our merry startings was a thing of my husband's early days, and added zest to every sport he undertook.

Coming from Michican, where there is a liberal dispensation of swamp and quagmire, having been taught by dear experience that Virginia had quicksands and sloughs into which one could disappear with great rapidity, and finally, having experienced Texas with its bayous, baked with a deceiving crust of mud, and its rivers with quicksand beds, very naturally I guided my horse around any lands that had even a depression. Indeed, he spoke volumes with his sensitive ears, as the turf darkened in hollows, and was ready enough to be guided by the rein on his satin-like neck, to the safer ground. It was a long time before I realized that all the Plains were safe. We chose no path, and stopped at no suspicion of a slough. Without a check on the rein, we flew over divide after divide, and it is beyond my pen to describe the wild sense of freedom that takes possession of one in the first buoyant knowledge that no impediment, seemingly, lies between you and the setting sun. After one has ridden over conventional highways, the beaten path marked out by fences, hedges, bridges, etc., it is simply an impossibility to describe how the blood bounds in the veins at the freedom of an illimitable sea. No spongy, uncertain ground checks the course over the Plains; it is seldom even damp, and the air is so exhilarating one feels as if he had never breathed a full breath before. Almost the first words General Sherman said to me out there were, "Child, you'll find the air of the Plains is like champagne," and so it surely was. Oh, the joy of taking in air without a taint of the city, or even the country, as we know it in farm life! As we rode on, speaking enthusiastically of the fragrance and purity of the atmosphere, our horses neighed and whinnied to each other, and snuffed the air, as if approving all that was said of that "land of the free." My husband could hardly breathe, from the very ecstasy of realizing that nothing trammeled him. He scarcely left the garrison behind him, where he was bound by chains of form and ceremony—the inevitable lot of an officer, where all his acts are under surveillance, where he is obliged to know that every hour in the day he is setting an example— before he became the wildest and most frolicsome of light-hearted boys. His horse and he were one, not only as he sat in the saddle, a part of the animal, swayed by every motion of the active, graceful beast, but such unison of spirit took possession of each, it was hard to believe that a human heart did not beat under the broad, splendid chest of the high-strung animal.

It were well if human hearts responded to our fondness, and came instantly to be *en rapport* with us, as did those dear animals when they flew with us out to freedom and frolic, over the divides that screened us from the conventional proprieties. My husband's horse had almost human ways of talking with him, as he leaned far out of the saddle and laid his face on the gallant animal's head, and there was a gleam in the eye, a proud little toss of the head, speaking back a whole world of affection. The General could ride hanging quite out of sight from the opposite side, one foot caught in the stirrup, his hand on the mane; and it made no difference to his beloved friend, he took any mode that his master chose to cling to him as a matter of course, and curveted and pranced in the loftiest, proudest way. His manner said as plainly as speech, " See what we two can do!" I rarely knew him to have a horse that did not soon become so pervaded with his spirit that they appeared to be absolutely one in feeling. I was obliged, usually, to submit to some bantering slur on my splendid Custis Lee. Perhaps a dash at first would carry the General and the dogs somewhat in advance. My side had a trick of aching if we started off on a gallop, and I was obliged to keep a tight rein on Custis Lee at first, as he champed at the bit, tossed his impatient head, and showed every sign of ignominious shame. The General, as usual, called out, " Come on, old lady! Hurry up that old plug of yours; I have one orderly; don't want another"—this because the soldier in attendance is instructed to ride at a certain distance in the rear. After a spurt of tremendous speed, back flew the master to beg me to excuse him; he was ready now to ride slowly till "that side of mine came round to time," which it quickly did, and then I revenged the insult on my swift Lee, and the maligner at last called out, "That's not so bad a nag, after all."

The horses bounded from the springy turf as if they really hated the necessity of touching the sod at all. They were very well matched in speed, and as on we flew were "neck by neck, stride by stride, never changing our place." Breathless at last, horses, dogs and ourselves made a halt. The orderly with his slow troop horse was a speck in the distance. Of course I had gone to pieces little by little, between the mad speed and rushing through the wind of the Plains. Those were ignominious days for women—thank fortune they are over! Custom made it necessary to disfigure ourselves with the awkward waterfall, and, no matter how luxuriant the hair, it seemed a necessity to still pile up more. With many a wrathful opinion regarding the fashion, the General took the hairpins, net and switch, and thrust them into the breast of his coat, as he said, "to clear the decks for action for another race." It was enough that he offered to carry these barbarities of civilization for me, without my bantering him about his ridiculousness if some accidental opening of his coat in the presence of the officers, who were then strangers, revealed what he scoffingly called "dead women's hair."

A fresh repinning, an ignoring of hairpins this time, regirthing of saddles, some proud patting of the horses' quiving flanks, passing of the hand over the full veins of their necks, praise of the beautiful distended, blood-red nostrils, and on we started for another race. If spur or whip had been used in speeding our horses, it would have spoiled the sport for me, as the effort and strain looks so cruelly like work; but the animals were as impatient for a run as we were to start them. It must be a rare moment of pleasure to all horse-lovers, to watch an animal flying over the ground,

without an incentive save the love of motion born in the
beast. When we came to certain smooth stretches on the
road, where we were accustomed to give the horses the rein,
they grew excited and impatient, and teased for the run if we
chanced to be earnestly talking and forgot to take it. How
fortunate is one who can ride a mythological Pegasus as well
as a veritable horse! There is nothing left for the less gifted
but to use others' words for our own enthusiasm:

" Now we're off, like the winds, to the plains whence they came;
And the rapture of motion is thrilling my frame!
On, on, speeds my courser, scarce printing the sod,
Scarce crushing a daisy to mark where we trod;
On, on, like a deer when the hounds' early bay
Awakes the wild echoes, away and away!
Still faster, still farther, he leaps at my cheer,
Till the rush of the startled air whirs in my ear! "

Buchanan Read not only made General Sheridan's splendid
black horse immortal, but his grateful owner kept that faithful beast, when it was disabled, in a paddock at Leavenworth, and then, when age and old wounds ended his life,
he perpetuated his memory by having the taxidermist set
him up in the Military Museum at Governor's Island, that
the boys of this day, to whom the war is only history, may remember what a splendid part a horse took in those days,
when soldiers were not the only heroes. I thank a poet for
having written thus for us to whom the horse is almost
human:

" I tell thee, stranger, that unto me
The plunge of a fiery steed
Is a noble thought—to the brave and free
It is music, and breath, and majesty—
'Tis the life of a noble deed;
And the heart and the mind are in spirit allied
In the charm of a morning's glorious ride."

There was a long, smooth stretch of land beyond Fort
Riley, where we used to speed our horses, and it even now

A SUSPENDED EQUESTRIENNE.

seems one of the fair spots of earth, it is so marked by happy hours.   In reality it was a level plain without a tree, and the dried buffalo-grass had then scarcely a tinge of green.   This neutral-tinted, monotonous surface continued for many un-varying miles.   We could do as we chose after we had passed out of sight of the garrison, and our orderly, if he happened to have a decent horse that could overtake us, kept drawing the muscles of his face into a soldierly expression, trying not to be so undignified as to laugh at the gamesomeness, the frolic, of his commanding officer.   What a relief for the poor fellow, in his uneventful life, to get a look at these pranks! I can see him now, trying to keep his head away and look unconscious, but his eyes turned in their sockets in spite of him and caught it all.   Those eyes were wild with terror one day, when our horses were going full tilt, and the General with one powerful arm, lifted me out of my saddle and held me poised in the air for a moment.   Our horses were so evenly matched in speed they were neck and neck, keeping close to each other, seemingly regardless of anything except the delight at the speed with which they left the country be-hind them.   In the brief moment that I found myself sus-pended between heaven and earth, I thought, with lightning rapidity, that I must cling to my bridle and keep control of my flying horse, and trust to good fortune whether I alighted on his ear or his tail.   The moment I was thus held aloft was an hour in uncertainty, but nothing happened, and it taught me to prepare for sudden raids of the commanding officer after that.   I read of this feat in some novel, but was incred-ulous until it was successfully practiced on me.   The Custer men were given to what their Maryland father called " tot-ing " us around.   I've seen them pick up their mother and carry her over the house as if she weighed fifty instead of one hundred and fifty pounds.   There was no chance for digni-fied anger with them.   No matter how indignant I might be, or how loftily I might answer back, or try one of those elo-quent silences to which we women sometimes resort in mo-ments of wrath, I was snatched up by either my husband or

Tom, and had a chance to commune with the ceiling in my airy flight up and down stairs and through the rooms.

One of our rides marked a day with me, for it was the occasion of a very successful exchange of horses. My husband used laughingly to refer to the transaction as unfortunate for him; but as it was at his suggestion, I clung with pertinacity to the bargain. My horse, Custis Lee, being a pacer, my husband felt in the fascination of that smooth, swift gait I might be so wedded to it I could never endure anything else; so he suggested, while we were far out on our evening ride, that we change saddles and try each other's horse. I objected, for though I could ride a spirited horse when I had come to know him, I dreaded the early stages of acquaintance. Besides, Phil was a high-strung colt, and it was a venturesome experiment to try him with a long riding-skirt, loaded with shot, knocking about his legs. At that time the safe fashion of short habits was not in vogue, and the high winds of Kansas left no alternative to loading our skirts. We kept opening the hem and inserting the little shot-bags as long as we lived there. Fortunately for me, I was persuaded into trying the colt. As soon as he broke into a long swinging trot, I was so enchanted and so hilarious with the motion, that I mentally resolved never to yield the honor temporarily conferred upon me. It was the beginning of an eternal vigilance for my husband. The animal was so high-strung, so quick, notwithstanding he was so large, that he sprang from one side of the road to the other on all fours, without the slightest warning. After I had checked him and recovered my breath, we looked about for a cause for this fright, and found only the dark earth where slight moisture had remained from a shower. In order to get the smoothest trotting out of him, I rode with a snaffle, and I never knew the General's eyes to be off him for more than an instant. The officers protested, and implored my husband to change back and give me the pacer. But his pride was up, and he enjoyed seeing the animal quivering with delight at doing his best under a light weight, and he had genuine love for the brute that, though so hard to manage in his hands, responded to my lightest touch or to my voice.

As time advanced and our regiment gained better and better horseflesh, it was a favorite scheme to pit Phil against new-comers. We all started out, a gay cavalcade of noisy, happy people, and the stranger was given the post of honor next to the wife of the commanding officer. Of course he thought nothing of this, as he had been at the right of the hostess at dinner. The other officers saw him take his place as if it were the most natural thing in the world, but in reality it was a deep-laid plot. Phil started off with so little effort that our visitor thought nothing of keeping pace for a while, and then he began to use his spurs. As my colt took longer and longer strides, there was triumph in the faces of the officers, and a gleam of delight in the General's eye. Then came the perplexity in my guest's face at a trotter outdoing the most splendid specimen of a loping horse, as he thought. A little glance from my husband, which incited me to give a sign and a low word or two that only Phil and I understood, and off we flew, leaving the mystified man urging his nag in vain. It was not quite my idea of hospitality so to introduce a new-comer to our horses' speed; but then he was not a transient guest, and the sooner he knew all our "tricks and our manners" the better, while it was beyond my power of self-denial to miss seeing the proud triumph in my husband's eyes as he rode up and patted the colt and received the little return of affection from the knowing beast. Phil went on improving in gait and swiftness as he grew in years, and I once had the courage, afterward, to speed him on the Government race-track at Fort Leavenworth, though to this day. I cannot understand how I got up to concert pitch; and I could never be induced to try such an experiment again. I suppose I often made as good time, trotting beside my husband's horse, but to go alone was something I was never permitted to do on a roadway. The General and brother Tom connived to get this bit of temporary courage out of me by an offhand conversation, as we rode toward the track, re-

garding what Phil might be made to do under the best circumstances, which I knew meant the snaffle-rein, a light
weight, and my hand, which the General had trained to be
steady. I tried to beg off and suggest either one of them for
the trial; but the curb which they were obliged to use, as
Phil was no easy brute to manage with them, made him
break his gait, and a hundred and seventy pounds on his
back was another obstacle to speed. It ended in my being
teased into the experiment, and though I called out, after
the first half-mile, that I could not breathe any longer, the
air rushed into my lungs so rapidly, they implored and urged
by gesture and enthusiastic praise, until I made the mile they
had believed Phil equal to in three minutes.

I wish I could describe what delight my husband took in his
horse life, what hours of recreation and untiring pleasure he got
out of our companionship with Jack Rucker, Phil and Custis
Lee. On that day we three and our orderly were alone on the
track, and such a merry, noisy, care-forgetting three as we
were! the General, with his stop-watch in hand, cheering me,
urging the horse wildly, clapping his hands, and hallooing with
joy as the animal responded to his expectation. Phil's coming
up to their boasts and anticipations was just a little episode
in our life that went to prove what a rare faculty he had of
getting much out of little, and of how persistently the boy
in him cropped out as soon as an opportunity came to throw
care aside. It is one of the results of a life of deprivation,
that pleasures, when they come, are rarities, and the enjoyment is intensified. In our life they lasted so short a time
that we had no chance to learn the meaning of satiety.

One of the hardest trials, in our first winter with the regiment, was that arising from the constantly developing tendency to hard drinking. Some who came to us had held up
for a time, but they were not restricted in the volunteer service, as a man who fought well was forgiven much else that
came in the rare intervals of peace. In the new state of affairs, as went the first few months of the regiment, so would
it go for all time. There was a regiment stationed in New

Mexico at that time, the record of which was shameful. We heard of its career by every overland train that came into our post, and from officers who went out on duty. General Sherman said that, with such a set of drunkards, the regiment, officers and all, should be mustered out of the service. Anything, then, rather than let our Seventh follow such a course. But I must not leave the regiment at that point in its history. Eventually it came out all right, ably officered and well soldiered, but it was the terror of the country in 1867. While General Custer steadily fought against drunkenness, he was not remorseless or unjust. I could cite one instance after another, to prove with what patience he strove to reclaim some who were, I fear, hopeless when they joined us. His own greatest battles were not fought in the tented field; his most glorious combats were those waged in daily, hourly fights on a more hotly contested field than was ever known in common warfare. The truest heroism is not that which goes out supported by strong battalions and reserve artillery. It is when a warrior for the right enters into the conflict alone, and dares to exercise his will in defiance of some established custom in which lies a lurking, deadly peril or sin. I have known my husband to almost stand alone in his opinion regarding temperance, in a garrison containing enough people to make a good-sized village. He was thoroughly unostentatious about his convictions, and rarely said much; but he stood to his fixed purpose, purely from horror of the results of drinking. I would not imply that in garrison General Custer was the only man invariably temperate. There were some on pledge; some temperate because they paid such a physical penalty by actual illness that they could not drink; some restrained because their best-loved comrade, weak in his own might, "swore off" on consideration that the stronger one of the two backed him up; some (God bless them!) refused because the woman they loved grieved, and was afraid of even one friendly glass. What I mean is, that the general custom, against which there is little opposition in any life, is, either to indulge in the social glass, or look leniently upon the habit. Without preaching or parading his own strength in having overcome the habit, General Custer stood among the officers and men as firm an advocate of temperance as any evangelist whose life is devoted to the cause.

I scarcely think I would have realized the constantly recurring temptations of my husband's life, had I not been beside him when he fought these oft-repeated battles. The pleasure he had in convivial life, the manner in which men and women urged him to join them in enjoyment of the sparkling wine, was enough to have swept every resolution to the winds. Sometimes the keen blade of sarcasm, though set with jewels of wit and apparent badinage, added a cut that my ears, so quickened to my husband's hard position, heard and grieved over. But he laughed off the carefully concealed thrust. When we were at home in our own room, if I asked him, blazing anew with wrath at such a stab, how he kept his temper, he replied, "Why notice it? Don't I know what I've been through to gain my victory? That fellow, you must remember, has fought and lost, and knows in his soul he'll go to the dogs if he doesn't hold up, and, Libbie, he can't do it, and I am sorry for him." Our brother Tom was less patient, less forbearing, for in one of his times of pledge, when the noble fellow had given his word not to taste a drop for a certain season if a man he loved, and about whom he was anxious, would do the same, he was sneered at by a brother officer, with gibes at his supposed or attempted superiority. Tom leaped across the table in the tent where they sat at dinner, and shook up his assailant in a very emphatic way. I laugh in remembrance of his choler, and am proud of it now. I, as "gentlewoman," descended from a line of decorous gentlemen and ladies, ought to be horrified at one man's seizing another by the collar and pouncing upon him, regardless of the Marquis of Queensbury rules. But I know that circumstances alter cases, and in our life an occasional good shaking was better than the slow justice of a tedious court-martial.

The General would not smile, but there was a noticeable twisting of his mustache, and he took himself out of the way to conceal his feelings, when I pointed my discerning finger at him and said, "You're laughing, your own self, and you think Tom was right, even if you don't say a word, and look so dreadfully commandery-officery at both of us!" The General did not keep himself aloof, and sometimes, in convivial scenes, when he joined in the increasing hilarity, was so infused with the growing artificial joviality, and grew jollier and jollier, that he was accused himself of being the wildest drinker of them all. But some one was sure to speak up and say, as the morning approached, "I have sat beside Custer the night through, and if he's intoxicated it's over water, for he has not tasted a drop of wine—more loss to him, I say."

Only a short time before the final battle, he dined in New York, at a house where General McDowell was also a guest. When no one else could hear, he told me, with a warning not to talk of it, that he had some one to keep him company, and described the bowl of ice that stood in the midst of the untouched semicircle of glasses before General McDowell, and how the ice seemed just as satisfactory as any of the rare beverages. We listened once to John B. Gough, and the General's enthusiasm over his earnestness and his eloquence was enhanced by the well-known fact of his failures, and the plucky manner in which he started anew. Everybody cries over Jefferson's *Rip Van Winkle*, even if they have never encountered drunkenness, and my husband wept like a child because of his intense sympathy for the weakness of the poor tempted soul, harrowed as he was by a Xantippe.

If women in civil life were taken among men, as army women are, in all sorts of festivities, they would get a better idea of what strength of purpose it requires to carry out a principle. At some army posts the women go to the sutler's store with their husbands, for billiards or amusements. There is a separate room for the soldiers, so we see nothing of those poor fellows who never can stay sober. The sutler's is not only the store, but it is the club-house for the garrison,

and I have known posts where the officers were so guarded
about their drinking, that women could go among them and
join in any amusement without being liable to the distress
that the sight of an intoxicated man invariably gives to a
sensitive woman. If I saw drunken soldiers reeling off after
pay-day, it was the greatest possible relief to me to know,
that out of hundreds only a few were married, as but a certain number of the laundresses were allowed to a company.
So no woman's heart was going to be wrung by unsteady
steps approaching her door, and the sight of the vacant eyes
of a weak husband. It took away half the sting and shock,
to know that a soldier's spree was not one that recoiled on
an innocent woman.

As I look back upon our life, I do not believe there ever
was any path so difficult as those men on the frontier trod.
Their failures, their fights, their vacillations, all were before
us, and it was an anxious life to be watching who won and
who lost in those moral warfares. You could not separate
yourself from the interests of one another. It was a network
of friendships that became more and more interwoven by
common hardships, deprivations, dangers, by isolation and
the daily sharing of joys and troubles. I am thankful for the
certainty that there is some one who scores all our fights and
all our victories ; for on His records will be written the story
of the thorny path over which an officer walked if he reached
the goal.

Women shielded in homes, supported by example, unconscious of any temptation save the mildest, will realize with
me what it was to watch the quivering mouth of a man who
voluntarily admitted that until he was fifty he knew he was
in hourly peril of being a drunkard. The tears blind me as I
go back in retrospection and think over the men that warred
against themselves.

In one respect, there never was such a life as ours ; it was
eminently one of partings. How natural, then, that the last
act before separation be one of hospitable generosity ! How
little we had to offer ! It was often almost an impossibility

to get up a good dinner. Then we had so many coming to us from a distance, that our welcome could not be followed up by any entertainment worthy of the name. Besides, there were promotions to celebrate, an occasional son and heir to toast, birthdays occurring so often, and nothing in the world that answered for an expression of hospitality and good feeling but an old straw demijohn behind the door. It was surprising what pertinacious lives the demijohns of the garrison had. The driver of the wagon containing the few appointments of an officer's outfit, was just as careful of the familiar friend as one could wish servants to be with the lares and penates of an æsthetic household. If he was rewarded with a drink from the sacred demijohn, after having safely preserved it over muddy roads, where the mules jerked the prairie-schooner out of ruts, and where, except for a protecting hand, the contents would have saturated the wagon, he was thankful. But such was his reverence for what he considered the most valuable possession of the whole wagon, virtue alone would have been sufficient reward. When in the regimental movings the crockery (the very heaviest that is made) was smashed, the furniture broken, carpets, curtains, clothes and bedding mildewed and torn, the old demijohn neither broke, spilled nor suffered any injury by exposure to the elements. It was, in the opinion of our lovers of good whiskey, a "survival of the fittest."

It never came to be an old story with me, that in this constant, familiar association with drinking, the General and those of his comrades who abstained could continue to exercise a marvelous self-control. I could not help constantly speaking to my husband of what he went through ; and it seemed to me that no liberty could be too great to extend to men who, always keeping their heads, were clear as to what they were about. The domestic lariat of a cavalryman might well be drawn in, if the women waiting at home were uncertain whether the brains of their liege lords would be muddled when absent from their influence.

CHAPTER XIII.

A MEDLEY OF OFFICERS AND MEN.

It was well we had our horses at Fort Riley for recreation, as walking was almost out of the question in autumn. The wind blew unceasingly all the five years we were in Kansas, but it seemed to do its wildest work in autumn. No one had told us of its incessant activity, and I watched for it to quiet down for days after our arrival, and grew restless and dull for want of exercise, but dared not go out. As the post was on a plateau, the wind from the two river valleys swept over it constantly. The flag was torn into ribbons in no time, and the storm-flag, made smaller, and used in rainy weather, had to be raised a good deal, while the larger and handsomer one was being mended. We found that the other women of the garrison, who were there when we arrived, ventured out to see one another, and even crossed the parade-ground, when it was almost impossible to keep on one's feet. It seems to date very far back, when I recall that our dresses then measured five yards around, and were gathered as full as could be pressed into the waistband. These seven breadths of skirt flew out in advance of us, if they did not lift themselves over our heads. My skirts wrapped themselves around my husband's ankles, and rendered locomotion very difficult for us both, if we tried to take our evening stroll. He thought out a plan, which he helped me to carry into effect, by cutting bits of lead in small strips, and these I sewed into the hem. Thus loaded down, we took our constitutional about the post, and outwitted the elements, which at first bade fair to keep us perpetually housed.

There was very little social life in garrison that winter. The

officers were busy studying tactics, and accustoming themselves to the new order of affairs, so very different from their
volunteer experience.   Had not everything been so novel, I
should have felt disappointed in my first association with the
regular army in garrison.   I did not then consider that the
few old officers and their families were really the regular
army, and so was somewhat disheartened regarding our future associates.   As fast as our own officers arrived, a part of
the regiment that had garrisoned Fort Riley before we came
went away; but it soon became too late in the season to send
the remainder.   The post was therefore crowded.   The best
manners with which all had made their début wore off, and
some jangling began.   Some drank too freely, and were
placed under arrest, or released if they went on pledge.
Nothing was said, of course, if they were sober enough for
duty; but there were some hopeless cases from the first.   For
instance, a new appointee made his entrance into our parlor,
when paying the visit that military etiquette requires, by
falling in at the door, and after recovering an upright position, proceeded to entangle himself in his sword again, and
tumble into a chair.   I happened to be alone, and was, of
course, very much frightened.   In the afternoon the officers
met in one of their quarters, and drew up resolutions that
gave the new arrival the choice of a court-martial or his resignation before night; and by evening he had written out
the papers resigning his commission.   Another fine-looking
man, whom the General worked long and faithfully to make
a sober officer, had really some good instincts.   He was so
glad to get into our home circle, and was so social, telling
the drollest stories of far Western life, where he had lived
formerly, that I became greatly interested in his efforts at
reformation.   He was almost the first to be court-martialed
for drunkenness on duty, and that was always a grief to us;
but in those early days of our regiment's history, arrest, imprisonment and trial had to go on much of the time.   The
officer to whom I refer was getting into and out of difficulty
incessantly.   He repented in such a frank, regretful sort of

way that my husband kept faith in his final reformation long
after it seemed hopeless. One day I asked him to dinner. It
was Thanksgiving, and on those days we tried to select the
officers that talked most to us of their homes and parents.
To my dismay, our reprobate came into the room with very
uncertain gait. The other men looked anxiously at him. My
husband was not in the parlor. I thought of other instances
where these signs of intoxication had passed away in a little
while, and tried to ignore his condition. He was sober
enough to see the concerned look in his comrades' faces, and
brought the tears to my eyes by walking up to me and saying, "Mrs. Custer, I'm sorry, but I think it would be best
for me to go home." Who could help being grieved for a
man so frank and humble over his failings? There were six
years of such vicissitudes in this unfortunate man's life, varied by brave conduct in the Indian campaigns, before the
General gave him up. He violated, at last, some social law
that was considered an outrage beyond pardon, which compelled his departure from the Seventh. That first winter,
while the General was trying to enforce one fact upon the
new-comers, that the Seventh must be a sober regiment, it
was a difficult and anything but pleasant experience.

Very few of the original appointments remained after a few
years. Some who served on to the final battle of 1876, went
through many struggles in gaining mastery of themselves.
The General believed in them, and they were such splendid
fighters, and such fine men when there was anything to occupy them, I know that my husband appreciated with all his
soul what trials they went through in facing the monotony
of frontier life. Indeed, he was himself enduring some hours
of torture from restlessness and inactivity. It is hard to
imagine a greater change than from the wild excitement of
the Virginia campaigns, the final scenes of the war, to the
dullness of Fort Riley. Oh! how I used to feel when my
husband's morning duties at the office were over, and he
walked the floor of our room, saying, "Libbie, what shall I
do?" There were no books to speak of, for the Seventh was

GENERAL CUSTER AT HIS DESK IN HIS LIBRARY.

then too new a regiment to purchase company libraries, as
we did later. . . . . My husband never cared much for
current novels, and these were almost the sole literature of
the households at that time.   At every arrival of the mail,
there was absolute contentment for a while.   The magazines
and newspapers were eagerly read, and I used to discover
that even the advertisements were scanned.   If the General
was caught at this, and accused of it, he slid behind his paper in mock humility, peeping roguishly from one side when
a voice, pitched loftily, inquired whether reading advertisements was more profitable than talking with one's wife?   It
was hard enough, though, when the heaps of newspapers lay
on the floor, all devoured, and one so devoted to them as he
was condemned to await the slow arrival of another mail.   The
Harper's Bazar fashion-pages were not scorned in that dearth
of reading, by the men about our fireside.   We had among
us a famous newspaper-reader; the men could not outstrip
her in extracting everything that the paper held, and the
General delighted in hunting up accounts of " rapscallions "
from her native State, cutting out the paragraphs, and sending them to her by an orderly.   But his hour of triumph was
brief, for the next mail was sure to contain an account of
either a Michigan or Ohio villain, and the promptness with
which General Custer was made aware of the vagabondage
of his fellow-citizens was highly appreciated by all of us.   He
had this disadvantage: he was a native of Ohio, and appointed to the Military Academy from there, and that State claimed him, and very proud we were to have them do so; but
Michigan was the State of his adoption during the war, he
having married there, and it being the home of his celebrated " Michigan brigade." . . .   He was enabled, by that
bright woman's industry, to ascertain what a large share of
the population of those States were adepts in crime, as no
trifling account, or even a pickpocket was overlooked.   I remember how we laughed at her one day.   This friend of ours
was not in the least sensational, she was the very incarna-
tion of delicate refinement.   All her reading (aside from

the search for Ohio and Michigan villains in the papers)
was of the loftiest type; but the blood rose in wild billows
over her sweet face when her son declared his mother such a
newspaper devotee that he had caught her reading the "per-
sonals." We knew it was a fib; but it proves to what
lengths a person might go from sheer desperation, when
stranded on the Plains.

Fortunately, I was not called much from home, as there
were few social duties that winter, and we devised all sorts of
trumpery expedients to vary our life. There was usually a
wild game of romps before the day was ended, We had the
strangest neighbors. A family lived on each floor, but the
walls were not thick, as the Government had wasted no material in putting up our plain quarters. We must have set
their nerves on edge, I suppose, for while we tore up stairs
and down, using the furniture for temporary barricades
against each other, the dogs barking and racing around,
glad to join in the fracas, the din was frightful.

The neighbors — not belonging to our regiment, I am
thankful to say, having come from a circle where the husband
brings the wife to terms by brute force—in giving a minute
description of the sounds that issued from our quarters, accounted for the mêlée to those of the garrison they could get
to listen, by saying that the commanding officer was beating
his wife. While I was inclined to resent such accusations,
they struck the General very differently. He thought it was
intensely funny, and the gossip passed literally in at one ear
and out at the other, though it dwelt with him long enough
to suggest something about the good discipline a man *might*
have if the Virginia law, never repealed, were now in vogue.
I felt sure it would fare badly with me; for, though the di-
mensions of the stick with which a man is permitted to beat
his wife are limited to the size of the husband's finger, my
husband's hands, though in good proportion, had fingers the
bones of which were unusually large. These strange fingers
were not noticeable until one took hold of them; but if they
were carefully studied, with the old English law of Virginia

in mind, there well might be a family mutiny. I tried to beg off from further visits to certain families of this stamp, but never succeeded; the General insisted on my going everywhere. One of the women asked me one day if I rose early. Not knowing why she asked, I replied that I feared it was often 9 o'clock before we awoke, whereupon she answered, in an affected voice, that "she never rose early—it was so plebeian."

It was very discouraging, this first encounter with what I supposed would be my life-long associates. There were many political appointments in the army then. Each State was entitled to its quota, and they were frequently given for favoritism, regardless of soldierly qualities. There were also a good many non-commissioned officers, who, having done good service during the war, were given commissions in the new regiments. For several years it was difficult to arrange everything so satisfactorily in social life that no one's feelings would be hurt. The unvarying rule, which my husband considered should not be violated by any who truly desired harmony, was to visit every one in their circle, and exclude no one from invitations to our house, unless for positively disgraceful conduct.

We heard, from other posts, of the most amusing and sometimes the most uncomfortable of experiences. If I knew any one to whom this incident occurred, I should not venture to make use of it as an example of the embarrassing situations in the new order of affairs in the reorganized army. The story is true; but the names, if I ever knew them, have long since faded out of memory. One of the Irish laundresses at a Western post was evidently infatuated with army life, as she was the widow of a volunteer officer—doubtless some old soldier of the regular army, who held a commission in one of the regiments during the war—and the woman drew the pension of a major's widow. Money, therefore, could not have been the inducement that brought her back to a frontier post. At one time she left her fascinating clothes-line and went into the family of an officer, to cook, but was

obliged to leave, from illness.   Her place was filled satisfactorily, and when she recovered and came back to the officer's
wife, she was told that the present cook was entirely satisfactory, but she might yet find a place, as another officer's wife
(whose husband had been an enlisted man, and had lately
been appointed an officer in the regular regiment stationed
there) needed a cook.   It seems that this officer's wife also had
been a laundress at one time, and the woman applying for
work squared herself off in an independent manner, placed
her arms akimbo, and announced her platform: " Mrs. Blank,
I ken work for a leddy, but I can't go there; there was a
time when Mrs. —— and I had our toobs side by side."

How often, in that first winter, I thought of my father's
unstinted praise of the regular army, as he had known it at
Sackett's Harbor and at Detroit, in Michigan's early days.
I could not but wonder what he would think, to be let down
in the midst of us.   He used to say, in reference to my future, " Daughter, marrying into the army, you will be poor
always ; but I count it infinitely preferable to riches with in-
ferior society.   It consoles me to think you will be always
associated with people of refinement."   Meanwhile, the General was never done begging me to be silent about any new
evidences of vulgarity.   There were several high-bred women
at Fort Riley ; but they were so discreet I never knew but
that they had been accustomed to such associations, until
after the queer lot had departed and we dared to speak confidentially to one another.

Soon after the officers began to arrive in the autumn, an
enlisted man, whom the General had known about in the
regular army, reported for duty.   He had reënlisted in the
Seventh, hoping ultimately for a commission.   He was soldierly in appearance, from his long experience in military life,
and excellently well versed in tactics and regimental discipline.   On this account he was made sergeant-major, the
highest non-commissioned officer of a regiment ; and, at his
request, the General made application almost at once for his
appointment as a lieutenant in the Seventh Cavalry.   The

application was granted, and the sergeant-major went to Washington to be examined. The examining board was composed of old and experienced officers, who were reported to be opposed to the appointment of enlisted men. At any rate, the applicant was asked a collection of questions that were seemingly unanswerable. I only remember one, "What does a regiment of cavalry weigh?" Considering the differences in the officers, men and horses, it would seem as if a correct answer were impossible. The sergeant-major failed, and returned to our post with the hopelessness before him of five years of association with men in the ranks ; for there is no escaping the whole term of enlistment, unless it is found that a man is under age. But the General did not give up. He encouraged the disappointed man to hope, and when he was ordered before the board himself, he went to the Secretary of War and made personal application for the appointment. Washington was then full of men and their friends, clamoring for the vacancies in the new regiments ; but General Custer was rarely in Washington, and was guarded in not making too many appeals, so he obtained the promise, and soon afterward the sergeant-major replaced the chevrons with shoulder-straps. Then ensued one of those awkward situations, that seem doubly so in a life where there is such marked distinction in the social standing of an officer and a private ; and some of the Seventh Cavalry made the situation still more embarrassing by conspicuous avoidance of the new lieutenant, carefully ignoring him except where official relations existed. This seemed doubly severe, as they knew of nothing in the man's conduct, past or present, to justify them in such behavior. He had borne himself with dignity as sergeant-major, living very much to himself, and performing every duty punctiliously. Shortly before, he had been an officer like themselves in the volunteer service, and this social ostracism, solely on account of a few months of service as an enlisted man, was absurd. They went back to his early service as a soldier, determined to show him that he was not " to the manner born." The single men had established a mess, and each bachelor officer who came was promptly called upon and duly invited to join them at table. There was literally no other place to be fed. There were no cooks to be had in that unsettled land, and if there had been servants to hire, the exorbitant wages would have consumed a lieutenant's pay. There were enough officers in the bachelors' mess to carry the day against the late sergeant-major. My husband was much disturbed by this discourteous conduct ; but it did not belong to the province of the commanding officer, and he was careful to keep the line of demarkation between social and official affairs distinct. Yet it did not take long for him to think a way out of the dilemma. He came to me to ask if I would be willing to have him in our family temporarily, and, of course, it ended in the invitation being given. In the evening, when our quarters filled up with the bachelor officers, they found the lieutenant whom they had snubbed established as one of the commanding officer's family. He remained as one of us until the officers formed another mess, as their number increased, and the new lieutenant was invited to join them. This was not the end of General Custer's marked regard for him, and as long as he lived he showed his unswerving friendship, and, in ways that the officer never knew, kept up his disinterested loyalty, making me sure, as years advanced, that he was worthy of the old adage, " Once a friend, always a friend." Until he was certain that there was duplicity and ingratitude, or that worst of sins, concealed enmity, he kept faith and friendships intact. At that time there was every reason in the world for an officer whose own footing was uncertain, and who owed everything to my husband, to remain true to him.

Many of the officers were learning to ride, as they had either served in the infantry during the war, or were appointed from civil life, and came from all sorts of vocations. It would seem that hardly half of the number then knew how to sit or even to mount a horse, and the grand and lofty tumbling that winter kept us in a constant state of merriment. It was too bad to look on and laugh ; but for the life of me I could

not resist every chance I had to watch them clambering up
their horses' sides, tying themselves hopelessly in their sabres,
and contorting their heels so wildly that the restive animal
got the benefit of a spur in unexpected places, as likely in his
neck as in his flank.   One officer, who came to us from the
merchant marine, used to insist upon saying to his brother
officers, when off duty and experimenting with his steed, "If
you don't think I am a sailor, see me shin up this horse's
foreleg."

Some grew hot and wrathy if laughed at, and that increased our fun.   Others were good-natured, even coming
into the midst of us and deliberately narrating the number of
times the horse had either slipped from under them, turned
them off over his head, or rubbed them off by running against
a fence or tree-trunk.   Occasionally somebody tried to hide
the fact that he had been thrown, and then there was
high carnival over the misfortune.   The ancient rule, that
had existed as far back as the oldest officer could remember,
was, that a basket of champagne was the forfeit of a first fall.
Many hampers were emptied that winter ; but as there were
so many to share the treat (and I am inclined to think, also,
it was native champagne, from St. Louis), I don't remember
any uproarious results, except the natural wild spirits of fun-
loving people.   After the secret was out and the forfeit paid,
there was much more courage among the officers in letting
the mishaps be known.   They did not take their nags off into
gullys where they were hidden from the post, and have it
out alone, but tumbled off in sight of the galleries of our quarters, and made nothing of a whole afternoon of voluntary
mounting and decidedly involuntary dismounting.   One of
the great six-footers among us told me his beast had tossed
him off half a dozen times in one ride, but he ended by conquering.   He daily fought a battle with his horse, and, in
describing the efforts to unseat him, said that at last the animal jumped into the creek.   How I admired his pluck and
the gleam in his eye ; and what a glimpse that determination
to master gave of his successful future ! for he won in resist-

ing temptation, and conquered in making himself a soldier, and his life, though short, was a triumph.

I am obliged to confess that to this day I owe a basket of champagne, for I belonged to those that went off the horse against their will and then concealed the fact. My husband and one of his staff were riding with me one day, and asked me to go on in advance, as they wanted to talk over something that was not of interest to me. I forgot to keep watch of my fiery steed, and when he took one of those mad jumps from one side of the road to the other, at some imaginary obstacle, not being on guard I lost balance, and found myself hanging to the saddle. There was nothing left for me but an ignominious slide, and I landed in the dust. The General found Phil trotting riderless toward him, was terribly frightened, and rode furiously toward where I was. To save him needless alarm, I called out, "All right!" from my lowly position, and was really quite unharmed, save my crushed spirits. No one can serve in the cavalry and not feel humiliated by a fall. I began to implore the two not to tell, and in their relief at my escape from serious hurt they promised. But for weeks they made my life a burden to me, by direct and indirect allusions to the accident when a group of us were together. They brought little All Right, the then famous Japanese acrobat, into every conversation, and the General was constantly wondering, in a seemingly innocent manner, "how an old campaigner *could* be unseated, under any circumstances." It would have been better to confess and pay the penalty, than to live thus under the sword of Damocles. Still, I should have deprived my husband of a world of amusement, and every joke counted in those dull days, even when one was himself the victim.

The Board in Washington then examining the officers of the new regiments, called old and new alike ; but in the General's case, as in that of most of the officers who had seen service before the war, or were West Point graduates, it was but a form, and he was soon back in our post.

He began then a fashion that he always kept up afterward,

of having regular openings of his trunk for my benefit. I was as interested in the contents as any child. First putting me under promise to remain in one spot without "peeking," as the children say, he took out from the trunk in our room article after article for me. They comprised everything a woman could wear, from gowns to stockings, with ribbons and hats. If all the gowns he brought were not made, he had dress-materials and stored-up recollections of the new modes of trimming. He enjoyed jokes on himself, and gave us all a laughable description of his discovering in the city some fashion that he had especially liked, when, turning in the crowded street, he followed at a respectful distance the woman wearing it, in order to commit to memory the especial style. Very naturally, he also took in the gait and figure of the stylish wearer, even after he had fixed the cut of her gown in his mind that he might eventually transfer it to me. Ah, how we tormented him when he described his discomfiture, and the sudden termination of his walk, when a turn in the street revealed the face of a negress !

I shall have to ask that a thought be given to our surroundings, to make clear what an immense pleasure a trunkful of finery was at that time. There were no shops nearer than Leavenworth, and our faces were set westward, so there seemed to be no prospect of getting such an outfit for years. There was no one in that far country to prevent the screams of delight with which each gift was received, and it is impossible to describe how jubilant the donor was over the success of his purchases. Brother Tom made a time always, because his name was left out, but he noted carefully if the General's valise held a new supply of neckties, gloves, etc., and by night he had usually surreptitiously transferred the entire contents to his own room. The first notification would be his appearance next morning at the breakfast-table wearing his brother's new things, his face perfectly solemn and innocent, as if nothing peculiar was going on. This sort of game never grew old, and it seemed to give them much more amusement than if the purchases were formally presented.

My husband confided to me that, knowing Tom would take all he could lay his hands on, he had bought twice as many as he needed. The truth is, it was only for the boyish fun they got out of it, for he always shared everything he had with his brother.

At some point in the journey East, the General had fallen into conversation with an officer who, in his exuberance of spirits at his appointment to the Seventh, had volunteered every detail about himself. He was coming from his examination at Washington, and was full of excitement over the new regiment. He had not the slightest idea who my husband was, only that he was also an officer, but in the course of conversation brought his name up, giving all the accounts he had heard of him from both enemies and friends, and his own impressions of how he should like him. The General's love of mischief, and curiosity to hear himself so freely discussed, led the unsuspecting man to ramble on and on, incited by an occasional query or reflection regarding the character of the Lieutenant-colonel of the Seventh. The first knowledge the Lieutenant had with whom he had been talking was disclosed to him when he came to pay the customary call on the return of the commanding officer at Fort Riley. His face was a study; perplexity and embarrassment reddened his complexion almost to a purple, and he moved about uneasily in his chair, abashed to think he had allowed himself to speak so freely of a man to that person's very face. My husband left him but a moment in this awkward predicament, and then laughed out a long roll of merriment, grasping the man's hand, and assured him that he must remember his very freely expressed views were the opinions of others, and not his own. It was a great relief to the Lieutenant, when he reached his quarters, to find that he had escaped some dire fate, either long imprisonment or slow torture; for at that time the volunteer officers had a deeply fixed terror of the stern, unflinching severity of regular officers. Again he became confidential, and told the bachelor mess. This was too good a chance to lose; they felt that some more fun

could still be extracted, and immediately planned a sham
trial. The good-natured man said his stupidity merited it,
and asked for counsel. The case was spun out as long as it
could be made to last. We women were admitted as audi-
ence, and all the grave dignity of his mock affair was a novelty.

The court used our parlor as a Hall of Justice. The counsel for the prisoner was as earnest in his defense as if great
punishment was to be averted by his eloquence. In the daytime he prepared arguments, while at the same time the
prosecuting attorney wrinkled his brows over the most con-
vincing assaults on the poor man, who, he vehemently asserted, ought not to go at large laden with such unpardonable
crime. The judge addressed the jury, and that solemn body
of men disappeared into our room, perching on the trunks,
the bed, the few chairs, to seriously discuss the ominous
"guilty" or "not guilty." The manner of the grave and dignified judge, as he finally addressed the prisoner, admonish-
ing him as to his future, sorrowfully announcing the decision
of the jury as guilty, and condemning him to the penalty of
paying a basket of champagne, was worthy of the chief ex-
ecutor of an Eastern court.

We almost regretted that some one else would not, by
some harmless misdemeanor, put himself within the reach of
such a court. This affair gave us the first idea of the clever
men among us, for all tried to acquit themselves at their best,
even in the burlesque trial.

Little by little it came out what varied lives our officers had
led heretofore. Some frankly spoke of the past, as they became acquainted, while others, making an effort to ignore
their previous history, were found out by the letters that came
into the post every mail, or by some one arriving who had
known them in their other life. The best bred among them
—one descended from a Revolutionary colonel and Governor
of a State, the other from Alexander Hamilton—were the
simplest and most unaffected in manner. The boaster and
would-be aristocrat of our number had the misfortune to

come face to face with a townsman, who effectually silenced further reference to his gorgeous past. There were men who had studied law ; there was one who had been a stump-speaker in Montana politics, and at last a judge in her courts; another who had been a sea-captain, and was distinguished from a second of his name in the regiment by being called always thereafter " Salt Smith," while the younger was "Fresh Smith," or, by those who were fond of him, "Smithie." There was also a Member of Congress, who, having returned to his State after the war, had found his place taken and himself quite crowded out. When this officer reported for duty, I could not believe my eyes. But a few months before, in Texas, he had been such a bitter enemy of my husband's, that, with all the caution observed to keep official matters out of my life, it could not be hidden from me. The General, when this officer arrived, called me into our room and explained that, finding him without employment in Washington when he went before the Board, he could not turn away from his appeal for a commission in the service, and had applied, without knowing he would be sent to our regiment. "And now, Libbie, you would not hurt my feelings by showing animosity and dislike to a man whose hair is already gray !" There was no resisting this appeal, and no disguising my appreciation of the manner in which he treated his enemies, so his words brought me out on the gallery with extended hand of welcome, though I would sooner have taken hold of a tarantula. I never felt a moment's regret, and he never forgot the kindness, or that he owed his prosperity, his whole future, in fact, to the General, and he won my regard by his unswerving fidelity to him from that hour to this.

There were some lieutenants fresh from West Point, and some clerks, too, who had tried to turn themselves into merchants, and groaned over the wretched hours they had spent, since the close of the war, in measuring tape. We had several Irish officers—reckless riders, jovial companions. One had served in the Papal army, and had foreign medals.

There was an Italian who had a long, strange career to draw upon for our amusement, and numbered, among his experiences, imprisonment for plotting the life of his king. There were two officers who had served in the Mexican War, and the ears of the subalterns were always opened to their stories of those days when, as lieutenants, they followed Gen. Scott in his march over the old Cortez highway to his victories and conquests. There was a Prussian among the officers, who, though expressing his approval of the justice and courtesy that the commanding officer showed in his charge of the garrison, used to infuriate the others by making invidious distinctions regarding foreign service and our own. We had an educated Indian as an officer. He belonged to the Six Nations, and his father was a Scotchman; but there was no Scotch about him, except that he was loyal to his trusts and a brave soldier, for he looked like any wild man of the Plains; and one of his family said to him, laughingly, " Dress you up in a blanket, and you couldn't be told from a Cheyenne or Arrapahoe." There was a Frenchman to add to the nationalities we represented, and in our heterogeneous collection one company might have its three officers with parentage from three of the four corners of the earth.

The immense amount of rank these new lieutenants and captains carried was amusing, for those who had served in the war still held their titles when addressed unofficially, and it was, to all appearances, a regiment made up of generals, colonels and majors. Occasionally, an officer who had served in the regular army many years before the war arrogantly lorded it over the young lieutenants. One especially, who saw nothing good in the service as it now was, constantly referred to "how it was done in the old First." Having a young fellow appointed from civil life as his lieutenant, who knew nothing of army tactics or etiquette, he found a good subject over whom to tyrannize. He gave this lad to understand that whenever the captain made his appearance he must jump up, offer him a chair, and stand attention. It was, in fact, a servile life he was mapping out for his subordinate.

If the lad asserted himself in the slightest way, the captain straightened up that Prussian backbone, tapped his shoulder-strap, and grandiloquently observed, "Remember the goolf" [gulf], meaning the great chasm that intervened between a shoulder-strap with two bars and one with none. Even one knowing little of military life is aware that the "goolf" between a captain and a second lieutenant is not one of great magnitude. At last the youth began to see that he was being imposed upon, and that other captains did not so hold themselves toward their inferiors in rank, and he confidentially laid the case before a new arrival who had seen service, asking him how much of a stand he might make for his self-respect without infringing on military rules. The reply was, "When next he tries that game on you, tell him to go to h— with his gulf." The young fellow, not lacking in spirit, returned to his captain well primed for the encounter, and when next the gulf was mentioned, he stretched up his six feet of admirable physique, and advised the captain to take the journey "with his gulf," that had been previously suggested by his friend.

This same young fellow was a hot-headed youth, though a splendid soldier, and had a knack of getting into little altercations with his brother-officers. On one occasion at our house during a garrison hop, he and another officer had some dispute about dancing with a young lady, and retired to the coat-room, too courteous to enter into a discussion in the presence of women. It occurred to them, as words grew hotter and insufficient for the gravity of the occasion, that it would be well to interview the commanding officer, fearing that they might be placed in arrest. One of them descended to the dancing-room, called the General one side, told the story, and asked permission to pound his antagonist, whom he considered the aggressor. The General, knowing well how it was himself, having, at West Point, been known as the cadet who said, "Stand back, boys, and let's have a fair fight!" gave his permission. The door of the coat-room closed on the contestants for the fair lady's favor, and they had it out alone. It must not, from this incident, be inferred that our officers belonged to a class whose idea of justice was " knocking down and dragging out," but, in the newness of our regiment, there seemed to be occasions when there was no recourse for impositions or wrongs, except in the natural way. The mettle of all was being tested with a large number of men turned suddenly from a free life into the narrow limits of a garrison. Where everybody's elbow knocked his neighbor's, and no one could wholly escape the closest sort of intercourse, it was the most natural consequence that some jarring and grating went on.

None of us know how much the good-nature that we possess is due to the fact that we can take refuge in our homes or in flight, sometimes, from people who rasp and rub us up the wrong way.

Our regiment was then a medley of incongruous elements, and might well have discouraged a less persevering man, in the attempt to mould such material into an harmonious whole. From the first, the effort was to establish among the better men, who had ambition, the proper *esprit de corps* regarding their regiment. The General thought over carefully the future of this new organization, and worked constantly from the first days to make it the best cavalry regiment in the service. He assured me, when occasionally I mourned the inharmonious feeling that early began to crop out, that I must neither look for fidelity nor friendship, in its best sense, until the whole of them had been in a fight together; that it was on the battle-field, when all faced death together, where the truest affection was formed among soldiers. I could not help noting, that first year, the change from the devotion of my husband's Division of cavalry in the Army of the Potomac, to these new officers, who, as yet, had no affection for him, nor even for their regiment. He often asked me to have patience, not to judge too quickly of those who were to be our companions, doubtless for years to come, and reminded me that, as yet, he had done nothing to win their regard or command their respect; he had come among offi-

cers and men as an organizer, a disciplinarian, and it was
perfectly natural they should chafe under restraints they had
never known before. It was a hard place for my husband to
fill, and a most thankless task, to bring that motley crowd
into military subjection. The mischief-makers attempted to
report unpleasant criticisms, and it was difficult to keep in
subjection the jealousy that existed between West Point
graduates, volunteer officers, and civil appointees. Of course
a furtive watch was kept on the graduates of the Military
Academy for any evidences of assumed superiority on their
part, or for the slightest dereliction of duty. The volunteer,
no matter how splendid a record he had made during the war,
was excessively sensitive regarding the fact that he was not a
graduated officer. My husband persistently fought against
any line of demarkation between graduates and non-gradu-
ates. He argued personally, and wrote for publication, that
the war had proved the volunteer officers did just as good
service as, and certainly were not one whit less brave than,
West Pointers. I remember how every little slip of a West
Pointer was caught at by the others. One morning a group
of men were gathered about the flag-staff at guard-mount,
making the official report as officer of the day and officer of
the guard, when a West Pointer joined them in the irreproachable uniform of a lieutenant, walking as few save
graduates ever do walk. He gravely saluted, but, instead of
reporting for duty, spoke out of the fullness of his heart,
" Gentlemen, it's a boy." Of course, not a man among them
was insensible to the honor of being the father of a first son
and heir, and all suspended military observances belonging
to the morning duties, and genuinely rejoiced with the new-
made parent; but still they gloated over the fact that there
had been, even in such a moment of excitement, this lapse of
military dignity in one who was considered a cut-and-dried
soldier.

An embarrassing position for General Custer was, that he
had under him officers much older than himself. He was
then but twenty-seven years of age, and the people who

studied to make trouble (and how rarely are they absent from any community !) used this fact as a means of stirring up dissension. How thankful I was that nothing could draw him into difficulty from that question, for he either refused to listen, or heard only to forget. One day he was deeply moved by the Major of our regiment, General Alfred Gibbs, who had commanded the brigade of regular cavalry in the Army of the Potomac during the war, and whose soul was so broad and his heart so big that he was above everything petty or mean. My husband called me into our room and shut the door, in order to tell me, quietly, that some gossip had endeavored to spread a report that General Gibbs was galled by his position, and unwilling to submit to the authority of so young a man. On hearing this, he came straightway to General Custer—ah, what worlds of trouble we would be saved if there were courage to inquire into slander!—and in the most earnest, frank manner assured him that he had never expressed such sentiments, and that their years of service together during the war had established an abiding regard for his soldierly ability that made it a pleasure to be in his regiment. This, from an officer who had served with distinction in the Mexican War, as well as done gallant service in an Indian campaign before the Civil War, was a most grateful compliment to my husband. General Gibbs was a famous disciplinarian, and he had also the quaintest manner of fetching every one to the etiquettical standard he knew to be necessary. He was witty, and greatly given to joking, and yet perfectly unswerving in the performance of the most insignificant duty. We have exhausted ourselves with laughter as he described, by contortions of feature and really extraordinary facial gymnastics, his efforts to dislodge a venturesome and unmilitary fly, that had perched on his nose when he was conducting a dress-parade. To lift his hand and brush off the intruder, with a long line of soldiers facing him, was an example he would scarcely like them to follow; and yet the tantalizing tickling of those fly-legs, slowly traveling over his moist and heated face, was almost too exas-

perating to endure. If General Gibbs felt the necessity of
reminding any one of carelessness in dress, it was managed
in so clever a manner that it gave no lasting offense. My
husband, absorbed in the drilling, discipline, and organization of the regiment, sometimes overlooked the necessity for
social obligations, and immediately came under the General's
witty criticisms. If a strange officer visited our post, and any
one neglected to call, as is considered obligatory, it was remarked upon by our etiquettical mentor. If the officers were
careless in dress, or wore semi-military clothes, something
quite natural in young fellows who wanted to load on everything that glittered, our General Etiquette made mention of
it. One wore an English forage-cap with a lot of gilt braid
on top, instead of the plain visored cap of the regulations.
The way he came to know that this innovation must be suppressed, was by a request from General Gibbs to purchase it
for his bandmaster. He himself was so strictly military that
he could well afford to hold the others up to the mark. His
coats were marvelous fits, and he tightly buckled in his increasing rotundity with a superb belt and clasp that had belonged to his grandfather, a Wolcott in the Revolutionary
War.

Most women know with what obstinate determination and
adoring fondness a man clings to some shabby article of wearing apparel. There was in our family an ancient dressing-
gown, not the jaunty smoking - jacket that I fortunately
learned afterward to make; but a long, clumsy, quilted mon-
strosity that I had laboriously cobbled out with very ignorant
fingers. My husband simply worshiped it. The garment
appeared on one of his birthdays, and I was praised beyond
my deserts for having put in shape such a success, and he
could hardly slide out of his uniform, when he came from the
office, quickly enough to enable him to jump into this soft,
loose abomination. If he had vanity, which it is claimed is
lodged somewhere in every human breast, it was spasmodic,
for he not only knew that he looked like a fright, but his family told him this fact, with repeated variations of derision.

When at last it became not even respectable, it was so ragged, I attempted to hide it, but this did no earthly good. The beloved possession was ferreted out, and he gaily danced up and down in triumph before his discomfited wife, all the rags and tags flaunting out as he moved. In vain General Gibbs asked me why I allowed such a disgraceful " old man's garment " about. The truth was, there was not half the discipline in our family that there might have been had we been citizens. A woman cannot be expected to keep a man up to the mark in every little detail, and surely she may be excused if she do a little spoiling when, after months of separation, she is returned to the one for whom her heart has been wrung with anxiety. No sooner are you together than there comes the ever-present terror of being divided again.

General Gibbs won at last in suppressing the old dressing-gown, for he begged General Custer to picture to himself the appearance of his entire regiment clad in long-tailed, ragged gowns modeled after that of their commanding officer ! In dozens of ways General Gibbs kept us up to the mark socially. He never drew distinctions between the old army and the new, as some were wont to do, and his influence in shaping our regiment in social as well as military affairs was felt in a marked manner, and we came to regard him as an authority, and to value his suggestions.

CHAPTER XIV.

THE COURSE OF TRUE LOVE.

SOON after my husband returned from Washington, he found that Ristori was advertised in St. Louis, and as he had been delighted with her acting when in the East, he insisted upon my going there, though it was a journey of several hundred miles. The young officers urged, and the pretty Diana looked volumes of entreaty at me, so at last I consented to go, as we need be absent but a few days. At that time the dreaded campaign looked far off, and I was trying to cheat myself into the belief that there might possibly be none at all.

Ristori, heard under any circumstances, was an event in a life; but to listen to her as we did, the only treat of the kind in our winter, and feeling almost certain it was the last of such privileges for years to come, was an occasion never to be forgotten.

I do not know whether Diana collected her senses enough to know, at any one time, that she was listening to the most gifted woman in histrionic art. A civilian lover had appeared on the scene, and between our young officers, already far advanced in the dazed and enraptured state, and the new addition to her retinue, she was never many moments without " airy nothings " poured into her ear. The citizen and the officers glowered on each other, and sought in vain to monopolize the inamorata. Even when the thoughtless girl put a military cap on the head of a civilian, and told him that an improvement in his appearance was instantly visible, he still remained, and held his ground valiantly. Finally the most desperate of them called me to one side, and implored my championship. He complained bitterly that he never

began to say what trembled on his tongue but one of those
interfering fellows appeared and interrupted him, and now,
as the time was passing, there remained but one chance before he went home, where he would again be among a dozen
other men who were sure to get in his way.   He said he had
thought over every plan, and if I would engage the interfering ones for a half hour, he would take Diana to the hotel
cupola, ostensibly to see the view, and if, after they were up
there, she saw anything but him, it would not be his fault;
for say his say he must.   No one could resist such a piteous
appeal, so I engaged the supernumerary men in conversation
as best I could, talking against time and eyeing the door as
anxiously as they did.   I knew, when the pair returned, that
the pent-up avowal had found utterance; but the coquetting
lass had left him in such a state of uncertainty that even
" fleeing to the house-top " had not secured his future.   So
it went on, suspense and agitation increasing in the perturbed hearts, but the dallying of this coy and skillful strategist,
wise beyond her years in some ways, seemed to prove that
she believed what is often said, that a man is more blissful
in uncertainty than in possession.

Our table was rarely without guests at that time.   A great
many of the strangers came with letters of introduction to
us, and the General superintended the arrangements for buf-
falo-hunts, if they were to be in the vicinity of our post.
Among the distinguished visitors was Prince Ourosoff,
nephew of the Emperor of Russia. He was but a lad, and only
knew that if he came west far enough, he was very likely to
find what the atlas put down as the " Great American Desert."   None of us could tell him much more of the Sahara
of America than of his own steppes in Russia.   As the years
have advanced, the maps have shifted that imaginary desert
from side to side.   The pioneer does such wonders in culti-
vating what was then supposed to be a barren waste, that we
bid fair in time not to have any Sahara at all.   I hardly wonder now at the surprise this royal scion expressed at finding
himself among men and women who kept up the amenities

of refined life, even when living in that subterranean home
which our Government provided for its defenders—the dug-
out. It seems strange enough, that those of us who lived
the rough life of Kansas's early days, did not entirely adopt
the careless, unconventional existence of the pioneer, but
military discipline is something not easily set aside.

Almost our first excursionists were such a success that we
wished they might be duplicated in those who flocked out
there in after years. Several of the party were old travelers,
willing to undergo hardships and encounter dangers to see
the country before it was overrun with tourists. They were
our guests, and the manner in which they beguiled our time
made their departure a real regret. They called themselves
" Gideon's Band." The youngest of the party, a McCook,
from the fighting Ohio family, was " Old Gid," while the
oldest of all answered when they called " Young Gid." As
they were witty, clever, conversant by actual experience with
most things that we only read of in the papers, we found
them a godsend.

When such people thanked us for what simple hospitality
we could offer, it almost came as a surprise, for we felt ourselves their debtors. After having written to this point in
my narrative of our gay visit from Gideon's Band, a letter in
response to one that I had sent to Mr. Charles G. Leland
arrived from London. I asked him about his poem, and
after twenty years, in which we never saw him, he recalls
with enthusiasm his short stay with us. I have only elimi-
nated some descriptions that he gives in the extract of the
private letter sent then from Fort Riley—descriptions of the
wife of the commanding officer and the pretty Diana.
Women being in the minority, it was natural that we were
never undervalued. Grateful as I am that he should so highly appreciate officers' wives, and much as I prize what he says
regarding " the influences that made a man, and kept him
what he was," I must reserve for Mr. Leland's correspondent
of twenty years back, and for myself, his opinion of frontier
women.

"LANGHAM HOTEL, PORTLAND PLACE,
"LONDON, W., June 14, 1887.

"DEAR MRS. CUSTER:—It is a thousand times more likely that
you should forget me than that I should ever forget you, though
it were at an interval of twice twenty years; the more so since I
have read your admirable book, which has revived in me the
memory of one of the strangest incidents and some of the most
agreeable impressions of a somewhat varied and eventful life. I
was with a party of gentlemen who had gone out to what was then
the most advanced surveyor's camp for the Pacific Railway, in
western Kansas. On returning, we found ourselves one evening
about a mile from Fort Riley, where we were to be the guests of
yourself and your husband. We had been all day in a so-called
ambulance or wagon. The one that I shared with my friend,
J. R. G. Hassard, of the New York *Tribune*, was driven by a
very intelligent and amusing frontiersman, deeply experienced in
Indian and Mexican life, named Brigham. Brigham thought, by
mistake, that we had all gone to Fort Riley by some other con-
veyance, and he was thirty or forty yards in advance, driving on
rapidly. We, encumbered with blankets, packs and arms, had no
mind to walk when we could 'wagon.' One man whistled, and
all roared aloud. Then one discharged his rifle. But the wind
was blowing away from Brigham towards us, and he heard nothing. The devil put an idea in my head, for which I have had
many a regret since then. *Infandum regina jubes renovare dolorem.*
('Thou, my queen, dost command me to revive a wretched sorrow.') For it occurred that I could send a rifle-ball so near to
Brigham's head that he could hear the whistle, and that this would
very naturally cause him to stop. If I could only know all, I
would sooner have aimed between my own eyes.

"'Give me a gun,' I said to Colonel Lambourn.

"'You won't shoot at him!' said the Colonel.

"'If you'll insure the mules,' I replied, 'I will insure the
driver.'

"I took aim and fired. The ambulance was covered, and I did
not know that Mr. Hassard, the best fellow in the world—*nemini
secúndus*—was sitting inside and talking to Brigham. The bullet
passed between their faces, which were a foot apart—less rather
than more.

"'What is that?' cried Hassard.

"'*Injuns!*' replied Brigham, who knew by many an experience how wagons were Apached, Comanchied, or otherwise aboriginated.

"'Lay down flat!'

"He drove desperately till he thought he was out of shot, and then put out his head to give the Indians a taunting war-whoop I shall never forget the appearance of that sunburned face, with gold ear-rings and a vast sombrero! What was his amazement at seeing only friends! I did not know what Brigham's state of mind might be toward me, but I remembered that he gloried in his familiarity with Spanish, so I said to him in the Castile-soap dialect, 'I fired that shot; is it to be hand or knife between us?' It is to his credit that he at once shook my hand, and said, '*La mano!*' He drove on in grim silence, and then said, 'I've driven for twelve years on this frontier, but I never heard, before, of anybody trying to stop one by shooting the driver.'

"Another silence, broken by the following remark: 'I wish to God there was a gulch any where between here and the fort! I'd upset this party into it d——n quick.'

"But I had a great fear. It was of General Custer and what he would have to say to me, for recklessly imperiling the life of one of his drivers, to say nothing of what might have happened to a valuable team of mules and the wagon. It was with perturbed feelings—and, *ay de mi!* with an evil conscience—that I approached him. He had been informed of the incident, but was neither angry nor vindictive. All he did was to utter a hearty laugh and say, 'I never heard before of such an original way of ringing a bell to call a man.'

"In a letter written about this time to a friend, I find the following:

"'We had not for many days seen a lady. Indeed, the only woman I had met for more than a week was a poor, sad soul, who, with her two child-daughters, had just been brought in by Lieutenant Hesselberger from a six-months' captivity of outrage and torture among the Apaches. You may imagine how I was impressed with Mrs. General Custer and her friend, Miss ——. . .

"'General Custer is an ideal—the ideal of frank chivalry, unaffected, genial humor, and that earnestness allied to originality which is so characteristic of the best kind of Western army man. I have not, in all my life, met with so many interesting types of character, as during this, my first journey to Kansas, but first among all, I place this trio.

" ' In the evening a great musical treat awaited me. I had once passed six months in Bavaria, where I had learned to love the zither. This instrument was about as well known twenty years ago in America, as a harp of a thousand strings. But there was at the fort a Bavarian soldier, who played charmingly on it, and he was brought in. I remember asking him for many of his best-loved airs. The General and his wife impressed me as two of the best entertainers of guests whom I ever met. The perfection of this rare talent is, to enjoy yourself while making others at their ease and merry, and the proof lies in this, that seldom, indeed, have I ever spent so pleasant an evening as that in the fort.'

" My personal experience of General Custer does not abound in anecdotes, but is extremely rich in my impressions of him, as a type and a character, both as man and gentleman. There is many a man whom I have met a thousand times, whom I hardly recollect at all, while I could never forget him. He was not only an admirable but an impressive man. One would credit anything to his credit, because he was so frank and earnest. One meets with a somewhat similar character sometimes among the Hungarians, but just such a man is as rare as the want of them in the world is great.

" With sincere regards, yours truly,

" CHARLES G. LELAND."

As Mr. Leland's poem, " Breitmann in Kansas," was inspired partly by the buffalo-hunt and visit at our quarters, I quote a few stanzas:*

" Vonce oopen a dimes, der Herr Breitmann vent oud West. Von efenings he was drafel mit some ladies und shendlemans, und he shtaid incognitus. Und dey singed songs dill py and py one of de ladies say: 'Ish any podies here ash know de crate pallad of "Hans Breitmann's Barty ?"' Den Hans said, 'I am

---

* From " Hans Breitmann's Ballads," by permission of Messrs. T. B. Peterson & Brothers, publishers.

dat rooster!' Den der Hans took a drink und a let pencil und a
biece of baper, und goes indo himself a little dimes, and den
coomes out again mit dis boem:

" Hans Breitmann vent to. Kansas;
   He drafel fast und far.
He rided shoost drei dousand miles
   All in one railroot car.
He knowed foost rate how far he goed—
   He gounted all de vile.
Dar vash shoost one bottle of champagne,
   Dat bopped at efery mile.

" Hans Breitmann vent to Kansas;
   He went in on de loud.
At Ellsvort in de prairie land,
   He found a pully croud.
He looked for bleeding Kansas,
   But dat's ' blayed out,' dey say;
De whiskey keg's de only dings
   Dat's bleedin' dere to-day.

" Hans Breitmann vent to Kansas;
   Py shings! I dell you vot,
Von day he met a crisly bear
   Dat rooshed him down, bei Gott!
Boot der Breitmann took und bind der bear,
   Und bleased him fery much—
For efry vordt der crisly growled
   Vas goot Bavarian Dutch!

" Hans Breitmann vent to Kansas!
   By donder, dat is so!
He ridit out upon de plains
   To chase de boofalo.
He fired his rifle at de bools,
   Und gallop troo de shmoke
Und shoomp de canyons shoost as if
   Der tyfel vas a choke!"

Not only were a large number of officers brought together that winter from varied walks in life and of different nationalities, but the men that enlisted ranged from the highest type of soldier to the lowest specimens of humanity recruited in the crowded cities. It often happened that enlisted men had served an honorable record as officers in the volunteer service. Some had entered the regular army because their life was broken up by the war and they knew not how to begin a new career; others had hopes of promotion, on the strength of their war record, or from the promises of influential friends. My heart is moved anew as I recall one man, who sank his name and individuality, his very self, it seemed, by enlistment, and as effectually disappeared as if he had flung himself into the river that rushed by our post. One night there knocked at the door of one of our officer's quarters a man who, though in citizen's dress, was at once recognized as an old comrade in the war. He had been a brigadier-general of volunteers. After he had been made welcome, he gave some slight account of himself, and then said he had about made up his mind to enlist. Our Seventh Cavalry officer implored him not to think of such a thing, pictured the existence of a man of education and refinement in such surroundings, and offered him financial help, should that be needed. He finally found the subject was adroitly withdrawn, and the conversation went back to old times. They talked on in this friendly manner until midnight, and then parted. The next day a soldier in fresh, bright blue uniform, passed the officer, formally saluting as he went by, and to his consternation he discovered in this enlisted man his friend of the night before. They never met again; the good-by of the midnight hour was in reality the farewell that one of them had intended it to be.

This is but one of many instances where superior men, for one reason or another, get into the ranks of our army. If they are fortunate enough to fall into the hands of considerate officers, their lot is endurable; but to be assigned to one who is unjust and overbearing is a miserable existence.

One of our finest men was so constantly looking, in his soldiers, for
the same qualities that he possessed, and insisted so upon the superiority of his men that the officers were wont to exclaim in good-
natured irony, "Oh, yes, we all
know that Hamilton's company is
made up of dukes and earls in
disguise."

There were some clever rogues
among the enlisted men, and the
officers were as yet scarcely able
to cope with the cunning of those
who doubtless had intimate acquaintance with courts of justice
and prisons in the Eastern States.
The recruiting officer in the cities
is not compelled, as in other occu-
pations, to ask a character from
a former employer. The Government demands able-bodied men,
and the recruiting sergeant casts
his critical eye over the anatom-

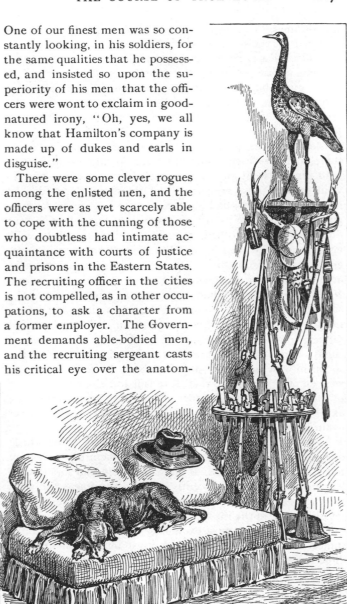

GUN-STAND IN GENERAL CUSTER'S LIBRARY.

ical outlines, as he would over the good points of a horse destined for the same service. The awful hereafter is, when the officer that receives this physical perfection on the frontier aims to discover whether it contains a soul.

Our guard-house at Fort Riley was outside the garrison a short distance, and held a goodly number of violators of the regulations. For several nights, at one time, strange sounds for such a place issued from the walls. Religion in the noisiest form seemed to have taken up its permanent abode there, and for three hours at a time singing, shouting and loud praying went on. There was every appearance of a revival among those trespassers. The officer of the day, in making his rounds, had no comment to pass upon this remarkable transition from card-playing and wrangling; he was doubtless relieved to hear the voice of the exhorters as he visited the guard, and indulged in the belief that the prisoners were out of mischief. On the contrary, this vehement attack of religion covered up the worst sort of roguery. Night after night they had been digging tunnels under the stone foundation-walls, removing boards and cutting beams in the floor, and to deaden the sound of the pounding and digging some of their number were told off to sing, pray and shout. One morning the guard opened the door of the rooms in which the prisoners had been confined, and they were empty! Even two that wore ball and chains for serious offences had in some manner managed to knock them off, as all had swum the Smoky Hill River, and they were never again heard from.

As with the history of all prisons, so it was of our little one. The greatest rogues were not incarcerated; they were too cunning to be caught. It often happened that some excellent soldiers became innocently involved in a fracas and were marched off to the guard-house, while the archvillain slipped into his place in the ranks and answered to his name at roll-call, apparently the most exemplary of soldiers. Several instances of what I thought to be unjust imprisonment came directly under my notice, and I may have been greatly influenced by Eliza's pleas in their behalf. We made the effort, and succeeded in extricating one man from his imprisonment. Whether he was in reality wronged, or had only worked upon our sympathies, will never be known, but he certainly made an excellent soldier from that time until the end of his enlistment. Eliza, in her own quaint way, is saying to me now: "Do you mind, Miss Libbie, how me and you got J——his parole? He used to come to our house with the rest of the prisoners, to police the yard and cut the wood, and they used to hang round my door; the guard could hardly get 'em away. Well, I reckon he didn't try very hard, for he didn't like hard-tack no better than they did. One of them would speak up the minute they saw me, and say, ' Eliza, you hain't got no hot biscuit, have you?' Hot biscuits for prisoners! do you hear *that*, Miss Libbie? The Ginnel would be standin' at the back window, just to catch a chance to laugh at me if I gave the prisoners anythin' to eat. He'd stand at that window, movin' from one foot to the other, craning of his neck, and when I did give any cold scraps, he just bided his time, and when he saw me he would say, ' Well, been issuin' your rations again, Eliza? How many apple-dumplin's and biscuit did they get this time?' Apple-dumplin's, Miss Libbie! He jest said that 'cause he liked 'em better than anythin' else, and s'posed I'd been givin' away some of his. But as soon as he had teased me about it, that was the end; he would go along about his way and pick up his book, when he had done his laugh. But, Miss Libbie, he used to kinder mistrust, if me and you was talkin' one side. He would say, ' What you two conspirin' up now? Tryin' to get some one out of jail, I s'pose.' I remember how we worked for J——. He came to me and told me I must ' try to get Mrs. Custer to work for him; two words from her would do him more good than all the rest,' and he would come along sideways by your window, carrying his ball over his arm with the chain adanglin', and look so pitiful like, so you would see him and beg him off." This affair ended entirely to Eliza's satisfaction. I saw the captain of his company;

for though it was against my husband's wish that I should have
anything to do with official matters, he did not object to this
intervention; he only laughed at my credulity. The captain
politely heard my statement of what Eliza had told me were
J——'s wrongs, and gave him parole. His sentence was rescinded eventually, as he kept his promises and was a most
faithful soldier. The next morning after J—— was returned
to duty and began life anew, one of the young officers saun-
tered into our quarters and, waving his hand with a little
flourish, said, "I want to congratulate you on having obtained the pardon of the greatest scamp in the regiment; he
wouldn't steal a red-hot stove, but would wait a mighty long
time for it to cool." Later in my story is my husband's mention, in his letters, of the very man as bearing so good a record that he sent for him and had him detailed at headquarters, for nothing in the world, he confessed, but because I
had once interceded for him.

Eliza kept my sympathies constantly aroused, with her piteous tales of the wrongs of the prisoners. They daily had
her ear, and she appointed herself judge, jury and attorney
for the defense. On the coldest days, when we could not
ride and the wind blew so furiously that we were not able to
walk, I saw from our windows how poorly clad they were, for
they came daily, under the care of the guard, to cut the wood
and fill the water-barrels. The General quietly endured the
expressions of sympathy, and sometimes my indignant pro-
tests against unjust treatment. He knew the wrathful spirit
of the kitchen had obeyed the natural law that heat must
rise, and treated our combined rages over the prisoners'
wrongs with aggravating calmness. Knowing more about
the guard-house occupants than I did, he was fortified by
facts that saved him from expending his sympathies in the
wrong direction. He only smiled at the plausible stories by
which Eliza was first taken in at the kitchen door. They
lost nothing by transmission, as she had quite an imagination
and decidedly a dramatic delivery; and finally, when I told
the tale, trying to perform the monstrously hard feat of telling

it as it was told to me, youth, inexperience and an emotional temperament made a narrative so absolutely distressing that the General was likely to come over bodily to our side, had he not recalled the details of the court-martial that had tried the soldier. We were routed, yet not completely, for we fell back upon his clothes, and pleaded that, though he was thought to be wicked, he might be permitted to be warm. But the colored and white troops had to leave the field, "horse, foot and dragoons," when, on investigation, we found that the man for whom we pleaded had gambled away his very shirt.

The unmoved manner in which my husband listened to different accounts of supposed cruelty—dropping his beloved newspaper with the injured air that men assume, while I sat by him, half crying, gesticulating, thoroughly roused in my defense of the injured one—was exasperating, to say the least; and then, at last, to have this bubble of assumed championship burst, and see him launch into such uproarious conduct when he found that the man for whom I pleaded was the archrogue of all—oh, women alone can picture to themselves what the situation must have been to poor me!

After one of these seasons of good-natured scoffing over the frequency with which I was taken in, I mentally resolved that, though the proof I heard of the soldier's depravity was too strong for me to ignore, there was no contesting the fact that the criminal was cold, and if I had failed in freeing him I might at least provide against his freezing. He was at that time buttoning a ragged blouse up to his chin, not only for warmth, but because in his evening game of poker, his comrade had won the undergarment, quite superfluous, he thought, while warmed by the guard-house fire. I proceeded to shut myself in our room, and go through the General's trunk for something warm. The selection that I made was unfortunate. There were some navy shirts of blue flannel that had been procured with considerable trouble from a gunboat in the James River the last year of the war, the like of which, in quality and durability, could not be found in any shop.

The material was so good that they neither shrunk nor pulled out of shape. The broad collar had a star embroidered
in solid silk in either corner. The General had bought these
for their durability, but they proved to be a picturesque addition to his gay dress; and the red necktie adopted by his
entire Third Division of Cavalry gave a dash of vivid color,
while the yellow hair contrasted with the dark blue of the
flannel. The gunboats were overwhelmed with applications
to buy, as his Division wished to adopt this feature of his
dress also, and military tailors had many orders to reproduce
what the General had "lighted upon," as the officers expressed it, by accident. Really, there was no color so good
for campaigning, as it was hard to harmonize any gray tint
with the different blues of the uniform. Men have a way of
saying that we women never seize their things, for barter or
other malevolent purposes, without selecting what they especially prize. But the General really had reason to dote
upon these shirts.

The rest of the story scarcely needs telling. Many injured
husbands, whose wardrobes have been confiscated for elee-
mosynary purposes, will join in a general wail. The men
that wear one overcoat in early spring, and carry another
over their arm to their offices, uncertain, if they did not observe this precaution, that the coming winter would not find
these garments mysteriously metamorphosed into lace on a
gown, or mantel ornaments, may fill in all that my story fails
to tell. In the General's case, it was perhaps more than
ordinarily exasperating. It was not that a creature who bargains for "gentlemen's cast-offs" had possession of something that a tailor could not readily replace, but we were then
too far out on the Plains to buy even ordinary blue flannel.

As I remember myself half buried in the trunk of the commanding officer, and suddenly lifted into the air with a shirt
in one hand, my own escape from the guard-house seems
miraculous. As it was, I was let off very lightly, ignoring
some remarks about its being "a pretty high-handed state
of affairs, that compels a man to lock his trunk in his own

family; and that, between Tom's pilfering and his wife's, the
commanding officer would soon be obliged to receive official
reports in bed."

There was very little hunting about Fort Riley in the winter. The General had shot a great many prairie chickens in
the autumn, and hung them in the wood-house, and while
they lasted we were not entirely dependent on Government
beef. As the season advanced, we had only ox-tail soup and
beef. Although the officers were allowed to buy the best
cuts, the cattle that supplied the post with meat were far
from being in good condition. One day our table was
crowded with officers, some of whom had just reported for
duty. The usual great tureen of soup was disposed of, and
the servant brought in an immense platter, on which generally reposed a large roast. But when the dish was placed
before the General, to my dismay there appeared in the centre of its wide circumference a steak hardly larger than a man's
hand. It was a painful situation, and I blushed, gazed uneasily at the new-comers, but hesitated about apologies as
they were my husband's detestation. He relieved us from
the awful silence that fell upon all, by a peal of laughter that
shook the table and disturbed the poor little steak in its
lonesome bed. Eliza thrust her head in at the door, and explained that the cattle had stampeded, and the commissary
could not get them back in time to kill, as they did daily at
the post. The General was perfectly unmoved, calling those
peculiar staccato "all right !" "all right !" to poor Eliza,
setting affairs at ease again, and asking the guests to do the
best they could with the vegetables, bread and butter, coffee
and dessert.

The next day beef returned to our table, but, alas ! the potatoes gave out, and I began to be disturbed about my house-
wifely duties. My husband begged me not to give it a
thought, saying that Eliza would pull us through the temporary famine satisfactorily, and adding, that what was good
enough for us was good enough for our guests. But an attack of domestic responsibility was upon me, and I insisted

upon going to the little town near us. Under any circumstances the General opposed my entering its precincts, as it was largely inhabited by outlaws and desperadoes, and to go for so small a consideration as marketing was entirely against his wishes. I paid dearly for my persistence; for when, after buying what I could at the stores, I set out to return, the chain bridge on which I had crossed the river in the morning had been swept away, and the roaring torrent, that had risen above the high banks, was plunging along its furious way, bearing earth and trees in its turbid flood. I spent several dreary hours on the bank, growing more uneasy and remorseful all the time. The potatoes and eggs that so short a time since I had triumphantly secured, seemed more and more hateful to me, as I looked at them lying in the basket in the bottom of the ambulance. I made innumerable resolves that, so long as my husband did not wish me to concern myself about providing for our table, I never would attempt it again; but all these resolutions could not bring back the bridge, and I had to take the advice of one of our officers, who was also waiting to cross, and go back to the house of one of the merchants who sold supplies to the post. His wife was very hospitable, as frontier men and women invariably are, and next morning I was down on the bank of the river early, more impatient than ever to cross. What made the detention more exasperating was that the buildings of the garrison on the plateau were plainly visible from where we waited. Then ensued the most foolhardy conduct on my part, and so terrified the General when I told him afterward, that I came near never being trusted alone again. The most vexing part of it all was that I involved the officer, who was in town by accident, in imminent danger, for when he heard what I was determined to do, he had no alternative but to second my scheme, as no persuasion was of any avail. I induced a sergeant in charge of a small boat to take me over. I was frantic to get home, as for some time preparations had been going on for a summer campaign, and I had kept it out of our day as much as I could.

The General never anticipated trouble, reasoning that it was bad enough when it came, and we both felt that every hour must hold what it could of enjoyment, and not be darkened a moment if we could help it. The hours of delay on the bank were almost insupportable, as each one was shortening precious time. I could not help telling the sergeant this, and he yielded to my entreaties—for what soldier ever refused our appeals? The wind drove through the trees on the bank, lashing the limbs to and fro and breaking off huge branches, and it required almost superhuman strength to hold the frail boat to the slippery landing long enough to lift me in. The soldier at the prow held in his muscular hands a pole with an iron pin at the end, with which he used all his energy to push away the floating logs that threatened to swamp us. It was almost useless to attempt to steer, as the river had a current that it was impossible to stem. The only plan was to push out into the stream filled with débris, and let the current shoot the boat far down the river, aiming for a bend in its shores on the opposite side. I closed my eyes to the wild rush of water on all sides, shuddering at the shouts of the soldiers, who tried to make themselves heard above the deafening clamor of the tempest. I could not face our danger and retain my self-control, and I was tortured by the thought of having brought peril to others. I owed my life to the strong and supple arms of the sergeant and the stalwart soldier who assisted him, for with a spring they caught the limbs of an overhanging tree, just at the important moment when our little craft swung near the bank at the river bend, and, clutching at branches and rocks, we were pulled to the shore and safely landed. Why the brave sergeant even listened to such a wild proposition I do not know. It was the maddest sort of recklessness to attempt such a crossing, and the man had nothing to gain. With the strange, impassable gulf that separates a soldier from his officers and their families, my imploring to be taken over the river, and my overwhelming thanks afterward, were the only words he would ever hear me speak. With the officer who shared the peril, it was dif-

ferent. When we sat around the fireside again, he was the
hero of the hour. The gratitude of the officers, the thanks
of the women putting themselves in my place and giving him
praise for encountering danger for another, were some sort
of compensation. The poor sergeant had nothing; he went
back to the barracks, and sank his individuality in the ranks,
where the men look so alike in their uniform it is almost impossible to distinguish the soldier that has acted the hero
from one who is never aught but a poltroon. After the excitement of the peril I had passed was over, I no longer wondered that there was such violent opposition to women traveling with troops. The lesson lasted me a long time, as I
was well aware what planning and preparation it cost to take
us women along, in any case, when the regiment was on the
move, and to make these efforts more difficult by my own
heedlessness was too serious a mistake to be repeated.

In spite of the drawbacks to a perfectly successful garrison,
which was natural in the early career of a regiment, the winter had been full of pleasure to me; but it came to a sad ending when the preparations for the departure of the troops
began. The stitches that I put in the repairs to the blue
flannel shirts were set with tears. I eagerly sought every opportunity to prepare the camping outfit. The mess-chest
was filled with a few strong dishes, sacks were made and filled
with coffee, sugar, flour, rice, etc., and a few cans of fruit and
vegetables were packed away in the bottom of the chest.
The means of transportation were so limited that every pound
of baggage was a matter of consideration, and my husband
took some of the space that I thought ought to be devoted
to comforts, for a few books that admitted of reading and re-
reading. Eliza was the untiring one in preparing the outfit
for the summer. She knew just when to administer comforting words, as I sighed over the preparations, and reminded
me that "the Ginnel always did send for you every chance
he got, and war times on the Plains wa'n't no wuss than in
Virginia."

There was one joke that came up at every move we ever

TROPHIES OF THE CHASE IN GENERAL CUSTER'S LIBRARY.

made, over which the General was always merry. The officers, in and out of our quarters daily, were wont to observe
the unusual alacrity that I displayed when orders came to
move. As I had but little care or anxiety about household
affairs, the contrast with my extreme interest in the arrangements of the mess-chest, bedding and campaigning clothes
was certainly marked. I longed for activity, to prevent me
from showing my heavy heart, and really did learn to be
somewhat successful in crowding a good deal into a small
space, and choosing the things that were most necessary.
As the officers came in unannounced, they found me flying
hither and thither, intent on my duties, and immediately saw
an opportunity to tease the General, condoling with him because, having exhausted himself in arduous packing for the
campaign, he would be obliged to set out totally unfitted for
the summer's hardships. After their departure, he was sure
to turn to me, with roguery in his voice, and asked if I had
noticed how sorry all those young fellows were for a man who
was obliged to work so hard to get his traps ready to move.

It was amusing to notice the indifferent manner in which
some of the officers saw the careful and frugal preparing for
the campaign. That first spring's experience was repeated
in every after preparation. There were always those who
took little or nothing themselves, but became experts at casual
droppings in to luncheon or dinner with some painstaking
provider, who endeavored vainly to get himself out of sight
when the halt came for eating. This little scheme was occasionally persisted in merely to annoy one who, having shown
some signs of parsimony, needed discipline in the eyes of
those who really did a great deal of good by their ridicule.
Among one group of officers, who had planned to mess together, the only provision was a barrel of eggs. It is only
necessary to follow a cavalry column over the crossing of one
creek, to know the exact condition that such perishable food
would be in at the end of the first day. There were two of
the "plebes," as the youngest of the officers were called—as
I recall them, bright, boyish, charming fellows—who openly

rebelled against the rebuffs they claimed were given them, when they attempted to practice the dropping-in plan at another's meals.

After one of these sallies on the enemy, they met the repulse with the announcement that if "those stingy old mollycoddles thought they had nothing to eat in their own outfit, they would show them," and took the occasion of one of their birthdays to prove that their resources were unlimited. Though the two endeavored to conceal the hour and place of this fête, a persistent watcher discovered that the birthday breakfast consisted of a bottle of native champagne and corn bread. The hospitality of officers is too well known to make it necessary to explain that those with any tendency to penuriousness were exceptions. An army legend is in existence of an officer who would not allow his hospitality to be set aside, even though he was very short of supplies. Being an officer of the old army, he was as formal over his repast as if it were abundant, and, with all ceremony, had his servant pass the rice. The guest, thinking it the first course, declined, whereupon the host, rather offended, replied, "Well, if you don't like the rice, help yourself to the mustard." This being the only other article on the bill of fare, there need be no doubt as to his final choice. When several officers decide to mess together on a campaign, each one promises to provide some one necessary supply. On one of these occasions, after the first day's march was ended, and orders for dinner were given to the servant, it was discovered that all but one had exercised his own judgment regarding what was the most necessary provision for comfort, and the one that had brought a loaf of bread instead of a demijohn of whiskey was berated for his choice.

In the first days of frontier life, our people knew but little about preparations for the field, and it took some time to realize that they were in a land where they could not live upon the country. It was a severe and lasting lesson to those using tobacco, when they found themselves without it, and so far from civilization that there was no opportunity of re-

plenishing their supply.   On the return from the expedition,
the injuries as well as the enjoyments are narrated.   Sometimes we women, full of sympathy for the privations that had
been endured, found that these *were* injuries ; sometimes we
discovered that imagination had created them.   We enjoyed,
maliciously I am afraid, the growling of one man who never
erred in any way, and consequently had no margin for any
one that did ; calculating and far-seeing in his life, he felt no
patience for those who, being young, were yet to learn those
lessons of frugality that were born in him.   He was still wrathful when he gave us an account of one we knew to be delightfully impudent when he was bent on teasing.   When the
provident man untied the strings of his tobacco-pouch, and
settled himself for a smoke, the saucy young lieutenant was
sure to stroll that way, and in tones loud enough for those
near to hear him, drawl out, "I've got a match ; if any other
fellow's got a pipe and tobacco, I'll have a smoke."

The expedition that was to leave Fort Riley was commanded
by General Hancock, then at the head of the Department of
the Missouri.   He arrived at our post from Fort Leavenworth
with seven companies of infantry and a battery of artillery.
His letters to the Indian agents of the various tribes give the
objects of the march into the Indian country.   He wrote :

"I have the honor to state, for your information, that I am
at present preparing an expedition to the Plains, which will
soon be ready to move.   My object in doing so at this time
is, to convince the Indians within the limits of this Department that we are able to punish any of them who may molest
travelers across the Plains, or who may commit other hostilities against the whites.   We desire to avoid. if possible, any
troubles with the Indians, and to treat them with justice, and
according to the requirements of our treaties with them ; and
I wish especially, in my dealings with them, to act through
the agents of the Indian Department as far as it is possible
to do so.   If you, as their agent, can arrange these matters
satisfactorily with them, we shall be pleased to defer the
whole subject to you.   In case of your inability to do so, I

would be pleased to have you accompany me when I visit the country of your tribes, to show that the officers of the Government are acting in harmony. I shall be pleased to talk with any of the chiefs whom we may meet. I do not expect to make war against any of the Indians of your agency, unless they commence war against us."

In General Custer's account, he says that "the Indians had been guilty of numerous thefts and murders during the preceding summer and autumn, for none of which had they been called to account. They had attacked the stations of the overland mail-route, killed the employees, burned the stations and captured the stock. Citizens had been murdered in their homes on the frontier of Kansas; and murders had been committed on the Arkansas route. The principal perpetrators of these acts were the Cheyennes and Sioux. The agent of the former, if not a party to the murder on the Arkansas, knew who the guilty persons were, yet took no steps to bring the murderers to punishment. Such a course would have interfered with his trade and profits. It was not to punish for these sins of the past that the expedition was set on foot, but, rather, by its imposing appearance and its early presence in the Indian country, to check or intimidate the Indians from a repetition of their late conduct. During the winter the leading chiefs and warriors had threatened that, as soon as the grass was up, the tribes would combine in a united outbreak along the entire frontier."

There had been little opportunity to put the expedition out of our minds for some time previous to its departure. The sound from the blacksmith's shop, of the shoeing of horses, the drilling on the level ground outside of the post, and the loading of wagons about the quartermaster and commissary storehouses, went on all day long. At that time the sabre was more in use than it was later, and it seemed to me that I could never again shut my ears to the sound of the grindstone, when I found that the sabres were being sharpened. The troopers, when mounted, were curiosities, and a decided disappointment to me. The horse, when prepared for the march, barely showed head and tail. My ideas of the dashing trooper going out to war, clad in gay uniform and curbing a curveting steed, faded into nothingness before the reality. Though the wrapping together of the blanket, over-coat and shelter-tent is made a study of the tactics, it could not be reduced to anything but a good-sized roll at the back of the saddle. The carbine rattled on one side of the soldier, slung from the broad strap over his shoulder, while a frying-pan, a tin-cup, a canteen, and a haversack of hardtack clat-tered and knocked about on his other side. There were pos-sibly a hundred rounds of ammunition in his cartridge-belt, which took away all the symmetry that his waist might other-wise have had. If the company commander was not too strict, a short butcher-knife, thrust into a home-made leather case, kept company with the pistol. It was not a murder-ous weapon, but was used to cut up game or slice off the bacon, which, sputtering in the skillet at evening camp-fire, was the main feature of the soldier's supper. The tin uten-sils, the carbine and the sabre, kept up a continual din, as the horses seemingly crept over the trail at the rate of three to four miles an hour. In addition to the cumbersome load, there were sometimes lariats and iron pichet-pins slung on one side of the saddle, to tether the animals when they grazed at night. There was nothing picturesque about this lumbering cavalryman, and, besides, our men did not then sit their horses with the serenity that they eventually attained. If the beast shied or kicked—for the poor thing was itself learning to do soldiering, and occasionally flung out his heels, or snatched the bit in his mouth in protest—it was a question whether the newly made Mars would land on the crupper or hang helplessly among the domestic utensils suspended to his saddle. How sorry I was for them, they were so bruised and lamed by their first lessons in horsemanship. Every one laughed at every one else, and this made it seem doubly try-ing to me. I remembered my own first lessons among fear-less cavalrymen—a picture of a trembling figure, about as un-certain in the saddle as if it were a wave of the sea, the hands

cold and nerveless, and, I regret to add, the tears streaming
down my cheeks! These recollections made me writhe when
I saw a soldier describing an arc in the air, and his self-freed
horse galloping off to the music of tin and steel in concert,
for no such compulsory landing was ever met save by a roar
of derision from the column. Just in proportion as I had
suffered for their misfortunes, did I enjoy the men when,
after the campaign, they returned, perfect horsemen and
with such physiques as might serve for a sculptor's model.

At the time the expedition formed at Fort Riley, I had
little realization what a serious affair an Indian campaign was.
We had heard of the outrages committed on the settlers, the
attacking of the overland supply-trains, and the burning of
the stage-stations; but the rumors seemed to come from so
far away that the reality was never brought home to me until
I saw for myself what horror attends Indian depredations.
Even a disaster to one that seemed to be of our own family,
failed to implant in me that terror of Indians which, a month
or two later, I realized to its fullest extent by personal danger. I must tell my reader, by going back to the days of the
war, something of the one that first showed us what Indian
warfare really was. It was a sad preparation for the campaign that followed.

After General Custer had been promoted from a captain to
a brigadier-general, in 1863, his brigade lay quietly in camp
for a few days, to recruit before setting out on another raid.
This gave the unusual privilege of lying in bed a little later
in the morning, instead of springing out before dawn. For
several mornings in succession, my husband told me, he saw
a little boy steal through a small opening in the tent, take
out his clothes and boots, and after a while creep back with
them, brushed and folded. At last he asked Eliza where on
earth that cadaverous little image came from, and she explained that it was " a poor little picked sparrow of a chile,
who had come hangin' aroun' the camp-fire, mos' starved,"
and added, "Now, Ginnel, you mustn't go and turn him off,
for he's got nowhar to go, and 'pears like he's crazy to wait

on you." The General questioned him, and found that the boy, being unhappy at home, had run away. Enough of his sad life was revealed to convince the General that it was useless to attempt to return him to his Eastern home, for he was a determined little fellow, and there was no question that he would have fled again. His parents were rich, and my husband evidently knew who they were; but the story was confidential, so I never knew anything of him, except that he was always showing signs of good-breeding, even though he lived about the camp-fire. A letter that my husband wrote to his own home at that time, spoke of a hound puppy that one of his soldiers had given to him, and then of a little waif, called Johnnie, whom he had taken as his servant. "The boy," he wrote, "is so fond of the pup he takes him to bed with him." Evidently the child began his service with devotion, for the General adds: "I think he would rather starve than to see me go hungry. I have dressed him in soldier's clothes, and he rides one of my horses on the march. Returning from the march one day, I found Johnnie with his sleeves rolled up. He had washed all my soiled clothes and hung them on the bushes to dry. Small as he is, they were very well done."

Soon after Johnnie became my husband's servant, we were married, and I was taken down to the Virginia farm-house, that was used as brigade headquarters. By this time, Eliza had initiated the boy into all kinds of work. She, in turn, fed him, mended his clothes, and managed him, lording it over the child in a lofty but never unkind manner. She had tried to drill him to wait on the table, as she had seen the duty performed on the old plantation. At our first dinner he was so bashful I thought he would drop everything. My husband did not believe in having a head and foot to the table when we were alone, so poor little Johnnie was asked to put my plate beside the General's. Though he was so embarrassed in this new phase of his life, he was never so intimidated by the responsibility Eliza had pressed upon him that he was absent-minded or confused regarding one point:

he invariably passed each dish to the General first. Possibly my husband noticed it. I certainly did not. There was a pair of watchful eyes at a crack in the kitchen-door, which took in this little incident. One day the General came into our room laughing, his eyes sparkling with fun over Eliza's description of how she had noticed Johnnie always serving the General first, and had labored with him in secret, to teach him to wait on the lady first. "It's manners," she said, believing that was a crushing argument. But Johnnie, usually obedient, persistently refused, always replying that the General was the one of us two that ranked, and he ought to be served first.

At the time of General Kilpatrick's famous raid, when he went to take Richmond, General Custer was ordered to make a détour in an opposite direction, in order to deceive the Confederate army as to the real object to be accomplished. This ruse worked so successfully, that General Custer and his command were put in so close and dangerous a situation it was with difficulty that any of them escaped. The General told me that when the pursuit of the enemy was hottest, and everyone doing his utmost to escape, he saw Johnnie driving a light covered wagon at a gallop, which was loaded with turkeys and chickens. He had received his orders from Eliza, before setting out, to bring back something for the mess, and the boy had carried out her directions with a vengeance. He impressed into his service the establishment that he drove, and filled it with poultry. Even in the mêlée and excitement of retreat, the General was wonderfully amused, and amazed too, at the little fellow's fearlessness. He was too fond of him to leave him in danger, so he galloped in his direction and called to him, as he stood up lashing his horse, to abandon his capture or he would be himself a prisoner. The boy obeyed, but hesitatingly, cut the harness, sprang upon the horse's unsaddled back, and was soon with the main column. The General, by his delay, was obliged to take to an open field to avoid capture, and leap a high fence in order to overtake the retreating troops.

He became more and more interested in the boy, who was such a combination of courage and fidelity, and finally arranged to have him enlist as a soldier. The war was then drawing to its close, and he secured to the lad a large bounty, which he placed at interest for him, and after the surrender, persuaded Johnnie to go to school. It was difficult to induce him to leave; but my husband realized what injustice it was to keep him in the menial position to which he desired to return, and finally left him, with the belief that he had instilled some ambition into the boy.

A year and a half afterward, as we were standing on the steps of the gallery of our quarters at Fort Riley, we noticed a stripling of a lad walking toward us, with his head hanging on his breast, in the shy, embarrassed manner of one who doubts his reception. With a glad cry, my husband called out that it was Johnnie Cisco, and bounded down the steps to meet him. After he was assured of his welcome, he told us that it had been impossible for him to stay away, he longed so constantly to be again with us, and added that if we would only let him remain, he would not care what he did. Of course, the General regretted the giving up of his school; but, now that he had made the long journey, there was no help for it, and he decided that he should continue with us until he could find him employment, for he was determined that he should not reënlist. The boy's old and tried friend, Eliza, at once assumed her position of " missus," and, kind-hearted tyrant ! gave him every comfort and made him her vassal, without a remonstrance from the half-grown man, for he was only too glad to be in the sole home he knew, no matter on what terms. Soon after his coming, the General obtained from one of the managers of the Wells Fargo Express Company a place of messenger; and the recommendation he gave the boy for honesty and fidelity was confirmed over and over again by the officers of the express line. He was known on the entire route from Ogden to Denver, and was entrusted with immense amounts of gold in its transmission from the Colorado mines to the States. Several times he came to our house for a vacation, and my husband had always the unvarying and genuine welcome that no one doubted when once given, and he did not fail to praise and encourage the friendless fellow. Eliza, after learning what the lad had passed through, in his dangers from Indians, treated him like a conquering hero, but alternately bullied and petted him still. At last there came a long interval between his visits, and my husband sent to the express people to inquire. Poor Johnnie had gone like many another brave employee of that venturesome firm. In a courageous defense of the passengers and the company's gold, when the stage was attacked, he had been killed by the Indians. Eliza kept the battered valise that her favorite had left with us, and mourned over it as if it had been something human. I found her cherishing the bag in a hidden corner, and recalling to me, with tears, how warm-hearted Johnnie was, saying that the night the news of her old mother's death came to her from Virginia, he had sat up till daybreak to keep the fire going. " Miss Libbie, I tole him to go to bed, but he said, ' No, Eliza, I can't do it, when you are in trouble: when I had no friends, and couldn't help myself, you helped me.' " After that, the lad was always " poor Johnnie," and many a boy with kinsfolk of his own is not more sincerely mourned.

As the days drew nearer for the expedition to set out, my husband tried to keep my spirits up by reminding me that the council to be held with the chiefs of the warlike tribes, when they reached that part of the country infested with the marauding Indians, was something he hoped might result in our speedy reunion. He endeavored to induce me to think, as he did, that the Indians would be so impressed with the magnitude of the expedition, that, after the council, they would accept terms and abandon the war-path. Eight companies of our own regiment were going out, and these, with infantry and artillery, made a force of fourteen hundred men. It was really a large expedition, for the Plains; but the recollections of the thousands of men in the Third Cavalry Divis-

ion, which was the General's command during the war, made
the expedition seem too small, even for safety.

No one can enumerate the terrors, imaginary and real,
that filled the hearts of women on the border in those desperate days. The buoyancy of my husband had only a momentary effect in the last hours of his stay. That time seemed
to fly fast; but no amount of excitement and bustle of preparation closed my eyes, even momentarily, to the dragging
hours that awaited me. Such partings are such a torture
that it is difficult even to briefly mention them. My husband
added another struggle to my lot by imploring me not to let
him see the tears that he knew, for his sake, I could keep
back until he was out of sight. Though the band played its
usual departing tune, "The Girl I Left Behind Me," if there
was any music in the notes, it was all in the minor key to the
men who left their wives behind them. No expedition goes
out with shout and song, if loving, weeping women are left
behind. Those who have not assumed the voluntary fetters
that bind us for weal or for woe, and render it impossible to
escape suffering while those we love suffer, or rejoicing
while those to whom we are united are jubilant, felt too keenly for their comrades when they watched them tear themselves from clinging arms inside the threshold of their homes,
even to keep up the stream of idle chaffing that only such
occasions can stop. There was silence as the column left the
garrison. Alas ! the closed houses they left were as still as
if death had set its seal upon the door; no sound but the
sobbing and moans of women's breaking hearts.

Eliza stood guard at my door for hours and hours, until I
had courage, and some degree of peace, to take up life again.
A loving, suffering woman came to sleep with me for a night
or two. The hours of those first wakeful nights seemed endless. The anxious, unhappy creature beside me said, gently,
in the small hours, "Libbie, are you awake?" "Oh, yes,"
I replied, "and have been for ever so long." "What are
you doing?" "Saying over hymns, snatches of poetry, the
Lord's Prayer backward, counting, etc., to try to put myself

to sleep." "Oh, say some rhyme to me, in mercy's name, for I am past all hope of sleep while I am so unhappy !" Then I repeated, over and over again, a single verse, written, perhaps, by some one who, like ourselves, knew little of the genius of poetry, but, alas ! much of what makes up the theme of all the sad verses of the world:

> " There's something in the parting hour
>   That chills the warmest heart;
> But kindred, comrade, lover, friend,
>   Are fated all to part.
> But this I've seen, and many a pang
>   Has pressed it on my mind—
> The one that goes is happier
>   Than he who stays behind."

Perhaps after I had said this, and another similar verse, over and over again, in a sing-song, droning voice, the regular breathing at my side told me that the poor, tired heart had found temporary forgetfulness; but when we came to the sad reality of our lonely life next day, every object in our quarters reminded us what it is to " stay behind." There are no lonely women who will not realize how the very chairs, or anything in common use, take to themselves voices and call out reminders of what has been and what now is. Fill up the time as we might, there came each day, at twilight, an hour that should be left out of every solitary life. It is meant only for the happy, who need make no subterfuges to fill up hours that are already precious.

CHAPTER XV.

A PRAIRIE FIRE.

IT was a great change for us from the bustle and excitement of the cavalry, as they prepared for the expedition, to the dull routine of an infantry garrison that replaced the dashing troopers. It was intensely quiet, and we missed the clatter of the horses' hoofs, the click of the curry-comb, which had come from the stables at the morning and evening grooming of the animals, the voices of the officers drilling the recruits, the constant passing and repassing of mounted men in front of our quarters; above all, the enlivening trumpet-calls ringing out all day, and we rebelled at the drum and bugle that seemed so tame in contrast. There were no more long rides for me, for Custis Lee was taken out at my request, as I feared no one would give him proper care at the post. Even the little chapel where the officers' voices had added their music to the chants, was now nearly deserted. The chaplain was an interesting man, and the General and most of the garrison had attended the services during the winter. Only three women were left to respond, and, as we had all been reared in other churches, we quaked a good deal, for fear our responses would not come in the right place. They did not lack in earnestness, for when had we lonely creatures such cause to send up petitions as at that time, when those for whom we prayed were advancing into an enemy's country day by day ! Never had the beautiful Litany, that asks deliverance for all in trouble, sorrow, perplexity, temptation, borne such significance to us as then. No one can dream, until it is brought home to him, how space doubles, trebles, quadruples, when it is impossible to see the little wire that,

fragile as it seems, chains one to the absent. It is difficult
to realize, now that our country is cobwebbed with telegraph lines, what a despairing feeling it was, in those days,
to get far beyond the blessed nineteenth-century mode of
communication. He who crosses the ocean knows a few
days of such uncertainty, but over the pathless sea of Western prairie it was chaos, after the sound of the last horse's
hoof was lost in the distance.

We had not been long alone when a great danger threatened us. The level plateau about our post, and the valley
along the river near us, were covered with dry prairie grass,
which grows thickly and is matted down into close clumps.
It was discovered one day, that a narrow thread of fire was
creeping on in our direction, scorching these tufts into shriv-
elled brown patches that were ominously smoking when first
seen. As I begin to write of what followed, I find it difficult; for even those living in Western States and Territories
regard descriptions of prairie-fires as exaggerated, and are
apt to look upon their own as the extreme to which they
ever attain. I have seen the mild type, and know that a
horseman rides through such quiet conflagrations in safety.
The trains on some of our Western roads pass harmless
through belts of country when the flames are about them;
there is no impending peril, because the winds are moderate.
When a tiny flame is discovered in Kansas, or other States,
where the wind blows a hurricane so much of the time, there
is not a moment to lose. Although we saw what was hardly
more than a suspicion of smoke, and the slender, sinuous,
red tongue along the ground, we women had read enough of
the fires in Kansas to know that the small blaze meant that
our lives were in jeopardy. Most of us were then unacquainted
with those precautions which the experienced Plainsman
takes, and, indeed, we had no ranchmen near us to set us
the example of caution which the frontiersman so soon learns.
We should have had furrows ploughed around the entire
post in double lines, a certain distance apart, to check the
approach of fire. There was no time to fight the foe with a

like weapon, by burning over a portion of the grass between the advancing blaze and our post. The smoke rose higher and higher beyond us, and curling, creeping fire began to ascend into waves of flame with alarming rapidity, and in an incredibly short time we were overshadowed with a dark pall of smoke.

The Plains were then new to us. It is impossible to appreciate their vastness at first. The very idea was hard to realize, that from where we lived we looked on an uninterrupted horizon. We felt that it must be the spot where some one first said, "The sky fits close down all around." It fills the soul with wonder and awe to look upon the vastness of that sea of land for the first time. As the sky became lurid, and the blaze swept on toward us, surging to and fro in waving lines as it approached nearer and nearer, it seemed that the end of the world, when all shall be rolled together as a scroll, had really come. The whole earth appeared to be on fire. The sky was a sombre canopy above us, on which flashes of brilliant light suddenly appeared as the flames rose, fanned by a fresh gust of wind. There were no screams nor cries, simply silent terror and shiverings of horror, as we women huddled together to watch the remorseless fiend advancing with what appeared to be inevitable annihilation of the only shelter we had. Every woman's thoughts turned to her natural protector, now far away, and longed with unutterable longing for one who, at the approach of danger, stood like a bulwark of courage and defense. The river was half a mile away, and our feet could not fly fast enough to reach the water before the enemy would be upon us. There was no such a thing as a fire-engine. The Government then had not even provided the storehouses and quarters with the Babcock Extinguisher. We were absolutely powerless, and could only fix our fascinated gaze upon the approaching foe.

In the midst of this appalling scene, we were startled anew by a roar and shout from the soldiers' barracks. Some one had, at last, presence of mind to marshal the men into line, and, assuming the commanding tone that ensures action and obedience in emergencies, gave imperative orders. Every one—citizen employees, soldiers and officers—seized gunny sacks, blankets, poles, anything available that came in their way, and raced wildly beyond the post into the midst of the blazing grass. Forming a cordon, they beat and lashed the flames with the blankets, so twisted as to deal powerful blows. It was a frenzied fight. The soldiers yelled, swore and leaped frantically upon beds of blazing grass, condensing a lifetime of riotous energy into these perilous moments. We women were not breathless and trembling over fears for ourselves alone: our hearts were filled with terror for the brave men who were working for our deliverance. They were men to whom we had never spoken, nor were we likely ever to speak to them, so separated are the soldiers in barracks from an officer's household. Sometimes we saw their eyes following us respectfully, as we rode about the garrison, seeming to have in them an air of possession, as if saying, "That's our captain's or our colonel's wife." Now, they were showing their loyalty, for there are always a few of a regiment left behind to care for the company property, or to take charge of the gardens for the soldiers. These men, and all the other brave fellows with them, imperiled their lives in order that the officers who had gone out for Indian warfare, might come home and find "all's well." Let soldiers know that a little knot of women are looking to them as their saviors, and you will see what nerves of iron they have, what inexhaustible strength they can exhibit.

No sooner had the flames been stamped out of one portion of the plain, than the whole body of men were obliged to rush off in another direction and begin the thrashing and tramping anew. It seemed to us that there was no such thing as conquering anything so insidious. But the wind, that had been the cause of our danger, saved us at last. That very wind which we had reviled all winter for its doleful howlings around our quarters and down the chimneys; that self-same wind that had infuriated us by blowing our hats off when we went out to walk, or impeded our steps by twisting our skirts into hopeless folds about our ankles—was now to be our savior. Suddenly veering, as is its fashion in Kansas, it swept the long tongues of flame over the bluffs beyond us, where the lonely coyote and its mate were driven into their lair. By this vagary of the element, that is never anywhere more variable than in Kansas, our quarters, our few possessions, and no doubt our lives, were saved. With faces begrimed and blistered, their clothes black with soot and smoke, their hands burnt and numb from violent effort, the soldiers and citizen employees dragged their exhausted bodies back to garrison, and dropped down anywhere to rest.

The tinge of green that had begun to appear was now gone, and the charred, smoke-stained earth spread as far as we could see, making more desolate the arid, treeless country upon which we looked   It was indeed a blackened and dismal desert that encircled us, and we knew that we were deprived of the delight of the tender green of early spring, which carpets the Plains for a brief time before the sun parches and turns to russet and brown the turf of our Western prairies.

As we sat on the gallery, grieving over this ruin of spring, Mrs. Gibbs gathered her two boys closer to her, as she shuddered over another experience with prairie fire, where her children were in peril. The little fellows, in charge of a soldier, were left temporarily on the bank of a creek. Imagine the horror of a mother who finds, as she did, the grass on fire and a broad strip of flame separating her from her children! Before the little ones could follow their first instinct, and thereby encounter certain death by attempting to run through the fire to their mother, the devoted soldier, who had left them but a moment, realizing that they would instantly seek their mother, ran like an antelope to where the fire-band narrowed, leaped the flame, seized the little men, and plunged with mad strides to the bank of the creek, where, God be praised! nature provides a refuge from the relentless foe of our Western plains.

In our Western prairie fires the flame is often a mile long, perhaps not rising over a foot high, but, sweeping from six to ten miles an hour, it requires the greatest exertion of the ranchmen, with all kinds of improvised flails, to beat out the fire. The final resort of a frontiersman, if the flames are too much for him to overcome, is to take refuge with his family, cattle, horses, etc., in the garden, where the growing vegetables make an effectual protection. Alas, when he finds it safe to venture from the green oasis, the crops are not only gone, but the roots are burned, and the ground valueless from the parching of the terrible heat. When a prairie fire is raging at ten miles an hour, the hurricane lifts the tufts of loosened bunch grass, which in occasional clumps is longer than the rest, carrying it far beyond the main fire, and thus starting a new flame. No matter how weary the pioneer may be after a day's march, he neglects no precautions that can secure him from fire. He twists into wisp the longest of the bunch grass, trailing it around the camp; the fire thus started is whipped out by the teamsters, after it has burned over a sufficient area for safety. They follow the torch of the leader with branches of the green willow or twigs of cottonwood bound together.

The first letters, sent back from the expedition by scouts, made red-letter days for us. The official envelope, stained with rain and mud, bursting open with the many pages crowded in, sometimes even tied with a string by some messenger through whose hands the parcel passed, told stories of the vicissitudes of the missive in the difficult journey to our post. These letters gave accounts of the march to Fort Larned, where a great camp was established, to await the arrival of the chiefs with whom the council was to be held. While the runners were absent on their messages to the tribes, some effort was made to protect the troops against the still sharp winds of early spring. The halt and partly permanent camp was most fortunate; for had the troops been on the march, a terrible snow-storm that ensued would have wrought havoc, for the cold became so intense, and the snow so blinding, it was only through great precautions that loss of life was pre-

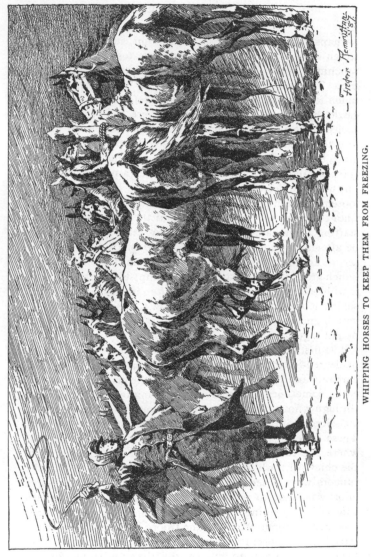

WHIPPING HORSES TO KEEP THEM FROM FREEZING.

vented. The animals were given an extra ration of oats, while the guards were obliged to take whips and strike at the horses on the picket-line, to keep them in motion and prevent them from freezing. The snow was eight inches deep, a remarkable fall for Kansas at that time of the year. As we read over these accounts, which all the letters contained, though mine touched lightly on the subject, owing to my husband's fixed determination to write of the bright side, we felt that we had hardly a right to our fires and comfortable quarters. There were officers on the expedition who could not keep warm. A number were then enduring their first exposure to the elements, and I remember that several, who afterward became stalwart, healthy men, were then partial invalids, owing to sedentary life in the States, delicate lungs or climatic influences.

In my husband's letters there was a laughable description of his lending his dog to keep a friend warm. The officer came into his tent after dark, declaring that no amount of bedding had any effect in keeping out the cold, and he had come to borrow a dog, to see if he could have one night's uninterrupted rest. Our old hound was offered, because he could cover such a surface, for he was a big brute, and when he once located himself he rarely moved until morning. My husband forgot, in giving Rover his recommendation, to mention a habit he had of sleeping audibly, besides a little fashion of twitching his legs and thumping his cumbrous tail, in dreams that were evidently of the chase, or of battles he was living over, in which "Turk," the bull-dog, was being vanquished. He was taken into the neighbor's tent, and induced to settle for the night, after the General's coaxing and pretense of going to sleep beside him. Later, when he went back to see how Rover worked as a portable furnace, he found the officer sound asleep on his back, emitting such nasal notes as only a stout man is equal to, while Rover lay sprawled over the broad chest of his host, where he had crept after he was asleep, snoring with an occasional interlude of a long-drawn snort, introduced in a manner peculiar to fox-

hounds. The next morning my husband was not in the least
surprised, after what he had seen the night before, to receive
a call from the officer, who presented a request to exchange
dogs. He said that when he made the proposal, he did not
expect to have a bedfellow that would climb up over his lungs
and crush all the breath out of his body. Instead of showing
proper sympathy, the General threw himself on his pallet
and roared with laughter.

All these camp incidents brightened up the long letters,
and kept me from realizing, as I read, what were the realities
of that march, undertaken so early in the season. But as the
day advanced, and the garrison exchanged the news contained in all the letters that had arrived from the expedition,
I could not deceive myself into the belief that the way of our
regiment had thus far been easy.

With all my endeavors to divide the day methodically, and
enforce certain duties upon myself, knowing well that it was
my only refuge from settled melancholy, I found time a laggard. It is true, my clothes were in a deplorable state,
for while our own officers were with us they looked to us to
fill up their leisure hours. The General, always devoted to
his books, could read in the midst of our noisy circle ; but I
was never permitted much opportunity, and managed to keep
up with the times by my husband's account of the important
news, and by the agreeable method of listening to the discussions of the men upon topics of the hour. If, while our circle was intact, I tried to sew, a ride, a walk or a game of
parlor croquet was proposed, to prevent my even mending
our clothing. Now that we were alone, it was necessary to
make the needle fly. Eliza was set up with a supply of blue-
checked gowns and aprons, while my own dresses were re-
constructed, the riding-habit was fortified with patches, and
any amount of stout linen thread disappeared in strengthen-
ing the seams ; for between the hard riding and the gales of
wind we encountered, the destruction of a habit was rapid.

Diana, with the elastic heart of a coquette, had not only
sped the parting, but welcomed the coming guest ; for hardly

had the sound of the trumpet died away, before a new officer began to frequent our parlor. It was then the fashion for men to wear a tiny neck-bow, called a butterfly tie. They were made on a pasteboard foundation, with a bit of elastic cord to fasten them to the shirt-stud. I knew of no pasteboard nearer than Leavenworth ; but in the curly head there were devices to meet the exigency. I found Diana with her lap full of photographs, cutting up the portraits of the departed beaux, to make ties for the next. Whether the new suitor ever discovered that he was wearing at his neck the face of a predecessor, I do not know ; but this I do remember, that the jagged, frayed appearance that the girl's dresses presented when turned inside out, betrayed where the silk was procured to make the neckties. She had clipped out bits of material where the skirt was turned in, and when we attempted to remodel ourselves and cut down the voluminous breadths of that time into tightly gored princesse gowns, we were put to it to make good the deficiencies, and " piece out " the silk that had been sacrificed to her flirtations.

Succeeding letters from my husband gave an account of his first experience with the perfidy of the Indians. The council had been held, and it was hoped that effectual steps were taken to establish peace. But, as is afterward related, the chiefs gave them the slip and deserted the village. Even in the midst of hurried preparations to follow the renegades, my husband stopped, in order that his departure might not make me depressed, to give an account of a joke that they all had on one of their number, who dared to eat soup out of an Indian kettle still simmering over the deserted fire. The General pressed the retreating Indians so closely, the very night of their departure, that they were obliged to divide into smaller detachments, and even the experienced Plainsmen could no longer trace a trail.

Meanwhile, as our officers were experiencing all sorts of new phases in life on their first march over the Plains, our vicissitudes were increasing at what seemed to be the peaceful Fort Riley. I had seen with dismay that the cavalry were

replaced by negro infantry, and found that they were to garrison the post for the summer. I had never seen negroes as soldiers, and these raw recruits had come from plantations, where
I had known enough of their life, while in Texas and Louisiana, to realize what an irresponsible, child's existence it was.
Entirely dependent on some one's care, and without a sense
of obligation of any kind, they were exempt from the necessity of thinking about the future. Their time had been spent
in following the directions of the overseer in the corn-field or
cotton brake by day, and beguiling the night with a coon-
hunt or the banjo. The early days of their soldiering were a
reign of terror to us women, in our lonely, unprotected
homes. It was very soon discovered that the officer who
commanded them was for the first time accustoming himself
to colored troops, and did not know how to keep in check
the boisterous, undisciplined creatures. He was a courteous,
quiet man, of scholarly tastes, and evidently entertained the
belief that moral suasion would eventually effect any purpose.
The negroes, doubtless discovering what they could do under
so mild a commander, grew each day more lawless. They
used the parade-ground, which our officers had consecrated
to the most formal of ceremonies, like dress-parades and
guard-mount, for a playground ; turning hand-springs all
over the sprouting grass, and vaulting in leap-frog over the
bent back of a comrade. If it were possible for people in the
States to realize how sacred the parade-ground of a Western
post is, how hurriedly a venturesome cow or loose horse is
marshaled off, how pompously every one performs the military duties permitted on this little square ; how even the
color-sergeant, who marches at measured gait to take down
and furl the garrison flag, when the evening gun announces
that the sun has been, by the royal mandate of military law,
permitted to set—they would then understand with what perturbation we women witnessed the desecration of what had
been looked upon as hallowed earth. The sacrilege of these
monkey acrobats turning somersaults over the ground, their
elongated heels vibrating in the air, while they stood upon

their heads in front of our windows, made us very indignant. When one patted "juba," and a group danced, we seemed transformed into a disconnected minstrel show. There was not a trace of the well-conducted post of a short time before.

All this frivolity was but the prelude to serious trouble. The joy with which the negroes came into possession of a gun for the first time in their lives would have been ludicrous had it not been extremely dangerous. They are eminently a race given over to display. This was exhibited in their attempts to make themselves marksmen in a single day. One morning we were startled by a shot coming from the barracks. It was followed by a rush of men out of the doors, running wildly to and fro, yelling with alarm. We knew that some disaster had occurred, and it proved to be the instant death of a too confiding negro, who had allowed himself to be cast for the part of William Tell's son. His accidental murderer was a man that had held a gun in his hand that week for the first time.

They had no sort of idea how to care for their health. The ration of a soldier is so large that a man who can eat it all in a day is renowned as a glutton. I think but few instances ever occur where the entire ration is consumed by one man. It is not expected, and, fortunately, with all the economy of the Government, the supply has never been cut down; but the surplus is sold and a company fund established. By this means, the meagre fare is increased by buying vegetables, if it happen to be a land where they can be obtained. The negroes, for the first time in possession of all the coffee, pork, sugar, and hardtack they wanted, ate inordinately. There was no one to compel them to cleanliness. If a soldier in a white regiment is very untidy the men become indignant, and as the voluminous regulations provide directions only for the scrubbing of the quarters and not of the men, they sometimes take the affair into their own hands, and, finding from their captain that they will not be interfered with, the untidy one is taken on a compulsory journey to the creek and " ducked " until the soldiers consider him

endurable. The negroes at that time had no idea of encountering the chill of cold water on their tropical skins,
and suffered the consequences very soon. Pestilence broke
out among them. Smallpox, black measles and other con-
tagious diseases raged, while the soldier's enemy, scurvy, took
possession. We were within a stone's-throw of the barracks.
Of course the illest among them were quarantined in hos-
pital-tents outside the garrison; but to look over to the infested barracks and realize what lurked behind the walls,
was, to say the least, uncomfortable for those of us who were
near enough to breathe almost the same air.

Added to this, we felt that, with so much indiscriminate
firing, a shot might at any time enter our windows. One
evening a few women were walking outside the garrison.
Our limits were not so circumscribed, at that time, as they
were in almost all the places where I was stationed afterward.
A sentinel always walked a beat in front of a small arsenal
outside of the post, and, overcome with the grandeur of
carrying a gun and wearing a uniform, he sought to impress
his soldierly qualities on anyone approaching by a stentorian
" Who comes thar?" It was entirely unnecessary, as it was
light enough to see the fluttering skirts of women, for the
winds kept our drapery in constant motion. Almost instantly
after his challenge, the flash of his gun and the whizz of a
bullet past us made us aware that our lives were spared only
because of his inaccurate aim. Of course that ended our evening walks, and it was a great deprivation, as the monotony
of a garrison becomes almost unbearable.

There was one person who profited by the presence of the
negro troops. Our Eliza was such a belle, that she would
have elevated them into too exalted a sphere to wait on us,
had she not been accustomed to constant adulation from the
officers' body-servants from the time, as she expressed it,
when she " entered the service." Still, it was a distraction,
of which she availed herself in our new post, to receive new
beaux, tire of them, quarrel and discard them for fresh victims. They waited on her assiduously, and I suspect they

dined daily in our kitchen, as long as their brief season of favor lasted. They even sought to curry favor with Eliza by gifts to me—snaring quail, imprisoning them in cages made of cracker-boxes, or bring dandelion greens or wild-flowers as they appeared in the dells. For all these gifts I was duly grateful, but I was very much afraid of a negro soldier, nevertheless.

At last our perplexities and frights reached a climax. One night we heard the measured tramp of feet over the gravel in the road in front of our quarters, and they halted almost opposite our windows, where we could hear the voices. No loud " Halt, who comes there!" rang out on the air, for the sentinel was enjoined to silence. Being frightened, I called to Eliza. To Diana and to me she was worth a corporal's guard, and could not be equaled as a defender, solacer and general manager of our dangerous situations—indeed, of all our affairs. Eliza ran up-stairs in response to my cry, and we watched with terror what went on. It soon was discovered to be a mutiny. The men growled and swore, and we could see by their threatening movements that they were in a state of exasperation. They demanded the commanding officer, and as he did not appear, they clenched their fists, and looked at the house as if they would tear it down, or at least break in the doors. It seemed a desperate situation to us, for the quarters were double, and our gallery had no division from the neighbors. If doors and windows were to be demolished, there would be little hope for ours. I knew of no way by which we could ask help, as most of the soldiers were colored, and we felt sure that the plan, whatever it was, must include them all.

At last Eliza realized how terrified I was, and gave up the absorbing watch she was keeping, for her whole soul was in the wrongs, real or fancied, of her race. Too often had she comforted me in my fears to forget me now, and an explanation was given of this alarming outbreak.

The men had for some time been demanding the entire ration, and were especially clamorous for all the sugar that

was issued. Very naturally, the captain had withheld the
supernumerary supplies, in order to make company savings
for the purpose of buying vegetables. A mutiny over sugar
may seem a small affair, but it assumes threatening proportions when a mob of menacing, furious men tramp up and down
in front of one's house, and there is no safe place of refuge,
nor any one to whom appeal can be made. Eliza kept up a
continuous comforting and reassuring, but when I reminded
her that our door had no locks, or, rather, no keys, for it was
not the custom to lock army quarters, she said, " La, Miss
Libbie, they won't tech you; you dun wrote too many letters
for 'em, and they'se got too many good vittels in your kitchen
ever to 'sturb you." Strong excitement is held to be the
means of bringing out the truth, and here were the facts revealed that they had been bountifully ted at our expense. I
had forgotten how much ink I had used in trying to put down
their very words in love-letters, or family epistles to the
Southern plantation. The infuriated men had to quiet down,
for no response came from the commanding officer. They
found out, I suppose from the investigations of one acting as
spy, and going to the rear of the quarters, that he had disappeared. To our intense relief, they straggled off until their
growling and muttering were lost in the barracks, where they
fortunately went to bed. No steps were taken to punish
them, and at any imaginary wrong, they might feel, from the
success of this first attempt at insurrection, that it was safe
to repeat the experiment. We women had little expectation
but that the summer would be one of carousal and open rebellion against military rule. The commanding officer,
though very retiring, was so courteous and kindly to all the
women left in the garrison, that it was difficult to be angry
with him for his failure to control the troops. Indeed, his
was a hard position to fill, with a lot of undisciplined, ignorant, ungoverned creatures, who had never been curbed, except by the punishment of plantation life.

Meanwhile my letters, on which I wrote every day, even if
there was no opportunity to send them, made mention of our

frights and uncertainties. Each mail carried out letters from
the women to the expedition, narrating their fears. We had
not the slightest idea that there was a remedy. I looked
upon the summer as the price I was to pay for the privilege
of being so far on the frontier, so much nearer the expedition than the families of officers who had gone East. With
all my tremors and misgivings, I had no idea of retreating
to safe surroundings, as I should then lose my hope of eventually going out to the regiment. It took a long time for our
letters to reach the expedition, and a correspondingly long
time for replies; but the descriptions of the night of mutiny
brought the officers together in council, and the best disciplinarian of our regiment was immediately despatched to our
relief. I knew but little of General Gibbs at that time; my
husband had served with him during the war, and valued his
soldierly ability and sincere friendship. He had been terribly wounded in the Indian wars before the Civil War, and
was really unfit for hard service, but too soldierly to be willing to remain at the rear. In a week after his arrival at our
post, there was a marked difference in the state of affairs.
Out of the seemingly hopeless material, General Gibbs made
soldiers who were used as guards over Government property
through the worst of the Indian country, and whose courage
was put to the test by frequent attacks, where they had to
defend themselves as well as the supplies. The opinion of
soldier and citizen alike underwent a change, regarding negroes as soldiers, on certain duty to which they were fitted.
A ranchman, after praising their fighting, before the season
was ended said, "And plague on my cats if they don't like it."

We soon found that we had reached a country where the
weather could show more remarkable and sudden phases in a
given time than any portion of the United States. The cultivation of the ground, planting of trees, and such causes,
have materially modified some of the extraordinary exhibitions that we witnessed when Kansas was supposed to be the
great American desert. With all the surprises that the elements furnished, there was one that we would gladly have

been spared.   One quiet day I heard a great rumbling in the
direction of the plateau where we had ridden so much, as if
many prairie-schooners, heavily laden, were being spirited
away by the stampede of mules.   Next, our house began to
rock, the bell to ring, and the pictures to vibrate on the wall.
The mystery was solved when we ran to the gallery, and
found the garrison rushing out of barracks and quarters;
Women and children ran to the parade-ground, all hatless,
some half-dressed.   Everybody stared at every one else,
turned pale, and gasped with fright.   It was an earthquake,
sufficiently serious to shake our stone quarters and overturn
the lighter articles, while farther down the gully the great
stove at the sutler's store was tumbled over and the side of
the building broken in by the shock.   There was a deep fissure in the side of the bank, and the waters of the Big Blue
were so agitated that the bed of the river twelve feet deep
was plainly visible.

The usual session of the "Did-you-evers" took place, and
resolutions were drawn up—not committed to paper, however—giving the opinion of women on Kansas as a place of
residence.   We had gone through prairie-fire, pestilence,
mutiny, a river freshet, and finally, an earthquake: enough
exciting events to have been scattered through a lifetime
were crowded into a few weeks.   Yet in these conclaves,
when we sought sympathy and courage from one another,
there was never a suggestion of returning to a well-regulated
climate.

CHAPTER XVI.

SACRIFICES AND SELF-DENIAL OF PIONEER DUTY—CAPTAIN
ROBBINS AND COLONEL COOK ATTACKED, AND FIGHT FOR
THREE HOURS.

IT is a source of regret, as these pages grow daily under
my hand, that I have not the power to place before the country the sacrifices ånd noble courage endured by the officers
and soldiers of our army in their pioneer work. I can only
portray, in the simplest manner, what I saw them endure
unmurmuringly, as I was permitted to follow in the marches
and campaigns of our regiment. I find that it is impossible
to make the life clear to citizens, even when they ask me to
describe personally something of frontier days, unless they
may have been over the Plains in their journeys to and from
the Pacific coast. Even then, they look from the windows
of the Pullman car on to the desert, white with alkali, over
which the heat rises in waves, and upon earth that struggles
to give even life to the hardy cactus or sage-brush. Then I
find their attention is called to our army, and I sometimes
hear a sympathetic tone in their voices as they say, "Ah !
Mrs. Custer, when I rode over that God-forgotten land, I began to see what none of us at the East ever realize—the terrible life that our army leads on the Plains." And only
lately, while I was in the West, a citizen described to me
seeing a company of cavalry, that had made a terrific march,
come in to the railroad at some point in Arizona. He told
me of their blistered faces, their bloodshot, inflamed eyes—
the result of the constant cloud of alkali dust through which
they marched—the exhaustion in every limb, so noticeable
in men of splendid vigor, with their broad chests, deep

throats, and muscular build, because it told what a fearful strain it must have been to have reduced such stalwart athletes to weakness. What effect it would have to introduce a body of such indomitable men in the midst of an Eastern city, tired, travel-stained, but invincible !

After all, if we who try to be their champions should succeed in making this transfer by some act of necromancy, the men would be silent about their sufferings. Among the few officers who have written of Plains life, there is scarcely a mention of hardships endured. As I read over my husband's magazine articles for the first time in many years, I find scarcely a reference to the scorching sun, the stinging cold, the bleak winds. His narrative reads like the story of men who marched always in sunshine, coming across clear streams of running water and shady woods in which to encamp. I have been there; through and through the breezy, buoyant tale I see the background—a treeless, arid plain, brackish, muddy water, sandy, sterile soil. The faces of our gallant men come up to me in retrospection, blistered and swollen, the eyes streaming with moisture from the inflaming dust, the parched lips cracked with fever of unquenched thirst, the hands, even, puffed and fiery with the sun-rays, day after day.

It seems heartless to smile in the midst of this vision, recalled to me of what I myself have seen, but I hear some civilian say, as they have often asked me equally inconsistent questions, "Well, why didn't they wear gloves?" Where all the possessions of a man are carried on the saddle, and the food and forage on pack-mules, it would be impossible to take along gloves to last from early spring till the stinging cold of late autumn. Thirst is an unconquerable foe. It is one of those enemies that may be vanquished on one field and come up, supported by legions of fresh desires, the very next day. I know nothing but the ever-present selfishness of our natures that requires such persistent fighting. Just fancy, for a moment, the joy of reaching a river or a stream on the Plains ! How easy the march seemed beside its banks! At

any moment one could descend, fill the canteen, and rejoin
the column. It is true the quality of the water was not of
the best, but there comes a time, out there, when quantity
triumphs. It seems so good to have enough of *anything*, for
the stinted supplies of all sorts make life seem always meagre
in a country with no natural resources. But woe be to the
man who puts his faith in a Western stream! They used to
take themselves suddenly out of sight, down somewhere into
the bowels of the earth, and leave the bed dry as dust, winding its tortuous way for miles, aggravating us by the constant
reminder of where water ought to be, but where it unfortunately was not. This sudden disappearance of water is supposed to be due to the depression of the rocky beds of the
streams. A deep sand absorbs the moisture from the surface,
and draws down into its depths all the stream. When the
bed again rises nearer the surface, the stream comes to sight
once more. Whoever, after the water disappeared, found
that he must drink or die, was obliged to stop and dig away
at the dry bed of the river until he found moisture. It was
a desperate man that attempted it; one whose throat had
become voiceless, whose mouth and lips ached with the
swelling veins of overheated blood; for, if one delayed behind the column for ever so short a time, he was reminded
of his insecurity by a flash from a pile of stones or a bunch
of sage-bush on the summit of a low divide. The wily foe
that lurks in the rear of a marching column has no equal in
vigilance.

And then, what a generous being a soldier is! How often
I have seen them pass the precious nectar—it seemed so then,
in spite of its being warm and alkaline; and I speak from experience, for they have given me a chance also—flavored
with poor whiskey sometimes, as that old tin receptacle which
Government furnishes holds coffee, whiskey or water, which-
ever is attainable. I fear that, had I scratched and dug slowly
into the soil with the point of a sabre, and scooped up a mini-
mum of water, my eye on the bluff near, watching and in
fear of an Indian, I should have remembered my own parched

throat and let the whole American army go thirsty. But I am thankful to say the soldier is made of different stuff. It is enough to weld strongest bonds of friendship, like those in our army, when it is share and share alike; and I am reminded of a stanza of soldier poetry:

"There are bonds of all sorts in this world of ours,
Fetters of friendship and ties of flowers,
And true-lover's knots, I ween;
The boy and the girl are bound by a kiss,
But there's never a bond of old friends like this—
We have drunk from the same canteen."

I have, among our Plains photographs, a picture of one of the Western rivers, with no sort of tree or green thing growing on its banks. It is the dreariest picture I ever saw, and as it appears among the old photographs of merry groups taken in camp or on porches covered with our garrison family, it gives me a shudder even now. Among the photographs of the bright side of our life, this is the skeleton at the feast which comes up so persistently.

Since all rivers and streams in the States are fringed with trees, it is difficult to describe how strange some of our Western water-ways appeared without so much as a border of shrubs or reeds. In looking over the country, as we ascended to a divide higher than the rest, the stream lay before us, winding on in the curving lines of our own Eastern rivers, but for miles and miles not a vestige of green bordered the banks. It seemed to me for all the world like an eye without an eyelash. It was strange, unnatural, weird. The white alkali was the only border, and that spread on into the scorched brown grass, too short to protect the traveler from the glare that was heightened by the sun in a cloudless sky. A tree was often a landmark, and was mentioned on the insufficient maps of the country, such as "Thousand-mile Tree," a name telling its own story; or, "Lone Tree," known as the only one within eighty miles, as was the one in Dakota, where so many Indians buried their dead.

What made those thirsty marches a thousand times worse was the alluring, aggravating mirage. This constantly deceived even old campaigners, and produced the most harrowing sort of illusions. Such a will-o'-the-wisp, too ! for, as we believed ourselves approaching the blessed water, imagined the air was fresher, looked eagerly and expectantly for the brown, shriveled grass to grow green, off floated the deluding water farther and farther away.

As I try to write something of the sacrifices of the soldier, who will not speak of himself, and for whom so few have spoken, there comes to me another class of heroes, for whom my husband had such genuine admiration, and in whose behalf he gave up his life—our Western pioneer. A desperate sort of impatience overcomes me when I realize how incapable I am of paying them proper tribute. And yet how fast they are passing away, with no historians! and hordes of settlers are sweeping into the western States and Territories, quite unmindful of the soldiers and frontiersmen, who fought, step by step, to make room for the coming of the overcrowded population of the East. My otherwise charming journeys West now are sometimes marred by the desire I feel for calling the attention of the travelers, who are borne by steam swiftly over the Plains, to the places where so short a time since men toilsomely traveled in pursuit of homes. I want to ask those who journey for pleasure or for a new home, if they realize what men those were who took their lives in their hands and prepared the way.* Their privations are for-

---

* My father went to Michigan early in 1800, and his long journey was made by stage, canal-boat and schooner. He was not only a great while in making the trip, but subject to privations, illness and fatigue, even when using the only means of travel in those early days. The man who went over the old California trail fared far worse. His life was in peril from Indians all the distance, besides his having to endure innumerable hardships. Those who pioneer in a Pullman car little know what the unbeaten track held for the first comers.

gotten, or carelessly ignored, by those who now go in and possess the land.   The graphic pens of Bret Harte and others, who have written of the frontier, arrest the attention of the Eastern man, and save from oblivion some of the noble characters of those early days.   Still, these poets naturally seized for portraiture the picturesque, romantic characters who were miners or scouts—the isolated instances of desperate men who had gone West from love of adventure, or because of some tragic history in the States, that drove them to seek forgetfulness in a wild, unfettered existence beyond the pale of civilization.

Who chronicles the patient, plodding, silent pioneer, who, having been crowded out of his home by too many laborers in a limited field, or, because he could no longer wring subsistence from a soil too long tilled by sire and grandsire; or possibly a returned volunteer from our war, who, finding all places he once filled closed up, was compelled to take the grant of land that the Government gives its soldiers, and begin life all over again, for the sake of wife and children! There is little in these lives to arrest the poetical fancy of those writers who put into rhyme (which is the most lasting of all history) the lives otherwise lost to the world.

How often General Custer rode up to these weary, plodding yeomen, as they turned aside their wagons to allow the column of cavalry to pass!   He was interested in every detail of their lives, admired their indomitable pluck, and helped them, if he could, in their difficult journeys.   Sometimes, after a summer of hardships and every sort of discouragement, we met the same people returning East, and the General could not help being amused at the grim kind of humor that led these men to write the history of their season in one word on the battered cover of the wagon—" Busted."

We were in Kansas during all the grasshopper scourge, when our Government had to issue rations to the starving farmers deprived of every source of sustenance.   What a marvel that men had the courage to hold out at all, in those exasperating times, when the crops were no sooner up than every vestige of green would be stripped from the fields! Then, too, the struggle for water was great. The artesian wells that now cover the Western States were too expensive to undertake with the early settlers. The windmills that now whirl their gay wheels at every zephyr of the Plains, and water vast numbers of cattle on the farms, were then unthought of. . . . A would-be settler in Colorado, in those times of deprivation and struggle, wrote his history on a board and set it up on the trail, as a warning to others coming after him: " Toughed it out here two years. Result: Stock on hand, five towheads and seven yaller dogs. Two hundred and fifty feet down to water. Fifty miles to wood and grass. Hell all around. God bless our home."

It would be too painful to attempt to enumerate the ravages made by the Indians on the pioneer; and God alone knows how they faced life at all, working their claims with a musket beside them in the field, and the sickening dread of returning to a desolated cabin ever present in their heavy hearts. There are those I occasionally meet, who went through innumerable hardships, and overcame almost insurmountable obstacles, and who attained to distinction in that land of the setting sun; but I find they only remember the jovial side of their early days. Not long since I had the privilege of talking with the Governor of one of our Territories. He was having an interview with some Mexican Senators by means of an interpreter, and after his business was finished, he turned to our party to talk with enthusiasm of his Territory. No youth could be more sanguine than he over the prospects, the climate, the natural advantages of the new country in which he had just cast his lines. All his reminiscences of his early days in other Territories were most interesting to me. General Custer was such an enthusiast over our glorious West, that I early learned to look upon much that I would not otherwise have regarded with interest, with his buoyant feeling. . . . I must qualify this statement, and explain that I could not always see such glowing colors as did he, while we suffered from climate, and were sighing for such

blessings as trees and water; but we were both heart and soul
with every immigrant we came across, and I think many a
half-discouraged pioneer went on his way, after encountering
my husband on the westward trail, a braver and more hopeful man.

How well I remember the long wait we made on one of the
staircases of the Capitol at Washington, above which hung
then the great picture by Leutze, "Westward the Course of
Empire Takes its Way." We little thought then, hardly
more than girl and boy as we were, that our lives would drift
over the country which the admirable picture represents.
The General hung round it with delight, and noted many
points that he wanted me to enjoy with him. The picture
made a great impression on us. How much deeper the impression, though, had we known that we were to live out the
very scenes depicted!

Coming back to the Governor: I cannot take time to write
his well-told story. The portion of the interesting hour that
made the greatest impression on me was his saying that the
happiest days of his life were those when, for fifteen hundred
miles, he walked beside the wagon containing his wife and
babies, and drove the team from their old home in Wisconsin
to a then unsettled portion of Ohio. The honors that had
come to him as senator, governor, statesman, faded beside
the joys of his first venture from home into the wilderness.
I saw him, in imagination, as I have often seen the pioneer,
looking back to the opening made in the front of the wagon
by the drawing over of the canvas cover to the puckered circle,
in which were framed the woman and babies for whom he
could do and dare. I fall to wondering if there is any affection like that which is enhanced or born of these sacrifices
in each other's behalf. I wonder if there can be anything
that would so spur a man to do heroic deeds as the feeling
that he walked in front of three dependent beings, and
braved Indians, starvation, floods, prairie-fire, and all those
perils that beset a Western trail; and to see the bright, fond
eyes of a mother, and the rosy cheeks of the little ones, look-

ing uncomplainingly out upon the desert before them—why, what could nerve a man's arm like that? Love grows with every sacrifice, and I believe that many a youthful passion, that might have become colorless with time, has been deepened into lasting affection on those lonely tramps over the prairies.

It has also been my good fortune lately to recall our Western life with an ex-governor of another Territory, a friend of my husband's in those Kansas days. What can I say in admiration of the pluck of those Western men? Even in the midst of his luxuriant New York life, he loves better to dwell on the early days of his checkered career, when at seven years of age he was taken by his parents to the land of the then great unknown. He had made a fortune in California, for he was a Forty-niner, and returned East to enjoy it. But as he lost his all soon afterward, there was nothing left for him to do but to start out again. His wife could have remained in comfort and security with her friends, but she preferred to share the danger and discomforts of her husband's life. Their first trip over the old trail to Denver (our stamping-ground afterward) was a journey from Missouri, the outfitting place at the termination of the last railway going West, taking sixty-four days to accomplish. The wife, brave as she was, fell ill, and lay on the hard wagon-bed the whole distance. The invincible father took entire care of her and of his children, cooking for the party of eleven on the whole route, and did guard duty a portion of every night. The Indians were hovering in front and in rear. Two of the party were too old to walk and carry a musket, so that on the five men devolved the guarding of their little train. Nine times afterward he and his wife crossed that long stretch of country before the railroad was completed, always in peril, and never knowing from hour to hour when a band of hostiles would sweep down upon them. He taught his children the use of fire-arms as soon as they were large enough to hold a pistol. His daughter learned, as well as his sons, to be an accurate marksman, and shot from the pony's back when he scampered at full speed over the prairies. For years and years, all his family were obliged to be constantly vigilant. They lived out a long portion of their lives on the alert for a foe that they knew well how to dread.

But the humorous comes in, even in the midst of such tragic days! How I enjoyed and appreciated the feelings of the Governor's wife, whom I had known as a girl, when she rebelled at his exercising his heretofore valuable accomplishment as cook, after he became Governor. How like a woman, and how dear such whimsicalities are, sandwiched in among the many admirable qualities with which such strong characters as hers are endowed! It seems that on some journey over the Plains they entertained a party of guests the entire distance. The cook was a failure, and as the route of travel out there is not lined with intelligence-offices, the only thing left to do for the new-made Governor, rather than see his wife so taxed, was to doff his coat and recall the culinary gifts acquired in pioneer life. The madame thought her husband, now a Governor, might keep in secrecy his gifts at getting up a dinner. But he persisted, saying that it was still a question whether he would make a good Governor, and as he was pretty certain he was a good cook, he thought it as well to impress that one gift, of which he was sure, upon his constituents.

The next letter from the expedition brought me such good news, that I counted all the frights of the past few weeks as nothing, compared with the opportunity that being in Fort Riley gave me of joining my husband. He wrote that the cavalry had been detached from the main body of the command, and ordered to scout the stage-route from Fort Hays to Fort McPherson, then the most invested with savages. A camp was to be established temporarily, and scouting parties sent out from Fort Hays. To my joy, my husband said in his letter that I might embrace any safe opportunity to join him there. General Sherman proved to be the direct answer to my prayers, for he arrived soon after I had begun to look confidently for a chance to leave for Fort Hays.

With the grave question of the summer campaign in his
mind, it probably did not occur to him that he was acting
as the envoy extraordinary of Divine Providence to a very anxious, lonely woman. While he talked with me occasionally of
the country, about which he was an enthusiast—and, oh, how
his predictions of its prosperity have come true already!—I
made out to reply coherently, but I kept up a very vehement,
enthusiastic set of inner thoughts and grateful ejaculations,
blessing him for every breath he drew, blessing and thanking
Providence that he had given the commander-in-chief of our
forces a heart so fresh and warm he could feel for others, and
a soul so loyal and affectionate for his own wife and family
that he knew what it was to endure suspense and separation.
He had with him some delightful girls, whom we enjoyed
very much. I cannot remember whether, in my anxiety to
go to my husband, my conversation led up to the subject—
doubtless it did, for I was then at that youthful stage of existence when the mouth speaketh out of the fullness of the
heart—but I do remember that the heart in me nearly leaped
out of my body when he invited me to go in his car to Fort
Harker, for the railroad had been completed to that next
post.

Diana crowded what of her apparel she could into her
trunk, and I had a valise, but the largest part of our luggage
was a roll of bedding, which I remember blushing over as it
was handed into the special coach, for there was no baggage-
car. It looked very strange to see such an ungainly bundle
as part of the belongings of two young women, and though
I was perfectly willing to sleep on the ground in camp, as I
had done in Virginia and Texas, I did not wish to court hardships when I knew a way to avoid them. Though we went
over a most interesting country, General Sherman did not
seem to care much for the outside world. He sat in the
midst of us, and entered into all our fun; told stories to
match ours, joined in our songs, and was the Grand Mogul
of our circle. One of the young girls was so captivating,
even in her disloyalty, that it amused us all immensely.

When we sang war-songs, she looked silently out of the window. If we talked of the danger we might encounter with Indians, General Sherman said, slyly, he would make her departure from earth as easy as possible, for he would honor her with a military funeral. She knew that she must, in such a case, be wrapped in the Stars and Stripes, and he did not neglect to tell her that honor awaited her if she died, but she vehemently refused the honor. All this, which would have been trying from a grown person, was nothing but amusement to us from a chit of a girl, who doubtless took her coloring, as the chameleon-like creatures of that age do, from her latest Confederate sweetheart.

In retrospection, I like to think of the tact and tolerance of General Sherman, in those days of furious feeling on both sides, and the quiet manner in which he heard the Southern people decry the Yankees. He knew of their impoverished and desolated homes, and realized, living among them as he did in St. Louis, what sacrifices they had made; more than all, his sympathetic soul saw into the darkened lives of mothers, wives and sisters who had given, with their idea of patriotism, their loved ones to their country. The truth is, he was back again among those people of whom he had been so fond, and no turbulent expressions of hatred and revenge could unsettle the underlying affection. Besides, he has always been a far-seeing man. Who keeps in front in our country's progress as does this war hero? Is he not a statesman as well as a soldier? And never have the interests of our land been narrowed down to any prescribed post where he may have been stationed, or his life been belittled by any temporary isolation or division from the rest of mankind. Every public scheme for our advancement as a nation meets his enthusiastic welcome. This spirit enabled him to see, at the close of the war, that, after the violence of wrath should have subsided, the South would find themselves more prosperous, and capable, in the new order of affairs, of immense strides in progress of all kinds.

I remember a Southern woman, who came to stay with

relatives in our garrison, telling me of her first encounter with General Sherman after the war. He had been a valued friend for many years; but it was too much when, on his return to St. Louis, he came, as a matter of course, to see his old friends. Smarting with the wrongs of her beloved South, she would not even send a message by the maid; she ran to the head of the stairs, and in an excited tone, asked if he for one moment expected she would speak, so much as speak, to a Yankee? The General went on his peaceful way, as unharmed by this peppery assault as a foe who is out of reach of our short-range Government carbines, and I can recall with what cordiality she came to greet him later in the year or two that followed. No one could maintain wrath long against such imperturbable good-nature as General Sherman exhibited. He remembered a maxim that we all are apt to forget, " Put yourself in his place."

Along the line of the railroad were the deserted towns, and we even saw a whole village moving on flat cars. The portable houses of one story and the canvas rolls of tents, which would soon be set up to form a street of saloons, were piled up as high as was safe, and made the strangest sort of freight train. The spots from which they had been removed were absolutely the dreariest of sights. A few poles, broken kegs, short chimneys made in rude masonry of small round stones, heaps of tin cans everywhere, broken bottles strewing the ground, while great square holes yawned empty where, a short time before, a canvas roof covered a room stored with clumsy shelves laden with liquor. Here and there a smoke-stained barrel protruded from the ground. They were the chimneys of some former dug-outs. I cannot describe how startled I was when I first came near one of these improvised chimneys, and saw smoke pouring out, without any other evidence that I was walking over the home of a frontier citizen. The roof of a flat dug-out is level with the earth, and as no grass consents to grow in these temporary villages, there is nothing to distinguish the upturned soil that has been used as a covering for the beams of the roof of a dwelling from any of the rest of the immediate vicinity. A portion of this moving village had already reached the end in the railroad, and named itself Ellsworth, with streets called by various high-sounding appellations, but marked only by stakes in the ground.

At Fort Harker we found a forlorn little post—a few log houses bare of every comfort, and no trees to cast a shade on the low roofs. The best of the quarters, belonging to the bachelor commanding officer, were offered to General Sherman and his party. We five women had one of the only two rooms. It seems like an abuse of hospitality, even after all these years, to say that the floor of uneven boards was almost ready for agricultural purposes, as the wind had sifted the prairie sand in between the roughly laid logs, and even the most careful housewife would have found herself outwitted if she had tried to keep a tidy floor. I only remember it because I was so amused to see the dainty women stepping around the little space left in the room between the cots, to find a place to kneel and say their prayers. I had given up, and gone to bed, as often before I had been compelled to tell my thanks to the Heavenly Father on my pillow, for already in the marches I had encountered serious obstacles to kneeling. The perplexed but devout women finally gave up attempting a devotional attitude, turned their faces to the rough wall, and held their rosaries in their fingers, while they sent up orisons for protection and guidance. They were reverential in their petitions; but I could not help imagining how strange it must seem to these luxuriously raised girls, to find themselves in a country where not even a little prayer could be said as one would wish. It must have been for exigencies of our life that Montgomery wrote the comforting definition that "Prayer is the soul's sincere desire," "The upward lifting of an eye," etc., and so set the heart at rest about how and where the supplication of the soul could be offered.

At Fort Harker we bade good-by to our delightful party, the frolic and light-heartedness departed, and the serious

side of existence appeared. I had but little realization that
every foot of our coming march of eighty miles was dangerous. We had an ambulance lent us, and accompanied a party
that had an escort. There were stage-stations every ten or
fifteen miles, consisting of rude log or stone huts, huddled
together for safety in case of attack. The stables for the relays of horses were furnished with strong doors of rough-
hewn timber, and the windows closed with shutters of similar
pattern. The stablemen and relays of drivers lived in no bet-

A MATCH BUFFALO HUNT.

ter quarters than the horses. They were, of course, intrepid
men, and there was no stint in arming them with good rifles
and abundance of ammunition. They were prepared for attack, and could have defended themselves behind the strong
doors—indeed, sustained a siege, for the supplies were kept
inside their quarters—had not the Indians used prepared arrows that could be shot into the hay and thus set the stables
on fire. These Plainsmen all had "dug-outs" as places of
retreat in case of fire. They were very near the stables, and
connected by an underground passage. They were about
four feet deep. The roof was of timbers strong enough to

hold four or five feet of earth, and in these retreats a dozen men could defend themselves, by firing from loopholes that were left under the roof-beams. Some of the stage-stations had no regular buildings. We came upon them without being prepared by any signs of human life, for the dug-outs were excavated from the sloping banks of the creeks. A few holes in the side-hill, as openings for man and beast, some short chimneys on the level ground, were all the evidence of the dreary, Columbarium homes.   Here these men lived, facing death every hour rather than earn a living in the monotonous pursuit of some trade or commonplace business in the States. And at that time there were always desperadoes who would pursue any calling that kept them beyond the reach of the law.

This dreary eighty miles over a monotonous country, varied only by the undulations that rolled away to Big Creek, was over at last, and Fort Hays was finally visible—another small post of log huts like Fort Harker, treeless and desolate, but the stream beyond was lined with white canvas, which meant the tents of the Seventh Cavalry.

Again it seemed to me the end of all the troubles that would ever enter into my life had come, when I was lifted out of the ambulance into my husband's tent. What a blessing it is that there is a halcyon time in sanguine youth, when each difficulty vanquished seems absolutely the last that will ever come, and when one trouble ends, the stone is rolled against its sepulchre with the conviction that nothing will ever open wide the door again.   We had much to talk about in camp.   The first campaign of a regiment is always important to them, and in this case, also, the council, the Indian village, and its final destruction, were really significant events. A match hunt they had carried out was a subject of interest, and each side took one ear in turn, to explain why they won, or the reasons they lost.   Mr. Theodore Davis, the artist whom the Harpers sent out for the summer, was drawing sketches in our tent, while we advised or commented. It seemed well, from the discussions that followed, that rules

GATHERING THE TONGUES

COUNTING THE TONGUES

GATHERING AND COUNTING
THE TONGUES.

for the hunt had been drawn up in advance. It was quite a ranking affair, when two full majors conducted the sides. As only one day was given to each side, the one remaining in camp watched vigilantly that the party going out held to the rule, and refrained from starting till sunrise, while the same jealous eyes noticed that sunset saw all of them in camp again. One of the rules was, that no shots should be counted that were fired when the man was dismounted. This alone was a hard task, as at that time the splendid racing of the horse at breakneck speed, with his bridle free on his neck, and both hands busy with the gun, was not an accomplished feat. The horses were all novices at buffalo-hunting, also, and the game was thin at that season—so thin that a bison got over a great deal of territory in a short time. I remember the General's telling me what an art it was, even after the game was shot, to learn to cut out the tongue. It was wonderful that there was such success with so much to encounter. The winning party kept their twelve tongues very securely hidden until the second day, when the losers produced the eleven they had supposed would not be outdone. My husband was greatly amused at one of our officers, who hovered about the camp-fires of the opposite party and craftily put questions to ascertain what was the result of the first day.

All this was told us with great glee. Diana's interests were centred in the success of that party with whom her best beloved, for the time, hunted. The officers regretted our absence at their great " feed," as they termed it, and it must, indeed, have been a great treat to have for once, in that starving summer, something palatable. Two wall-tents were put together so that the table, made of rough boards, stretching through both, was large enough for all. Victors and vanquished toasted each other in champagne, and though the scene was the plainest order of banquet, lighted by tallow candles set in rude brackets sawed out of cracker-box boards and fastened to the tent-poles, and the only draping a few cavalry guidons, the evening brightened up many a dreary day that followed. Gallant Captain Louis McLane Hamilton, who afterward fell in the battle of the Washita, was the hero of the hour, and bore his honors with his usual modesty. Four out of twelve buffaloes was a record that might have set a less boastful tongue wagging over the confidences of the evening camp-fire. I do not think he would have permitted Mr. Davis to put his picture in the illustration if he could have helped it. He was gifted with his pencil also; he drew caricatures admirably, and after a harmless laugh had

gone the rounds, he managed, with the utmost adroitness, to
get possession of the picture and destroy it, thus taking away
the sting of ridicule, which constant sight of the caricature

SUPPER GIVEN BY THE VANQUISHED TO THE VICTORS OF THE
MATCH BUFFALO HUNT.

might produce. How I came into possession of one little
drawing is still a mystery, but it is very clever. Among our
officers was one who had crossed the Plains as a citizen a
year or two previous, and his habit of revealing mines of

frontier lore obtained on this one trip was somewhat tiresome to our still inexperienced officers. At last, after all had
tried chasing antelope, and been more and more impressed
in their failures with the fleetness of that winged animal,
Captain Hamilton made a sketch representing the boaster as
shooting antelope with the shot-gun. The speck on the horizon was all that was seen of the game, but the booted and
spurred man kneeling on the prairie was admirable. It
silenced one of the stories, certainly, and we often wished
the pencil could protect us further from subsequent statements airily made on the strength of the one stage-journey.

I had arrived in the rainy season, and such an emptying of
the heavens was a further development of what Kansas could
do. But nothing damped my ardor; no amount of soakings
could make me think that camping-ground was not an Elys-
ian field. The General had made our tent as comfortable
as possible with his few belongings, and the officers had sent
in to him, for me, any comfort that they might have chanced
to bring along on the march. I was, it seemed, to be especially honored with a display of what the elements could do
at night when it was too dark to grope about and protect
our tent. The wind blew a tornado, and the flashes of lightning illumined the tent and revealed the pole swaying ominously back and forth. A fly is an outer strip of canvas
which is stretched over the tent to prevent the rain from
penetrating, as well as to protect us in the daytime from the
sun. This flapped and rattled and swung loose at one end,
beating on the canvas roof like a trip-hammer, for it was
loaded with moisture; and the wet ropes attached to it, and
used to guy it down, were now loose, and lashed our rag
house in an angry, vindictive manner. My husband, accustomed to the pyrotechnic display of the elements, slept
soundly through the early part of the storm. But lightning
"murders sleep" with me, and, consequently, he was awakened by a conjugal joggle, and on asking, "What is it?"
was informed, "It lightens!" Often as this statement was
made to him in his sudden awakenings, I do not remember

his ever meeting it with any but a teasing, laughing reply, like: " Ah ! indeed; I am pleased to be informed of so important a fact. This news is quite unexpected," and so on, or " When, may I inquire, did you learn this ? " On this occasion, however, there was no attempt to quiet me or delay precautions. Feeling sure that we were in for it for the night, he unfastened the straps that secured the tent in front, and crept out to hammer down the tent-pins and tether the ropes. But it was of no earthly use. After fruitless efforts of·his own, he called the guard from their tents, and they went energetically to work with the light of our lantern. Ropes wrenched themselves away from the tent-pins, straps broke, whole corners of the tent were torn out, even while the men were hanging with all their might to the upright poles to try and keep the ridge-pole steady, and clinging to the ropes to keep them from loosening entirely and sailing off in the air with the canvas.

In the midst of this fracas, with the shouts of the soldiers calling to one another in the inky darkness, the crash of thunder and the howling of the tempest, the wife of a brave soldier was hiding her head under the blankets, and not one sound emerged from this temporary retreat. The great joy of getting out to camp at last was too fresh to extract one word, one whimper of fear from under the bedding. The sunniest day at Fort Riley could not be exchanged, could not even be mentioned in the same breath, with that tornado of wind and rain.

The stalwart arms of the soldiers failed at last. Their brawny chests were of no more use, thrust against the tent-poles, than so many needles. Over went the canvas in a heap, the General and his men hanging on to the ridge-pole to clear it from the camp bed and save any accident.

The voices of officers in an adjoining tent called out to come over to them. One, half dressed, groped his way to us and said there was yet room for more in his place, and, besides, he had a floor. It was a Sibley, which, having no corners with which those Kansas breezes can toy, is much more secure. I was rolled in the blankets and carried through the blinding rain to our hospitable neighbors'. The end of a tallow dip gave me a glimpse only of many silent forms rolled in blankets and radiating from the centre like the spokes of a wagon wheel. The officer owning this tent had taken the precaution, while at Leavenworth, to have a floor made in sections, so that it could be easily stowed away in the bottom of a prairie-schooner in marching.

My husband laid me down, and we were soon two more spokes in the human wheel, and asleep in a trice. Next morning I wakened to find myself alone, with a tin basin of water and a towel for my toilet beside me. My husband had to dress me in his underclothing, for everything I had was soaked. My shoes were hopeless, so I was dropped into a pair of cavalry boots, and in this unpicturesque costume, which I covered as best I could with my wet dress, I was carried through the mud to the dining-tent, and enthroned *à la* Turk, on a board which the cook produced from some hiding-place, where he had kept it for kindlings. There were not a few repetitions of this stormy reception in the years that followed, for Kansas continued its weather vagaries with unceasing persistency, but this, being my first, is as fresh in my mind as if it occurred but yesterday.

The tent might go down nightly for all I cared then. Every thought of separation departed, and I gave myself up to the happiest hours, clamping about the tent in those old troop boots, indifferent whether my shoes *ever* dried. The hours flew too fast, though, for very soon preparations began for a scout, which my husband was to command. It took a great deal of comforting to reconcile me to remaining behind. The General, as usual, had to beg me to remember how blessed we were to have been permitted to rejoin each other so early in the summer. He told me, over and over again, that there was nothing, he felt, that I would not encounter to come to him, and that if he was detained, he would send for me. Eliza and a faithful soldier were to be left to care for us. The cavalry departed, and again the days lengthened out longer and longer, until each one seemed forty-eight hours from sun to sun. We could scarcely take a short walk in safety. The Indians were all about us, and daily the sentinels were driven in, or attempts were made to stampede the horses and mules grazing about the post. The few officers remaining, in whose care we were placed, came or sent every day to our tents, which were up the creek a short distance, to inquire what they could do for our comfort. Mrs. Gibbs, with her boys, had joined her husband, and we were their neighbors.

It seemed, sometimes, as if we *must* get outside of our prescribed limits, the rolling bluffs beyond, tinged with green and beginning to have prairie flowers, looked so tempting. One evening we beguiled an officer, who was sitting under our tent fly, which was stretched in front for a shade, to take us for a little walk. Like many another man in the temporary possession of wheedling women, he went with us a little, and "just a little farther." Diana would have driven all thought of everything else save herself out of the gravest head. At last our escort saw the dark coming on so fast he insisted upon going home, and we reluctantly turned. As we came toward the post, the shadows were deepening in the twilight, and the figures of the sentinels were not visible. A flash, followed by a sound past our ears, that old campaigners describe as never to be forgotten when first heard, was the warning that we three were taken for Indians and fired upon by the sentinel. Another flash, but we stood rooted to the spot, stunned by surprise. The whizz and zip of the bullet seemed to be only a few inches from my ear. Still we were dazed, and had not the officer gained his senses our fate would have been then and there decided. The recruit, probably himself terrified, kept on sending those deadly little missives, with the terrible sound cutting the air around us. Our escort shouted, but it was too far for his voice to carry. Then he told us to run for our lives to a slight depression in the ground, and throw ourselves on our faces. I was coward enough to burrow mine in the prairie-grass, and for once in

my life was devoutly grateful for being slender. Still, as I lay
there quaking with terror, my body seemed to rise above the
earth in such a monstrous heap that the dullest marksman,
if he tried, might easily perforate me with bullets. What
ages it seemed while we waited in this prostrate position,
commanded by our escort not to move! The rain of bullets
at last ceased, and blessed quiet came, but not peace of mind.
The officer told us he would creep on his hands and knees
through the hollow portions of the plain about the post, approach by the creek side, and inform the sentinels along the
line, and as soon as they all knew who we were he would
return for us. With smothered voices issuing from the grass
where our faces were still crushed as low as we could get
them, we implored to be allowed to creep on with him. We
prayed him not to leave us out in the darkness alone. We
begged him to tell us how he could ever find us again, if once
he left us on ground that had no distinctive features by which
he could trace his way back. But he was adamant: we must
remain; and the ring of authority in his tone, besides the cul-
prit feeling we had for having endangered his life, kept us
still at last. As we lay there, our hearts' thumping seemed
to lift us up in air and imperil anew our wretched existence.
The pretty, rounded contour of the girl, which she had naturally taken such delight in, was now a source of agony to
her, and she moaned out, " Oh! how high I seem to be above
you! Oh, Libbie, do you think I lie as flat to the ground as
you do?" and so on, with all the foolish talk of frightened
women.

When at last our deliverer came, my relief at such an escape was almost forgotten in the mortification I felt at having
made so much trouble; and I thought, with chagrin, how
quickly the General's gratitude to find we had escaped the
bullets would be followed by temporary suspension of faith
regarding my following out his instructions not to run risks
of danger and wander away from the post. I wrote him an
abject account of our hazardous performance. I renewed
every promise. I asked to be trusted again, and from that

time there were no more walks outside the beat of the sentinel.

An intense disappointment awaited me at this time, and took away the one hope that had kept up my spirits. I was watching, from day to day, an opportunity to go to my husband at Fort McPherson, for he had said I could come if any chance offered. I was so lonely and anxious, I would gladly have gone with the scout who took despatches and mail, though he had to travel at night and lie in the ravines all day to elude the sharp eyes of the Indians. I remember watching Wild Bill, as he reported at the commanding officer's tent to get despatches for my husband, and wishing with all my heart that I could go with him. I know this must seem strange to people in the States, whose ideas of scouts are made up from stories of shooting affrays, gambling, lynching and outlawry. I should have felt myself safe to go any distance with those men whom my husband employed as bearers of despatches. I have never known women treated with such reverence as those whom they honored. They were touched to see us out there, for they measured well every danger of that country; and the class that followed the moving railroad towns were their only idea of women, except as they caught glimpses of us in camp or on the march. In those border-towns, as we were sometimes compelled to walk a short distance from the depot to our ambulance, the rough characters in whom people had ceased to look for good were transformed in their very attitude as we approached. Of course, they all knew and sincerely admired the General, and, removing their hats, they stepped off the walk and cast such looks at me as if I had been little lower than the angels. When these men so looked at me, my husband was as proud as if a President had manifested pleasure at sight of his wife, and amused himself immensely because I said to him, after we were well by, that the outlaws had seemed to think me possessed of every good attribute, while to myself my faults and deficiencies appeared to rise mountains high. I felt that if there was a Christian grace that my mother had not striven

to implant in me, I would cultivate it now, and try to live up
to the frontier citizen's impression of us as women.

I think the General would have put me in the care of any
scout that served him, just as readily as to place me in the
keeping of the best officer we had.   There was not a trust he
reposed in them that they did not fulfill.   Oh, how hard
it was for me to see them at that time, when starting
with despatches to my husband, swing themselves into the
saddle and disappear over the divide! I feel certain, with
such an end in view as I had, and with the good health that
the toughening of our campaigns had given me, I could have
ridden all night and slept on the horse-blanket in the ravines
daytimes, for a great distance.   Had I been given the opportunity to join my husband by putting myself in their charge,
there would not have been one moment's hesitation on my
part.   I knew well that when "off duty" the scout is often
in affrays where lynching and outlawry are every-day events
of the Western towns; but that had no effect upon these
men's sense of honor when an officer had reposed a trust in
them.   Wild Bill, California Joe, Buffalo Bill, Comstock,
Charlie Reynolds, and a group of intrepid men besides, who
from time to time served under my husband, would have defended any of us women put in their charge with their lives.

I remember with distinctness what genuine admiration and
gratitude filled my heart as these intrepid men rode up to my
husband's tent to receive orders and despatches.   From my
woman's standpoint, it required far more and a vastly higher
order of courage to undertake their journeys than to charge
in battle.   With women, every duty or task seems easier
when shared by others.   The most cowardly of us might be
so impressionable, so sympathetic, in a great cause that we
saw others preparing to defend, that it would become our
own; and it is not improbable that enthusiasm might take
even a timid woman into battle, excited and incited by the
daring of others, the bray of drums, the clash of arms, the
call of the trumpet.   But I doubt if there are many who
could go off on a scout of hundreds of miles, and face death

alone. It still seems to me supreme courage. Imagine, then, my gratitude, my genuine admiration, when my husband sent scouts with letters to us, and we saw them in returning swing lightly into the saddle and gallop off, apparently unconcerned, freighted with our messages of affection.

Something better than such a journey awaited me, it seemed, when two of our Seventh Cavalry officers, Captain Samuel Robbins and Colonel William W. Cook, appeared in camp at the head of a detachment of cavalry and a small train of wagons for supplies. The General had told them to bring me back, and an ambulance was with the wagons, in which I was to ride. It did not take me long to put our roll of bedding and my valise in order; and to say anything about the heart in me leaping for joy is even a tame expression to describe the delight that ran through every vein in my body. To ascend such heights of joy means a corresponding capability of descent into a region of suffering, about which I do not, even now, like to think, for the memory of my disappointment has not departed after all these years. The commanding officer of the department was at the post temporarily, and forbade my going. There is a hateful clause in the Army Regulations which gives him control of all camp-followers as well as troops. I ran the whole gamut of insubordination, mutiny, and revolt, as I threw myself alone on the little camp-bed of our tent. This stormy, rebellious season, fought out by myself, ended, of course, as everything must that gives itself into military jurisdiction, as I was left behind in spite of myself; but I might have been enlisted as a soldier for five years, and not have been more helpless. I put my fingers into my ears, not to hear the call " Boots and Saddles!" as the troops mounted and rode away. I only felt one relief; the officers would tell the General that nothing but the all-powerful command forbidding them to take me had prevented my doing what he knew I would do if it was in my power. I had time also to use my husband as a safety-valve, and pour out my vials of wrath against the officer detaining me, in a long letter filling pages with regret that I was prevented going to him.

The Indians were then at their worst. They roamed up and down the route of travel, burning the stations, running off stock, and attacking the stages. General Hancock had given up all aggressive measures. The plan was, to defend the route taken for supplies, and protect the stage company's property so far as possible. The railroad building was almost entirely abandoned. As our officers and their detachment were for a time allowed to proceed quietly on their march to McPherson, they rather flattered themselves they would see nothing of the enemy. Still, every eye watched the long ravines that intersect the Plains and form such fastnesses for the wily foe. There is so little to prepare you for these cuts in the smooth surface of the plain, that an ungarded traveler comes almost upon a deep fissure in the earth, before dreaming that the lay of the land was not all the seeming level that stretches on to sunset. These ravines have small clumps of sturdy trees, kept alive in the drought of that arid climate by the slight moisture from what is often a buried stream at the base. The Indians know them by heart, and not only lie in wait in them, but escape by these gullies, that often run on, growing deeper and deeper till the bed of a river is reached.

In one of these ravines, six hundred savages in full war-dress were in ambush, awaiting the train of supplies, and sprang out from their hiding-place with horrible yells as our detachment of less than fifty men approached. Neither officer lost his head at a sight that was then new to him. Their courage was inborn. They directed the troops to form a circle about the wagons, and in this way the little band of valiant men defended themselves against attack after attack. Not a soldier flinched, nor did a teamster lose control of his mules, though the effort to stampede them was incessant. This running fight lasted for three hours, when suddenly the Indians withdrew. They, with their experienced eyes, first saw the reinforcements coming to the relief of our brave fellows, and gave up the attack.

The first time I saw Colonel Cook after this affair, he said: "The moment I found the Indians were on us, and we were in for a fight, I thought of you, and said to myself, 'If she were in the ambulance, before giving an order I would ride up and shoot her.'" "Would you have given me no chance for life," I replied, "in case the battle had gone in your favor?" "Not one," he said. "I should have been unnerved by the thought of the fate that awaited you, and I have promised the General not to take any chances, but to kill you before anything worse could happen." Already, in these early days of the regiment's history, the accounts of Indian atrocities perpetrated on the women of the frontier ranches, had curdled the blood of our men, and over the camp-fire at night, when these stories were discussed, my husband had said to the officers that he should take every opportunity to have me with him, but there was but one course he wished pursued; if I was put in charge of any one in the regiment, he asked them to kill me if Indians should attack the camp or the escort on the march. I have referred in general terms to this understanding, but it was on this occasion that the seriousness with which the General's request was considered by his brother officers first came home to me.

CHAPTER XVII.

A FLOOD AT FORT HAYS.

BEFORE General Custer left for Fort McPherson, he removed our tents to a portion of that branch of Big Creek on which the post was established. He selected the highest ground he could find, knowing that the rainy season was not yet over, and hoping that, if the camp were on a knoll, the ground would drain readily and dry quickly after a storm. We were not a great distance from the main stream and the fort, but still too far to recognize anyone that might be walking in garrison. The stream on which we were located was tortuous, and on a bend above us the colonel commanding, his adjutant and his escort were established. Between us and the fort, General and Mrs. Gibbs were camped, while the tents of a few officers on detached duty were still farther on. The sentinel's beat was along a line between us and the high ground, where the Indians were likely to steal upon us from the bluffs. This guard walked his tour of duty on a line parallel with the stream, but was too far from it to observe the water closely. Each little group of tents made quite a show of canvas, as we had abundance of room to spread out, and the quartermaster was not obliged to limit us to any given number of tents. We had a hospital tent for our sitting-room, with a wall-tent pitched behind and opening out of the larger one, for our bedroom. There was a wall-tent for the kitchen, near, and behind us, the " A " tent for the soldier whom the General had left to take care of us in his absence. We were as safely placed, as to Indians, as was possible in such a country. As is the custom in military life, the officers either came every day, or sent to know if I could think of anything they could do for my comfort. The General had thought of everything, and, besides, I did my best not to have any wants. I was as capable of manufacturing needs as anyone, and could readily trump up a collection in garrison, but I was rendered too wary by the uncertainty of my tenure of that (to me) valuable little strip of ground that held my canvas house, to allow my presence to be brought home to those gallant men as a trouble or a responsibility. The idea that I might have to retreat eastward was a terror, and kept in subjection any passing wish I might indulge to have anything done for me. I would gladly have descended into one of the cellar-like habitations that were so common in Kansas then, and had my food handed down to me, if this would have enabled the officers to forget that I was there, until the expedition returned from the Platte. Yet the elements were against me, and did their best to interfere with my desire to obliterate myself, as far as being an anxiety to others was concerned.

One night we had retired, and were trying to believe that the thunder was but one of those peculiar menacing volleys of cloud-artillery that sometimes passed over harmlessly; but we could not sleep, the roar and roll of thunder was so alarming. There is no describing lightning on the Plains. While a storm lasts, there seems to be an incessant glare. To be sure, there is not the smallest flash that does not illumine the tent, and there is no way of hiding from the blinding light. In a letter written to my husband while the effect of the fright was still fresh on my mind, I told him "the heavens seemed to shower down fire upon the earth, and in one minute and a half we counted twenty-five distinct peals of thunder." There seemed to be nothing for us to do but to lie quaking and terrified under the covers. The tents of the officers were placed at some distance from ours intentionally, as it is impossible to speak low enough, under canvas, to avoid being heard, unless a certain space intervenes. It is the custom to allow a good deal of ground to intervene, if the guard is so

posted as to command the approach to all the tents. The
result was, that we dared not venture to try to reach a neighbor; we simply had to endure the situation, as no cry could
be heard above the din of the constantly increasing storm.
In the midst of this quaking and misery, the voice of some
officers outside called to ask if we were afraid. Finding that
the storm was advancing to a tornado, they had decided to
return to us and render assistance if they could, or at least
to quiet our fears. The very sound of their voices calmed us,
and we dressed and went into the outer tent to admit them.
The entrance had been made secure by leather straps and
buckles that the General had the saddler put on; and in
order to strengthen the tents against these hurricanes, which
we had already learned were so violent and sudden, he had
ordered poles at each corner sunk deep into the ground.
These, being notched, had saplings laid across either side,
and to these the tent-ropes were bound. We were thus
seemingly secured between two barriers. He even went
further in his precautions, and fastened a picket-rope, which
is a small cable of itself, to either end of the ridge-pole,
stretching it at the front and rear, and fasting it with an iron
pin driven into the ground. As we opened two or three of
the straps to admit the officers and Eliza, who always overcame every obstacle to get to me in danger, the wind drove
in a sheet of rain upon us, and we found it difficult to strap
the opening again. As for the guy-ropes and those that tied
the tent at the sides, all this creaking, loosening cordage
proved how little we could count upon its stability. The
great tarpaulin, of the heaviest canvas made, which was
spread over our larger tent and out in the front for a porch,
flapped wildly, lashing our poor little "rag house" as if in a
fury of rage. Indeed, the whole canvas seemed as if it might
have been a cambric handkerchief, for the manner in which
it was wrenched and twisted above and on all sides of us.
The tallow candle was only kept lighted by surrounding it
with boxes to protect its feeble flame from the wind. The
rain descended in such sheets, driven by the hurricane, that

it even pressed in the tent-walls; and in spite of the trenches, that every good campaigner digs about the tent, we were almost inundated by the streams that entered under the lower edge of the walls.

The officers, finding we were sure to be drenched, began to fortify us for the night. They feared the tent would go down, and that the ridge-pole of a hospital-tent, being so much larger than that of a wall-tent, would do some fatal injury to us. They piled all the available furniture in a hollow square, leaving a little space for us. Fortunately, some one, coming down from the post a few days before, had observed that we had no table. There was no lumber at the post, and the next best thing was to send us a zinc-covered board which had first served for a stove ; secondly, with the addition of rude supports, as our table, and now did duty in its third existence as a life-preserver ; for the ground was softening with the moisture, and we could not protect our feet, except for the narrow platform on which we huddled. At last the booming of the thunder seemed to abate somewhat, though the wind still shrieked and roared over the wide plain, as it bore down upon our frail shelter. But the tent, though swaying and threatening to break from its moorings, had been true to us through what we supposed to be the worst of the tempest, and we began to put some confidence in the cordage and picket-pins. The officers decided to return to their tents, promising to come again should there be need, and we reluctantly permitted them to go. Eliza put down something on which we could step over the pools into the other tent, and we fell into bed, exhausted with terror and excitement, hardly noticing how wet and cold we and the blankets were.

Hardly had we fallen into a doze, when the voice of the guard at the entrance called out to us to get up and make haste for our lives ; the flood was already there ! We were so agitated that it was difficult even to find the clothes that we had put under the pillow to keep them from further soaking, much more to get into them. It was then impossible to remain inside of the tent. We crept through the opening, and, to our horror, the lightning revealed the creek—which we had last seen, the night before, a little rill in the bottom of the gully—now on a level with the high banks. The tops of good-sized trees, which fringed the stream, were barely visible, as the current swayed the branches in its onward sweep. The water had risen in that comparatively short time thirty-five feet, and was then creeping into the kitchen tent, which, as usual, was pitched near the bank. I believe no one attempted to account for those terrific rises in the streams, except as partly due to water-spouts, which were common in the early days of Kansas. I have seen the General hold his watch in his hand after the bursting of a rain-cloud, and keep reckoning for the soldier who was measuring with a stick at the stream's bed, and for a time it recorded an inch a minute.

Of course the camp was instantly astir after the alarm of the guard. But the rise of the water is so insidious often, that a sentinel walking his beat a few yards away will sometimes be unconscious of it until the danger is upon the troops. The soldiers, our own man, detailed as striker, and Eliza, were not so "stampeded," as they expressed it; as to forget our property. Almost everything that we possessed in the world was there, much of our property being fortunately still boxed. I had come out to camp with a valise, but the wagon-train afterward brought most of our things, as we supposed we had left Fort Riley forever. The soldiers worked like beavers to get everything they could farther from the water, upon a little rise of ground at one side of our tents. Eliza, the coolest of all, took command, and we each carried what we could, forgetting the lightning in our excitement.

The officers who had come to us in the early part of the tempest now returned. They found their own camp unapproachable. The group of tents having been pitched on a bend in the crooked stream, which had the advantage of the circle of trees that edged the water, was now found to be in the worst possible locality, as the torrent had swept over the narrow strip of earth and left the camp on a newly made island, perfectly inaccessible. The lives of the men and horses stranded on this little water-locked spot were in imminent peril. The officers believed us when we said we would do what we could to care for ourselves if they would go at once, as they had set out to do, and find succor for the soldiers. It was a boon to have something that it was necessary to do, which kept us from absolute abandonment to terror. We hardly dared look toward the rushing torrent ; the agony of seeing the water steal nearer and nearer our tent was almost unendurable. As we made our way from the heap of household belongings, back and forth to the tent, carrying burdens that we could not even have lifted in calmer moments, the lightning became more vivid and the whole arc above us seemed aflame. We were aghast at what the brilliant light revealed. Between the bluffs that rose gradually from the stream, and the place where we were on its banks, a wide newly made river spread over land that had been perfectly dry, and, as far as any one knew, had never been inundated before. The water had overflowed the banks of the stream above us, and swept across the slight depression that intervened between our ground and the hills. We were left on that narrow neck of land, and the water on either side of us, seen in the lightning's glare, appeared like two boundless seas. The creek had broken over its banks and divided us from the post below, while the garrison found themselves on an island also, as the water took a new course down there, and cut them off from the bluffs. This was a misfortune to us, as we had so small a number of men and sorely needed what help the post could have offered.

While we ran hither and thither, startled at the shouts of the officers and men as they called to one another, dreading some new terror, our hearts sinking with uncontrollable fright at the wild havoc the storm was making, the two dogs that the General valued, Turk, the bull-dog, and Rover, his favorite fox-hound, broke their chains and flew at each other's throat. Their warfare had been long and bloody, and they meant that night to end the contest. The ferocity of the bull-dog was not greater than that of the old hound. The soldiers sprang at them again and again to separate them. The fangs of each showed partly buried in the other's throat, but finally, one powerful man choked the bull-dog into re-laxing his hold. The remnants of the gashed and bleeding contestants were again tied at a secure distance, and the soldiers renewed their work to prevent the tents from falling. I remember that in one gale, especially furious, seventeen clung to the guy-rope in front and saved the canvas from downfall.

But, after all, something worse awaited us than all this fury of the elements and the dread of worse to come to ourselves ; for the reality of the worst that can come to anyone was then before us without a warning. There rang out on the air, piercing our ears even in the uproar of the tempest, sounds that no one, once hearing, ever forgets. They were the de-spairing cries of drowning men. In an instant our danger was forgotten ; but the officers and men were scattered along the stream beyond our call, and Eliza was now completely unnerved. We ran up and down the bank, wringing our hands, she calling to me, "Oh, Miss Libbie ! what shall we do ? What shall we do ?" We tried to scream to those dark forms hurrying by us, that help might come farther down. Alas ! the current grew more furious as the branch poured into the main stream, and we could distinguish, by the oft-repeated glare of the lightning, the men waving their arms imploringly as they were swept down with tree-trunks, masses of earth, and heaps of rubbish that the current was drifting by. We were helpless to attempt their rescue. There can be few moments in existence that hold such agonizing suffering as those where one is appealed to for life, and is powerless to give succor. I thought of the ropes about our tent, and ran to unwind one ; but they were lashed to the poles, stiff with moisture, and tied with sailors' intricate knots. In a frenzy, I tugged at the fastenings, bruising my hands and tearing the nails. The guy-ropes were equally unavailable, for no knife we had could cut such a cable.

Eliza, beside herself with grief to think she could not help the dying soldiers with whom she had been such a favorite, came running to me where I was insanely struggling with the cordage, and cried, "Miss Libbie, there's a chance for us with one man. He's caught in the branches of a tree; but I've seen his face, and he's alive. He's most all of him under water, and the current is a-switchin' him about so he can't hold out long. Miss Libbie, there's my clothes-line we *could* take, but I can't do it, I can't do it! Miss Libbie, you wouldn't have me to do it, would you? For where will we get another?" The grand humanity that illumined the woman's face, full of the nobility of desire to save life, was so interwoven with frugality and her inveterate habit of protecting our things, that I hardly know how the controversy in her own mind would have ended if I had not flown to the kitchen tent to get the clothes-line. The current swayed the drowning man so violently he was afraid to loosen his hold of the branches to reach the rope as we threw it to him over and over again, and it seemed momentarily that he must be torn from our sight. The hue of death was on his face—that terrible blue look—while the features were pinched with suffering, and the eyes starting from their sockets. He was naked to the waist, and the chill of the water, and of those hours that come before dawn, had almost benumbed the fingers that clutched the branches. Eliza, like me, has forgotten nothing that happened during that horrible night, and I give part of her story, the details of which it is so difficult for me to recall with calmness :

"Miss Libbie, don't you mind when we took the clothes-line an' went near to him as we could get, he didn't seem to understan' what we was up to? We made a loop and showed it to him, when a big flash of lightnin' came and made a glare, and tried to call to him to put it over his head. The noise of the water, and the crashin' of the logs that was comin' down, beside the thunder, drownded out our voices. Well, we worked half an hour over that man. He thought you and me, Miss Libbie, couldn't pull him in—that we wasn't strong enough. He seemed kind o' dazed-like; and the only way I made him know what the loop was for, I put it on over my body and made signs. Even then, he was so swept under that part of the bank, and it was so dark, I didn't think we could get him. I could hear him bubblin', bellowin', drownin' and gaggin'. Well, we pulled him in at last, though I got up to my waist in water. He was cold and blue, his teeth chatterin'; he just shuck and shuck, and his eyes was perfectly wild. We had to help him, for he could hardly walk to the cook tent. I poured hot coffee down him; and, Miss Libbie, you tore aroun' in the dark and found your way to the next tent for whisky, and the lady that never was known to keep any before, had some then. And I wrapped the drownded man in the blouse the Ginnel give me. It was cold, and I was wet and I needed it, Miss Libbie; but didn't that man, as soon as ever his teeth stopped a-chatterin', jest get up and walk off with it? And, Miss Libbie, the Ginnel wrote to you after that, from some expedition, that he had seen the soldier Eliza gave her clothes-line to save, and he sent his thanks and asked how I was, and said I had saved his life. I just sent back word, in the next letter you wrote the Ginnel, to ask if that man said anything about my blouse he wore off that night. You gave one of the Ginnel's blue shirts to a half-naked, drownded man. We saved two more and wrapped 'em in blankets, and you rubbed 'em with red pepper, and kept the fire red-hot, and talked to them, tryin' to get the shiver and the scare out of 'em. I tell you, Miss Libbie, we made a fight for their lives, if ever any one did. The clothes-line did it all. One was washed near to our tent, and I grabbed his hand. We went roun' with our lanterns, and it was so dark we 'spected every moment to step into a watery grave, for the water was so near us, and the flashes of lightnin' would show that it was a-comin' on and on. Turk and Rover would fight just by looking at each other, and in all that mess they fell on each other, an' I was sure they was goin' to kill each other, and, oh, my! the Ginnel would have taken on so about it! But the soldiers dragged them apart."

Seven men were drowned near our tent, and their agonizing cries, when they were too far out in the current for us to throw our line, are sounds that will never be stilled. The men were from the Colonel's escort on the temporary island above us. The cavalrymen attempted, as the waters rose about them, to swim their horses to the other shore; but all were lost who plunged in, for the violence of the current made swimming an impossibility. A few negro soldiers belonging to the infantry were compelled to remain where they were, though the water stood three feet in some of the tents. When the violence of the storm had abated a little, one of the officers swam the narrowest part of the stream, and, taking a wagon-bed, made a ferry, so that with the help of soldiers that he had left behind holding one end of the rope he had taken over, the remaining soldiers were rescued and brought down to our little strip of land. Alas! this narrowed and narrowed, until we all appeared to be doomed. The officers felt their helplessness when they realized that four women looked to them for protection. They thought over every imaginable plan. It was impossible to cross the inundated part of the plain, though their horses were saddled, with the thought that each one might swim with us through the shallowest of the water. They rode into this stretch of impassable prairie, but the water was too swift, even then, to render it anything but perilous. They decided that if the water continued to rise with the same rapidity we would be washed away, as we could not swim, nor had we strength to cling to anything. This determined them to resort to a plan that, happily, we knew nothing of until the danger was passed. We were to be strapped to the Gatling guns as an anchorage. These are, perhaps, the lightest of all artillery, but might have been heavy enough to resist the action of what current rose over our island. There would have been one chance in ten thousand of rescue under such circumstances, but I doubt if being pinioned there, watching the waves closing around us, would have been as merciful as permitting us to float off into a quicker death.

While the officers and men with us were working with all
their might to save lives and property, the little post was beleaguered.   The flood came so unexpectedly that the first
known of it was the breaking in of the doors of the quarters.
The poorly built, leaky, insecure adobe houses had been heretofore a protection, but the freshet filled them almost instantly
with water.   The quarters of the laundresses were especially endangered, being on even lower ground than the officers'
houses.   The women were hurried out in their night-dresses,
clasping their crying children, while they ran to places
pointed out by the officers, to await orders.   Even then, one
of our Seventh Cavalry officers, who happened to be temporarily at the garrison, clambered up to the roof of an adobe
house to discover whether the women of his regiment were
in peril.   The same plan for rescue was adopted at the post
that had been partly successful above.   A ferry was improvised out of a wagon-bed, and into this were collected the
women and children.   The post was thus emptied in time to
prevent loss of life.   First the women, then the sick from the
hospital, and finally the drunken men; for the hospital liquor
was broken into, and it takes but a short time to make a soldier helplessly drunk.   The Government property had to be
temporarily abandoned, and a great deal was destroyed or
swept away by the water.   It was well that the camp women
were inured to hardship, for the condition in which the cold,
wet, frightened creatures landed, without any protection from
the storm, on the opposite bank, was pitiful.   One laundress
had no screams of terror or groans of suffering over physical
fright; her wails were loud and continuous because her savings had been left in the quarters, and facing death in that
frail box, as she was pulled through the turbid flood, was
nothing to the pecuniary loss.   It was all the men could do to
keep her from springing into the wagon-bed to return and
search for her money.

On still another branch of Big Creek there was another
body of men wrestling with wind and wave.   Several companies, marching to New Mexico, had encamped for the

night, and the freshet came as suddenly upon them as upon all of us. The colonel in command had to seize his wife, and wade up to his arms in carrying her to a safe place. Even then, they were warned that the safety was but temporary. The ambulance was harnessed up, and they drove through water that almost swept them away, before they reached higher ground. There was a strange coincidence about the death, eventually, of this officer's wife. A year afterward they were encamped on a Texas stream, with similar high banks, betokening freshets, and the waters rose suddenly, compelling them to take flight in the ambulance again; but this time the wagon was overturned by the current, and the poor woman was drowned.

When the day dawned, we were surrounded by water, and the havoc about us was dreadful. But what a relief it was to have the rain cease, and feel the comfort of daylight! Eliza broke up her bunk to make a fire, and we had breakfast for everybody, owing to her self-sacrifice! The water began to subside, and the place looked like a vast laundry. All the camp was flying with blankets, bedding and clothes. We were drenched, of course, having no dry shoes even, to replace those in which we had raced about in the mud during the night. But these were small inconveniences, compared with the agony of terror that the night had brought. As the morning advanced, and the stream fell constantly, we were horrified by the sight of a soldier, swollen beyond all recognition, whose drowned body was imbedded in the side of the bank, where no one could reach it, and where we could not escape the sight of it. He was one who had implored us to save him, and our failure to do so seemed even more terrible than the night before, as we could not keep our fascinated gaze from the stiffened arm that seemed to have been stretched out entreatingly.

Though we were thankful for our deliverance, the day was a depressing one, for the horror of the drowning men near us could not be put out of our minds. As night came on again, the clouds began to look ominous; it was murky, and it rained a little.

A BUFFALO UNDECIDED AS TO AN ATTACK ON GENERAL CUSTER.

At dark word came from the fort, to which some of the officers had returned, that we must attempt to get to the high ground, as the main stream, Big Creek, was again rising. All the officers were alarmed. They kept measuring the advance of the stream themselves, and guards were stationed at intervals, to note the rise of the water and report its progress. The torch-lights they held were like tiny fire-flies, so dark was the night. An ambulance was driven to our tent to make the attempt to cross the water, which had abated there slightly, and, if possible, to reach the divide beyond. One of the officers went in advance, on horseback, to try the depth of the water. It was a failure, and the others forbade our going, thinking it would be suicidal. While they were arguing, Diana and I were wrapping ourselves in what outside garments we had in the tent. She had been plucky through the terrible night, writing next morning to the General that she never wished herself for one moment at home, and that even with such a fright she could never repay us for bringing her out to a life she liked so much. Yet as we tremblingly put on our outside things, she began to be agitated over a subject so ridiculous in such a solemn and dangerous hour, that I could not keep my face from what might have been a smile under less serious circumstances. Her trepidation was about her clothes. She asked me anxiously what she should do for dresses next day, and insisted that she must take her small trunk. In vain I argued that we had nowhere to go. We could but sit in the ambulance till dawn, even if we were fortunate enough to escape to the bluff. She still persisted, saying, "What if we should reach a fort, and I was obliged to appear in the gown I now wear?" I asked her to remember that the next fort was eighty miles distant, with enough water between it and us to float a ship, not to mention roving bands of Indians lying in wait; but this by no means quieted her solicitude about her appearance. At last I suggested her putting on three dresses, one over the other, and then taking, in the little trunk from which she could not part, the most necessary garments and gowns. When I

went out to get into the wagon, after the other officers had
left, and found our one escort determined still to venture, I
was obliged to explain that Diana could not make up her
mind to part with her trunk. He was astounded that at such
an hour, in such a dangerous situation, clothes should ever
enter anyone's head. But the trunk appeared at the entrance
of the tent, to verify my words. He argued that with a
wagon loaded with several people, it would be perilous to
add unnecessary weight in driving through such ground.
Then, with all his chivalry, working night and day to help
us, there came an instant when he could no longer do justice
to the occasion in our presence; so he stalked off to one side,
and what he said to himself was lost in the growl of the
thunder.

The trunk was secured in the ambulance, and Diana, Eliza
and I followed. There we sat, getting wetter, more frightened and less plucky as the time rolled on. Again were we
forbidden to attempt this mode of escape, and condemned to
return to the tent, which was vibrating in the wind and
menacing a downfall. No woman ever wished more ardently
for a brown-stone front than I longed for a dug-out. Any
hole in the side of a bank would have been a palace to me,
living as I did in momentary expectation of no covering at
all. The rarest, most valuable of homes meant to me something that could not blow away. Those women who take
refuge in these days in their cyclone cellar—now the popular
architecture of the West—will know well how comforting it
is to possess something that cannot be readily lifted up and
deposited in a neighboring county.

With the approach of midnight, there was again an abate-
ment in the rain, and the water of the stream ceased to creep
toward us; so the officers, gaining some confidence in its
final subsidence, again left us to go to their tents. For three
days the clouds and thunder threatened, but at last the sun
appeared. In a letter to my husband, dated June 9, 1867, I
wrote: "When the sun came out yesterday, we could almost
have worshipped it, like the heathen. We have had some

dreadful days, and had not all the officers been so kind to us, I do not know how we could have endured what we have. Even some whom we do not know have shown the greatest solicitude in our behalf. We are drenching wet still, and everything we have is soggy with moisture. Last evening, after two sleepless nights, Mrs. Gibbs and her two boys, Alphie and Blair, Diana and I, were driven across the plain, from which the water is fast disappearing, to the coveted divide beyond. It is not much higher, as you know, than the spot where our tents are; but it looked like a mountain, as we watched it, while the water rose all around us. Some of the officers had tents pitched there, and we women were given the Sibley tent with the floor, that sheltered me in the other storm. We dropped down in heaps, we were so exhausted for want of sleep, and it was such a relief to know that at last the water could not reach us." The letter (continued from day to day, as no scouts were sent out) described the moving of the camp to more secure ground. It was incessant motion, for no place was wholly satisfactory to the officers. I confessed that I was a good deal unnerved by the frights, that every sound startled me, and a shout from a soldier stopped my breathing almost, so afraid was I that it was the alarm of another freshet—while the clouds were never more closely watched than at that time.

A fresh trouble awaited me, for General Hancock came to camp from Harker, and brought bad news. The letter continues: " The dangers and terrors of the last few days are nothing, compared with the information that General Hancock brings. It came near being the last proverbial ' straw.' I was heart-sick, indeed, when I found that our schemes for being together soon were so ruthlessly crushed. General Hancock says that it looks as if you would be in the Department of the Platte for several months—at which he is justly indignant—but he is promised your return before the summer is ended. He thinks, that if I want to go so badly, I may manage to make you a flying visit up there; and this is all that keeps me up. The summer here, so far separated from

you, seems to stretch out like an arid desert. If there were
the faintest shadow of a chance that I would see you here
again, I would not go, as we are ordered to. I will come
back here again if I think there is the faintest prospect of
seeing you. If you say so, I will go to Fort McPherson on
the cars, if I get the ghost of an opportunity."

Eliza, in ending her recollections of the flood at Fort Hays,
says, " Well, Miss Libbie, when the water rose so, and the
men was a-drownin', I said to myself in the night, if God
spared me, that would be the last of war for me; but when
the waters went down and the sun came out, then we began
to cheer each other up, and were willing to go right on from
there, if we could, for we wanted to see the Ginnel so bad.
But who would have thought that the stream would have
risen around the little knoll as it did? The Ginnel thought
he had fixed us so nice, and he had, Miss Libbie, for it was
the knoll that saved us. The day the regiment left for Fort
McPherson the Ginnel staid behind till dark, gettin' everythin' in order to make you comfortable, and he left at 12
o'clock at night, with his escort, to join the troops. He'd
rather ride ride all night than miss that much of his visit
with you. Before he went, he came to my tent to say good-
by. I stuck my hand out, and said, 'Ginnel, I don't like to
see you goin' off in this wild country, at this hour of the
night.' . . . 'I have to go,' he says, 'wherever I'm called.
Take care of Libbie, Eliza,' and puttin' spurs to his horse,
off he rode. Then I thought they'd certainly get him, ridin'
right into the mouth of 'em. You know how plain the sound
comes over the prairie, with nothin', no trees or anythin', to
interfere. Well, in the night I was hearin' *quare* sounds.
Some might have said they was buffalo, but on thy went,
lumpety lump, lumpety lump, and they was Indians ! Miss
Libbie, sure as you're born, they was Indians gettin' out of
the way, and, oh ! I was so scart for the Ginnel."

CHAPTER XVIII.

ORDERED BACK TO FORT HARKER.

AFTER the high-water experience, our things were scarcely dry before I found, for the second time, what it was to be under the complete subjection of military rule. The fiat was issued that we women must depart from camp and return to garrison, as it was considered unsafe for us to remain. It was an intense disappointment; for though Fort Hays and our camp were more than dreary after the ravages of the storm, to leave there meant cutting myself off from any other chance that might come in my way of joining my husband, or of seeing him at our camp. Two of the officers and an escort of ten mounted men, going to Fort Harker on duty, accompanied our little cortège of departing women. At the first stage-station the soldiers all dismounted as we halted, and managed by some pretext to get into the dug-out and buy whiskey. Not long after we were again *en route* I saw one of the men reel on his saddle, and he was lifted into the wagon that carried forage for the mules and horses. One by one, all were finally dumped into the wagons by the teamsters, who fortunately were sober, and the troopers' horses were tied behind the vehicles, and we found ourselves without an escort. Plains whiskey is usually very rapid in its effect, but the stage-station liquor was concocted from drugs that had power to lay out even a hard-drinking old cavalryman like a dead person in what seemed no time at all. Eliza said "they only needed to smell it, 'twas so deadly poison." A barrel of tolerably good whiskey sent from the States was, by the addition of drugs, made into several barrels after it reached the Plains.

The hours of that march seemed endless. We were help-less, and knew that we were going over ground that was hotly contested by the red man. We rose gradually to the summit of each divide, and looked with anxious eyes into every de-pression; but we were no sooner relieved to find it safe, than my terrors began as to what the next might reveal. When we came upon an occasional ravine, it represented to my frightened soul any number of Indians in ambush.

In that country the air is so clear that every object on the brow of a small ascent of ground is silhouetted against the deep blue of the sky. The Indians place little heaps of stones on these slight eminences, and lurk behind them to watch the approach of troops. Every little pile of rocks seemed, to my strained eyes, to hide the head of a savage. They even appeared to move, and this effect was heightened by the waves of heat that hover over the surface of the earth under that blazing sun. I was thoroughly frightened, doubt-less made much more so because I had nothing else to think of, as the end of the journey would not mean for me what the termination of ever so dangerous a march would have been in the other direction. Had I been going over such country to join my husband, the prospect would have put temporary courage into every nerve. During the hours of daylight the vigilance of the officers was unceasing. They knew that one of the most hazardous days of their lives was upon them. They felt intensely the responsibility of the care of us; and I do not doubt, gallant as they were, that they mentally pronounced anathemas upon officers who had want-ed to see their wives so badly that they had let them come into such a country. When we had first gone over the route, however, its danger was not a circumstance to this time. Our eyes rarely left the horizon; they were strained to discern signs that had come to be familiar, even by our hearing them discussed so constantly; and we, still novices in the experi-ence of that strange country, had seen for ourselves enough to prove that no vigilance was too great. If on the monoto-nous landscape a whirl of dust arose, instantly it was a matter of doubt whether it meant our foe or one of the strange eccentricities of that part of the world.   The most peculiar communions are those that the clouds seem to have with the earth, which result in a cone of dust whirlpooling itself straight in the air, while the rest of the earth is apparently without commotion, bearing no relation to the funnel that seems to struggle upward and be dissolved into the passing wind.   With what intense concentration we watched to see it so disappear !   If the puff of dust continued to spread, the light touching it into a deeper yellow, and finally revealing some darker shades, and at last shaping itself into dusky forms, we were in agony of suspense until the field-glasses proved that it was a herd of antelopes fleeing from our approach.   There literally seemed to be not one inch of the way that the watchful eyes of the officers, the drivers, or we women were not strained to discover every object that specked the horizon or rose on the trail in front of us.

With all the terror and suspense of those dragging miles, I could not be insensible to the superb and riotous colors of the wild flowers that carpeted our way.   It was the first time that I had ever been where the men could not be asked, and were not willing, to halt or let me stop and gather one of every kind.   The gorgeousness of the reds and orange of those prairie blossoms was a surprise to me.   I had not dreamed that the earth could so glow with rich tints.   The spring rains had soaked the ground long enough to start into life the wonderful dyes that for a brief time emblazon the barren wilderness.   The royal livery floats but a short period over their temporary domain, for the entire cessation of even the night dews, and the intensity of the scorching sun, shrivels the vivid, flaunting, feathery petals, and burns the venturesome roots down into the earth.   What presuming things, to toss their pennants over so inhospitable a land !   But what a boon to travelers like ourselves to see, for even the brief season, some tint besides the burnt umber and yellow ochre of those plains!   All the short existence of these flowers is condensed into the color, tropical in richness; not

one faint waft of perfume floated on the air about us. But it
was all we ought to have asked, that their brilliant heads appear out of such soil.   This has served to make me very appreciative of the rich exhalation of the Eastern gardens. I
do not dare say what the first perfume of the honeysuckle is
to me, each year now; nor would I infringe upon the few
adjectives vouchsafed the use of a conventional Eastern
woman when, as it happened this year, the orange blossoms,
white jessamine and woodbine wafted their sweet breaths in
my face as a welcome from one garden to which good fortune led me. I remember the starvation days of that odor-
less life, when, seeing rare colors, we instantly expected rich
odors, but found them not, and I try to adapt myself to the
customs of the country, and not rave, but, like the children,
keep up a mighty thinking.

Buffalo, antelope, blacktail deer, coyote, jack-rabbits,
scurried out of our way on that march, and we could not
stop to follow. I was looking always for some new sight,
and, after the relief that I felt when each object as we neared
it turned out to be harmless, was anxious to see a drove of
wild horses.   There were still herds to be found between the
Cimmaron and the Arkansas rivers. The General told me
of seeing one of the herds on a march, spoke with great admiration and enthusiasm of the leader, and described him as
splendid in carriage, and bearing his head in the proudest,
loftiest manner as he led his followers. They were not large;
they must have been the Spanish pony of Cortez' time, as
we know that the horse is not indigenous to America. The
flowing mane and tail, the splendid arch of the neck, and the
proud head carried so loftily, give the wild horses a larger,
taller appearance than is in reality theirs. Few ever saw the
droves of wild horses more than momentarily. They run
like the wind.

After the introduction of the dromedary into Texas, many
years since, for transportation of supplies over that vast territory, one was brought up to Colorado. Because of the immense runs it could make without water, it was taken into

A BUFFALO AT BAY. (FROM A PHOTOGRAPH TAKEN ON THE SPOT.)

the region frequented by the wild horses, and when they were sighted, the dromedary was started in pursuit. Two were run down, and found to be nearly dead when overtaken. But the poor dromedary suffered so from the prickly-pear filling the soft ball of its feet, that no farther pursuit could ever be undertaken.

I had to be content with the General's description, for no wild horses came in our way. But there was enough to satisfy any one in the way of game. The railroad had not then driven to the right and left the inhabitants of that vast prairie. Our country will never again see the Plains dotted with game of all sorts. The railroad stretches its iron bands over these desert wastes, and scarcely a skulking coyote, hugging the ground and stealing into gulches, can be discovered during a whole day's journey.

As the long afternoon was waning, we were allowed to get out and rest a little while, for we had reached what was called the " Home Station," so called because at this place there was a woman, then the only one along the entire route. I looked with more admiration than I could express on this fearless creature, long past the venturesome time of early youth, when some dare much for excitement. She was as calm and collected as her husband, whom she valued enough to endure with him this terrible existence. How good the things tasted that she cooked, and how different the dooryard looked from those of the other stations! Then she had a baby antelope, and the apertures that served as windows had bits of white curtains, and, altogether, I did not wonder that over the hundreds of miles of stage-route the Home Station was a place the men looked forward to as the only reminder of the civilization that a good woman establishes about her. There was an awful sight, though, that riveted my eyes as we prepared to go on our journey, and the officers could not, by any subterfuge, save us from seeing it. It was a disabled stage-coach, literally riddled with bullets, its leather hanging in shreds, and the woodwork cut into splinters. When there was no further use of trying to conceal it from us, we

were told that this stage had come into the station in that
condition the day before, and the fight that the driver and
mail-carrier had been through was desperate.   There was no
getting the sight of that vehicle out of my mind during the
rest of the journey.   What a friend the darkness seemed, as
it wrapped its protecting mantle about us, after the long
twilight ended! yet it was almost impossible to sleep, though
we knew we were comparatively safe till dawn.   At daybreak
the officers asked us to get out, while the mules were watered
and fed, and rest ourselves, and though I had been so long
riding in a cramped position, I would gladly have declined.
Cleanliness is next to godliness, and, one of our friends said,
"With a woman, it is before godliness," yet that was an occasion when I would infinitely have preferred to be numbered with the great unwashed.   However, a place in the little
stream at the foot of the gully was pointed out, and we took
our tin basin and towel and freshened ourselves by this early
toilet; but there was no lingering to prink, even on the part
of the pretty Diana.   Our eyes were staring on all sides, with
a dread impossible to quell, and back into the ambulance we
climbed, not breathing a long, free breath until the last of
those terrible eighty miles were passed, and we beheld with
untold gratitude the roofs of the quarters at Fort Harker.
    I felt that we had trespassed as much as we ought upon the
hospitality of the commanding officer of the post, and begged to be allowed to sleep in our ambulance while we remained
in the garrison.   He consented, under protest, and our wagon
and that of Mrs. Gibbs were placed in the space between two
Government storehouses, and a tarpaulin was stretched over
the two.   Eliza prepared our simple food over a little camp-
fire.   While the weather remained good, this was a very comfortable camp for us—but when, in Kansas, do the elements
continue quiet for twenty-four hours?   In the darkest hour
of the blackest kind of night the wind rose into a tempest,
rushing around the corners of the buildings, hunting out with
pertinacity, from front and rear, our poor little temporary
home.   The tarpaulin was lifted on high, and with ropes and

picket-pins thrashing on the canvas it finally broke its last moorings and soared off into space. The rain beat in the curtains of the ambulance and soaked our blankets. Still, we crept together on the farther side of our narrow bed and, rolled up in our shawls, tried to hide our eyes from the lightning, and our ears from the roar of the storm as it swept between the sheltering buildings and made us feel as if we were camping in a tunnel.

Our neighbor's dog joined his voice with the sobs and groans of the wind, while in the short intervals of quiet we called out, trying to get momentary courage from speech with each other. The curtain at the end of the ambulance jerked itself free, and in came a deluge of rain from a new direction. Pins, strings and four weak hands holding their best, did no earthly good, and I longed to break all military rule and scream to the sentinel. Not to speak to a guard on post is one of the early lessons instilled into every one in military life. It required such terror of the storm and just such a drenching as we were getting, even to harbor a thought of this direct disobedience of orders. Clutching the wagon-curtains and watching the soldier, who was revealed by the frequent flashes of lightning as he tramped his solitary way, might have gone on for some time without the necessary courage coming to call him, but a new departure of the wind suddenly set us in motion, and I found that we were spinning down the little declivity back of us, with no knowledge of when or where we would stop. Then I did scream, and the peculiar shrillness of a terrified woman's voice reached the sentinel. Blessed breaker of his country's laws! He answered to a higher one, which forbids him to neglect a woman in danger, and left his beat to run to our succor.

Our wagon was dragged back by some of the soldiers on night duty at the guard-house, and was newly pinioned to the earth with stronger picket-pins and ropes, but sleep was murdered for that night. Of course the guard reported to the commanding officer, as is their rule, and soon a lantern or two came zigzagging over the parade-ground in our direc-

tion, and the officers called to know if they could speak with
us. There was no use in arguing. Mrs. Gibbs and her boys,
Diana drenched and limp as to clothes, and I decidedly moist,
were fished out of our watery camp-beds, and with our arms
full of apparel and satchels, we followed the officers in the
dark to the dry quarters, that we had tried our best to decline
rather than make trouble.

It was decided that we must proceed to Fort Riley, as there
were no quarters to offer us ; and tent-life, as I have tried to
describe it, had its drawbacks in the rainy season. Had it
not meant for me ninety miles farther separation from my
husband, seemingly cut off from all chance of joining him
again, I would have welcomed the plan of going back, as Fort
Harker was at this time the most absolutely dismal and melancholy spot I remember ever to have seen. A terrible and
unprecedented calamity had fallen upon the usually healthful
place, for cholera had broken out, and the soldiers were dying by platoons. I had been accustomed to think, in all the
vicissitudes that had crowded themselves into these few
months, whatever else we were deprived of, we at least had a
climate unsurpassed for salubrity, and I still think so. For
some strange reason, right out in the midst of that wide,
open plain, with no stagnant water, no imperfect drainage,
no earthly reason, it seemed to us, this epidemic had suddenly appeared, and in a form so violent that a few hours of
suffering ended fatally. Nobody took dying into consideration out there in those days ; all were well and able-bodied,
and almost everyone was young who ventured into that new
country, so no lumber had been provided to make coffins.
For a time the rudest receptacles were hammered together,
made out of the hardtack boxes. Almost immediate burial
took place, as there was no ice, nor even a safe place to keep
the bodies of the unfortunate victims. It was absolutely necessary, but an awful thought neverthelesss, this scurrying
under the ground of the lately dead, perhaps only wrapped
in a coarse gray army blanket, and with the burial service
hurriedly read, for all were needed as nurses, and time was

too precious to say even the last words, except in haste. The officers and their families did not escape, and sorrow fell upon every one when an attractive young woman who had dared everything in the way of hardships to follow her husband, was marked by that terrible finger which bade her go alone into the valley of death. In the midst of this scourge, the Sisters of Charity came. Two of them died, and afterward a priest, but they were replaced by others, who remained until the pestilence had wrought its worst; then they gathered the orphaned children of the soldiers together, and returned with them to the parent house of their Order in Leavenworth.

I would gladly have these memories fade out of my life, for the scenes at that post have no ray of light except the heroic conduct of the men and women who stood their ground through the danger. I cannot pass by those memorable days in the early history of Kansas without my tribute to the brave officers and men who went through so much to open the way for settlers. I lately rode through the State, which seemed when I first saw it a hopeless, barren waste, and found the land under fine cultivation, the houses, barns and fences excellently built, cattle in the meadows, and, sometimes, several teams ploughing in one field. I could not help wondering what the rich owners of these estates would say, if I should step down from the car and give them a little picture of Kansas, with the hot, blistered earth, dry beds of streams, and soil apparently so barren that not even the wildflowers would bloom, save for a brief period after the spring rains. Then add pestilence, Indians, and an undisciplined, mutinous soldiery who composed our first recruits, and it seems strange that our officers persevered at all. I hope the prosperous ranchman will give them one word of thanks as he advances to greater wealth, since but for our brave fellows the Kansas Pacific Railroad could not have been built; nor could the early settlers, daring as they were, have sowed the seed that now yields them such rich harvests.

We had no choice about leaving Fort Harker. There was

no accommodation for us—indeed we would have hampered the already overworked officers and men ; so we took our departure for Fort Riley.   There we found perfect quiet ; the negro troops were reduced to discipline, and everything went on as if there were no such thing as the dead and the dying that we had left a few hours before.   There was but a small garrison, and we easily found empty quarters, that were lent to us by the commanding officer.

Then the life of watching and waiting, and trying to possess my soul in patience, began again, and my whole day resolved itself into a mental protest against the slowness of the hours before the morning mail could be received.   It was a doleful time for us ; but I remember no uttered complaints as such, for we silently agreed they would weaken our courage.   If tears were shed, they fell on the pillow, where the blessed darkness came to absolve us from the rigid watchfulness that we tried to keep over our feelings.   My husband gladdened many a dark day by the cheeriest letters.   How he ever managed to write so buoyantly was a mystery when I found afterward what he was enduring.   I rarely had a letter with even so much as a vein of discontent, during all our separations.   At that time came two that were strangely in contrast to all the brave, encouraging missives that had cheered my day.   The accounts of cholera met our regiment on their march into the Department of the Platte ; and the General, in the midst of intense anxiety, with no prospect of direct communication, assailed by false reports of my illness, at last showed a side of his character that was seldom visible.   His suspense regarding my exposure to pestilence, and his distress over the fright and danger I had endured at the time of the flood at Fort Hays, made his brave spirit quail, and there were desperate words written, which, had he not been relieved by news of my safety, would have ended in his taking steps to resign.   Even he, whom I scarcely ever knew to yield to discouraging circumstances, wrote that he could not and would not endure such a life.

Our days at Fort Riley had absolutely nothing to vary them

after mail time. I sat on the gallery long before the time of distribution, pretending to sew or read, but watching constantly for the door of the office to yield up next to the most important man in the wide world to me. The soldier whose duty it was to bring the mail became so inflated by the eagerness with which his steps were watched, that it came near being the death of him when he joined his company in the autumn, and was lost in its monotonous ranks. He was a ponderous, lumbering fellow in body and mind, who had been left behind by his captain, ostensibly to take care of the company property, but I soon found there was another reason, as his wits had for some time been unsettled, that is—giving him the benefit of a doubt—if he ever had any. Addled as his brain might be, the remnant of intelligence was ample in my eyes if it enabled him to make his way to our door. As he belonged to the Seventh Cavalry, he considered that everything at the post must be subservient to my wish, when in reality I was dependent for a temporary roof on the courtesy of the infantry officer in command. If I even met him in our walks, he seemed to swell to twice his size, and to feel that some of the odor of sanctity hung around him, whether he bore messages from the absent or not.

The contents of the mail-bag being divided, over six feet of anatomical and military perfection came stalking through the parade-ground. He would not demean himself to hasten, and his measured steps were in accordance with the gait prescribed in the past by his sergeant on drill. He appeared to throw his head back more loftily as he perceived that my eyes followed his creeping steps. He seemed to be reasoning. Did Napoleon ever run, the Duke of Wellington ever hasten, or General Scott quicken his gait or impair his breathing by undue activity, simply because an unreasoning, impatient woman was waiting somewhere for them to appear? It was not at all in accordance with his ideas of martial character to exhibit indecorous speed. The great and responsible office of conveying the letters from the officer to the quarters had been assigned to him, and nothing, he determined,

THE ADDLED LETTER-CARRIER.

should interfere with its being filled with dignity. His country looked to him as its savior. Only a casual and condescending thought was given to his comrades, who perhaps at that time were receiving in their bodies the arrows of Indian warriors. No matter how eagerly I eyed the great official envelope in his hand, which I knew well was mine, he persisted in observing all the form and ceremony that he had decided was suitable for its presentation. He was especially particular to assume the " first position of a soldier," as he drew up in front of me. The tone with which he addressed me was deliberate and grandiloquent. The only variation in his regulation manners was that he allowed himself to speak before he was spoken to. With the flourish of his colossal arm, in a salute that took in a wide semicircle of Kansas air, he said, "Good morning, Mrs. Major-General George Armstrong Custer." He was the only gleam of fun we had in those dismal days. He was a marked contrast to the disciplined enlisted man, who never speaks unless first addressed by his superiors, and who is modesty itself in demeanor and language in the presence of the officers' wives. The farewell salute of our mail-carrier was funnier than his approach. He wheeled on his military heel, and swung wide his flourishing arm, but the "right about face" I generally lost, for, after snatching my envelope from him, unawed by his formality, I fled into the house to hide, while I laughed and cried over the contents.

CHAPTER XIX.

THE FIRST FIGHT OF THE SEVENTH CAVALRY.

THE first fight of the Seventh Cavalry was at Fort Wallace. In June, 1867, a band of three hundred Cheyennes, under Roman Nose, attacked the stage-station near that fort, and ran off the stock. Elated with this success, they proceeded to Fort Wallace, that poor little group of log huts and mud cabins having apparently no power of resistance. Only the simplest devices could be resorted to for defense. The commissary stores and ammunition were partly protected by a low wall of gunny-sacks filled with sand. There were no logs near enough, and no time if there had been, to build a stockade. But our splendid cavalry charged out as boldly as if they were leaving behind them reserve troops and a battery of artillery. They were met by a counter-charge, the Indians, with lances poised and arrows on the string, coming on swiftly in overwhelming numbers. It was a hand-to-hand fight. Roman Nose was about to throw his javelin at one of our men, when the cavalryman, with his left hand, gave a sabre-thrust equal to the best that many good fencers can execute with their sword-arm. With his Spencer rifle he wounded the chief, and saw him fall forward on his horse.

The post had been so short of men that a dozen negro soldiers, who had come with their wagon from an outpost for supplies, were placed near the garrison on picket duty. While the fight was going on, the two officers in command found themselves near each other on the skirmish-line, and observed a wagon with four mules tearing out to the line of battle. It was filled with negroes, standing up, all firing in the direction of the Indians. The driver lashed the mules with his black-snake, and roared at them as they ran. When the skirmish-line was reached the colored men leaped out and began firing again. No one had ordered them to leave their picket-station, but they were determined that no soldiering should be carried on in which their valor was not proved. The officers saw with surprise that one of the number ran off by himself into the most dangerous place, and one of them remarked, " There's a gone nigger, for a certainty ! " They saw him fall, throw up his hands, kick his feet in the air, and then collapse—dead to all appearances. After the fight was over, and the Indians had withdrawn to the bluffs, the soldiers were called together and ordered back to the post. At that moment a negro, gun in hand, walked up from where the one supposed to be slain had last been seen. It was the dead restored to life. When asked by the officer, " What in thunder do you mean, running off at such a distance into the face of danger, and throwing up your feet and hands as if shot ? " he replied, " Oh, Lord, Massa, I just did dat to fool 'em. I fot deyed try to get my scalp, thinkin' I war dead, and den I'd jest get one of 'em."

The following official report, sent in from some colored men stationed at Wilson's Creek, who were attacked, and successfully drove off the Indians, will give further proof of their good service, while at the same time it reveals a little of other sides of the negro, when he first began to serve Uncle Sam:

" All the boys done bully, but Corporal Johnson—he flinked. The way he flinked was, to wait till the boys had drove the Injuns two miles, and then he hollered, ' Gin it to 'em ! ' and the boys don't think that a man that would flink that way ought to have corporal's straps."

In order to give this effort at military composition its full effect, it would be necessary to add the official report of a cut-and-dried soldier. No matter how trifling the duty, the stilted language, bristling with technical pomposity, in which every military move is reported, makes me, a non-combatant, question if the white man is not about as absurd in his way as the darkey was in his.

NEGROES FORM THEIR OWN PICKET-LINE.

Poor Fort Wallace ! In another attack on the post, where several of our men were killed, there chanced to be some engineers stopping at the garrison, *en route* to New Mexico, where a Government survey was to be undertaken. One of them, carrying a small camera, photographed a sergeant lyon the battle-ground after the enemy had retreated. The body was gashed and pierced by twenty-three arrows. Everything combined to keep that little garrison in a state of siege, and a gloomy pall hung over the beleaguered spot.

As the stage-stations were one after another attacked, burned, the men murdered and the stock driven off for a distance of three hundred miles, the difficulty of sending mail became almost insurmountable. Denver lay out there at the foot of the mountains, as isolated as if it had been a lone island in the Pacific Ocean. Whenever a coach went out with the mail, a second one was filled with soldiers and led the advance. The Seventh Cavalry endeavored to fortify some of the deserted stage-stations; but the only means of defense consisted in burrowing underground. After the holes were dug, barely large enough for four men standing, and a barrel of water and a week's provision, it was covered over with logs and turf, leaving an aperture for firing. Where the men had warning, they could " stand off " many Indians, and save the horses in another dug-out adjacent.

After a journey along the infested route, where one of our officers was detailed to post a corporal and four men at the stations when the stage company endeavored to reinstate themselves, he decided to go on into Denver for a few days. The detention then was threatening to be prolonged, and at the stage company's headquarters the greatest opposition was encountered before our officer could induce them to send out a coach. Fortunately, as it afterward proved, three soldiers who had orders to return to their troop, accompanied him. The stage company opposed every move, and warned him that he left at his own risk. But there was no other alternative, as he was due and needed at Fort Wallace. At one of the stage-stations nearest Denver a woman still endeavored to brave it out; but her nerve deserted her at last, and she implored our officer to take her as far as he went on her way into the States. Her husband, trying to protect the company's interests, elected to remain, but begged that his wife might be taken away from the deadly peril of their surroundings. Our officer frankly said there was very little chance that the stage would ever reach Fort Wallace. She replied that she had been frightened half to death all summer, and was sure to be murdered if she remained, and might as well die in the stage, as there was no chance for her at the station.

Every revolution of the wheels brought them into greater danger. The three soldiers on the top of the stage kept a lookout on every side, while the officer inside sat with rifle in hand, looking from the door on either side the trail. Even with all this vigilance, the attack, when it came, was a surprise. The Indians had hidden in a wash-out near the road. Their first shot fatally wounded one of the soldiers, who, dropping his gun, fell over the coach railing, and with dying energy, half swung himself into the door of the stage, gasping out a message to his mother. Our officer replied that he would listen to the parting words later, helped the man to get upon the seat, and, without a preliminary, pushed the woman down into the deep body of the coach, bidding her, as she valued the small hope of life, not to let herself be seen. As has been said before, those familiar with Indian warfare know well with what redoubled ferocity the savage fights, if he finds that a white woman is likely to fall into his hands. It is well known, also, that the squaws are ignored if the chiefs have a white woman in their power, and it brings a more fearful agony to her lot, for when the warriors are absent from the village, the squaws, wild with jealousy, heap cruelty and exhausting labor upon the helpless victim. All this the frontier woman knew, as we all did, and it needed no second command to keep her imperiled head on the floor of the coach.

The instant the dying soldier had dropped his gun, the

driver—ah, what cool heads those stage-drivers had!—seized
the weapon, thrusting his lines between his agile and muscular knees, inciting his mules, and every shot had a deadly
aim.   The soldiers fired one volley, and then leaped to the
ground as the officer sprang from the stage door, and following beside the vehicle, continued to fire as they walked.
The first two shots from the roof of the coach had killed two
Indians hidden in the hole made by the wash-out.   By that

AN ATTACK ON A STAGE-COACH.

means our men got what they term the "morale" on them,
and though they pursued, it was at a greater distance than it
would have been had not two of their number fallen at the
beginning of the attack.

This running fire continued for five miles, when, fortunately
for the little band, one of the stage stations, where a few men
had been posted on our officer's trip out, was reached at last.
Here a halt was made, as the Indians congregated on a bluff
where they could watch safely.   The coach was a wreck.
The large lamps on either side of the driver's seat were shat-

tered completely, and there were six bullet-holes between the roof and the wooden body of the coach.   When the door of the stage was opened, and the crouching woman lifted her face from the floor and was helped out, she was so unmoved, so calm, the officer and soldiers were astonished at her nerve. She looked about, and said, "But I don't see any Indians yet." The officer told her that if she would take the trouble to look over on the bluff, she would find them on dress parade.   Then she told him about her experience in the stage. The dying soldier had breathed his last soon after he fell into the coach, and all the five miles his dead body kept slipping from the seat on to the prostrate woman.   In vain she pushed it one side; the violence with which the vehicle rocked from side to side, as the driver urged his animals to their utmost speed, made it impossible for her to protect herself from contact with the heavy corpse, that rolled about with the plunging of the coach.   All this, repeated without agitation, with no word of fear for the remaining portion of the journey, which, happily, was safely finished, drew from our officer, almost dumb with amazement at the fortitude displayed, a speech that would rarely be set down by the novelist who imagines conversations, but which is just what is likely to be said in real life—" By Jove! you deserve a chromo!"

One troop of the Seventh Cavalry was left to garrison Fort Wallace, while the remainder of the regiment was scouting. The post was then about as dreary as any spot on earth. There were no trees; only the arid plain surrounded it, and the sirocco winds drove the sands of that desolate desert into the dug-outs that served for the habitation of officers and men.   The supplies were of the worst description.   It was impossible to get vegetables of any kind, and there was, therefore, no preventing the soldier's scourge, scurvy, which the heat aggravated, inflaming the already burning flesh. Even the medical supplies were limited.   None of the posts at that time were provided with decent food—that is, none beyond the railroad.   I remember how much troubled my husband was over this subject, when I joined him at Fort

Hays. The bacon issued to the soldiers was not only rancid, but was supplied by dishonest contractors, who slipped in any foreign substance they could, to make the weight come up to the required amount; and thus the soldiers were cheated out of the quantity due them, as well as imposed upon in the quality of their rations. It was the privilege of the enlisted men to make their complaints to the commanding officer, and some of them sent to ask the General to come to the company street and allow them to prove to him what frauds were being practiced. I went with him, and saw a flat stone, the size of the slices of bacon as they were packed together, sandwiched between the layers. My husband was justly incensed, but could promise no immediate redress. The route of travel was so dangerous that it was necessary to detail a larger number of men to guard any train of supplies that attempted to reach those distant posts. The soldiers felt, and justly too, that it was an outrage that preparations for the arrival of so large a number of troops had not been perfected in the spring, before the whole country was in a state of siege. The supplies provided for the consumption of those troops operating in the field or stationed at the posts had been sent out during the war. It was then 1867, and they had lain in the poor, ill-protected adobe or dug-out storehouse all the intervening time—more than two years. At Forts Wallace and Hays there were no storehouses, and the flour and bacon were only protected by tarpaulins. Both became rancid and moldy, and were at the mercy of the rats and mice. A larger quantity of supplies was forwarded to that portion of the country the last year of the war than was needed for the volunteer troops sent out there, and consequently our Seventh Cavalry, scouting day and night all through that eventful summer, were compelled to subsist on the food already on hand. It was the most mistaken economy to persist in issuing such rations, when it is so well known that a well-filled stomach is a strong background for a courageous heart. The desertions were unceasing. The nearer the troops approached the mountains, the more the men took themselves off to the mines.

In April of that year no deaths had occurred at Fort Wallace, but by November there were sixty mounds outside the garrison, covering the brave hearts of soldiers who had either succumbed to illness or been shot by Indians. It was a fearful mortality for a garrison of fewer than two hundred souls. If the soldiers, hungry for fresh meat, went out to shoot buffalo, the half of them mounted guard to protect those who literally took their lives in their hands to provide a few meals of wholesome food for themselves and their comrades. At one company post on the South Platte, a troop of our Seventh Cavalry was stationed. In the mining excitement that ran so high in 1866 and 1867, the captain woke one morning to find that his first sergeant and forty out of sixty men that composed the garrison, had decamped, with horses and equipments, for the mines. This left the handful of men in imminent peril from Indian assaults. The wily foe lies hidden for days outside the garrison, protected by a heap of stones or a sage-bush, and informs himself, as no other spy on earth ever can, just how many souls the little group of tents or the quarters represent. In this dire strait a dauntless sergeant, Andrews, offered to go in search of the missing men. He had established his reputation as a marksman in the regiment, and soldiers used to say that "such shooting as Andrews did, got the bulge on everybody." He was seemingly fearless. The captain consented to his departure, but demurred to his going alone. The sergeant believed he could only succeed if he went into the mining-camp unaccompanied, and so the officer permitted him to go. He arrested and brought away nine, traveling two hundred miles with them to Fort Wallace. There was no guard-house at the post, and the commanding officer had to exercise his ingenuity to secure these deserters. A large hole was dug in the middle of the parade-ground and covered with logs and earth, leaving a square aperture in the centre. The ladder by which they descended was removed by the guard when all were in, and the Bastile could hardly be more secure than this ingenious prison.

Two separate attacks were made by three hundred Dog-soldiers (Cheyennes) to capture Fort Wallace that summer. During the first fight, the prisoners in their pit heard the firing, and knew that all the troops were outside the post engaged with the Indians. Knowing their helplessness, their torture of mind can be imagined. If the enemy succeeded in entering the garrison, their fate was sealed. The attacks were so sudden that there was no opportunity to release these men. The officers knew well enough, that, facing a common foe, they might count on unquestionable unity of action from the deserters. Some clemency was to be expected from a military court that would eventually try them, but all the world knows the savage cry is "No quarter!" In an attack on a post, there is only a wild stampede at the sound of the "General" from the trumpet. There is a rush for weapons, and every one dashes outside the garrison to the skirmish-line. In such a race, every soldier elects to be his own captain till the field is reached. I have seen the troops pour out of a garrison, at an unexpected attack, in an incredibly short time. No one stands upon the order of his going, or cares whose gun or whose horse he seizes on the way. Once the skirmish-line is formed, the soldierly qualities assert themselves, and complete order is resumed. It is only necessary to be in the midst of such excitement, to realize how readily prisoners out of sight would be forgotten.

After the fight was over, and the Indians were driven off, the poor fellows sent to ask if they could speak with the commanding officer, and when he came to their prison for the interview, they said, "For God's sake, do anything in future with us that you see fit—condemn us to any kind of punishment, put balls and chains on all of us—but whatever you do, in case of another attack, let us out of this hole and give us a gun!" I have known a generous-minded commanding officer to release every prisoner in the guard-house and set aside their sentences forever, after they have shown their courage and presence of mind in defending a post from Indians, or other perils, such as fire and storms.

The brave sergeant who had filled the pit with his captures, asked to follow a deserter who had escaped to a settlement on the Saline River.   He found the man, arrested him, and brought him away unaided.   When they reached the railway at Ellsworth, the man made a plea of hunger, and the sergeant took him to an eating-house.   While standing at the counter, he took the cover from a red-pepper box and furtively watching his chance, threw the contents into the sergeant's eyes, completely blinding him.   The sergeant was then accounted second only to Wild Bill as a shot, and not a whit less cool.   Though groaning with agony, he lost none of his self-possession.   Listening for the footfall as the deserter started for the door, he fired in the direction, and the man fell dead.

Our regiment was now passing through its worst days. Constant scouting over the sun-baked, cactus-bedded Plains, by men who were as yet unacclimated, and learning by the severest lessons to inure themselves to hardships, made terrible havoc in the ranks.   The horses, also fresh to this sort of service, grew gaunt, and dragged their miserably fed bodies over the blistering trail.   Here and there along the line a trooper walked beside his beast, wetting, when he could, the flesh that was raw from the chafing of the saddle, especially when the rider is a novice in horsemanship.

Insubordination among the men was the certain consequence of the half-starved, discouraged state they were in. One good fight would have put heart into them to some extent, for the hopelessness of following such a will-o'-the-wisp as the Indians were that year, made them think their scouting did no good and might as well be discontinued.   Some of the officers were poor disciplinarians, either from inexperience or because they lacked the gift of control over others, which seems left out of certain temperaments.   Alas! some had no control over themselves; and no one could expect obedience in such a case.   In its early days the Seventh Cavalry was not the temperate regiment it afterward became. Some of the soldiers in the ranks had been officers during

the war, and they were learning the lesson, that hard summer, of receiving orders instead of issuing them.   There were
a good many men who had served in the Confederate army,
and had not a ray of patriotism in enlisting; it was merely a
question of subsistence to them in their beggared condition.

There were troopers who had entered the service from a
romantic love of adventure, with little idea of what stuff a
man must be made if he is hourly in peril, or, what taxes the
nerves still more, continually called upon to endure privation.

The mines were evidently the great object that induced
the soldier to enlist that year.   The Eastern papers had wild
accounts of the enormous yield in the Rocky Mountains, and
free transportation by Government could be gained by enlisting.   At that time, when the railroad was incomplete, and
travel almost given up on account of danger to the stages;
when the telegraph, which now reaches the destination of
the rogue with its warning far in advance of him, had not
even been projected over the Plains—it was the easiest sort
of escape for a man, for when once he reached the mines he
was lost for years, and perhaps died undiscovered.

Recruits of the kind sent to us would, even under favor-
able circumstances, be difficult material from which to evolve
soldierly men; and considering their terrible hardships, it
was no wonder the regiment was nearly decimated.   In enlisting, the recruit rarely realizes the trial that awaits him of
surrendering his independence.   We hear and know so much
in this country of freedom that even a tramp appreciates it.
If a man is reasonably subordinate, it is still very hard to become accustomed to the infinitesimal observances that I have
so often been told are "absolutely necessary to good order
and military discipline."   To a looker-on like me, it seemed
very much like reducing men to machines.   The men made
so much trouble on the campaign—and we knew of it by the
many letters that came into garrison in one mail, as well as
by personal observation, when in the regiment—that I did
not find much sympathy in my heart for them.   In one night,
while I was at Fort Hays, forty men deserted, and in so bold

and deliberate a manner, taking arms, ammunition, horses, and quantities of food, that the officers were roused to action, for it looked as if not enough men would be left to protect the fort. A conspiracy was formed among the men, by which a third of the whole command planned to desert at one time. Had not their plotting been discovered, there would not have been a safe hour for those who remained, as the Indians lay in wait constantly. My husband, in writing of that wholesale desertion in the early months of the regiment's history, makes some excuse for them, even under circumstances that would seem to have put all tribulation and patience out of mind.

After weary marches, the regiment found itself nearing Fort Wallace with a sense of relief, feeling that they might halt and recruit in that miserable but comparatively safe post. They were met by the news of the ravages of the cholera. No time could be worse for the soldiers to encounter it. The long, trying campaign, even extending into the Department of the Platte, had fatigued and disheartened the command. Exhaustion and semi-starvation made the men an easy prey. The climate, though so hot in summer, had heretofore been in their favor, as the air was pure, and, in ordinary weather, bracing. But with cholera, even the high altitude was no protection. No one could account for the appearance of the pestilence; never before or since had it been known in so elevated a part of our country. There were those who attributed the scourge to the upturning of the earth in the building of the Kansas Pacific Railroad; but the engineers had not even been able to prospect as far as Wallace on account of the Indians. An infantry regiment, on its march to New Mexico, halted at Fort Wallace, and even in their brief stay the men were stricken down, and with inefficient nurses, no comforts, not even wholesome food, it was a wonder that there was enough of the regiment left for an organization. The wife of one of the officers, staying temporarily in a dug-out, fell a victim, and died in the wretched underground habitation in which an Eastern farmer would refuse to shelter his stock.

It was a hard fate for our Seventh Cavalry mén. Their camp, outside the garrison, had no protection from the remorseless sun, and the poor fellows rolled on the hot earth in their small tents, without a cup of cold water or a morsel of decent food. The surgeons fought day and night to stay the spread of the disease, but everything was against them. The exhausted soldiers, disheartened by long, hard, unsuccessful marching, had little desire to live when once seized by the awful disease.

With the celerity with which evil news travels, much of what I have written came back to us. Though the mails were so uncertain, and travel was almost discontinued, still the story of the illness and desperate condition of our regiment reached us, and many a garbled and exaggerated tale came with the true ones. Day after day I sat on the gallery of the quarters in which we were temporarily established, watching for the first sign of the cavalryman who brought our mail. Doubtless he thought himself a winged Mercury. In reality, no snail ever crept so slowly. When he began his walk toward me, measuring his regulation steps with military precision, a world of fretful impatience possessed me. I wished with all my soul I was, for the moment, any one but the wife of his commanding officer, that I might pick up my skirts and fly over the grass, and snatch the parcel from his hand. When he finally reached the gallery, and swung himself into position to salute, my heart thumped like the infantry drum. Day after day came the same pompous, maddening words: "I have the honor to report there are no letters for Mrs. Major-General George Armstrong Custer." Not caring at last whether the man saw the flush of disappointment, the choking breath, and the rising tears, I fled in the midst of his slow announcement, to plunge my wretched head into my pillow, hoping the sound of the sobs would not reach Eliza, who was generally hovering near to propose something that would comfort me in my disappointment.

She knew work was my panacea, and made an injured mouth over the rent in her apron, which, in her desires to keep me occupied, she was not above tearing on purpose. With complaining tones she said, " Miss Libbie, ain't you goin' to do no sewin' for me at all? 'Pears like every darkey in garrison has mo' clo'es than I has "—forgetting in her zeal the abbreviation of her words, about which her "ole miss" had warned her. Sewing, reading, painting, any occupation that had beguiled the hours, lost its power as those letterless days came and went. I was even afraid to show my face at the door when the mail-man was due, for I began to despair about hearing at all. After days of such gloom, my leaden heart one morning quickened its beats at an unusual sound— the clank of a sabre on our gallery and with it the quick, springing steps of feet unlike the quiet infantry around us. The door, behind which I paced uneasily, opened, and with a flood of sunshine that poured in, came a vision far brighter than even the brilliant Kansas sun. There before me, blithe and buoyant, stood my husband! In an instant, every moment of the preceding months was obliterated. What had I to ask more? What did carth hold for us greater than what we then had? The General, as usual when happy and excited, talked so rapidly that the words jumbled themselves into hopeless tangles, but my ears were keen enough to extract from the medley the fact that I was to return at once with him.

Eliza, half crying, scolding as she did when overjoyed, vibrated between kitchen and parlor, and finally fell to cooking, as a safety-valve for her overcharged spirits. The General ordered everything she had in the house, determined, for once in that summer of deprivations, to have, as the soldiers term it, one "good, square meal."

After a time, when my reason was again enthroned, I began to ask what good fortune had brought him to me. It seems that my husband, after reaching Fort Wallace, was overwhelmed with the discouragements that met him. His men dying about him, without his being able to afford them relief, was something impossible for him to face without a struggle for their assistance. A greater danger than all was yet to be encountered, if the right measures were not taken immediately. Even the wretched food was better than starvation, and so much of that had been destroyed, with the hope of the arrival of better, that there was not enough left to ration the men, and unless more came they would starve, as they were out then two hundred miles from the railroad. If a scout was sent, his progress was so slow, hiding all day and traveling only by night, it would take so long that there might be men dying from hunger as well as cholera, before he could return with aid. And, besides this scarcity of food, the medical supplies were insufficient. The General, prompt always in action, suddenly determined to relieve the beleaguered place by going himself for medicines and rations. He took a hundred men to guard the wagons that would bring relief to the suffering, and in fifty-five hours they were at Fort Hays, one hundred and fifty miles distant. It was a terrible journey. He afterward made a march of eighty miles in seventeen hours, without the horses showing themselves fagged ; and during the war he had marched a portion of his Division of cavalry, accompanied by horse artillery, ninety miles in twenty-four hours.

My husband, finding I had been sent away from Fort Hays, and believing me to be at Fort Harker, a victim of cholera, determined to push on there at night, leaving the train for supplies to travel the distance next day. Colonel Custer and Colonel Cook accompanied him. They found the garrison in the deepest misery, the cholera raging at its worst, the gloom and hopelessness appalling. My husband left the two officers to load the wagons, and fortunately, as the railroad had reached Fort Harker, the medical and commissary supplies were abundant. It took but a few hours to reach Fort Riley.

He knew from former experience that I would require but a short time to get ready—indeed, my letters were full of assurances that I lived from hour to hour with the one hope that I might join him, and these letters had met him at Forts Hays and Harker. He knew well that nothing we might encounter could equal the desolation and suspense of the days that I was enduring at Fort Riley.

My little valise was filled long before it was necessary for us to take the return train that evening. With the joy, the relief, the gratitude, of knowing that God had spared my husband through an Indian campaign, and averted from him the cholera ; and now that I was to be given reprieve from days of anxiety, and nights of hideous dreams of what might befall him, and that I would be taken back to camp—could more be crowded into one day? Was there room for a thought, save one of devout thankfulness, and such happiness as I find no words to describe ?

There was in that summer of 1867 one long, perfect day. It was mine, and—blessed be our memory, which preserves to us the joys as well as the sadness of life !—it is still mine, for time and for eternity.

END.